Breaking Through the Access Barrier

Breaking Through the Access Barrier argues that the policies designed to address inequalities in college access are failing to address underlying issues of inequality. This book introduces academic capital formation (ACF), a groundbreaking new theory defined by family knowledge of educational options and the opportunities for pursuing them. The authors suggest focusing on intervention programs and public policy to promote improvement in academic preparation, college information, and student aid.

This textbook offers:

- a new construct—academic capital—that integrates and draws upon existing literature on influencing access to college
- practical advice for better preparation and intervention
- real student outcomes, databases, and interviews taken from exemplary intervention programs
- empirical research illuminating the role of class reproduction in education and how interventions (financial, academic, and networking) can reduce student barriers
- quantitative and qualitative analysis of the importance and effectiveness of several major policy interventions

Written for courses on higher education policy and policy analysis, readers will find *Breaking Through the Access Barrier* offers valuable advice for working within new policy frameworks and reshaping the future of educational opportunities and access for underrepresented students from disadvantaged backgrounds.

Edward P. St. John is Algo D. Henderson Collegiate Professor of Higher Education at the University of Michigan.

Shouping Hu is Professor of Higher Education at Florida State University.

Amy S. Fisher is a doctoral candidate at the Center for the Study of Higher and Postsecondary Education, the University of Michigan.

Breaking Through the Access Barrier

How Academic Capital Formation Can Improve
Policy in Higher Education

Edward P. St. John
Shouping Hu
Amy S. Fisher

Routledge
Taylor & Francis Group

NEW YORK AND LONDON

First published 2011
by Routledge
270 Madison Avenue, New York, NY 10016

Simultaneously published in the UK
by Routledge
2 Park Square, Milton Park, Abingdon, Oxon OX14 4RN

Routledge is an imprint of the Taylor & Francis Group, an informa business

Typeset in Minion by EvS Communication Networx, Inc.
Printed and bound in the United States of America on acid-free paper by Edwards Brothers, Inc.

Library of Congress Cataloging in Publication Data
St. John, Edward P.
Breaking through the access barrier : how academic capital formation can improve policy in higher education / by Edward P. St. John, Shouping Hu, Amy S. Fisher.
p. cm.
Includes bibliographical references and index.
1. Minorities—Education (Higher)—United States. 2. College preparation programs—United States. 3. Academic achievement—United States. I. Hu, Shouping. II. Fisher, Amy. III. Title.
LC3727.S69 2010
378.1'982694—dc22
2010014524

ISBN 13: 978-0-415-80032-7 (hbk)
ISBN 13: 978-0-415-80033-4 (pbk)
ISBN 13: 978-0-203-84901-9 (ebk)

CONTENTS

LIST OF TABLES

LIST OF FIGURES

PREFACE

The access barrier can be conceived in many ways. Viewing it as a threshold of entry into college is the conventional way, but misses the many challenges low-income, first-generation college students face as they navigate pathways into and through college. Their parents may not advocate for them to get into advanced courses or encourage them to think in terms of becoming prepared for college. Applications for 4-year colleges are due early in the senior year of high school and to have a realistic expectation of being accepted into a quality college requires years of academic preparation and the ability to pay. If low-income students overcome these obstacles and get accepted into college, they often face new challenges. Integrating into the seemingly foreign culture of academe can be very difficult, especially if their families have no prior experience with college and thus may find it difficult to offer emotional and monetary support. In other words, many families do not have academic capital sufficient to navigate this treacherous journey.

Given the social and system aspects of transcending these obstacles, we view the process of "breaking through the access barrier" as a process that involves systemic change and academic capital formation. *Academic capital* refers to the social processes that underlie family knowledge of educational options, strategies to pursue them, and career goals that require a college education. Illumination of academic capital formation processes among low-income families provides a basis for rethinking how educational reforms, student aid, and encouragement can empower low-income students to break through barriers to preparation, access, and college success. After completing the studies for this book on the educational pathways traveled by successful low-income students, it became apparent that systemic changes that empower social engagement by students and their parents in high schools and colleges are central to breaking through the access barrier. This barrier holds back students with no prior family experience with college who may not obtain the level of academic preparation required for entry. Providing the necessary courses in high school, student aid, and information on college options for students and their parents are only partial remedies to the access challenge. It is also necessary to rebuild the human side of the educational system, especially by providing a caring and supportive environment for first-generation college students and their parents.

In *Breaking Through the Access Barrier: How Academic Capital Formation Can Improve Policy in Higher Education* we examine comprehensive interventions that combine student aid and support services for low-income students. A theory of academic capital formation is proposed, tested, and refined based on analyses of both quantitative and qualitative data on students who were eligible for three exemplary and comprehensive intervention programs: Indiana's Twenty-first Century Scholars (TFCS), Washington State Achievers (WSA), and Gates Millennium Scholars (GMS). As comprehensive reforms, these programs provide financial aid, support services, and encouragement to low-income students in high school and college. The analyses of quantitative data on students eligible for these programs—recipients and nonrecipients—examine processes that encourage family engagement, academic preparation during high school, careful thought about college choices, engaged learning during college, and, ultimately, academic success; it is interviews with students, however, that provide the most compelling information. The chapters in part I focus on the ways low-income students build academic capital, followed in part II by discussions of how reformers and policymakers can craft strategies to improve educational opportunities for low-income students.

By examining how interventions by schools, colleges, community organizations, foundations, and state agencies foster academic capital formation, we can envision a new generation of innovation and reform. Building understanding of the academic capital formation process, as voiced by underrepresented students who are blazing pathways to academic success, provides information that can inform the design of interventions and strategies used by advocates and interventionists. Too often, previous research has either focused on actions students *should* take to be successful—like completing advanced courses in high school or submitting applications for college and student aid—or has been critical of the systemic barriers that prevent students from achieving these goals. Obstacles facing underrepresented students include:

- Attending high schools that don't offer advanced courses;
- Tracking schemes within schools that systematically deny underrepresented students access to advanced courses;
- School environments that do not feel welcoming to students and their families;
- Financial aid policies that make it necessary for low-income students to work long hours and borrow excessively to pay for college.

Fixing these problems involves a major systemic change. States are currently engaged in transforming comprehensive high school systems into an academic systems that prepare all students for college and the global labor market. This book focuses on the social aspects of systemic transformation: the process of engaging parents and students in preparation, finding colleges that fit, and navigating pathways through educational systems. Studying how pioneering students have navigated around these obstacles, we gain a different perspective on new pathways and more supportive ways to design future interventions.

By focusing on linkages between public policies and academic capital formation processes, we hope to inform policy makers about the consequences of mandates, funding decisions, and other political actions. In policy research, a distinction is often made between the study of policy development, the analysis of policy options, and studies of policy results. Policy choices are seldom based on these analyses; instead, they are usually based on politically constructed arguments. In fact, in recent decades research has been used in the political process through *rationale building* (St. John, 2006a; St. John & Parsons, 2004), which diminishes its value as an instrument of political advocacy. During this period, the debates about policies on college access have been dominated by academic and financial rationales, which have largely overlooked social aspects of capital formation in families.

The book is written as a text for researchers and students interested in improving postsecondary opportunity. Research that tests and builds new theory can be used to educate new professionals, including administrators and faculty. *Breaking Through the Access Barrier* can be used in policy courses that include a focus on postsecondary outcomes. It can also be used in graduate courses in education, sociology, and economics that aim to provide graduate students with frames for research that cuts across disciplinary boundaries and envisions new approaches to investigating critical social problems, including academic preparation, college choice, and educational attainment by underrepresented students.

ACKNOWLEDGMENTS

Inequality in college access has become a national concern and numerous groups are actively engaged in crafting possible remedies to the challenge. *Breaking Through the Access Barrier* examines three major interventions that have a record of success. The book would not have been possible without the opportunity to collaborate with other researchers in projects that supported the studies that provide the basis for the volume.

The Bill and Melinda Gates Foundation funded the Washington State Achievers (WSA) Program and research initiatives that provided the central data sources for research on WSA. Deborah Wilds, Peter Bloch Garcia, and Margot Tyler were program officers who worked with program administration and research advisors on the development of a research program to inform program development. Lorraine Soleagui, Director of Research and Evaluation at the College Success Foundation, provided support over time including a review of earlier drafts of this book. Several research organizations collected the survey and interview data we used for the studies of WSA: the National Opinion Research Center (NORC) at the University of Chicago collected longitudinal data on applicants to WSA; Charles Hirschman of the University of Washington collected surveys of high school and college students in Washington; and Stanford Research International conducted interviews and focus group studies on WSA students.

The Gates Foundation also sponsored the Gates Millennium Scholars Program and supported the development of databases used in our research. Deborah Wilds, Peter Bloch Garcia, and Margot Tyler supported the work of research advisors to design research studies. Contracting agencies that collected data for the studies of GMS were the NORC which collected longitudinal studies of applicants to GMS and the American Institutes of Research (AIR) which conducted focus groups with GMS students. In addition, the Gates Foundation supported most of the analyses of databases on GMS and WSA students presented in part II. The Foundation's program officers worked with research advisory committees from 2000 through 2009. Collaboration and discussions with Walter Allen, Shirley Hune, Sylvia Hurtado, William Sedlacek, John Tippiconic, and William Trent were sources of insight and inspiration throughout this extended process.

Lumina Foundation for Education supported three studies of Indiana's Twenty-first Century Scholars Program (TFCS). The major study was completed in 2008 and involved collaboration among researchers from the University of Michigan, Indiana University-Purdue University Indianapolis (IUPUI), and Purdue University. Mary Williams was the project manager at Lumina Foundation. Andrew Koch and other members of the Purdue University research team made their interviews and summaries available to our research team. The Indiana Commission on Higher Education and the State Student Assistance Commission of Indiana provided databases for the studies of Twenty-first Century Scholars.

A grant from the Ford Foundation for Projects Promoting Equity in Higher Education has supported the production of the book, from proposal development through final manuscript revision. Phyllis Stillman served as editor throughout the process of developing this book.

We gratefully acknowledge this support, financial and collegial, in the development of the book. However, the analyses and interpretations are the authors' and do not represent policies or positions of the funding organizations and researchers.

1

INTRODUCTION

Every year, many thousands of middle-class parents take their children, aspiring college students, to visit college campuses. Most of these parents use their own college knowledge, or academic capital, to encourage their children to prepare for college. Academic capital[1] is defined as social processes that build family knowledge of educational and career options and support navigation through educational systems and professional organizations. Parental support usually starts with reading to children in early childhood and continues with parents encouraging their children to complete advanced preparatory courses in high school, to apply to a range of colleges based on their interests, and to see what types of scholarships are offered. But this type of cross-generation support—academic capital transmitted across generations—is not available to most children whose parents did not attend college, a replicating pattern in many low-income families. College knowledge along with other forms of academic capital acquired by individuals and transmitted by families and communities serve as forces that reproduce the elite and middle classes in society. It is possible that carefully designed and administered interventions that ensure an opportunity to attend college and provide support services at critical points along the way can empower low-income children and their parents to acquire academic capital and take the necessary steps toward college.

Academic capital played a central role in expanding the middle class, from the GI Bill after World War II through the start of the neoliberal transformation in the early 1980s and the cross-generation uplift that resulted in a massive expansion of higher education (Bound & Turner, 2002). Academic capital acquisition—access to support systems and networks of people to expand opportunities—has been beyond the reach of most families that do not have college knowledge or the resources to pay for college. This has been especially problematic during the past 3 decades of escalating costs and the declining purchasing power of need-based grants (St. John, 2003, 2006a). However, a few successful reforms—including the Twenty-first Century Scholars (TFCS), Washington State Achievers (WSA), and the Gates Millennium Scholars Program (GMS)—have shown that academic capital formation can be developed through social, educational, and financial interventions. A thoughtful examination of student and parent experiences with these comprehensive interventions can provide a basis for rethinking the core process of overcoming inequalities in educational attainment.

Reducing inequality in educational opportunity was central to the development of a federal role in education in 1965 and remained so through the 1970s. In the 1980s, however, the focus of public education policy shifted toward emphasizing "excellence" and away from focusing on equal opportunity. It is crucial to examine how schools changed during these 3 decades of nearly constant reform, as well as to consider the impact of the new standards and requirements. Unfortunately, there was a decline in high school graduation rates between 1980 and 2000, along with the formation of large differentials in college-going rates for Hispanics and African Americans compared to Whites (St. John, 2003, 2006a), the best available indicator of disparity in access across racial/ethnic and income groups. At the very least, the reforms did not work as intended in schools serving low-income students. It is time to dig deeper into the linkages between the features of policies and interventions and the ways they link to outcomes. An examination of the ways social, educational, and financial interventions relate to the formation of academic capital can, at least potentially, inform the refinement of policies that encourage interventions and the intervention strategies themselves.

Breaking Through the Access Barrier reexamines the three successful reform initiatives mentioned above that combined guarantees of student aid with comprehensive support services. These programs have a record of success in improving academic preparation, enrollment in 4-year colleges, and educational attainment. As an introduction, we first consider why policy researchers and educational practitioners should focus on the policy puzzle of college access. Next, we summarize the theory of academic capital formation that emerged, and conclude by outlining the rest of the book.

THE POLICY PUZZLE

Three decades of public policies have addressed the access challenge with the goal of substantially raising, possibly doubling, the percentage of youth who enroll in and complete college. These policies have resulted in a puzzling, disjointed pattern: decline of need-based grants and rise of loans and merit aid (and of need-based aid with merit features); implementation of standards-driven reforms coupled with alignment of teaching and course content in secondary schools; and the emergence of numerous organizations that provide information and encouragement to students. This combination of policies has not had the desired effect of improving access to educational pathways leading to 4-year degrees. Trends show, in fact, that fewer students are graduating from high school. While more of the students who do graduate meet college preparatory criteria, many are not finding their way into 4-year colleges due to funding, limited access, or a lack of knowledge. The disjointed nature of public policy reveals two underlying problems: linkages between the various policies aimed at improving access were seldom designed in cohesive and complementary ways; and the social processes of change in schools and cross-generation uplift were seldom even considered.

Recently, federal policy in higher education in the United States has refocused on public accountability as a means of regulating preparation for, access to, and attainment of higher education. The College Opportunity Act of 2008 (P. L. 110-315)—the most recent reauthorization of the Higher Education Act, the major federal program in higher education—focused federal programs on student academic preparation, college success, and accountability. The framing of this new law was influenced by two strands of research: studies of the impact of student financial aid (e.g., Advisory Committee on Student Financial Assistance, 2002; Heller 1997, 2002; McPherson & Schapiro, 1998) and educational research that examined how high school courses correlated with college outcomes (e.g., Adelman, 1995, 1999, 2004; Berkner & Chavez, 1997; Choy, 2002a; Pelavin & Kane, 1990). Advocacy for accountability (e.g., Conklin & Curran, 2005; U.S. Department of Education, 2006) eventually became a means of linking these two rationales.

A question of major concern in this book is: Does the current policy framework provide a basis for schools, colleges, and states to piece together strategies for breaking through the access barrier? Our argument is that it is necessary to adjust intervention methods and public policies to facilitate academic capital formation in families historically denied college access because of attendance at poor schools, paltry need-based aid, and a social environment that reinforces transitions from school to work, welfare, prison, and other pathways instead of to college. We recognize parents want the best for their children, but there is already substantial evidence that sometimes the educational system undermines this intent, especially for low-income, first-generation college students (Brantlinger, 1994; Levin, 1996; Oakes, 1985; St. John, Griffith, & Allen-Haynes, 1997). We dig deeper into the problem to figure out possible remedies. To provide a perspective on how this policy puzzle has developed since 1980, we examine the evolution of the rationales for financial aid, academic preparation, and public accountability as means of promoting access to higher education by examining the three main rationales underlying the three major strategies for promoting access.

Financial Aid Rationale

Student financial aid became the cornerstone of federal education policy under the Higher Education Act of 1965 (P. L. No. 89-329). At the time, human capital theory and research (Becker, 1964; Schultz, 1969) influenced the creation of the early grant, loan, and work-study programs (Gladieux & Wolanin, 1976). Between 1965 and 1978, economic research on enrollment had a substantial influence on the creation and funding of federal need-based grants (Hansen & Weisbrod, 1967, 1969; McPherson, 1978; National Commission on the Financing of Postsecondary Education, 1973), including Pell as the major federal need-based program after 1972. Subsequent economic research that focused exclusively on the implementation of Pell grants found the new program did not increase enrollment rates as much as had been expected (Hansen, 1983; Kane, 1995; Manski & Wise, 1983). Regrettably, this research overlooked cuts in other federal grant programs. Total federal grant aid actually declined slightly during the period (St. John, 2003). While economists puzzled over the flat enrollment rate and the rise of Pell funding, the United States entered a period of near-equal enrollment opportunity and lower cost. A cost-efficient remedy to the access challenge was found in the 1970s, but only a few economists noticed (e.g., McPherson & Schapiro, 1991a, 1991b).

Unfortunately, the criticisms of Pell grants made it easier to shift the emphasis from grants to loans in the early 1980s, a consequence of the apparent paradox of aid awards continuing to rise while research did not confirm efficacy (Hearn, 1993). The framing of this paradox is somewhat puzzling, given that federal tax dollars spent on aid declined because loans were much less costly than grants (McPherson & Schapiro, 1991b; St. John, 2003). Pell grants declined in real dollars and a substantial unmet need gap opened for low-income students. At the same time, the focus of access research shifted to the role of academic preparation, so the decline in the purchasing power of the Pell grants went largely unnoticed. Research had a more substantial influence on education policy during this period when it documented correlations between high school courses completed and collegiate outcomes than did research on student aid (e.g., Adelman, 1995; Choy, 2002a, 2002b). Publications of the American Council on Education, for example, argued that preparation was the primary access challenge (King, 1999a, 1999b, 1999c, 2002) and posited that low-income families' failure to apply for available aid was the real financial problem (King, 2004).

It was not until the Advisory Committee on Student Financial Assistance released papers on student aid and college access by hosting national meetings and encouraging publications on the topic (e.g., Heller, 2002) that a federal agency refocused on the access challenge for low-income students. There had been a few published studies documenting that the decline in federal aid had increased inequality (McPherson & Schapiro, 1991b, 1993; St. John, 1994; St. John & Elliott, 1994), but this research did not alter the erosion of funding for federal grant programs; Pell grants continued to decline.

With the decline in federal grants, state funding for need-based aid became especially important for ensuring opportunity for college enrollment by low-income students, especially as tuition charges rose. Between 1998 and 2004, the ratio of state funding for need-based aid per full time equivalent (FTE) student declined slightly (Figure 1.1). During the same period, the ratio of first-time freshmen to high school graduates also declined at about the same rate. The fact is that enrollment rates have remained highly sensitive to student aid funding. However, there was variability across states because states funded at different levels while federal grants were awarded with the same criteria across states. The parallel trend (the correlation between aid funding and enrollment) was visible evidence that enrollment was related, at least in part, to funding for students.

What is surprising about the trends is the change in the general pattern between 2004 and 2006. During this period, there was an increase in the college-continuation rate (ratio of high school graduates in the spring to first-time freshman college enrollment the next fall), from 52% of the graduating class in 2004 to 62% in 2006, even though the ratio of state funding for student aid to tuition declined. This break in the pattern suggests that the changes in high school graduation requirements influenced the percentage of the graduating cohort who went on to college.

In spite of the overall gain in access, the percentage of students going on to more costly 4-year colleges did not increase at the same rate, especially for minorities. Therefore, it appears that while gains in preparation resulted in improved college access, opportunities for low-income students continue to be constrained because of financial conditions in many states.

Academic Preparation Rationale

When Pell grant funding became uncertain in the early 1980s and enrollment of minority students began to waver, the National Association for Equal Opportunity (NAFEO), an association of private historically Black colleges, went to President Reagan and asked for research on the reasons for the decline. The report from this research focused on academic preparation and emphasized a correlation between middle school algebra and college outcomes (Pelavin & Kane, 1988, 1990). A flood of reports followed showing similar relationships (Adelman, 1995, 1999, 2004; Berkner & Chavez, 1997; Choy, 2002a, 2002b).

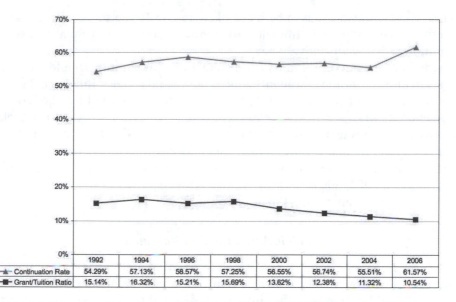

	1992	1994	1996	1998	2000	2002	2004	2006
Continuation Rate	54.29%	57.13%	58.57%	57.25%	56.55%	56.74%	55.51%	61.57%
Grant/Tuition Ratio	15.14%	16.32%	15.21%	15.69%	13.62%	12.38%	11.32%	10.54%

Figure 1.1 National trends in college continuation rates for high school graduates and grant/tuition ratio. Data from Postsecondary Education Opportunity, NCES Integrated Postsecondary Education Data System, and National Association of State Student Grant & Aid Programs. © 2009 Project Promoting Equity in Urban and Higher Education, NCID at the University of Michigan.

A pattern had been established: The new rationale argued that increasing requirements for high school graduation, especially in math, would improve college access.

States rapidly adopted policies based on these arguments (Table 1.1), and by 2000 all states had adopted new math standards. But while there was an obvious correlation between course completion and college success, requiring more math courses did not increase college enrollment, especially in 4-year colleges (St. John, 2006a). The number of states requiring three or more math courses for high school graduation rose from 11 in 1990 to 28 in 2005. The number of states that required exit exams for graduation had dropped in the 1990s, but increased again in the early 2000s. The average math SAT scores in the United States improved between 2000 and 2005, a period when the percentage of students taking the SAT increased. In combination, these trends suggest that improving high school graduation requirements was linked to improvements in student achievement. However, college enrollment rates actually declined during this period (St. John, 2006a)—as the pool of qualified students expanded, college enrollment rates declined. High school graduates were more prepared, but access to the 4-year colleges for which they prepared remained elusive.

Basing policy primarily on correlations between preparation and college success was ill conceived. Massive and extensive policy changes were implemented by 2005. The improvement in college-going rates after 2004, as noted above, appears to support the proposition that improvement in preparation results in improved enrollment rates.[2] Unfortunately, these gains were limited to access to 2-year colleges in most states, not because of limited preparation but because of financial conditions.

Improving preparation for students without giving adequate attention to whether they can afford to pay for college is not a well-conceived policy. Common sense should tell everyone that both academic preparation and the ability to pay for college are important. The new standards for high school graduation are based on enrollment in 4-year colleges while students seem to be more likely to enroll in a less costly 2-year college. These trends suggest there is difficult work ahead for advocates of equal access based on preparation rather than ability to pay.

Researchers and advocates who focus primarily on preparation should recognize how changes in public funding of students, high schools, and colleges influence the outcomes they advocate (i.e., enrollment in 4-year colleges), just as those of us who have focused on student aid should recognize the gains in access to 2-year colleges attributable to the new policy. Both groups need to be concerned about academic success in 2-year *and* 4-year colleges and opportunities for transfer between the two systems. About a decade ago, the balanced access model was proposed as a framework for assessing both rationales (St. John, 2002, 2003), and the framework is proving its worth given the trends noted and other research using the model.

Public Accountability Rationale

We are now in a new period of public policy, one that emphasizes accountability as a means of ensuring improvement in access to and success in higher education. The reauthorized HEA links continued funding for student aid to improved student outcomes, much as No Child Left Behind (NCLB; 2001) created an accountability scheme for public K-12 schools. This represents a further complication and convolution of rationales: Suddenly colleges must achieve certain outcomes in order to maintain their federal funding for grants, but if these grants are not fully funded in the first place, the outcomes are not possible, at least for students who cannot afford to pay for college without the funding.

In *A Call for Leadership*, the Bush administration's U.S. Department of Education (2006) combined the notion of public accountability with advocacy for improvements in academic preparation and the funding of student aid. This was the first policy report in many years to emphasize both student aid and preparation. At first glance, we may conclude a new compromise was reached. However, these sorts of political arrangements never quite seem to turn out as advocated. The key issue in ensuring access, at least if 4 decades of research in economics is right, is the funding of student aid, an argument made by economic historians (e.g., Fogel, 2000; Friedman, 2005), but such arguments have not had an influence on federal policy for decades. Holding colleges and universities accountable for certain outcomes when the federal government makes no real commitment to funding students is an impossible situation we will explore in part II.

Will new policies be developed as a result of the Department of Education's report, and will they positively influence access to and academic success in college? It is not possible to answer such questions without better knowledge of future funding for student aid and school reform. In spite of the stimulus package (http://www.recovery.gov/), we cannot predict federal, state, or institutional budgets in the short or long term. We don't know whether grant programs will be funded, or whether colleges will constrain prices. One lesson from No Child Left Behind seems to be that commitments for federal funding do not guarantee improved funding even when there is adherence to accountability schemes.[3] Policy analysts may want to ponder how to rearrange the incentives in policy to ensure opportunity.

What is missing from the current set of discourses on research and policy? There is very little understanding in the policy literature of the ways in which academic policies since 1990 have influenced the expectations and behaviors of parents and children in low-income families. Our intent in this book is to reframe research and inform advo-

Table 1.1 State Policy Indicators for Selected Years, 1990–2005

	1990	1995	2000	2005
Policy Related Variables				
State-established content standards in math	7	46	50	50
Require 3 or more math courses for graduation	11	12	21	28
Require 1 or 2 math courses for graduation	33	31	24	17
Require at least Algebra I or above	0	2	12	22
High School Curriculum is locally controlled	6	7	5	5
Offer an honors diploma	15	17	19	22
Exam required for high school diploma*	15**	12	14	19
Percentage of schools participating in AP*§	45%	51%	58%	62%
Percentage of students taking SAT∞	42%*	41%	44%	49%
9th Grade cohort size (millions)	3.2	3.32	3.79	3.96
Outcomes of Interest				
SAT Verbal mean	500	504	505	508
SAT Math mean	501	506	514	520
SAT Combined	1001	1010	1019	1028

*   Based upon numbers reported in 1991.
**   This number is higher than anticipated but cannot be externally validated.
§   Reflects the median percentage for AP and the median dollars per FTE for K-12 expenditures.
†   Dollars reported are unadjusted.
∞   These numbers reflect the national figures reported by Educational Testing Service.
Source: Promoting Equity in Higher Education Project, National Center for Institutional Diversity (NCID),
         University of Michigan, Ann Arbor.

cacy by focusing on the social processes that empower cross-generation uplift through academic capital formation by illuminating the college knowledge that emerges from social engagement before and during college. Past research has been critical of the post-secondary-encouragement literature in higher education because it failed to consider the role of finances (St. John, 2003). In part I of this book, we reconsider the social processes involved in educational attainment based on the study of low-income students. This provides a means of reconsidering the role of engagement, just as the balanced access model provided a framework for considering both academic and financial policies.

An alternative to using data to "hold campuses accountable" involves using state student record databases to examine challenges at campuses and to provide guidance in the design and testing of interventions to address these challenges. St. John and Musoba (2011) have adapted the balanced access model to provide a framework for promoting academic success for underrepresented students in higher education. They revised the model based on a research process that involved using assessment research with state student record data to inform teams from campuses about challenges to success faced by their students. The research on campus-level interventions illustrates an alternative to top-down notions of accountability and that it is possible to adapt practice to improve the academic success of students who would not have been able to enroll in the past. Trends indicate that gains in access are possible, so strategies for promoting academic success should be a high priority.

This book aims to inform readers interested in rethinking research paradigms and refining intervention strategies and public policies. We do not advocate for any particular policy or strategy, but encourage thoughtful responses to policy changes which are both frequent and disjointed. A commitment to social justice in policy and action underlies our work (St. John, 2003, 2006, 2009b). We recognize that all practitioners working in high schools, colleges, and public agencies governing these organizations must build and act upon their own understandings of social processes that can overcome barriers to success for low-income students and to present this information in ways that can inform reformers and policy advocates. We return to the problems of policy and practice in part II.

EMERGENT THEORY OF ACADEMIC CAPITAL FORMATION

The studies in part I were organized to conceptualize, test, and build a new theory of academic capital formation. We used a critical-empirical approach to framing research (St. John, 2007, 2009b) starting with propositions we tested using both quantitative and qualitative data on students in three successful programs. In our work on the critical transitions—outcomes important in policy research—we started with the well-established balanced access model (St. John, 2003, 2006a), but continued to evolve the core concepts and test policy linkages. In addition, we used a set of qualitative analyses to examine the social process—starting with concepts in theories of human capital, social capital, and social class reproduction—within the core processes of preparation, college transition, and engagement during college. We summarize the policy and social dimensions of the emergent theory below.

Academic Capital and Educational Transitions

The balanced access model provided the initial framework for examining how K-12 reforms, postsecondary encouragement, and public financing of higher education influence critical educational transitions as outcomes often considered important in public policy on education (St. John, 2006a). More recently, the framework was revised to examine how college campuses can intervene to expand opportunities for underrepresented students to achieve academically (St. John & Musoba, 2010). In this book, we consider how policy influences the same educational outcomes, but focus on the outcomes as being integral to a social process of uplift in first-generation college families. The emergent framework of academic capital formation links policies to outcomes, educational transitions that involve social action within the lives of students and their families (Figure 1.2).

By using the three programs and comparison groups, we could assess policy linkages. We looked across all of the outcomes using a mixed-methods approach for Washington State Achievers (WSA), but we had both quantitative and qualitative data on only precollege outcomes for Twenty-first Century Scholars (TFCS) and college-related outcomes for Gates Millennium Scholars (GMS). The mixed-methods approach provides insights into significant linkages and the meaning of linkages for students and parents, but we do not make causal inferences from our work;[4] however, when such studies are available, we do refer to them.

Based on the understandings reached from research on educational attainment, this book started with a set of propositions about the ways in which the critical transitions incorporated social and cultural capital into the steps in the academic pipeline.[5] The three programs studied focused on low-income students, so our model was tailored to

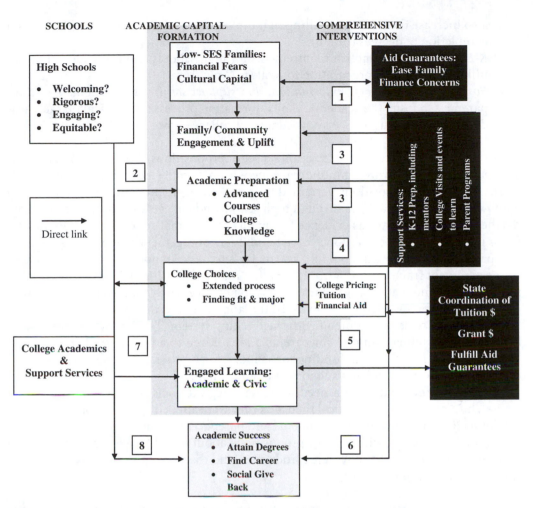

Figure 1.2 Academic capital formation reconsidered: The roles of K-12 policies and comprehensive interventions.

this group. We reconstructed these concepts into a set of initial propositions about critical transitions[6] that focused on family knowledge, inclusive of the parent learning about school and college and the student taking the steps necessary to prepare for college.

The studies in part II consider the roles of public policy on graduation requirements and educational interventions in promoting the formation of academic capital among students from low-income families. While our primary focus is on the critical transitions in academic capital formation, the process of overcoming barriers to educational opportunity that foster inequality cannot be illuminated without also considering the role of interventions. Three specific types can be identified from reviews of government interventions (St. John, 2006a):

- *Financial aid*, including guarantees that financial need will be met by government or foundation grants, can encourage academic capital formation in low-income families if it eases concerns about college costs (link 1 in Figure 1.2) and facilitates enrollment in the college of choice (link 4). Meeting financial need means providing support adequate to overcome financial barriers, in which case it would also increase the odds of enrolling in more costly or selective colleges (link 5) and completion of degrees (link 6).

- *K-12 policies* that establish requirements for high schools and fund education can influence academic preparation for college (link 2).
- *Postsecondary outreach, information, and support services* for students and their parents can foster the academic capital formation processes of critical literacy, academic preparation, college knowledge, and college choice (link 3).

We tested these linkages by examining a set of propositions about educational transitions as processes involving human agency within families, schools, and social networks. The initial propositions pertained to family engagement, which we found could empower students to navigate through high school and college and parents to advocate for their children. There was evidence to support the original conceptions of linkages 1 (guarantees easing concerns about costs) and 2 (encouragement empowering students and parents to navigate high school). The major alteration in policy linkage 2, as stated in the emergent framework (Figure 1.2), is that K-12 policies link to the culture of high schools. We found that raising requirements did not necessarily make schools more welcoming places for low-income students. In Indiana, we found that parents' advocacy for children was necessary to contend with the tracking system; TFCS provided the college knowledge and human support for parents and children to advocate for better classes. In contrast, the supplemental funding for school reform provided to WSA high schools created a more welcoming and supportive environment.

Previous reviews indicated a need to better integrate social constructs from social capital, human capital, and critical theory as they were applied to educational outcomes (St. John, 2006b). To explore how students and parents experienced the key educational transitions, we started with a set of propositions about social processes, derived from theories of social capital and social reproduction and the alternative of cross-generation uplift. The first proposition:

- Family and community engagement in forming college knowledge provides one mechanism for overcoming social barriers to access.

The studies in chapter 3 examine how parents and students learned about educational opportunities within their school and community contexts. Easing concerns about college costs early on empowers low-income parents who lack experience in higher education to build academic capital by acquiring college knowledge that enables their children to self-navigate through high school and college. We concluded that when interventions actually enable students to take action through social agency, the interventions were experienced as empowering.

Two of the programs studied included outreach opportunities for students and families. Indiana's TFCS provided direct services to parents and students through regional centers placed around the state, while WSA in Washington provided services to students as a school-based process. Both quantitative and qualitative studies of the two programs confirm a relationship between involvement in interventions and subsequent outcomes (e.g., improved access to advanced courses, gains in expectations of college, and so forth). Encouragement services were frequently mentioned in interviews for both programs. There was also empirical evidence of parental empowerment by programs in the TFCS. We conclude there is a relationship, but our methods preclude claims of causality.[7]

In addition, we found that there were differences in the way engagement worked in the two programs. In WSA, there was more emphasis on mentors and teacher connectivity to students, while in Twenty-first Century Scholars, family involvement and advocacy played a larger role. Based on these differences we conclude that the structure of interventions along with the care shown by interventionists makes a difference in the extent of student and parent engagement in preparation and advocacy as a form of empowered social agency.

The second proposition:

- Academic preparation, a process that involves taking advanced courses and building knowledge of college options, involves family engagement and support.

This proposition focuses on the ways engagement influences completion of advanced courses in high school, an important link given the emphasis now being placed on raising graduation requirements. We found that encouragement of students played a crucial role in the process, extending concepts of preparation beyond the education tautology that completion of advanced courses in math and other subjects relates to future attainment by recasting the process as integral to academic capital formation. Chapter 4 examines academic preparation as a process related to family knowledge of college, financial expectations, and information exchange.

In both WSA and TFCS there was evidence of greater completion of advanced courses by students involved in the precollege programs, but it is not possible to claim causality because of the self-selection problem.[8] Not only did students in these programs take advanced courses at higher rates than peers, they discussed their involvement in the outreach programs as a factor in their gaining access. Access to courses involves advocacy to change teachers and courses and may involve repeating courses even when school counselors express doubt.

The proposition held up for TFCS: Parents were actively engaged in advocating for their children in schools (Lumina, 2008; St. John & Musoba, 2010). However, a different pattern was evident for WSA, where the connection between teachers and students proved more crucial, at least in the interviews. Thus, we once again conclude that the design of programs along with the care of practitioners play significant roles in gaining access to advanced courses.

College enrollment and the opportunity to attend a 4-year college are critical outcomes. Not only is there a threshold of access for many students, evident in the percentage of students going on to 2-year colleges, but preparation for and the ability to enroll in 4-year colleges is also important. The third proposition, centered on college choice, is:

- College choice is the process of searching for colleges, taking exams, applying for admission, and choosing a college. Hossler's theory of college choice (e.g., Hossler, Schmit, & Vesper, 1999) provides a workable frame for considering the role of information in encouraging and enabling college choice as a process of expanding opportunity. At this step, families need to weigh the costs and benefits of available options. Chapter 5 examines college choice as a capital formation process.

The analyses of quantitative data using predictive models confirm the linkage between the amount of aid available to students and college enrollment. This is consistent with a longstanding research tradition in economics and the finance of higher education. The more interesting finding pertained to student experiences with the college choice process. Analyses of interviews with students in WSA and GMS found that:

- Money made a difference in college choice and transfer. Having a guarantee of aid made it possible for students to reassess their choices and change colleges if their first choice did not work for them.
- Choice of a college and a major program was an intertwined process for students during their first 2 years of college. Students discussed their experiences as a process of finding a fit that worked for them.

We concluded that the initial college choice, search for majors of interest, and decision to transfer during or after the first 2 years of college were part of a process of "finding fit." Our concept of fit was constructed from students' experiences with the system and the people in it as well as finding meaningful academic connections; this represents a reconstruction of conventional theory of student choice and persistence (e.g., Braxton, 2000; Hossler, Schmit, & Vesper, 1997; Tinto, 1993).

Based on prior research on GMS and WSA, we decided to examine the linkage between academic and civic engagement given the encouragement and aid provided through the programs. Fortunately, both programs had survey data on student engagement during college.

The fourth proposition:

- Engaged learning is a process that involves students in learning opportunities with faculty on campus and civic service in the community that empowers students to develop and use skills that support cross-generation uplift. This concept of engagement is derived from theory and research on college students (Pascarella & Terenzini, 2005). Chapter 6 examines concepts of engaged learning, academic and civic, by college students as a capital formation process helping students to build a better self-understanding and rethink their future opportunities. Engagement is not absolutely necessary for attainment but it helps, and it builds cross-generation academic capital.

Previous studies of GMS found a relationship between student aid funding and student engagement during college (St. John, 2008; St. John, Rowley, & Hu, 2009); our analyses supported this proposition of linkage, but cannot confirm causality.

The focus on social processes provided substantial insight into the meaning of engagement with respect to social class transformation within family systems, a critical part of the preparation and college-transition processes. Student engagement during college was part of a reformation of self-understanding that led to inner concepts of giving back to family, community, and society.

The fifth proposition focuses narrowly on core educational processes and the alignment between different levels of education:

- Academic success is a capital formation process that results, in part, from engagement during college along with knowledge of educational requirements and social expectations in college. The definition of college success is inclusive of academic capital formation and is, therefore, more than degree attainment. *Alignment* of state education policies and college admissions requirements (i.e., taking the right courses in high school) can increase the odds of academic achievement and the opportunity to engage academically during college. The concept of alignment is consistent with efforts to change high school offerings and graduation requirements to ease the transition between high school and college (e.g., Conklin & Curran, 2005). In addition to examining student experiences in choosing majors and completing college, the analyses in chapter 7 consider congruity and discontinuities in student experiences as they make education and career choices during their college years.

The key indicator of academic success is degree attainment. Analyses of quantitative data did not indicate statistically significant differences in persistence rates for students in the three programs and comparison students. There are substantial difficulties with measurement of the statistical significance of student aid in persistence. Our quantitative analyses indicate that both financial and academic support during college improved engagement during college, such as WSA and GMS, but neither of the programs had significantly higher degree completion rates.[9] We also found a complex pattern of social relationships that merits further investigation, including meaningful transitions from college to work.

In addition, social giveback[10] emerged as a compelling concept in the GMS and WSA programs, both of which provide generous financial support along with different forms of mentorship and social support. We were interested to find how students developed a sense of giveback based on the combination of monetary and social support.

ACADEMIC CAPITAL FORMATION IN LOW-SES FAMILIES

The studies in part II examine the social processes evident within each of the critical transitions. The underlying logic of this and other research using the balanced access model on student outcomes (St. John, 2003, 2006a) has been that the system itself and experiences of the system are different aspects of the same phenomenon, a proposition rooted in Habermas's critical theory of communicative action (1984, 1987, 1990). The availability of extensive interview data for the three programs makes it possible to examine the experiential aspect of each of the critical transitions rather than merely reducing them to policy outcomes.

Theory Reconstruction

We used a critical-empirical approach to studying these social processes within each outcome in a three-step process:

1. A review of theories of social capital (Coleman, 1988), class reproduction (e.g., Bourdieu, 1977, 1990), and human capital (Becker, 1964, 1975) to discern claims about social processes related to educational attainment. Six initial constructs emerged from this review process.
2. An examination of interviews in relation to quantitative findings for each of the outcomes. We developed alternative conceptions of each proposition: one related to reproduction and the other related to uplift.[11] This process may seem repetitive to some readers, but we think the benefit of the approach outweighs the risk.[12]

3. A reconstruction of understanding looking at each of the constructs and across them. A reconstructed understanding of social processes emerged that was embedded in academic capital formation.

Social capital theory posits that networking, trust, and information enable building college knowledge and overcoming structural barriers to educational opportunity (Coleman, 1988). However, Coleman takes a functionalist position, embedding the role of social capital within social structures. The alternative of looking at social capital formation and social structures in schools and families as an interdependent process is consonant with Habermas's theory of communicative action (1984, 1987). Specifically, we examine how the processes of networking, building trust, and constructing meaning from information and encouragement generate agency among students who overcome the cultural barriers to education by forming academic capital.

The concept of cultural capital is that family and community knowledge transmission reproduces social class in terms of educational attainment. These cultural barriers to academic capital formation can potentially be overcome through educational, networking, and financial interventions, concepts crucial in reconstructing the steps to building academic capital. Bourdieu (1990) focuses on cultural capital transmitted through the family. In the analyses in this book, we focus on how interventions that inform families transform cultural capital as an extension of family literacy.[13]

We also look at the cultural barriers related to each of the processes that can inhibit academic capital formation. We consider how habitual patterns within families (or habitus) are conveyed or transformed across generations as parents and students learn to engage in the academic capital formation process. In addition, individual habits related to resiliency and the ability to navigate systems are considered within the concept of noncognitive variables, which can be used for college selection as articulated by William Sedlacek (2004).

Economic human capital theory implies that easing family concerns about college costs can empower them to build knowledge of options. Gary S. Becker's statement of human capital theory (1964) argued that individuals make choices about education based on a consideration of both costs of college and expected earnings; however, a potential problem is that it is unclear whether or not students and families actually do (Paulsen & St. John, 1997). Specifically, low-income families may preclude consideration of college, especially higher-cost colleges that are more competitive and may require leaving home. In theory, family support services could be developed to empower families without prior experience with college (cross-generation college knowledge) to gain this knowledge and make informed judgments as an explicit process. In this book, we reexamine the assumption that easing concerns about college costs for parents and children from low-income families by providing a guarantee of student aid to cover the cost of attendance can enable students to consider a broader range of options. Specifically, we consider how aid guarantees provide hope which leads to social action by parents and children as forms of social agency.

More generally, we view these social processes as having the potential for cross-generation uplift of social class. There is a dilemma with focusing on the possibility of class reproduction in that it can result in a focus on deficits. To contend with this possibility while also dealing with the prospect of reproduction of class as a force difficult to overcome through social policy or educational intervention, we hypothesized both reproductive patterns related to each of the critical transitions and related social processes. A concept of "class maintenance" emerged as a better way to explain reproduction of class as a caring social process.

Initially, we based our argument on the Western concepts of justice and cross-generation uplift. In his theory of justice, John Rawls (1971) argued that cross-generation uplift was crucial and that taxation provided means of achieving the goal of extending rights to the least advantaged. While this principle is worthy, the public often is unwilling to pay taxes at a level that supports college opportunity (St. John, 2003). Redefining the concepts of justice to consider basic educational opportunity as a right for all (college preparation and equal opportunity to attend) is necessary (St. John, 2006a).

The standard of adequate education to support a family, a basic human capability (Nussbaum, 1999), has been redefined in the early 21st century to include higher levels of math education and other knowledge normally associated with at least 2 years of college (St. John, 2006a). Based on the concept of human capabilities along with research testing the assumptions of social capital formation, we can develop subsidiary propositions about academic capital formation.

Emergent Theory

A reconstructed theory of academic capital formation emerged (Figure 1.3) that combined social processes and pattern transformation. These four social processes[14] engage students in overcoming barriers.

- *Easing Concerns about Costs*: Concern about college costs is an inhibiting force for low-income families, especially when parents have no personal knowledge of college. Aid guarantees provide a way to overcome these fears.
- *Supportive Networks in Schools and Communities*: Mentors, teachers, and community leaders can help students and their parents overcome fears about pursuing an education and paying for it, easing the process of learning about college.
- *Navigation of Systems*: Navigation through barriers requires the ability to deal with classism and racism. It builds knowledge that is transferable across educational transitions and can be conveyed through mentorship and social networks.
- *Trustworthy Information*: Accurate information received from people at critical times emerges as important in the process of overcoming educational barriers.

These academic capital formation (ACF) social processes emerged from the analyses but are rooted in core concepts in human and social capital theory. These concepts are largely postpositivist constructs.[15] The mechanisms can exist in social groups and can even be created through successful education and social interventions. However, these processes generally are not present in communities with little family and community history of educational success. Educational failure, like educational success, can reinforce replication patterns.

The construct of easing concerns about costs has emerged over time in studies of college access and was refined in these studies. The qualitative studies of students in the three comprehensive programs reinforce this process as underlying decisions about preparation, college transition, engagement, and academic success, both as a goal to navigate toward and as a process that reconstructs into values that support uplift for the next generation. In addition, the concepts on navigation of systems and social networks

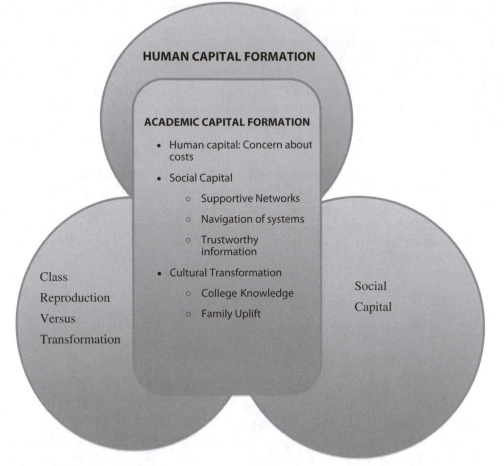

Figure 1.3 Social processes integral to academic capital formation.

supporting transition emerged from social capital theory informed by theories of the African American tradition (e.g., Siddle Walker, 1996) and William Sedlacek's concept of system navigation (2004).

Underlying the concept of academic capital formation is a conceptual tension between class reproduction and class uplift. The notions of cultural capital and habitus as originally constructed examined classist social organizations (Bourdieu, 1977) and are the root of critical theories (Macey, 2000). Given the growing percentage of the U. S. population living in poverty, it is important not to overlook forces that reinforce and expand the underclass.

Our studies focus on students engaged in forming academic capital, making it possible to discern patterns of social behavior that promote this process. Two patterns of social behavior[16] emerged as underpinnings of the ACF process:

- *College Knowledge*: A form of cultural capital that includes the capacity to envision one's self and family members as college students, building understanding of the roles of courses and majors in preparation for graduate education and the workforce, and the ability to use human and information resources to discern and pursue appropriate pathways through educational systems.

- *Family Uplift*: A pattern of behavior within family systems and extended networks that supports the acquisition of college knowledge, navigation of education and employment systems, and expansion of educational opportunity across generations.

Academic capital formation is a complex set of social processes and behavioral patterns that reinforce individual and family commitments to and actualization of cross-generation uplift. By definition, first-generation college students are making a first-time transition in family education, which can lead to social and economic class transformation.

The process of uplifting families across social classes is complicated by prevailing economic conditions. In the U.S. economy after World War II it was possible for families to transition into middle-income status through becoming a part of the working class. In the late 20th century, working-class jobs in the United States generally became pathways to poverty and regress from middle-income to low-income status to become the working poor, as the economics of production shifted to information and service (Fogel, 2000; B. Friedman, 2005). Attaining a college education may be a way through this economic challenge in families, a way to maintain middle-income status across generations. This requires adopting new family behaviors, tacit patterns that reinforce building college knowledge.

ABOUT THIS BOOK

The overarching questions addressed in this book are:

- How do social processes created within educational systems and related to support networks empower first-generation college students to navigate their way through the access barrier?
- What approaches to educational policy and public finance encourage the development of these social processes?

To address these questions, we conduct a set of quantitative and qualitative studies using extant databases (surveys, administrative records, focus group interview transcripts, and, in one instance, summaries of focus group interviews) on three successful large-scale comprehensive interventions—Twenty-first Century Scholars, Washington State Achievers, and Gates Millennium Scholars.

We avoided making the overly simplistic assumption that successful interventions are easily replicated and instead assumed that successful interventions were created by change agents who learned from past experiences and the research. In the history of these programs, there were many adaptations; some worked and others did not. The stories of program adaptation are only partially told in this text because our aim is not to document programs, although we do describe the features of these programs so they can be compared and analyzed. Our approach involves specifying and investigating the features of the three programs using the core transitions in academic capital formation.

Part I includes the studies completed to address questions about critical transitions and related social processes. Chapter 2 describes the critical-empirical methods we used to deconstruct, test, and reconstruct claims. The analytic chapters (3–7) examine quantitative evidence related to critical outcomes focusing on evidence of impact along with qualitative evidence related to social processes, and on building an understanding of their role in outcomes.

The two chapters in part II return to the role of public policy. Chapter 8 reconsiders the role of ACF as a social process in promoting educational attainment, considering implications for institutional practice and design of interventions. Finally, chapter 9 returns to policy strategies for promoting ACF as part of efforts to improve educational attainment, including attainment by first-generation college students.

Part I
Academic Capital Formation

2

REFRAMING

What social processes facilitate educational attainment among low-income families with no history of higher education? And, how can interventions be designed by reformers and supported by policymakers to accelerate these processes? These are critical questions because the majority of low-income students either drop out of high school or, if they graduate, fail to enroll in college. In fact, only about half of the low-income students who graduate from high school prepared for college, based on national standards, actually enroll in 4-year colleges (Advisory Committee on Student Financial Assistance, 2002). After a quarter century of policies that promote simplistic school reforms like imposing higher graduation standards as solutions to the access challenge, there is greater inequality in postsecondary opportunity now than there was in the 1970s. To make the new college preparatory high school system work better for underrepresented students and to increase their chances of academic success in college, we need to consider how to facilitate the social aspects of academic transitions for low-income and first-generation college students.

This chapter frames our research studies that link educational transitions and social processes. First, we compare the features of the three exemplary programs and how we used the quantitative databases to examine linkages between programs and specific outcomes. Each of the analytic chapters examines critical outcomes using reviews of prior studies to inform our use of quantitative methods to document differences in the key policy-related outcomes for participants in the three programs compared to similar nonparticipants, to determine whether participation in the programs was associated with higher rates of academic success. Second, we describe the process used to frame the quantitative analyses of outcomes, considering how the features of the programs related to program outcomes and develop our initial hypotheses about academic capital formation. We reviewed the literature on human capital, social capital, and critical theory on social reproduction to derive a set of core claims about social processes as an initial conceptual frame to examine social process in the analytic chapters. Third, we describe the process used to analyze qualitative data to test and refine the core concepts of academic capital formation. The result is an iterative reframing process that posits hypotheses and tests them in relation to the evidence in the qualitative analyses of interviews.[1] We conclude with a summary of the databases and analyses used in each of the analytic chapters.

STUDY OF EXEMPLARY PROGRAMS

Since our focus was on how programs were constructed to promote access and academic success for underrepresented students, it was necessary to examine how specific features linked to specific outcomes. The Washington State Achievers (WSA) program is discussed first because we had data related to each of the transitions for this program. Next, we look at the Twenty-first Century Scholars Program (TFCS) that focuses on encouraging preparation and enrollment. The Gates Millennium Scholars Program (GMS), which focused on college choice and academic success in undergraduate and graduate education, is examined.

The Washington State Achievers Program

The Washington State Achievers (WSA) program is a comprehensive encouragement program funded by the Bill and Melinda Gates Foundation. The program provides a guarantee of supplemental aid to 500 low-income students chosen from high-poverty high schools in Washington. WSA has consistently set income eligibility at 30% of the state average income; students from income-eligible families could apply for the program. Noncognitive variables, like ability to deal with racism and to navigate the system, were also used in the selection of applicants (Bial, 2004; Sedlacek, 2004, 2006). WSA students receive supplemental mentoring and coaching during high school and college.

Program Features. The features of the WSA program are summarized in Table 2.1. In addition, large grants were given to high schools to support school reforms, including offering more college preparatory courses and developing small schools within large high schools. The students included in the studies in this book graduated before the school reforms were fully implemented, but did benefit from increased emphasis on college preparatory courses. The WSA recipients received a commitment for last dollar grants for students enrolling in Washington colleges and universities. WSA meets need after other grants, up to specified limits.[2]

Databases. A series of surveys of high school seniors in Tacoma, WA high schools (2000, 2002, and 2003), along with follow-ups the next fall to determine college enrollment, were conducted by Charles Hirschman at the University of Washington. The first year the program was administered, a survey of seniors in Tacoma high schools was conducted, and two of these schools were in WSA. The Gates Foundation funded a follow-up to determine who had gone to college. Two years later, the survey was expanded to include more high schools, some with a closer socioeconomic status (SES) match to the WSA schools. In combination, these surveys provide an excellent source of information on family background and high school courses and are an excellent resource for the analyses of family engagement (chapter 3), academic preparation (chapter 4), and college choice (chapter 5).

Prior Research. The Gates Foundation has funded a set of cohort-tracking studies that followed WSA applicants (selected and nonselected students) through early adulthood.

Table 2.1 Washington State Achievers: Program Features that Link to Academic Capital Formation for Low-Income Students

Potential Linkage	Program Features
1. Easing concerns about college costs in middle school can improve aspirations for low-income families.	The program provides information about aid to students in middle school and high school; students selected[1] in junior year of high school.
2. Educational reforms and funding can improve preparation.	The WSA program provides grants to high schools to support school restructuring. Students are encouraged to complete advanced courses (i.e., International Baccalaureate [IB]) by the Washington Education Foundation.
3. Encouragement and information on academic programs and student aid can improve preparation.	The WSA program provides mentors for WSA students and encouragement to complete advanced courses.
4. Coordinated state financing (need-based aid sufficient to tuition) can ease the burden for campuses to meet financial need with grant aid.	Washington has maintained coordination between funding for student grants and tuition charged, but the policy has not always been followed. The WSA program provides a supplemental guarantee to students receiving awards.
5. Coordinated state finance policies and institutional grants can improve access and opportunity to enroll in selective four-year colleges for prepared, low- and middle-income students.	Washington has a policy aimed at coordinating tuition and state grants, but grants have not been consistently funded.[2] However, supplemental aid provided by the WSA program allows families a better margin of financial resources.
6. Coordinated state finance policies can improve the odds of persistence and degree attainment by low- and middle-income students.	Washington has a policy aimed at coordinating tuition and state grants, but grants have not been consistently funded. Supplemental financial support provided by WSA, coupled with the improvements in preparation, can influence engagement during college and degree attainment.

1   Noncognitive variables (Sedlacek, 2004) are used in selecting students for the WSA program.
2   St. John (1999) used state student records to examine the effects of aid in different academic years with different levels of state grant funding. Findings indicated there was more equity in opportunity to persist across racial/ethnic groups in years when the grant program was better funded.

The results of these studies indicate that aid improves the odds of enrolling in 4-year colleges and persisting (St. John & Chung, 2004b). In addition, funding and improved opportunities to attend college of choice have improved both academic and social engagement during college. While being selected for WSA is significantly associated with improved preparation (St. John & Hu, 2006, 2007), it is not clear which features of the program—high school courses, aid guarantees, or both—were associated with improved access (opportunity to enroll as well as enrollment in 4-year colleges). The analyses in part I use databases developed by the Gates Foundation.

The University of Chicago's National Opinion Research Center (NORC) conducted a freshman survey of about 1,000 students in the 2000 and 2002 cohorts who applied for WSA, about half of whom received awards. This survey instrument included questions about academic and civic engagement from the National Survey of Student Engagement (NSSE), along with other information related to the college experience. This provided excellent information on student engagement, a critical part of the academic capital formation process. The NORC data was used in analyses of engaged learning (chapter 6) and academic success (chapter 7).

Quantitative Methods.[3]   The statistical methods used to analyze the data are discussed in the chapters. Most of the chapters discuss descriptive statistics. Multivariate analyses are included in appendices for readers interested in reviewing them. The aims of the quantitative analyses in this book are to establish extent of difference between awardees and nonawardees (a process reliant on descriptive statistics); examine patterns of behavior using multivariate methods as appropriate to supplement prior studies (detailed in the appendices); and reference the relationship between our findings and the causal analyses that have been completed by others.

Twenty-first Century Scholars Program

Program Features.   The Twenty-first Century Scholars Program is a state program in Indiana that provides aid guarantees to low-income students who take a pledge in the sixth to eighth grades to prepare for college and remain drug free. The state guarantees aid sufficient to meet tuition costs and provides encouragement and support services for students who take the pledge and their families. The features of the program as they relate to the linkages to human capital formation are presented in Table 2.2.

To be eligible for Twenty-first Century Scholars, students must be enrolled in an Indiana middle school and be eligible for the federal free or reduced cost lunch program, which means that eligible students must be from low-income families. When the program was first implemented in 1995, eligibility for this program was not closely monitored in Indiana schools, but a more rigorous test of eligibility was implemented for the high school class of 2000. Students who were included in studies of engagement, preparation, and enrollment were more recent cohorts subject to this more rigorous review of financial eligibility; students in the 1999 high school cohort used to examine persistence and degree completion were not subject to the same level of rigor. Since 2005, about 30% of Indiana's students signed up for the program (Lumina, 2008). Students took a pledge to complete high school, maintain at least a C average, remain crime and drug free, and apply for college and financial aid. In return, they received a commitment from the state for aid and grants equaling tuition at public colleges (even if they chose to attend a private college) and access to an array of support services (e.g., help with homework, counseling, college visits).

For the years studied in this book, students who applied for the Scholars Program did not have to meet any academic standard other than a minimum GPA.[4] When they signed up for the program, they received a financial commitment that should have been sufficient to ease parental concerns about college costs. By following this group, we can examine behaviors and outcomes related to academic capital formation by students who were willing to take a minimal step toward the goal of attending college. This represents an excellent group of low-income students to study with respect to academic capital formation.

Prior Research.   The prior research on the Twenty-first Century Scholars and other policies in Indiana evolved from collaborations among the Indiana Commission for Higher Education (ICHE), the Indiana Education Policy Center, and the Lumina Foundation for Education. The ICHE has collected student records for years, providing

Table 2.2 Twenty-first Century Scholars: Program Features that Link to Academic Capital Formation for Low-Income Students

Potential Linkage	Program Feature
1. Easing concerns about college costs early on can improve aspirations for low-income families.	Students in the Free and Reduced Lunch Program can take the Scholars Pledge to prepare for college and stay drug free which ensures tuition support if they fulfill their obligations and apply for student aid.
2. Education funding and reforms can improve preparation.	Indiana requires all high schools to offer a college preparatory curriculum and provides supplemental funding to schools based on the number of students who complete advanced high school diplomas.
3. Encouragement and information on academic programs and student aid can improve preparation.	State Students' Assistance Agency of Indiana (SSACI) provides support services to Scholars and their parents, including homework support, campus visits, and parent groups.
4. Coordinated state financing (need-based aid equaling tuition) can ease the burden on campuses to meet the financial needs of low-income students.	Provides grants for Twenty-first Century Scholars equaling tuition in public colleges or a subsidy for students in private colleges. State of Indiana requires that the maximum grant award be no larger than tuition charges.
5. Coordinated state finance policies and institutional grants can improve access and opportunity for prepared, low- and middle-income students to enroll in more selective 4-year colleges.	Indiana indexes the maximum award for state grants to tuition in public colleges. Additional costs for Scholars are relatively modest.
6. Coordinated state finance policies can improve the odds of persistence and degree attainment by low- and middle-income students.	The State of Indiana has delivered on its commitment to Twenty-first Century Scholars and fully funded state grant programs. In addition, colleges provide support services for Scholars which can improve academic and civic engagement during college and improve the odds of persistence.

Source: Adrianna Kezar (Ed.). (2010). *Recognizing and Serving Low-Income Students in Higher Education.* NY: Routledge.

a basis for evaluating the impact of the state's grant programs on persistence (St. John, Hu, & Weber, 2000, 2001). The initial study of the impact of the Twenty-first Century Scholarships found that scholars had the same odds of persisting as other aid recipients (St. John, Musoba, & Simmons, 2003). After this study was initially presented at a conference, two program officers from the Lumina Foundation requested another study of the program that focused on enrollment. With financial support from Lumina it was possible to develop a cohort file for a survey of eighth-grade students who graduated from high school and enrolled in college in 1999, examining the effects of taking the scholars pledge on preparation, enrollment, and persistence. These studies found that the program substantially improved the odds low-income students would apply for college and student aid, enroll in college, and enroll in a 4-year college (Musoba, 2004; St. John, Musoba, Simmons, Chung, Schmit, et al., 2002). A follow-up study found that Twenty-first Century Scholars persisted over 4 years as well as did other aid recipients and other low-income aid recipients (St. John, Gross, Musoba, & Chung, 2006).

In addition, Lumina funded the development of a 2000 cohort with data from the College Board surveys and ICHE student record systems. The results of studies using this cohort (e.g., St. John, Carter, Chung, & Musoba, 2006) provided an initial assessment of state policies on preparation, access, and student success. This research indicates that the comprehensive reform approach used in Indiana—the combination of high school curriculum reform, coordinated state finance policies, and aid guarantees coupled with support services for low-income students provided by the Twenty-first Century Scholars Program—contributed to improvement in high school preparation and college enrollment by Indiana high school students.

Databases. This book takes a next step in the process. The Lumina Foundation (2008) funded follow-up studies with the 1999 and 2000 cohorts, along with the development of new cohorts for 2004 and 2005 high school graduates. These quantitative databases were used for the studies discussed in this book, with analyses generated by a University of Michigan research team. In addition, a team of researchers at Purdue University conducted and analyzed interviews with middle and high school students and their parents (Enersen, Servaty-Seib, Pistilli, & Koch, 2008). The analyses presented in part I use quantitative data to discern the ways that state policies and the Scholars Program have influenced academic capital formation by low-income families.

The college cohorts studied in the Twenty-first Century Scholars Program (TFCS) consisted of students who made it to college, unlike the great majority of low-income students. Students who enrolled as freshmen in 2004 and 1999 were studied using student records from the Indiana Commission on Higher Education's Student Information System (SIS). Information on precollege behavior was also available for the two groups.

The 2004 cohort was used for analysis of family engagement (chapter 3) and academic preparation (chapter 4). For this cohort, we had data collected by the TFCS Program that tracked every engagement in the program, including each time a parent or student took part in any of the services offered. This provided an excellent source of information to examine patterns of parent engagement among Scholars. However, no similar records were maintained for students who did not sign up, so we did not have a comparison group for these analyses. We constructed a database on student and parent engagement that included information on student use of counseling services, homework support, and other services along with data on parent involvement (St. John, Fisher, Daun-Barrett, Lee, & Williams, 2008).

The 1999 cohort was used for analyses of degree attainment (chapter 7), and we were able to follow this group through college if they enrolled in a public college. For the 1999 cohort, we had access to an eighth grade survey completed by most students in Indiana public schools; however, low-income students were more likely to be absent on the days these surveys were administered, so it is highly likely the survey does not provide information thorough enough to choose an ideal comparison group. There is also no way to discern which of the non-Scholar respondents would have been eligible for the program since no questions were asked about the federal lunch program or family income. Nevertheless, the 1999 survey can be considered to be a baseline for Indiana students. We used propensity score matching (PSM) as a means of selecting comparable students for the analysis of persistence and degree attainment.

In addition, a research team at Purdue University conducted focus-group interviews with students who had taken the Scholars pledge along with interviews of parents and service providers at regional centers. The researchers conducted interviews and compiled a report with descriptive information from the interviews, *Twenty-first Century Scholars, Their Parents and Guardians, and the Sites that Serve Them* (Enersen et al., 2008). This qualitative data proved invaluable in the analysis of family engagement (chapter 3) and academic preparation (chapter 4).

Gates Millennium Scholars Program

Program Features. The Bill and Melinda Gates Foundation initiated the Gates Millennium Scholars (GMS) Program to provide grants for undergraduate and graduate education for 20 cohorts of high-achieving, low-income students (Table 2.3). The selection process focuses on low-income students and guarantees aid (related to link 1), emphasizes preparation (related to link 2), and a selection process that uses noncognitive variables (related to link 3). However, since awards are made during the senior year, later for most of the first cohort, our analyses do not focus on the first three links. The intent of the program is to improve college opportunity (linkage 5) and degree attainment (linkage 6) for a new generation of leaders.

The Gates Millennium Scholars Program (GMS) provides generous last dollar awards with no award caps during undergraduate years. Graduate education is supported in selected fields (engineering, science, math, library/information science, and public health). With the easing of concerns about cost, students are able to make choices based on their interests rather than monetary considerations such as whether they will have

Table 2.3 Gates Millennium Scholars: Program Features that Link to Academic Capital Formation for Low-Income Students

Potential Linkage	Program Feature
1. Easing concerns about college costs early on can improve aspirations for low-income families.	Applicants must be Pell eligible. Selected students are guaranteed a scholarship meeting need at any undergraduate college and funding for study in selected graduate fields.
2. Education funding and reforms can improve preparation.	Students must meet minimum GPA requirements (3.3 on a 4.0 scale) and complete preparatory curriculum.
3. Encouragement and information on academic programs and student aid can improve preparation.	Partner organizations provide information and select students by racial/ethnic group using noncognitive variables.
4. Coordinated state financing (need-based aid equaling tuition) can ease the burden on campuses to meet the financial needs of low-income students.	If selected, students receive guaranteed scholarships as last dollar grants that meet need after other grants and scholarships.
5. Coordinated state finance policies and institutional grants can improve access and opportunity to enroll in more selective four-year colleges for prepared, low- and middle-income students.	GMS encourages students to apply to and enroll in selective colleges and universities. There is no cap on the maximum award, so costs are removed as a barrier to enrollment in selective colleges.
6. Coordinated state finance policies can improve the odds of persistence and degree attainment by low- and middle-income students.	GMS provides leadership conferences at which students are introduced to career paths related to high priority fields and provides support services as part of the annual award process.

sufficient earning potential to repay debt after college. Easing concerns about student debt can also influence patterns of academic and civic engagement during college, as well as choices about going on to graduate education after college.

Prior Research. Students in this program differ fundamentally from those in the other two programs. Students were required to have a minimum grade point average and letters of recommendation. African American, Latino/a, Asian American, and American Indian students were selected using noncognitive variables (Sedlacek & Sheu, 2004). Low-income students with this level of achievement are outstanding and do not represent the typical low-income students who make up the other two groups.

The GMS Program has been extensively studied using the quantitative databases described briefly below. There have been two edited volumes on GMS (St. John, 2004; Trent & St. John, 2008). A report by the Institute for Higher Education Policy (2010) summarizes some of the most recent research.

Databases. Longitudinal studies were conducted for samples of qualified applicants (recipients and nonrecipients) in the 2000, 2001, and 2002 cohorts by the University of Chicago's National Opinion Research Center (NORC). These surveys have been used in prior studies of patterns of college access and success (St. John, 2008; St. John & Chung, 2004a; Trent & St. John, 2008). Analyses of these cohort databases are used here to examine college choices, academic and civic engagement during college, and patterns of academic success. In addition, we used logical and statistical models that considered students' reasons for their college choices, as a form of habitus, on these outcomes, a step that provides further insights into patterns of academic capital formation (i.e., how lived family experiences and perceptions influence engagement and academic success in college). An advisory team of researchers[5] designed longitudinal surveys that could be used to track students, and NORC developed a longitudinal tracking system. We used survey data for the 2000, 2001, and 2002 cohorts. The surveys asked questions about student engagement and other topics related to college experiences. In addition, follow-up surveys for the 2000 and 2001 cohorts included information on graduation. NORC survey data were analyzed in the chapters on college choice (chapter 5), engaged learning (chapter 6), and academic success (chapter 7).

In quantitative analyses of the GMS cohorts, we examined how state finance policies (as state level variables) influenced student outcomes (as individual level variables) in hierarchical linear models. This provided additional insight into how state finance policies (i.e., tuition charges and funding for need-based grants) influenced the formation of academic capital, especially engaged learning (link 5) and academic success (link 6). The capacity to examine interviews with GMS students and information on GMS and comparison students helps build a more comprehensive understanding of the role of finances in academic capital formation.

FRAMING ACF SOCIAL PROCESSES

To generate a set of claims about social processes related to student transitions, we went back to the early foundational literature: Gary Becker's (1964) concepts of reasoning about educational choices in his formulation of human capital theory, James Coleman's (1988) conceptions of mechanisms of social capital, and Pierre Bourdieu's (1990) concepts of cultural capital and habitus. While these basic concepts have many reconstructions, such as McDonough's (1997) analysis of habitus, we went back to the original conceptions to generate testable claims rather than contending with the many nuanced reinterpretations.[6]

Part of the problem is that the American literature on educational outcomes and related social process has largely been framed within positivist and functionalist notions. Early concepts of social attainment (e.g., Blau & Duncan, 1967) and human capital (G. S. Becker, 1964), for example, had implicit assumptions of cross-generation uplift. Cross-generation uplift was framed in the 1960s when there was great movement toward class uplift in the United States. In contrast, since 1980 cross-generation social regress has been a possibility for all of our poorest, and many of our less-poor citizens (e.g., Friedman, 2005).

Given the tendency to recreate concepts to promote success and minimize barriers, it was necessary to step back and take a postprogressive stance (St. John, 2009b) that recognizes that social progress, status maintenance, and social regress are all possible across generations in most families. Fortunately, we had focus group interview data for students in the three programs. This section first describes the core constructs and then summarizes the claims examined and the qualitative data used for this purpose.

Human Capital

The financial aspect of college access is central to low-income families because they lack the ability to pay for most 4-year colleges without financial support in the form of need-based or merit aid. Human capital theory not only frames public investment in higher education in terms of need-based student aid, it also provides a basis for framing concerns about costs. Both roles of human capital are examined below.

Public Finance of Higher Education in an Economic Frame. Economic theory has had a substantial influence on federal policy in higher education since the 1960s and, to a somewhat lesser extent, on state policy. The theory of human capital argues that governments can make investment decisions based on expected returns (Becker, 1964); if citizens have higher earnings based on education, they will pay higher taxes. This rationale has been used to assess the returns from social and educational programs (Levin & McEwan, 2000). Cost-effectiveness also theoretically applies to individual decisions about education. The argument has long been that individuals consider the costs and benefits of educational investment, especially going to college (Becker, 1964; Hansen & Weisbrod, 1967). In fact, the notion that federal and state student aid can improve college enrollment by low-income students, a claim for which there is substantial evidence (Heller, 1997; Leslie & Brinkman, 1988; Paulsen, 2001a, 2001b), is predicated on the idea that students make choices based on a consideration of their ability to pay for college and economic gains they can expect from attaining a college degree.

Given the well-documented relationship between student aid and college enrollment, especially for low-income students in higher cost 4-year colleges, the decline in state and federal investment in need-based student financial aid in recent decades is troubling. The major federal grant program, Pell grants, has declined in recent decades in relation to college costs. In the late 20th and early 21st centuries, the costs of attending public colleges have increased faster than the maximum award under the Pell program. In some years, the Pell maximum actually declined in real dollars (Figure 2.1). Whether or not there is other grant aid available to fund the gap between costs and Pell award

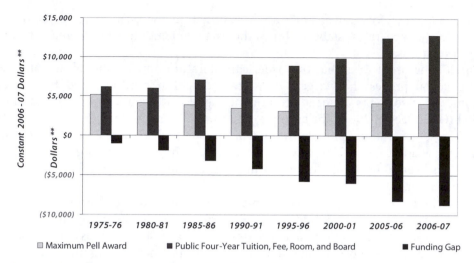

Figure 2.1 The gap between the actual maximum Pell award and university attendance costs.
** Dollar amounts adjusted to July 2006 to June 2007 (CPI-U). Data from Collge Board *Trends in College Pricing 2005*, Table 4a; *Trends in College Pricing 2007*, Table 4b; *Trends in Student Aid 2005*, Table 8a; *Trends in Student Aid 2007*, Table 8b. Source: St. John, 2009b, p. 50.

amounts for low-income families depends on state student aid policy and the availability of need-based grants. For the typical low-income student, the work-loan burden was well in excess of $8,000 per year by the turn of the century (Advisory Committee on Student Financial Assistance, 2002; Hartle, Simmons, & Timmons, 2005), even among students with other forms of grant aid. While some students receive sufficient grant aid to pay for costs, most do not. High-prestige colleges make the commitment to fully fund low-income students (e.g., University of North Carolina, Princeton, Stanford, and so forth), but the vast majority of college-prepared, low-income students do not have access to these institutions.

These financial trends correspond with the inequality in college enrollment rates evident during the same period (see Figure 2.2). In the middle 1970s, African Americans and Hispanics of traditional college age enrolled in college at about the same rate as Whites, an indication that the student aid system was working well after more than a decade of federal policy emphasizing need-based aid. However, gaps eventually reopened. Two new policy trajectories occurred: (1) a decline in student aid (as noted above); and (2) federal policies that emphasize higher standards for graduation put new pressures on all schools, but were a much more difficult burden for underfunded urban schools. Of the two policy changes, the shift in student aid is a more plausible explanation of the differential in enrollment opportunity.

The inequality in college enrollment opportunity is not just a problem for minority populations with histories of poverty. Low-income Whites and Asian Americans face similar difficulties in paying for college, but these populations overall have lower percentages of poverty. Of course, financial aid is not the only barrier for low-income families, but as long as the financial barriers continue, it will be more difficult for low-income families to pay for college than middle- and upper-income families. Research on students in the states with comprehensive interventions provides an opportunity to examine the complex processes of academic capital formation in low-income families whose concerns about college costs have been eased or removed altogether.

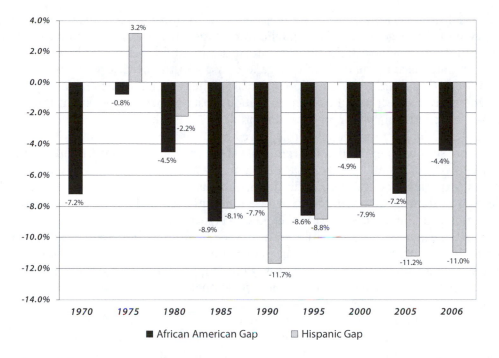

Figure 2.2 Differences in college enrollment rates for African Americans and Hispanics compared to White high school graduates. Source: St. John, 2009b, p. 50.

Social Construct 1: Concerns about College Costs. While economic research typically focuses on price response in enrollment and persistence, such analyses of the direct effects of student aid overlook the ways that financial conditions influence perceptions of college costs, the social processes influenced by these concerns, and related social behaviors. It has long been evident that concerns about ability to pay for college influence college choice and persistence (Cabrera, Nora, & Castañeda, 1993; Paulsen & St. John, 2002; St. John, Cabrera, Nora, & Asker, 2000; St. John, Paulsen, & Starkey, 1996). However, the role that financial concerns play among parents and children in low-income families in determining precollege behavior has not been adequately examined. Data on concerns about college costs have been hard to collect in part because so many low-income children do not apply for college.

Some research shows that many families do not know the exact costs of college or have information about many student aid programs (King, 1999a, 1999b, 1999c, 2004). The core substance argument, as promoted in publications by the American Council on Education (ACE),[7] is that information on aid applications can help solve the access problem. On the other hand, finding out about costs can dissuade parents if the costs after aid are higher than they can afford. The problem is that, in most states, available need-based financial aid—state and federal grants, plus subsidized loans[8]—is lower than the cost of attendance. To attend 4-year colleges, low-income families must borrow from both subsidized and unsubsidized loan programs, as other ACE reports have documented (Hartle et al., 2005).

Thus, whether or not they know the exact net cost of college after student aid, low-income parents know from their own experience—the "trustworthy" sources of information in their social networks—that college costs are a problem. In fact, local knowledge generated from networks may be more accurate, with respect to the financial struggles of paying for college, than official public information that claims students can afford college if they apply for aid. Simplistic information that focuses on aid being available without emphasizing the costs of college after aid and the need to work and manage money can disguise the net cost of attendance for the typical low-income family.

One crucial aspect of family concerns about costs is that worries about the ability to pay can constrain college preparation and negate even the possibility of enrollment. In academic capital formation, the role played by family concerns about costs is deeper and more serious than implied in arguments about information sources and reliability. Many low-income children are born into families with no experience of college and, in fact, experiences of failure in education. Schools are often perceived as unfriendly places by parents, who often do not believe their children will have a fair opportunity in school or in life (St. John, Griffith, & Allen-Haynes, 1997). Out of love,[9] parents may think it is best to protect their children from the potential for hurt that goes along with shattered dreams. While this is not the pattern for all low-income families—many persevere through adversity and find their way into higher education, taking the necessary steps to prepare, apply, enroll, and persist—it is nonetheless part of the culture of many families with no history of college.

A second crucial aspect of concerns about costs is that it can influence engagement during college as well as degree attainment. Even when students make it into college, inadequate student aid and financial concerns can limit course taking, either to minimize tuition costs by taking fewer credits or lack of time related to having to work to pay tuition. Concerns about costs are often the artifact of inadequate aid, and they can have a ripple effect. Certainly the research on persistence shows perceptions of inability to pay and having chosen a college for financial reasons have an influence on persistence (St. John, Cabrera, et al., 2000). In addition, there is evidence that these same concerns are associated with engagement in civic and social activities during college (St. John, 2008; St. John, Rowley, & Hu, 2009), which can also have an impact on persistence and success.

The guarantees of student aid in the three comprehensive programs featured in this book allow families to think about college for their children, encourage their children to take the courses necessary to prepare for college, and ease hardships during the college years. Concerns about costs are a focus of the studies included in this book to discern the role these attitudes play, along with the direct effects of money or the lack of it. It is complicated to discern the difference between a concerned attitude about costs and an actual lack of finances. Certainly, attitudes are influenced by experience, so there is a form of validity within the lived culture. The speculation is that concerns about cost are related to lack of knowledge about things like potential aid and scholarship programs (e.g., King, 1999a, 1999b). However, a very real problem is created if people *could* find a way to pay for college but fail to do so because their concerns are overwhelming. Thus the challenges are to, (a) find realistic ways to deal with problems in paying for college, (b) inform people about potential solutions to their financial concerns, but at the same time (c) prepare low-income families for the financial hardships they still may have to endure during the college years.

Social Capital

Social capital theory is widely used to frame research on preparation, enrollment, and persistence by low-income students (Allen, 1992; Allen, Harris, & Dinwiddie, 2008;

Tierney & Venegas, 2007). For example, Tierney and Venegas (2007) have developed a framework for examining the role information plays in promoting preparation for and application to college. This type of research illustrates the importance of social capital theory as a lens for examining challenges in preparation and other academic capital formation processes. In his original article on social capital theory, James Coleman wrote:

> Social capital is defined by its function. It is not a single entity but a variety of different entities, with two elements in common: they all consist of some aspect of social structures, and they facilitate action of actors—whether persons or corporate actors—within the structure. (1988, p. S98)

Thus, social capital theory is consonant with the functionalist tradition of sociology with a lineage from Max Weber to great American sociologists, including Talcott Parsons and James Coleman. Habermas (1987) criticized the functionalist tradition as treating the process—the actions of actors or lifeworld experiences of people—as dependent on structure. He distinguished human systems (e.g., formal organizations and their subsystems) from the lifeworld (the experiences of people interacting within organizations). Our approach in this book involves testing concepts of social capital theory informed by Habermas's critiques of functionalist reasoning.

Habermas distinguished the system and the lifeworld as different and related, but argued that experience should not be subordinate to the system. When researchers carry forward an implicit assumption of subordination of experience to structure, the barriers to the formation of social capital might be insurmountable without changes in structure. For example, Coleman (1988) describes the move of a Jewish family from the United States to Israel to become part of a more supportive environment so their children could have enhanced opportunities. This supports the argument that to increase the odds of success change from one social system to another may be required. Conceptually, it is similar to Coleman's earlier concepts of White flight from urban centers due to busing and even to the more recent movement of middle-income African Americans from cities to suburbs. While we recognize that such structural changes will introduce students to new, contextualized social settings, we are interested in the social processes students experience within their life context, how the processes are experienced, and whether comprehensive interventions can transform trajectories toward class maintenance (reproduction) or either uplift or downward movement.

It is necessary to question the functionalist view of social structure implicit in Coleman's original view: Will system changes (e.g., raising standards for high school graduation) facilitate academic access? Or is it also necessary to change microsystems (e.g., adding better support from schools)? Many of the proponents of social capital theory argue it is possible to alter systems, or cultures, of organizations. For example, Tierney (2006) focuses on the role of trust in facilitating organizational change in higher education. He argues that colleges that have a shared sense of trust with their students are more effective. The alternative is to offer support to help students navigate through systems they do not experience as supportive. This approach involves focusing on human process along with systemic change.

So we also ask: Can encouragement organizations outside of schools provide services that actually alter the trajectory of students, transforming a student not expecting to attend college to one able to find pathways into and through the advanced courses necessary for college preparation? This book focuses on the ways social capital processes change when aid guarantees and support services are provided. The studies in this book examine the roles of support organizations outside of schools, along with the roles of teachers and other personnel in schools.

Social Construct 2: Trust. Coleman (1988) defines trustworthiness within the context of mutual obligation: "This form of social capital depends on two elements: trustworthiness of the social environment, which means the obligations will be paid, and the actual extent of obligations held" (p. S102). He uses examples of extended families with a patriarch and a "club" such as the U.S. Senate in which members, as "insiders," depend on each other for payback. This concept is problematic when considering uplift or transition into college. If the trust networks (i.e., families and local communities) do not include elders who know about and have experience with the advantages of education, information about college may seem like false advertising because it does not fit with lived social experiences. Certainly the concept of trust, as it is applied to people and building meaningful personal understanding options, is an important concept that should be examined.

Yet Coleman's second notion of trust as mutual obligation could imply a quid pro quo, making the assumption that people form trust as a result of learning the obligations of payback. In the alternate critical conception of social capital, we must question the implied assumption of quid pro quo. Habermas (1990) has argued that the notion of quid pro quo embodies a form of preconventional moral reasoning that creates social problems. If quid pro quo is the core notion of trust in society, there is reason to question the very ideas of charity and the public good. We don't think this morally problematic position is the intent of many proponents of social capital theory, but we need to be careful to consider the possibility that systems of mutual obligation have an inherent inequality of power relations when children are in exchanges with adults, even teachers and parents.

Both assumptions—trust of environment and mutual obligations—hold implied positives. They assume mutual obligation rather than value-based action, or social agencies based on a sense of social justice and "doing what is right." Certainly, it is possible to be supportive of others without expecting an obligatory reciprocity. In fact, the monotheistic faith traditions—Judaism, Christianity, and Islam—hold basic tenets that encourage actions based on values.[10] While many people of faith do not act according to the espoused values of their faiths, there is a strong emphasis on the role of faith traditions in sociology (e.g., Durkheim, 1951). We think it is important to recognize the assumptions theorists make about social structures and value systems.

Given the structure and value-interpretive positions embedded in this foundational conception of social capital theory, it is important to recognize the implicit moral problem. By examining the roles of structure and trust as potentially class maintaining or transforming forces in the academic capital formation process, we attempt to create conceptual space to consider these problems. Further, we need to probe the concept of obligation, since all of these comprehensive programs have an obligation tethered to the financial guarantee in the form of meeting certain academic or social requirements.

If we take Coleman's assertions literally, then it seems reasonable to argue that the concept of trustworthy information is forged within families, schools, and other social structures where people have grown up. For example, if parents do not think they can pay for college after loans and grant awards, a condition facing many low-income families, it is likely that children will hold this same view because their concepts of trustworthy information would be influenced by, if not constructed through, the family. Thus, the belief that college costs too much—a potentially serious problem for many parents who would have entered college since 1990[11] (i.e., the period of the Pell gap, Figure 2.1)—could be the most trustworthy information children receive, at least without structural alterations (e.g., change of communities).

Two forms of structural change are embedded in the comprehensive intervention programs: (1) they introduce new people with whom trust can be constructed (i.e., counselors or mentors) into the child's social system; and (2) they provide the parent and child with alternative possibilities (e.g., financial aid guarantees) that ease their concerns about cost. In the first instance, the family ethos may not change unless the child is able to share information that eases the parents' concern. In the second instance, the parents' change of attitude and acceptance of opportunities within the environment can facilitate transformation of opportunity for their children.

Social Construct 3: Information. Coleman describes information in relation to action: "An important form of social capital is the potential for information that is inherent in social relations. Information is important in providing a basis for action. But acquisition of information is costly" (1988, p. S104). Coleman cites examples of people who gain information about fashion or current events from trusted others. He argues that information accrued through social encouragement can alter cultural and social processes, resulting in improved educational access. He also assumes that socially constructed information provides a basis for new forms of social action.

If information about college options is provided free of charge early in a child's education, it could alter the engagement of parents and children in the pursuit of educational options and academic preparation. There is certainly evidence that *official information* about college preparation, along with alterations in graduation requirements (structural changes), have improved preparation nationally. Between 2000 and 2006 there were improvements in the number of students taking advanced courses, the number of students taking college entrance exams, math scores on these exams, and high school graduation rates (St. John, Pineda, & Moronski, 2009). The fact that high school graduation rates improved in the past decade reversed a trend in prior decades (St. John, 2006a). These recent trends indicate a possible link between policy changes and an improvement in college preparation during this century. However, college enrollment rates for high school graduates actually declined during this same period, at least partly because too many students were applying for too few spots. More students were being prepared for college in a context of less opportunity for college enrollment. These conditions—the increased numbers of dropouts, prepared students not going to 4-year colleges, and students who return to the community after dropping out of college—provide another source of free *unofficial information* for school children.

Given arguments about official information disseminated as part of encouragement programs (e.g., Perna, 2005b), we think it is important to consider both the official and unofficial socially constructed information that students receive, using the criterion of validity of the information in the lives of students as communicated in interviews. Proponents of information and encouragement run the risk of making overly positivist assumptions about the role and value of official information. We need to understand how the meaning of information is socially constructed and shared within communities through new narratives about college. The research studies examined in this book provide some evidence of families through interviews with children and, in a few instances, their parents. The analyses attempt to discern the social conditions of information and access to it. Students who were a part of interventions—like Twenty-first Century Scholars and Washington State Achievers—had access to information that was not available to students not chosen for the programs, some of whom are included in data examined in chapters 3 through 7.

Social Construct 4: Networks.   Another mechanism in Coleman's theory of social capital is norms within social networks, which he views as a form of power and source of action: "When a norm exists and is effective, it constitutes a powerful, though sometimes fragile, form of social capital" (p. S104). To illustrate, Coleman compares graduation rates in private and Catholic high schools. He argues: "the low dropout rates of Catholic schools, the absence of low dropout rates in other private schools, and the independent effect of frequency of religious attendance all provide evidence of the importance of social capital outside the school, in the adult community surrounding it, for this outcome of education" (1988, p. S115). Using this example, it appears that the norms that reinforce educational attainment are situated, at least in part, in the adult networks in which children live.

Coleman's discussion of Catholic schools is similar to analyses of social integration by Emile Durkheim in *Suicide* (1951). Durkheim compared the suicide rates of Catholics and Protestants in European nations, tested different explanations for lower suicide rates by Catholics, and concluded that social integration, rather than faith, explained these differences. Durkheim's argument, as adapted by Tinto (1975), has had a substantial influence on research on college students. The college persistence research consistently notes correlations between integration and persistence (Braxton & Lien, 2000; Pascarella & Terenzini, 2005). Coleman's concept gives us a more critical lens than the traditional concept of social integration used in higher education research.

Coleman rests his argument on the idea that norms, as social processes, can be fragile in action. But there is also an implied positivity embedded in this argument, the linking of norms with the concept of effectiveness. Coleman recognizes that "effective" norms may or may not exist. We focused on the norms that were evident among the high achieving students we studied, as described in interviews, setting aside the implicit positivity embedded in notions of effectiveness. The concept of effectiveness is another manifestation of the functionalist position in Coleman's theory. Taking a critical position required us to consider different patterns, from those that could reinforce the status quo to those that could transform. However, we don't claim that the new patterns observed are norms.[12]

Low-income communities, like all communities, have norms based on shared information and experiences. To make claims about efficacy of norms requires us to make judgments about interpretation of information before we consider how families construct meaning as part of the interpretive process. If a community's norms do not reinforce college-going or engaged learning during college, it is important to discern why they exist and whether they help maintain the communities in question, including the supportive and caring norms within those communities. Norms of behavior within families can be caring in intent and action even when they don't support educational attainment (St. John, Griffith, et al., 1997; Wooden, 2007). If we assume "effective" means going to college, then a norm that does not support going to college would be "ineffective" and should be altered. We first need to understand the meaning of the norm and its value within its social system before considering efficacy or whether altering the norm is even desirable.

It is apparent from research on the parents of children in high-poverty schools that they love their children even if they have personal fears of school based on their own experiences (St. John, Griffith, et al., 1997). A crucial question is: How can networks that do not support preparation for and enrollment in college be transformed to provide this support? This question maintains a positive attitude toward college-going without projecting negativity onto behavior that reproduces a status quo other than college. This brings us back to questions about the cultures underlying social capital that may reinforce reproduction of educational dropout.

Social Class Reproduction versus Cross-Generation Uplift

Class reproduction provides a conceptual basis for framing the underlying cultural forces that reinforce conveyance of social class—and educational attainment—across generations. If economic capital refers to the financial resources within families and societies that enable people to attain educationally, and social capital refers to the structures and experiences within society that foster or inhibit educational attainment, class reproduction can be seen as an underlying process that reproduces social status and education levels as aspects of social class. In periods of social instability, class reproduction may be conducive to social maintenance, such as the Hindu caste system in India that had existed for centuries before the British colonial period. Erik Erikson (1969) argued, for example, that British occupation inhibited the evolution of Hindu traditions that might have gradually transformed into a more socially just faith tradition.

The United States went through a period of class uplift between World War II and the election of Ronald Reagan, with the creation of the middle class. Western European countries went through similar transitions in the 20th century. Now Western democracies are in a neoliberal period with evidence of regression with respect to social equity (Fogel, 2000; Friedman, 2005; Harvey, 2005). In this context, there can be transitions for families up and down the social hierarchy. Education as a form of capital within families plays an important role. It is reasonable to assume that low-income families with a history of higher education have a different knowledge about preparation for and access to college than the majority of low-income families who lack this educational opportunity. Cultural capital, as explained by Pierre Bourdieu (1990), provides a construct that explains this form of transferable family knowledge. Bourdieu also uses the concept of habitus to depict the recurrent cultural patterns in families and communities that reproduce social class.

The espoused value placed on increasing educational attainment—as endorsed by advocacy groups promoting education as a strategy for economic development (Commission on the Skills of the American Workforce, 2007)—seems to contradict regressive tendencies evident in contemporary Western democracies. That is, greater emphasis is being placed on educational outcomes at the same time that it is more difficult for low-income families to acquire the financial resources to pay for college. All too frequently, low-income parents must obtain unsubsidized loans from private lenders to pay for their children to attend public 4-year colleges (Hartle et al., 2005). This means that families already facing unstable economic conditions may have to put themselves at greater financial risk. It also means some families—the lowest income families in states that do not provide sufficient need-based aid—must take serious financial risks for one or more of their children to have any hope of rising up in class in an apparently regressive period.

These conditions are further complicated by the recent problems with the global economy. For nearly 4 decades middle-income families have borrowed on their homes to pay for college, a strategy that gave them access to low-cost, tax-deductable financial capital. The decline in the value of homes and in lending capital which started in 2008 and appears likely to extend into the foreseeable future will make it more difficult for low- and middle-income families to borrow money to pay for college. Some of the obstacles to attending college are worsening while the costs of college still appear to be rising. The potential for cross-generation regression in social class and educational attainment is painfully clear.

To make matters more problematic, working-class occupations are in transition. In the economy of the mid-20th century there were many middle-income jobs that could be attained with a high school education. In the early 21st century, having at least some college is considered necessary to attain a job with earnings sufficient to support a family. To maintain their social class, working-class families with no history of higher education may have to encourage their children to attain at least a 2-year or technical college degree in order for them to be able to find employment consonant with their expectations. These conditions, abundantly evident in the early 21st century, mean that cross-generation stability—the habitus of working-class families—may be severely challenged at the same time low-income families are seeking an education for economic survival. Class reproduction can have a different meaning in this time of economic and social instability—class downgrade. Within this context, we should consider the roles of cultural capital and habitual patterns of families and students as individuals within families.

Social Construct 5: Cultural Capital. We can understand cultural capital as the accumulated knowledge of education in the family system. Bourdieu's (1990) conception of cultural capital, on which most of these interpretations are based, is:

> Just as economic wealth cannot function as capital except in relation to an economic field, so cultural competence in all of its forms is not constituted as cultural capital until it is inserted into the objective relations set up between the system of economic production and the system producing the producers (which is itself constituted by the relationship between the education system and the family). When a society lacks both the literacy that would enable it to preserve and accumulate in objectified form the cultural resources inherited from the past, and also the educational system that would give its agents the aptitudes and dispositions required for symbolic reappropriation of those resources, it can only preserve them in their incorporated state. (pp. 124–125)

This definition places the concept of cultural capital at the nexus of the educational and family systems, with family knowledge being constructed by experience with education. In this context, it is possible to see how changing education systems might influence the views of parents. For example, do parents view the introduction of a more rigorous curriculum as supportive of or detrimental to their children? The answer probably depends on the culture of the family and the ways in which the educational changes are communicated and understood. Certainly the correlation of high school dropout with the new educational standards (St. John, 2006a) suggests that at least some families do not view all changes toward stiffer requirements as a positive development.

Some families may lack the capacity—what Bourdieu refers to as "the literacy that would enable it to preserve and accumulate in objective form the cultural resources inherited from the past" (1990, p. 125)—to benefit from changes in the educational system or to realistically take advantage of new opportunities. This particular definition, the one we work with in this book, confronts us with interesting questions with respect to the role of children and parents in relation to changing education systems.

It is necessary to distinguish maintenance of status across generations from uplift, a step that is sometimes missing when researchers attempt to apply indicators of cultural capital in studies of student outcomes. A middle-class family in Connecticut with prior college experience is likely to encourage college for their children as a matter of status maintenance. Similarly, a working-class family in Gary, Indiana, with no prior college experience may expect their students to learn a trade rather than risk status to go on to college. The Gary family would be changing status, potentially upwardly, if they encouraged their child to attend college and their child was successful in college. On the other hand, a typical Connecticut family would probably view the notion of trade school as a form of downward mobility. Part of the problem with putting variables related to college knowledge and encouragement into a regression is that it assumes the variables have equal value for both groups,[13] while in fact college encouragement is status maintenance for one family and status uplift for the other. If we assume the working-class family wants college for their children, then we can also assume a value of cross-generation uplift. However, it is important to test such assumptions by listening to—and decoding—what children and their parents actually say.

When educational systems change in ways unfamiliar to parents, the family system may resist the change. This could be due to values about status maintenance if parents expect their children to have the same quality of education they had. In fact, it is possible that student departure from high school could be attributable to parental disbelief that a curriculum change is intended for their children. Alternatively, families may fear new and more advanced education because they don't understand it. For example, adding new requirements for advanced math can result in students taking math courses their parents don't understand. If parents cannot help with math homework, then both child and parent may be confronted by new challenges especially since some of the student's peers will be able to rely on their parents for help with homework, creating an inherent inequality.

It is possible that interventions can overcome this sort of challenge. For example, setting up mechanisms for students and parents to get help with homework, a feature of Indiana's Twenty-first Century Scholars Program, could provide a partial solution for parents who aspire for cross-generation uplift but can't help with homework, but such an assumption must hold up to evidence. At the very least, it is important to consider how families, as systems with caregivers to children, understand and respond to upgrading educational offerings or requirements. This process would seem complicated even if all families had access to excellent education, but not all high schools are equal or excellent; when standards are raised, that does not mean all students have access to an education that meets the standard.

Most low-income families live near and enroll in K-12 schools that struggle to meet new educational standards. Children are often confronted by the need to acquire new forms of literacy—to place value on learning complex computations in math or abstract and unfamiliar notions in science and literature—at the same time their teachers may be struggling to understand how best to teach these same concepts. The problem of changing educational systems (e.g., a high school that historically provided vocational training being required to offer a college preparatory curriculum) complicates cultural capital because stasis is no longer possible. Educators must adapt to providing new forms of knowledge, a process that may be overwhelming—recall that Bourdieu argues for "the educational system that would give its agents the aptitudes and dispositions" (1990, p. 125)—at the same time their students are struggling to accumulate that new knowledge.

This interactive notion of cultural capital formation and its complexity is important for understanding how low-income families engage in academic capital formation and whether there are sound ways to organize interventions and formulate policies to encourage these transitions. We work with the concept of cultural capital to focus on the interaction between the cultures of learning in families in relation to the change processes embedded in the educational systems and the intervention programs with which they interact.

Social Construct 6: Habitual Patterns. Underlying the process of reproduction in Bourdieu's sociology is the concept of habitus. Bourdieu (1990) describes habitus as a tacit, replicating, internal patterning system that predetermines strategy:

> The *habitus* explains the paradoxes of objective meaning without subjective intention. It is the source of these strings of "moves" which are objectively organized strategies without being the product of genuine strategic intention—which would presuppose at least that they be apprehended as one among possible strategies. (p. 62)

According to this definition, habitus refers to recurring behaviors or sequences of strategic moves patterned through culturally transmitted habit rather than intention. By extension, the sum of family and community habits can undermine college enrollment by reproducing patterns such as high school to work or early pregnancy as a way out of school or other patterns of dropout (McDonough, 1997). There can be culturally transmitted forces that actually discourage cross-generation uplift. For example, working-class families that value status maintenance across generations may have fears about risking limited family financial capital on education that costs more than can be borrowed or earned during the college years.

However, families can also transmit a pattern of cross-generation uplift, evident in the historical African American tradition (Siddle Walker, 1996). In this pattern, families steer through prejudice and support their children to do better than their parents, persevering through a system that often has inherent prejudice that constrains uplift. There is a conscious intention of breaking through barriers of class within a culturally transmitted commitment to uplift, conveyed through parents wanting more opportunity for their children than they had themselves and support communities that share these values. This pattern of commitment has been observed in some African American schools engaging in reform (Allen-Hynes, St. John, & Cadray, 2003; St. John, Griffith, et al., 1997; Wooden, 2007).

The analyses of interviews focus on two types of documented patterns within families and communities: (1) *replicating patterns* that reinforce the level of educational attainment across generations within families; or, (2) *transforming patterns* that support uplift across generations *within an extended family*. Our research considers low- and moderate-income families with students who are mostly first-generation college. We thought about the ways both reproduction and transformation were framed.

First, while focused on transitions within families as contrasted to the questions related to school class transformation in society, providing a focus that links critical theories to programs that aim to promote educational gains for individuals, we were careful not to degrade efforts to maintain social class. A concept of status maintenance emerged that was more compatible with observed behaviors than was a notion of class reproduction as externally imposed. Behaviors that seek to maintain social status may be considered a reproductive process when great social value is being placed on improving high school preparation, but placing too much emphasis on the new behaviors can blind us to reasons why families seek to maintain class.

Second, since notions of class transformation are beyond the normal language of education reform, we also considered the ways engagement in comprehensive intervention programs can empower parents and children to shift from status maintenance to habits that reinforce uplift. We considered the noncognitive variables studied by Sedlacek (2004) that distinguish children who have a capacity for personal uplift expressed through self-navigation of educational and social systems. We examined the role of replication/status maintenance, transformation/uplift, and self-navigation as processes that help prepare students for going to college, as well as the role of self-navigation throughout the college years as students make choices about engagement in social and civic activities, decide on and change majors, and persist through or leave college. The two programs that included qualitative data on retention—WSA and GMS—used noncognitive variables for selection, so the study of students in these programs provides information on self-navigation skills.

The concept of easing concerns about costs can be explained in relation to habitual patterns. Specifically, if parents have concerns they will not be able to pay for a 4-year college even with student financial aid, it is highly likely that they will convey these concerns to their children, which could affect preparation. Two of the exemplary programs studied in this volume—Twenty-first Century Scholars and Washington State Achievers—provided early aid guarantees for high school students, which has the potential of inducing change in perceptions, a major barrier to college access, which can also influence preparation (i.e., taking advanced courses and acquiring college knowledge).

We focus on discerning different types of habitual patterns evident among different groups of low-income families, including but not limited to concerns about costs. By comparing how different groups of low-income students make educational choices and engage in educational processes, we hope to learn more about the habitual patterns that reinforce gains in educational attainment among low-income, first-generation students. Interventions that aim to increase attainment among first-generation college families must recognize the importance of altering habitual patterns. The aim should not be to encourage the individual to leave the community, but should include an emphasis on giving back, using the acquired cultural capital to recreate opportunities across generations within families and communities. This type of giveback, without the expectation of quid pro quo, seems necessary for social progress.

ANALYSIS OF ACF SOCIAL PROCESSES

The method used in analyses of social processes related to academic capital formation is presented in three parts: focus group data on the programs; initial constructs examined; and methods of testing and reconstructing the constructs stated above.

Focus Group Data

Focus group interviews were conducted as part of the ongoing research on each of these successful programs. While none of the programs had random assignment of awards, which would have permitted a more scientific study of the causal impact of the financial aid portion of the programs, focus-group interviews were conducted on award recipients for each of the programs.

Washington State Achievers. In addition to the quantitative databases, the Gates Foundation contracted with SRI International to conduct interviews with students who received WSA awards. The transcribed interviews were made available for this study. They provide a thick and rich source of information in the students' voices about family engagement, high school preparation, family college knowledge, college choices, and engagement during college.

The transcribed data, *Focus Group and Life History Interview Transcription*, includes eight case histories and 100 focus groups involving about 50 students (Hilberg, Joshi, & Means, 2006), Achievers who had attained 4 years of college. The case histories were especially helpful because they asked questions related to the sequence of academic capital formation (ACF) processes, making it possible to track a group of students through the process with retrospective interviews. The focus group interviews added student voices to further illustrate and extend patterns observed from the case histories. The interviews were used in the analyses of family and community engagement (chapter 3), academic preparation (chapter 4), college choice (chapter 5), engaged learning (chapter 6), and academic success (chapter 7).

Twenty-first Century Scholars Program. Part of the Lumina Foundation (2008) study of the TFCS program, included a team from Purdue University which conducted focus group interviews with high school students and their parents. The researchers provided portions of transcripts and summary analyses (Enersen et al., 2008). The reported interviews and analyses were examined in the chapters on family engagement (chapter 3) and preparation (chapter 4). Since there was some prior grouping of interviews into topical areas, we cite the authors with each reference of the text.

Gates Millennium Scholars. Focus groups were conducted and transcribed for the Gates Foundation by the American Institutes of Research (AIR). The facilitator asked questions about application for the program, college experiences, and other topics. These interviews provided an excellent information source about student perceptions, motivations, and experiences related to academic capital formation. The focus group transcripts were analyzed in the chapters on college choice (chapter 5), engaged learning (chapter 6), and academic success (chapter 7).

Initial Constructs Examined

Six constructs are used throughout the chapters in part I: concerns about costs, networking, trust, information, cultural capital, and habitual patterns. Based on the initial review, we can hypothesize about a generic set of conditions in low-income families without a history of higher education (Table 2.4), a set of propositions about the barriers facing most low-income students. There was extensive transcription of spoken text in

Table 2.4   Hypothesized Challenges to Academic Capital Formation in Low-Income Families

Concept	Conditions Facing Many Low-Income Families
Concerns about Costs	For low-income families in most states, the costs of public four-year colleges place them out of reach without institutional, state and federal aid. Awareness of financial constraints represents an informed position
Networking	Family networks situated in schools and work settings provide limited exposure to college learning environments; parents and children may have high aspirations and low expectations
Trust	Framed by cross-generation experience of families within communities. Depending on context, there may be school and community support for uplift.
Information	Information from family and friends may be viewed as more trustworthy than information from educators. Trustworthy and accessible information on opportunities can raise expectations; new information technologies provide potential basis for building trust and accessing information informing educational choices.
Cultural Capital	First-generation-college families do not have experiential knowledge of college that can be passed along across generations; most visible signs of education attainment are embedded in local patterns of success among people who are familiar (e.g., doctors, lawyers, teachers)
Habitual Patterns	The routines of families, including attitudes toward education and work expressed in daily actions, are conveyed and reinforced as part of family life. Some students develop capacity to navigate educational and social systems.

the working paper prepared by the Purdue team, along with their summative interpretations. We treated the transcribed text and their summative statements as material for review. We cited the researchers each time their text is referenced as means of respecting their grouping of data as a prior step in the process of data grouping and analysis of qualitative text.

The Six Constructs

First, in the current social context there are educational and financial reforms to improve college access. The interventions studied were implemented in contexts influenced by state efforts to increase educational standards, introduce new grant schemes emphasizing aspects of merit, and other reforms. The low public investment in need-based grants relative to college costs in most states has created a cross-generation perception that enrollment in a 4-year college is beyond the means of most low-income families. Since there have been shortfalls in funding for need-based aid since 1980, it is reasonable to expect that parents faced these severe conditions when they were in high school and expect their children to face similar hardships and financial barriers.

The status quo for most low-income families, based on generations of experience, is that 4-year colleges are not affordable. To alter this condition, families could make structural changes, like moving to states that have more generous student aid programs. However, knowledge of these options is beyond the information networks of most low-income families, so concerns about costs remain problematic as both a real and perceived barrier to opportunity. WSA, GMS, and TFCS all had guarantees of financial aid: As a result, financial barriers were removed, which created opportunities that altered students' prospects compared to other low- and moderate-income, first-generation college students.

Second, the family and social networks of students whose parents did not go to college usually do not include a large number of trusted others with knowledge of the benefits of college. Family relations with schools, including whether parents feel welcome (St. John, Griffith, et al., 1997) are part of the social context that can add to perceived barriers to education. Having alliances with trusted others who have knowledge of education and occupations that require an education may be crucial to overcoming this structural barrier.

Students in the three intervention programs receive supplemental services that alter this pattern: TFCS provides a statewide network of service centers to support preparation; WSA provides mentors in high school, the community, and college, as well as support personnel through the College Success Foundation; and GMS provides Scholars with an opportunity to attend a leadership conference along with support services. As part of this study, we examine the ways these networks and services alter the social process related to academic capital formation.

Third, trusting the educational system to provide a quality education and the state to fund college education represents a leap of faith for many low-income families. When the communities of trust and care within which children are raised distrust public officials and educators, it is difficult to persevere through the educational system. Since a majority of low-income students in the United States do not complete high school, there is good reason for distrust of education and educators. A challenge facing educators and education systems is to overcome this distrust by building trustworthy reforms—changes people can depend on to deliver what they claim.

Fourth, official and unofficial information play roles in reinforcing or overcoming distrust of educational systems and educators. There has been the ideological belief among some quasi-government officials that providing information about student aid can overcome the financial barriers to access, but this position ignores decades of inadequate student aid in most states. When the rhetoric of public information and the realities of social life are incongruent (i.e., when the notion that applying for financial aid will take care of affordability problems proves to be untrue), the official rhetoric is understandably not considered trustworthy. In this context, finding accurate information about what to prepare for and how to pay for college represents a major challenge for low-income families; even when the information provided is trustworthy, these families often lack the practical literacy to learn from official rhetoric about how to overcome these barriers.

Students in the three intervention programs faced dramatically different situations from the typical low-income family. They had aid guarantees that were trustworthy. They had additional sources of information—peers, service providers, and media (i.e., Web pages) associated with their programs—that further enhanced opportunity. In addition, the three interventions provided a supplemental network of service providers and opportunities to interact with other students, giving students in these programs additional opportunities to build new, trustworthy relationships. Further, the money provided increased the time available to network and build relationships during college since students did not have to work. The combination of monetary guarantees and support services could alter the systemic relationship between schools and families (parents and students).

Fifth, cultural capital represents the family knowledge of education, including residuals from bad experiences within education systems, conveyed across generations. In families with histories of high educational attainment, cultural capital provides a resource that supports educational attainment across generations. The reverse can be true in families without such histories of higher learning. The culture of the family with regard to education can be conveyed through the sharing of family experiences. Positive interactions between families and schools is crucial to facilitating the formation of the cultural capital needed to complete high school, prepare for and enroll in college, and experience college success.

An overarching question was whether engagement in the comprehensive programs that provide aid and support services actually provided a catalyst to alter cultural capital or overcome barriers associated with lack of it. To address this question, it was important to consider whether participation in one of the three interventions could alter the family pattern, shifting it in the direction of supporting uplift, and giving parents and children a stronger commitment to overcoming educational barriers.

Finally, the habitual patterns of life, conveyed through formal learning and life experiences, can either encourage cross-generation uplift or inhibit it. Engagement by educators and mentors as trusted others may be necessary to empower a family to transform habitual patterns from distrusting educational systems to collaborating with educators and mentors in pursuit of education. The assumption that all parents love their children (Levin, 1996) may be a necessary element of transformative education change.

The two precollege interventions—TFCS and WSA—provide opportunities to alter these patterns through additional support. When educators and parents engage in practices that show care for children, the odds of creating patterns that support and enable educational attainment increase.

In addition, the two programs that provide support services during college—WSA and GMS—select students based on noncognitive variables. This selection process leads to the choice of students with strong self-navigation abilities and provides the opportunity to examine how self-navigation, supplemented by support through comprehensive programs, alters engagement during college.

These six constructs were treated as guiding questions in the analysis of interview data to examine social processes across the sequence of ACF; inquiry into social processes within ACF is a secondary purpose of this book. We reexamine the constructs in relation to study findings in chapter 8. Our aim is to construct understandings that can inform the refinement of interventions and the redesign of public policies, our focus in chapter 9. We used the quantitative analysis to discern whether there was a relationship between program participation and intended outcomes. Using the constructs to guide questions that focus on the qualitative inquiries created an opening for alternative conceptions to emerge.

Analysis of Focus Group Data

The analyses of social processes related to each of the transitions used the critical-empirical approach to test and refine claims derived from different theoretical perspectives as they apply to each of these transitions. The critical-empirical approach involves thinking critically about the claims of competing theories as they apply to a social or educational problem, using appropriate quantitative and qualitative methods to test the claim conceptually, and reconstruct new or refined claims that can be further tested (St. John, 2007, 2009b). The method was derived from the critical analytic approach

Habermas (1984, 1987, 1990) used to develop and extend the theory of communicative action, but does not use or extend this theory per se. The purpose is to test how well claims about phenomena hold up to evidence, qualitative or quantitative, rather than to provide statistical proof of cause. We used qualitative methods to test conceptual claims (as core constructs) from social capital, human capital, and critical theories of social reproduction and transformation. Using this approach, we recognize that causal logic overlooks the roles of social agency and human action. We consider human behaviors, such as teacher or parent advocacy for a child, as socially situated but not determined by the individual's background and context and encouraged or empowered by interventions but not guaranteed by them.

The analyses of core processes focused on the core components of each transition in the academic-capital-formation framework: family engagement, academic preparation, college choice, engaged learning, and college success. The following four steps were used in the two comprehensive interventions examined in each of the analytic chapters—chapter 3 (family engagement), chapter 4 (academic preparation), chapter 5 (college choice), chapter 6 (engagement, both academic and civic/social), and chapter 7 (persistence/attainment).

First, the six social constructs (concerns about costs, information, trust, networking, cultural capital, and habitual patterns) were reexamined to discern a set of hypothesized patterns as specific processes of academic capital formation related to each transition. The qualitative method relied on breaking down the general statement about each claim into a possible process that related to: (a) status maintenance or class replication, and (b) family uplift as a process of acquiring higher education by the first generation in a family.

For family engagement, preparation, and college transitions, we had three initial propositions related to each process, one related to status maintenance and two related to uplift. For college engagement and college success we broke each of the six claims into miniclaims related to academic and civic/social engagement during college. The student's family can be a force that supports preparation and college going as pattern changing or one that reinforces a working-class family culture or another pattern that could be replicated across generations. Status maintaining patterns (i.e., replication) might include encouragement to go to work after college, encouragement to learn a trade (e.g., technical school), or encouragement to stay close to home and attend college part time, possibly to try it out. Our aim was to explore the meanings of status maintenance and cross-generation uplift. These transitions involve communication within families, which made it possible to gain new insights from a detailed breakdown of qualitative data.

Engagement during college, including engagement in academic processes in college, is beyond the experience typically found within families of first-generation college students. So we explored the academic and social dimensions of engaged learning during college as processes that might support uplift. Of course, support, pull back, and silence from families is possible, but these forces would not be directly involved in engaged learning. However, if students had to work excessive hours, they would have less opportunity to take advantage of learning opportunities outside of class or of opportunities for civic service than students who did not have to work as much. Survey questions about engagement during college provided a tight link between the quantitative analysis of academic and social engagement and the analysis of the interviews. For academic success, we considered academic and social engagement and goals after college along two dimensions: expectation or experience of graduate education and career preferences as part of the academic dimension; and social and civic responsibilities. Each analysis includes a table specifying these minipropositions.

Second, the portions of the transcripts related to each transition and minipropositions were coded. The interview data were reviewed several times. As part of a process, the interviews were first bracketed in relation to segments of conversations about each transition. Next, comments were classified into how they were related to the six constructs (concerns about costs, trust, networks, information, cultural capital, and family patterns), then these chunks of text were further broken down and coded in relation to each of the minipropositions. This resulted in distinct sets of interview material related to each topic. For TFCS, the cluster summary statements were analyzed along with the transcripts.

Rather than analyze chunks of interview text to see if concepts held up, the analyses focused on concepts that emerged. Since the three programs had different features and different types of students, analyses discerned themes that emerged within each cluster. Using this approach, we could explore how the voices of students—including the shared perceptions voiced and validated in exchanges within focus groups—conveyed their experiences within each aspect of the social processes related to college.

To some readers this approach might seem repetitive, a potential problem with thick and rich qualitative analyses. However, we encourage readers to ponder the evidence presented about each part of the thematic analyses, to test whether the analyses and conclusions hold up. To us, this seemed the best way to validate constructs.

Third, we compared findings from quantitative analysis outcomes with qualitative data on social processes for each comprehensive program to build an understanding of the role the intervention played in the social processes related to the transitional outcomes. These analyses provided intermediate, program-based constructs focused on how the features of each program related to the outcomes observed. This step constructed understanding about the qualitative and quantitative data for each program to build a summative understanding of how each program functions, focusing on how social processes were transformed within the lives of students, and how the navigational skills of students evolved.

The WSA program included retrospective case histories, which provided an opportunity to explore how students' self-understanding changed over time as well as the linking structures across program features. In contrast, the focus group interviews for TFCS and GMS provided more extensive voices, providing opportunities to make comparisons across groups. The interviews with parents of TFCS students provided an opportunity to compare working-class families to families that lived in poverty. GMS included race-based focus groups, so it was possible to develop themes related to racial/ethnic group difference in social process, including differences in orientation toward uplift. The richness of the data provided the opportunity to make many different types of comparisons across groups and programs.

Finally, we examined the full set of analyses across the programs in each chapter[14] (i.e., analyses of differences to comparison groups). As a conclusion to each of the analytic chapters, it was possible to look across the analyses for each transition as an educational outcome and interrelated social processes enabled by specific program features (e.g., aid guarantees, mentors and so forth). In addition, multivariate analyses of program effects are appended to each for the analytic chapters.

SUMMARY OF APPROACH

The programs compared for each of the academic formation processes, along with the data sources and program features, are presented in Table 2.5. Using both qualitative and quantitative data, Twenty-first Century Scholars and Washington State Achievers are compared on family and community engagement, academic preparation, and college choice, and Washington State Achievers and Gates Millennium Scholars are compared for engaged learning and academic success. In addition, quantitative indicators of outcomes related to academic success (5-year and 6-year degree attainment rates) were examined for Twenty-first Century Scholars. These analyses provide a thorough, multifaceted comparison of the programs along with an exploration of academic capital formation as a social process underlying educational attainment.

The systematic analysis of social processes embedded in education yields insights into academic capital formation as a set of interrelated social processes that foster cross-generation uplift in low-income families. The aims of these analyses are to: (1) inform policy development related to the design of interventions; (2) provide information necessary for the revision of public policy to enable more families to transform educational opportunity; and (3) provide a foundation for a new generation of research on interventions that aim to improve educational opportunity for underrepresented students.

Table 2.5 Summary of Programs Compared, Data Sources, and Program Features for each of the Academic Capital Formation Processes

Process	Programs & Data Sources	Features
Family and Community Engagement **(Chapter 3)**	Washington State Achievers • Surveys of high school seniors in WSA and comparison schools • Case histories and focus group interviews	• Income eligibility • Selects on noncognitive variables • Guarantees Scholarship • Provides school service • Provides mentors
	Twenty-first Century Scholars • Cohort files for students and parents (2004 senior class) • Focus group interviews with students, parents and service providers	• Income eligibility • Voluntary pledge to prepare and keep out of trouble • State guarantees scholarship • Service centers support parents & students (including college visits)
Academic Preparation **(Chapter 4)**	Washington State Achievers • Surveys of high school seniors in WSA and comparison schools • Case histories and focus group interviews	• Income eligibility • Elects on noncognitive variables • Guarantees Scholarship • Provides school service • Funds school reforms • Provides mentors
	Twenty First Century Scholars • Cohort files for students and parents (2004 senior class) • Focus group interviews with students and parents	• Income eligibility • Voluntary pledge • State guarantees scholarship • Service centers support parents and students (including homework support) • Voluntary engagement in support services

Process	Programs & Data Sources	Features
College Choice **(Chapter 5)**	Washington State Achievers • Surveys of high school seniors in WSA and comparison schools • Case histories and focus group interviews	• Funds awards for in-state public and private colleges (last dollar with maximum award) • Supports application process • Requires application for student aid programs • Transfers possible (in-state, plus out-of-state after two years)
	Gates Millennium Scholars • Surveys of Freshmen (2000, 2001, & 2002) • Focus group interviews	• Selects high school seniors using noncognitive variables • Student must meet academic threshold and be Pell eligible • Guarantees scholarship that meets need after all other grant/scholarship aid (no loans required) • Transfers possible
Engaged Learning **(Chapter 6)**	Washington State Achievers • NORC Surveys of WSA applicants (awardees and non-awardees) • Case histories and focus group interviews	• Guaranteed scholarships (undergraduate only) • Transfer options (in-state, plus out-of-state after two years) • College mentors • Foundation mentors • Network support
	Gates Millennium Scholars • Surveys of Freshmen (2000, 2001, & 2002) • Focus group interviews	• Guaranteed scholarship (undergraduate, plus graduate in selected fields) • Leadership conferences
Academic Success **(Chapter 7)**	Washington State Achievers • Program reports • NORC Surveys of WSA applicants (awardees and non-awardees) • Case histories and focus group interviews	• Guaranteed scholarships (undergraduate only) • Transfer options (in-state, plus out-of-state after two years) • College mentors • Foundation mentors • Network support
	Gates Millennium Scholars • Surveys of Freshmen (2000, 2001, and 2002) with follow-up surveys • Focus group interviews • Six-year persistence rates for the 2000 cohort and five-year persistence rates for the 2001 cohort.	• Guaranteed scholarships (undergraduate, plus graduate in selected fields) • Leadership conferences
	Twenty-first Century Scholars • Tracking of 1999 cohort (6 year persistence	• Guaranteed aid • Support services in some colleges

3

FAMILY AND COMMUNITY ENGAGEMENT

Family engagement is an early part of the formation of academic capital within low-income, first-generation families involved in two of the exemplary programs. The selection mechanisms differ for the two programs, setting up different patterns of family engagement from the outset. Washington State Achievers (WSA) are chosen as juniors in high school using noncognitive variables (Sedlacek & Sheu, 2006) and teacher recommendations. In contrast, Twenty-first Century Scholars (TFCS) signed up students for the program, requiring parent signatures, between the sixth and eighth grade. Scholars were encouraged to take a college preparatory curriculum in high school, and they and their parents had opportunities to learn about college requirements and visit campuses. The comparison of the two programs enables an exploration of how relieving concerns about college costs interacts with student and family engagement to form academic capital prior to high school graduation. Before examining the programs, we identify anticipated patterns, or hypotheses, related to the ways program involvement might alter academic capital formation.

Before starting the analysis, we acknowledge the research stance on access. On the one hand, gaining entry to any college represents a breakthrough for many students. Further, completion of a degree—2-year or 4-year—is an important accomplishment, evidence of breaking through the barriers to access. On the other hand, access to 4-year colleges is frequently denied to low-income and working-class children, even if their parents had some prior college. Therefore, we also consider gaining access to and completing a 2-year degree to be an indication of breaking through the access barriers, especially for prepared low-income students. We consider both forms of access as crucial.

REFRAMING FAMILY AND COMMUNITY ENGAGEMENT

The gap in academic capital between wealthy and poor families has early and sustained effects on differentials in achievement by children unless there are appropriately targeted interventions during school. The gap in academic capital begins in the home if, for example, parents do not read to their children before they go to school. Literacy reforms in early elementary grades can narrow the gap (Manoil, 2008; St. John, Loescher, & Bard-zell, 2003), yet the gap usually widens in middle and high school.

Family engagement in rearing and supporting their children in life transitions, including education after high school, is complex because of the barriers both actual and perceived by educators and parents. To start our exploration of family engagement (Table 3.1), we hypothesize three patterns of academic capital formation before under-taking the analysis of interviews. These hypotheses were based on literature reviews, but were also informed by our experiences with the research on related topics. These three hypothesized concepts could be a progression of steps in ACF. The one-time interviews did not permit testing of the sequential possibility. In fact, aspects of all three hypoth-eses were evident in interviews, so they are not mutually exclusive propositions.

The hypotheses guided the examination of qualitative data, but hypothesis testing was not explicitly used; rather, the hypotheses focused the inquiry and new themes emerged. Some of the these were consistent with the hypotheses, but most were not. At some point in the process of learning about colleges, the question of affordability emerges for fami-lies, especially if families struggle economically on a daily basis.

Table 3.1 Hypothesized Constructs for Family and Community Engagement for Basic Patterns Reinforcing No College, Low-Income Families Making Transitions (1), and Low-Income Families with Opportunities to Engage in Comprehensive Programs (2)

Concepts	Family Engagement (From)	Family Engagement (To)
Concerns about Costs	Allowing concerns about college costs to discourage preparation and application for college	• 1. Making informed decisions about options based on information • 2. Taking additional steps if there is funding available
Networking	Engaging in family, community, and religious activities that reinforce the status quo, that do not give a sense of hope or raise expectations	• 1. Seeking out opportunities in the community; moving to communities that have support structures • 2. Engaging in trustworthy programs, especially when it reduces college costs
Trust	Trust in others is critical to success whether or not college is perceived to be an option; some people lack trusted others who are supportive of educational attainment	• 1. Finding mentors in school and community • 2. Building trustworthy networks to gain access to information
Information	The quality of information on college options and costs varies; often it is deceptive (i.e. high-cost loans may seem the only option for college, even when student apply through appropriate means)	• 1. Realistic assessment of costs is critical to avoid high debt with little hope of college attainment • 2. Ability to choose four-year colleges depends on opportunity (e.g.. being in state with generous grants)
Cultural Capital	Recurring patterns of failure in education within families can discourage expectations and support alternatives to college	• 1. Family engagement in learning about options can overcome barriers • 2. Engaging civic and educational opportunities create knowledge of cultural expectations
Habitual Patterns	Replicating patterns of parent and student engagement can reinforce low expectations and poor performance	• 1. Seeking new networks that support transformation • 2. Taking advantage of options and providing cross-generation support

McDonough (1997) and Hossler, Schmit, and Vesper (1999) provide insight into the role of socioeconomic status (SES) in family engagement, providing explanations for the ways family differences influence opportunity. Previously, researchers have found that support personnel in outreach programs like WSA and TFCS can promote preparation (Levine & Nidiffer, 1996), and school personnel can create cultures of exchange with parents (Stanton-Salazar, 1997). There is also strong evidence that family engagement is crucial among academically successful African American students, providing encouragement as well as role models (Harbowski, Maton, Green, & Grief, 2002; Harbowski, Maton, & Grief, 1998). This prior research illustrates the importance of examining: (a) the ways engagement programs encourage low-income parents to provide the type of support typically provided by high SES families; and (b) the ways teachers and community service providers encourage and support parents and children in their preparation for college and college choice.

Family engagement in education is also crucial because low-income and minority students often do not have access to the best courses and teachers (Oakes & Saunders, 2004, 2008). Even in schools that appear to be diverse, minority students are often in segregated classrooms offering courses that meet lower educational standards (Oakes, 2008). In this context, it is crucial that parents and educators become advocates.

This chapter examines the basic social processes that underlie family and community engagement as an academic capital formation process. Based on the critical review of theory (prior chapter), we hypothesized a potential progression regarding the six constructs inhibiting college enrollment (concerns about costs, networking, trust, information, cultural capital, and habitual patterns) from a first response (alternative 1) to a more effective response (alternative 2) (see Table 3.1):

- *Basic constructs inhibiting college access.* We hypothesized social processes related to the basic frame of action for the six constructs as they pertain to family engagement: concerns about college costs, networking, information, trust, cultural capital, and habitual patterns. Without intervention, a pattern of status maintenance could occur that reinforces cross-generation patterns of leaving school before or after high school graduation, transitioning from school to work, or enrolling in a 2-year or technical or "trade" program. We expected to find this pattern in recollections of interviewees about their circumstances before program involvement.
- *Alternative 1*: The conditions under which families might engage in promoting preparation and college opportunities with or without a financial guarantee of aid. For example, parents might acquire information regarding how difficult it would be to pay for a 4-year college, learning more about realistic opportunities (a form of family knowledge before program involvement). We can reasonably expect some of these patterns to have been evident among WSA families prior to selection into the program.
- *Alternative 2*: An activist model of parent and child action (social agency) would enable engagement in activities related to college preparation and exploring college alternatives when programs are in place to provide support services and aid guarantees. We expected to find some evidence of these patterns among interviewees in both programs.

Since the interviews were with students and, in the case of TFCS, parents engaged in the interventions, we don't have a comparison group per se. We tried to discern whether the hypothetical pattern was evident. We assumed that respondents could describe situations related to two or three of the claims. Our approach was to use these hypothetical statements as guides for sorting among quotes, then examining the quotes to see if there was a related pattern. A reconstruction of these initial hypotheses emerged from the analyses.

The sections on the two programs in this chapter review descriptive data related to students who applied for each program, along with evidence from qualitative studies. These analyses aim to inform conceptual understanding of academic capital formation, rather than to confirm hypotheses. The conclusion compares patterns of engagement evident among students in the two programs.

WASHINGTON STATE ACHIEVERS

For the WSA program, we had survey data on students who applied for the program and students who did not. The analyses of the population compare WSA students to the students in their schools who applied but did not receive WSA awards and students who did not apply, providing background information on the population. Analyses of interviews follow with subsections for each of the social constructs.

Population

The Washington State Achievers program (WSA) was the first large-scale program to combine comprehensive school reform (i.e., implementation of the small schools concept) with student financial aid guarantees. Students receiving grants during the 2000 academic year, the cohort interviewed, were chosen late in the academic year, even after completing high school in a few instances. We used the Hirschman survey of the 2002 cohort, the first year for which we had data on WSA applicants and other students in WSA and comparison schools. Next, a table from a study published by Emeka and Hirschman (2006) is presented to illustrate the role the selection process played relative to variables associated with social capital.

The surveys were completed by high school seniors at both WSA and comparison schools, so we had a comparison group. The WSA schools received large grants to undergo school reform (e.g., transition to small schools), and their low- and middle-income students could apply for Scholarships; the non-WSA (comparison) schools received no support.

In 2002, the survey of all students in Tacoma high schools resulted in 143 awardees and only 30 students who applied but did not receive awards, illustrating that during the start-up process there were not an excessive number of applicants. Most of the students responding to the survey, about 90% of high school seniors (Emeka & Hirschman, 2006), had aspirations to attain 4-year degrees. However, there was a larger gap between aspirations for and expectations of receiving a 4-year degree for students in the WSA schools than for students in the non-WSA schools. In addition, the WSA schools had substantially higher percentages of students whose parents had not gone to college (Table 3.2). This illustrates that in Tacoma, schools with lower SES populations received the awards consistent with the intent of the program.

The WSA awardees were similar in SES to other students within their schools. About one third had parents who had attained 4-year degrees, similar to the average in their schools. Surprisingly, the nonselected WSA applicants had lower levels of parental education, so the selection process may have been somewhat biased. Selected students came from majority minority schools, and a higher percentage of the selected students were Hispanic and African American compared to White. However, only a few applicants did not receive awards during this school year. Thus, selection was largely an artifact of nomination.

A higher percentage of WSA awards than nonapplicants had taken advanced courses in high school; the selected students also had higher grades. Most of the students in the initial WSA cohort were nominated by teachers and most nominated students were selected. Yet many of the students in WSA schools had not had access to the advanced courses, consistent with the tracking of low-income students in high schools (Oakes, 2008). In making their decisions about whom to nominate, teachers apparently considered those they thought had a good chance to make it academically in college, even if they had not been tracked into the best curriculum, a privilege often retained by the high-SES students.

There was substantial evidence in the case histories and focus group interviews related to the progression hypothesized in Table 3.1. The case histories were for the first cohort of students receiving awards. Students in this group were selected during their senior year, after they had completed most of their college preparation process. An examination of interviews with students in this group provides insight into how they formed academic capital prior to selection.

Concerns about Costs

Initial Concerns.   The fact that students apply for WSA is a prima facie indicator of family concerns about college costs. A summative preview of the backgrounds of the case study students:

- John, a White male, had a father who had not gone to college and a mother who had attended for 2 years. He was a highly motivated student with a supportive family.
- Leslie, a White female from a broken home, heard about the scholarship late in her senior year in high school and began to apply to colleges only after that. She indicated she would not have gone to college after high school had it not been for the award.
- Liliya was an immigrant from Eastern Europe who came to the United States while in high school. Her biggest challenge was to learn English so she could go on to community college.
- Missy had been a foster child after an extremely difficult childhood. She did not expect to go to college, but did apply to one college after receiving the award.
- Monica was a high-achieving Hispanic student raised by her mother who had inspired her. She had been student body president.
- Oscar, an immigrant from China, enrolled in the tech-prep program when he came to the United States. He expected to go directly into a community college and take technical courses.
- Seth, a White male, was the first in his family to go to college. After receiving the award, his parents encouraged him to make campus tours and go on to college.
- Sky Warrior, an American Indian who had experienced legal problems, had always had high educational aspirations but did not have family support, either financial or emotional.

Table 3.2 Comparison of Students in WSA and Comparison Schools for 2002

Variable	Value	All Schools	Non-WSA Schools	WSA Schools			
				All WSA Schools	Non-Applicants	Applicants	Awardees of
Education Aspiration	To Attain a 4-year Degree	72.5%	74.3%	70.8%	64.5%	52.8%	92.3%
	No	27.5%	25.7%	29.2%	35.5%	47.2%	7.7%
Education Expectation	To Attain a 4-year Degree	63.1%	67.3%	59.2%	51.9%	36.1%	84.6%
	No	36.9%	32.7%	40.8%	48.1%	63.9%	15.4%
Lost Aspiration	Lost Aspiration	10.3%	7.9%	12.5%	13.9%	16.7%	7.7%
	No	89.7%	92.1%	87.5%	86.1%	83.3%	92.3%
Financial Aid Application	Applied for Financial Aid	47.1%	44.1%	50.0%	39.6%	38.9%	81.1%
	No	52.9%	55.9%	50.0%	60.4%	61.1%	18.9%
Education Plan After High School	Planning to Continue Education	76.9%	78.5%	75.2%	68.9%	72.2%	93.0%
	No	23.1%	21.5%	24.8%	31.1%	27.8%	7.0%
Gender	Men	44.1%	44.8%	43.5%	46.0%	58.3%	32.9%
	Women	55.9%	55.2%	56.5%	54.0%	41.7%	67.1%
Ethnicity	African American	17.0%	11.2%	22.4%	21.3%	16.7%	26.6%
	Hispanic	9.8%	7.6%	11.8%	12.6%	13.9%	9.1%
	Asian American	18.0%	13.8%	21.8%	17.8%	33.3%	29.4%
	American Indian	4.6%	4.7%	4.4%	4.1%	8.3%	4.2%
	White	50.6%	62.7%	39.6%	44.2%	27.8%	30.7%
Father's Education	Four-year College and higher	22.0%	28.7%	15.5%	19.3%	8.3%	7.0%
	Lower than Four-year College	78.0%	71.3%	84.5%	80.7%	91.7%	93.0%
Mother's Education	Four-year College and higher	19.8%	25.5%	14.4%	17.0%	0.0%	11.2%
	Lower than Four-year College	80.2%	74.5%	85.6%	83.0%	100.0%	88.8%
Family Structure	Living with Both Parents	57.7%	61.4%	54.2%	57.1%	72.2%	42.0%
	No	42.3%	38.6%	45.8%	42.9%	27.8%	58.0%
Home Language	Other than English	26.2%	8.2%	33.6%	29.6%	55.6%	39.2%
	English	73.8%	81.8%	66.4%	70.4%	44.4%	60.8%
Cumulative Grades in High School	Mostly A	23.3%	26.5%	20.4%	19.3%	2.7%	28.0%
	Mostly B	46.1%	46.5%	45.6%	42.6%	52.8%	51.7%
	Mostly C	25.5%	22.1%	28.7%	31.4%	38.9%	18.9%
	Mostly D	5.1%	4.9%	5.3%	6.7%	5.6%	1.4%
AP/Honors/ IB Courses	Taken or Taking	45.3%	49.3%	41.6%	37.0%	33.3%	55.9%
	No	54.7%	50.7%	58.4%	63.0%	66.7%	44.1%
% of Sample		100.0%	48.2%	51.8%	35.5%	3.3%	13.0%
N		1,097	529	568	389	36	143

Some of these students had emotional support in their families to make cross-generation educational transitions, while others found social support outside the home, overcoming doubt in their families. A few may have made it into 4-year colleges without the award, but easing the concerns about costs made it possible for all of them to consider more alternatives than would have been otherwise possible. These cases are used below to explore the role of family and community engagement in relation to receiving the scholarship. In addition, focus group interviews are used to explore some of the issues. The analyses focus on emergent themes.

Finding Out about Options.   There was a consistent pattern of expanding the college search process after selection for WSA, even though selection was late in the senior year for many of the case history students. Most applied for college after selection so their choices were limited by this timing. They all received encouragement from a teacher or counselor in high school; school personnel and mentors played critical roles in encouraging students to apply. The critical role of school personnel was the biggest surprise in reading the transcripts, given that prior research had indicated WSA students already had higher social capital than their peers (Emeka & Hirschman, 2006); we did not expect this kind of intervention would have been needed.

Missy received the WSA award after high school ended; she illustrates the role school personnel played during the process. She had an interest in college early on and emotional support from her father, but she had a traumatic childhood. Her father died when she was young. Her mother was an alcoholic. Missy went through a period of being homeless before being placed in a foster home. A high school teacher insisted Missy apply to WSA. Missy commented, "I really started taking it seriously, like, okay, I'm applying for scholarships." She applied to one college.

Taking Additional Steps.   The first WSA cohort included students who had taken steps to prepare for college, although most did not expect to go to a 4-year college. Oscar's technical preparation program in high school provided an internship at Boeing Corporation. Students in the program were strongly encouraged to enter a community college and to work at Boeing. The scholarship empowered Oscar to consider alternatives. As part of his involvement in WSA, he visited the University of Washington campus and commented, "So it was helpful when they actually get you to different places for tours." He changed his goals after receiving the award and visiting campuses, as did several other students. In his interviews, Oscar expressed some guilt about having left the Boeing program, but he also realized that he was an example of success.

Networking

The studies of student selection for WSA indicate that the selected students had strong encouragement (Emeka & Hirschman, 2006) and social skills (Sedlacek & Sheu, 2006) in spite of difficult family circumstances.

Family and Social Organizations.   While parents were not always the primary source of support, some of the students indicated their parents or caregivers had encouraged their educational aspirations. In addition, WSA students tried to encourage their peers and family members. Seth noted, "I was the first to graduate," but went on to say he had two younger brothers in WSA and college. Missy indicated her experience in a foster home helped her break out of a dysfunctional homeless pattern. She commented, "I had to ask for help...I learned about a healthy relationship, healthy boundaries." Most of the WSA students were first-generation college students, playing the role of bringing college knowledge to the family rather than benefiting from already-acquired family knowledge.

Support from Community and Schools.   Other social organizations were also important to many WSA students. Churches and religious organizations provided social support for many. More than half talked about the support they received from their churches or about their involvement in religious student groups. As indicated above, many students benefited from the support networks of teachers, counselors, and others in their schools. One student had been a student body president. Sports teams also played a role, especially for White males; for example, John played football.

Exposure to Opportunities.   In precollege years, students found images of possible educational and career pathways from their limited exposure to college opportunities. Liliya's case represents exposure to a career pathway. After a serious family car accident, Liliya explained, "my whole family after an accident, we were in a hospital…. [T]he health personnel were doing a really good job and so I wanted to be part of that team." In Missy's case, WSA provided an unexpected opportunity for college: she could hardly believe it was real. She had not allowed herself to dream about college until it appeared possible after receiving notice of program acceptance after high school graduation. She said, "That's when I realized, okay, this is probably going to happen. And even then I wasn't 100% until I moved into the dorm and started my first day of classes."

Trust

Although many of these students had limited exposure to educational and career pathways, they found people in their families and in the educational system they could trust; these advisors played a role in opening doors to WSA and college opportunity.

Trusted Others.   Most students who graduate from high school can enroll in open-access community colleges, yet there are forces in families, schools, and communities that discourage college enrollment. These discouraging messages can be explicitly or implicitly sent. Even Achievers had to overcome a feeling that college was not for them.

Parents discourage their children from considering 4-year colleges for various reasons. For example, concerns about costs can motivate guidance from parents to enroll in a community college, a response which may be situated in love and care (i.e., not wanting a child to be hurt by obvious barriers to opportunity). Access to 4-year colleges, even for the academically prepared, is often thought to be beyond the reach of many low-income families. For example, in a focus group one of the students said, "My mom was like, 'Well, just go to community college, stay by the family,' and I got the scholarship and it was, like, last minute."

Teachers were often a source of support but not in all cases. For example, one student in a focus group observed, "Teachers in high school told me that the military was my only choice, so I actually signed up to go in…I had like 3 days left to figure it out, if I was really going or not and the scholarship came through." He added, "Teachers are constantly telling you that you are not going to make it…. So it wasn't until the scholarship that I actually decided to go to the college, to the university." In this instance, trusted others were recommending military service rather than college and the aid award actually made the difference. The focus groups were composed of students in later cohorts, so many had applied on their own initiative.

The key insight from these and other similar comments is that networks of trusted others are not always supportive of enrollment in a 4-year college, especially for low-income students. In many cases, trusted others encourage college-qualified students to consider alternatives to 4-year colleges. These discouraging comments come from people who care for the child and are probably intending to provide a realistic assessment of opportunities available; they also illustrate a social pattern of status maintenance.

Mentors.　Most of these students had mentors—teachers, counselors, and other trusted people in their lives—who provided the advice and encouragement to apply for college and student aid. Liliya, an immigrant, explained how her English teachers encouraged her not only to learn the language but also to go on to college. Yet, when WSA students did so, they often did not find the same level of support. In a focus group interview, a student explained how she had not received the support she needed:

> Well, this particular advisor…was director of the Computer Science department and I went in and, you know, I took my test and everything…. I went in and I said, you know, I have this and in Upward Bound…we built Websites and stuff…. Well, I felt that I was limited because I was not told about the computer literacy exam and I could have tested out of that…I was placed in the lowest possible level on computer literacy.

In this case, the transition from supplemental programs that support college readiness (i.e., Upward Bound) to college was not seamless. This same student explained how the event affected her educational plans:

> I don't know why [I was placed in such a low-level class]. My mom said that it was because I was an African American woman and so him being a Caucasian male…he wanted to make it more difficult and so it frustrated me…. I ended up changing my major because I was never even, he was supposed to be my advisor…. He was not very available, was not very open to discussion even about questions nonrelated to computer science. And I changed…but I thought that was a strong limitation on what I could have done and I am upset about that.

What is disheartening about the comment is how the neglect of a professor can be interpreted as racism. The fact that trustworthy support is not always provided once a student is in college may not be surprising to many of us who teach in college. There is often little training for advising, especially regarding mentoring students from underrepresented groups. Certainly the process of building authentic trust with students is as crucial for professionals in college—professors and advisors—as it is in high school.

Information

The interviews with case history students illustrate that the meaning of information was constructed through a lens of students' lived experiences. Often their social support networks reinforced status maintenance, even though trusted others may have encouraged students to take steps that could help them break through barriers to attainment.

Trustworthy Information.　The concept of quality of information was abundantly evident from the interviews, especially the focus groups where students had the chance to engage in exchange. A sequence of comments in a focus group discussing a College Mentor Coordinator (CMC), a staff person in the College Success Foundation:

1. "For me, the CMC was actually a really good source. She helped me out quite a bit as far as looking at being in school or doing this job, you know, or whatever, you know. She helped me in that sense."

2. "Well, the CMC kind of allowed me to think outside the box, think outside the perspective at times when I was really narrow…This is my last resort where I have to go back home because my family is breaking down or whatever, you know, just instilling the fact that separating from yourself, from your family, or your job, you know, school, you know, just finish it off or whatever."

3. "Aside from the CMC…my mentor [from Upward Bound] at the time…we were already friends because we were in the same high school program, transition program, Upward Bound. So it was easier to communicate with her about things that were going on, and she's also experienced some of the same things because she came from the same area that I lived in."

This exchange is extremely informative with respect to the role that trust and information, in combination, played in reconstructing understanding of college opportunities among these students. In the first comment, a student talks about how a professional advisor helped her to consider options while she was in school, although the issue was to find work.

In the next comment, a student reveals an underlying issue, "thinking outside the box." This student indicated her family was "breaking down" and that the CMC had given her an image of possibilities beyond this current reality. Like many of the students interviewed, she came from a dysfunctional family.

Another student provides an even more revealing comment about how meaningful information is conveyed. In addition to the CMC (a professional within the scholarship program), a person from Upward Bound who had lived in the student's neighborhood, became an important mentor who could be trusted because she came from similar circumstances.

The three comments illustrate that trusted information is received from trusted others: people who provide meaningful information which conveys that alternative pathways really are possible. These students reveal the social constructions of information within life contexts. The trustworthiness of information is related to the way it is conveyed and the relationship with the people who convey it.

Realistic Self-Assessment. It takes a new self-assessment to see beyond the options one expects to realize. This process of reaching new understandings of self—new and realistic self-assessments that reveal something different is possible—is complicated because it involves taking risks. Expectations are created within families and schools. Raising or changing expectations can be set in motion by life experiences; it involves thinking and seeing beyond life as it was structured in everyday environments.

Oscar, who had been in an internship as part of his technical preparation program, indicated that he had expected to get an A.A. degree as part of that program. The campus visits opened up new possibilities. He observed, "So a lot of those things…are actually helping you make a decision." Experiences that take students outside of circumstances they know can be gained by visiting new places, like Oscar's visit to 4-year campuses, or by being encouraged to "think outside the box" as was expressed by the second student above.

Financial Opportunity.   Low-income families use available resources to function, to make it day-to-day or week-to-week. When resources are limited, children and parents learn to live within constraints. In a focus group a student commented, "Some of us… come from families who're on welfare." He added, "For me it had to do with growing up and having nothing to [having] like a huge amount of money. But definitely it helped me a lot with everyday expenses and things like that." These comments illustrate how having money from the scholarship that he needed to manage gave him the opportunity to learn how to handle money, a life lesson.

The issue of having been given money for college does not stop at personal management of money. Another student described her experience in this way:

> My family, they just, I won't ask them just because of my pride, I guess. I just, I don't want to ask, because, like, my brother and sister are not in college at all. My sister has got, like, four kids and is one year older than me and my brother got one kid and he's got so many problems. That they both look at me like, um, mom and dad. I don't accept Christmas money, birthday money from them just because my brother and sister…because they think that just because I'm in college, it's, like, completely me. So it's just, like, I am not going to give them any reason to. I want to try to do this all on my own."

She wanted to make sure any available family financial support went to siblings who had not had the chance to go to college; she did not want them to resent her because of her opportunity. Having been provided with an experience that was beyond the shared expectations of the family, this student experienced a changed role in her family.

The evidence from analysis of national surveys indicates that low-income families support their children long after high school, providing help with housing and family expenses (Schoeni & Ross, 2005). Ironically, the average amount of support provided to non-college-going children is often as much as the net cost of college (the actual cost of college minus aid).

Cultural Capital

Academic capital is constructed at the intersection of the family and school. Ideally, both family and school environments support striving for greater opportunity, for uplift to new life opportunities, but this is not always the case. Below we explore how these patterns of educational encouragement compare and contrast as alternate forms of cultural capital.

Recurring Patterns of Encouragement and Discouragement.   The implicit assumption in social attainment theory is that educational and career opportunities correspond with the education and career attainment of parents (Alexander & Eckland, 1974; Blau & Duncan, 1967). The concept of social capital (Coleman, 1988; Emeka & Hirschman, 2006) expands this notion to include other social processes that function as supportive mechanisms. The concept of cultural capital as a status maintenance force introduces the idea that families and schools can discourage high expectations.

School reform and outreach to students can alleviate discouragement. To illustrate this social mechanism and the ambiguities it creates, we can compare two examples from the case histories. Leslie was from a broken, dysfunctional home. When discussing her life experience, she commented, "I mean, that was kind of a struggle, to do it on my own.... So I kind of had the stress of that, family stresses." Contrast this with Liliya, a student who had to learn English as a high school senior, but had family support. She commented that her mother "taught me that education is, like, the first thing you have to do." Leslie achieved her dreams in spite of a family that was not supportive, while Liliya received the family and school support she needed to overcome language and cultural barriers. Both families were poor economically, neither had prior collegiate education, and both faced many barriers, but there was a difference in the social mechanism—the support of educational attainment as part of the family and school experiences—for the two students. This distinction between family as source of stress and family as source of support plays out through preparation and college transition.

The distinction is important: Some students make it through barriers *without* visible family and school support and prepare in spite of an unsupportive environment, while others make it, at least in part, *because of* support. For many of the WSA students who did not have family support, another adult reached out and recognized an inner quality in the student—appropriately stated as visible indicators of a noncognitive variable— and recommended these students for selection for WSA, as was the case in Levine and Nidiffer's study (1996). The WSA program provided more than the promise of money. Mentors and other supportive adults gave these students a chance to see themselves differently.

The encouragement literature hypothesizes that cultural capital is built through the interventions (King, 1999a, 1999b; Perna, 2005a, 2005b). There was confirmatory evidence: The interviews revealed that students gained new understandings of self in relation to education as a consequence of their involvement in precollege programs, interactions with teachers, and involvement in other community-based organizations. But the links between information and learning about college were formed mostly through social processes rather than through reading posted or printed information.

Inner Sense of Self.   While teachers, counselors, and trusted others provided information and support, most WSA students and applicants had an inner sense of self which was evident to the adults who encouraged them to apply and wrote recommendations for them. Case history students demonstrated an inner resilience, often expressed in recollections going back to early childhood.

Seth, a student who traveled a somewhat more conventional path, commented: "I went to, like, church camp, and my counselor happened to be going into a seminary. And we became pretty good friends, always being pen pals and such, and this is, before the Internet...I was going to be, like, the hippest pastor there ever was. So it was like an ongoing joke throughout my childhood." Seth describes an image of a career path, a professional pathway that could become an outcome of college, which was a guiding force for him. Similar stories were told in most of the case studies.

Early Engagement in Learning Opportunities.   Many WSA recipients described an early interest in education. Sky Warrior said, with pride, that he was the first in his family to learn to read. After years of hardship, a period of being homeless with her mother, and life in a foster home, Missy recollected: "My dad taught me to read. I learned how to read when I was 4 or something." This early nurturing became part of her personal narrative. John, a more traditional student who engaged in a range of high school activities, recalled: "My parents bought a set of encyclopedias when I was in kindergarten. And

I would just sit and, like, read these things and I liked that stuff." While the WSA students ran into educational barriers as they progressed through school, many had an inner desire to learn and attain educationally that saw them through.

The case history students faced difficult circumstances along the way, yet their inner sense of self had formed early in life, traits that may have been recognized by the noncognitive criteria used by teachers to recommend students. Most described events in their lives that could have discouraged them altogether but did not. Perhaps it is not surprising that children with these inner experiences would have been recognized by teachers and mentors and selected for WSA using noncognitive variables focusing on these qualities. There is certainly a congruence evident in these life sequences, from inner yearning to the ability to take advantage of options that emerged during school.

Intermediate Reconstruction. What is compelling about these cases is the extent to which self-navigation toward educational access was an inner force. Yet a shared sense of uplift among students and parents was not as evident. The selection process came from the school and did not require parental action. These insights alerted us to look for individual navigation as a process of moving through social systems, consistent with the noncognitive variables (Sedlacek, 2004).

Habitual Patterns

Another way to examine the inner strength of WSA students is through the lens of the habitual patterns developed through family life, school, and the expression of the inner self in these environments. The concept of habitus as habitual patterns situated in the individual life context is examined below.

Family Expectations. Ideally, students would develop aspirations with the support of their families, but this is not always the case. Sometimes WSA students had to navigate a path that confounded family expectations.

Sky Warrior's parents laughed when he talked about college, but he was determined, "So pretty much as soon as I learned about the concept of college...I was interested in it." But his parents did not share the dream, "So, yea, they were like, no way this little kid is going to high school." In contrast, Oscar chose engineering much as his father had before him: "He was an engineer before, although it was kind of different.... He kind of talked to me about it...more or less like a certificate." So Oscar followed his father's path into engineering, a form of reproduction of fields, but he also had the opportunity for uplift, to alter the trajectory from a 2-year program to a 4-year college.

These cases represent very different habitual patterns, but both young men found their own way into a 4-year college and exceeded family expectations. Oscar's family was a source of support; Sky Warrior made it without family support.

Supportive Networks and Patterns of Transformation. Social experiences in schools have long been associated with college access and eventual success, including sports and other student activities (Jackson, 1978; Paulsen, 1990). But these earlier studies also found that higher-SES students were more likely to go to college.

Some WSA students engaged in traditional support networks during high school. For example, John recalled, "I played football…I was in Knowledge Bowl, which was like the nerd bowl." However, most WSA students did not follow this conventional pattern of engagement within schools.

Religion also played a role in social networking and uplift for half of the students included in the case studies. Leslie, a female student from a broken home, commented that her religion "always encouraged women to go on to school in case of a crisis in the family so that we are able to take care of ourselves in the family [if] something were [to] happen to our spouse." Even though this is a socially conservative church, this communicated belief illustrates an embedded understanding of human capabilities (e.g., Nussbaum, 2004).

This finding on religious organizations raises the prospect of comparing students with religious foundations to those without as a more contemporary way to conceive of the role of religion in capital formation than the older tradition of focusing on Catholicism. Catholicism has been noted as a factor in social integration and reduction of suicide (Durkheim, 1951), and Catholic schools have been cited as providing social capital (Coleman, 1988). These seminal works define a role for religion in social integration, but limit it to Catholicism because of its strong social mechanisms. However, other religions play a role in social formation and should also be considered in studies that focus on the link between involvement in religious organizations and a patterning process that reinforces college going.

The role of educational networks in creating opportunity should not be overlooked. Both traditional patterns (e.g., sports) and alternative patterns (e.g., religion) illustrate the role of networks, consistent with Coleman's hypothesis (1988). While financial support is part of the WSA story, especially with respect to the ability to pay for 4-year colleges, it is not the only story. A compelling portrait of support by counselors, teachers, and other adults emerges from the discussion above.

Taking Advantage of Options. Some students knew they would make it because of family support; others lacked family support but overcame that and other barriers. Some students were on trajectories toward 2-year colleges before the award, while others were not. But all of the students exhibited a capacity to navigate toward success.

Monica had family support, but she was also aware of the need to change her life through education: "I guess the number one thing, like, I always wanted to not live a life that I was living and not like, get stuck in a dead end street and seeing people around me who didn't go anywhere and just wanting a better life. And my mom told me I could do it. I just didn't want to be there. So, I guess that was the motivating factor." This was strong motivation to create a new path, to take advantage of options. The Achievers award opened the gate to this path

The focus group interviews reinforced the image of WSA as life changing. One student commented, "Actually I wasn't going to college and the Achievers Scholar came out, Achiever Scholarship. I was in the first year…I got it and so I went." Whether or not the program altered the trajectory, the award enhanced opportunity. Another focus group student observed, "I can say I am an Achiever Scholar, so like, I want to portray the scholarship, like, you know, good, so it makes me strive harder." In fact, a strong desire to make it, to overcome barriers, is evident with most of the WSA students interviewed.

Pathways to Engagement

An image of school and community engagement emerged from the quantitative and qualitative analyses. The students themselves lacked the prior family experience that would normally be seen among college students, but the WSA selection process used noncognitive variables to select students with resilience and an ability to navigate systems. As was evident in the stories told by Achievers, their selection was often the result of having these qualities recognized by teachers and counselors who encouraged them to apply. Selection into the WSA program not only provided a guarantee of financial support, ensuring affordability, but also provided access to a support network.

These stories illustrate a deceptive component of the access barrier: Low-income students who are prepared still may be steered toward 2-year colleges. If this happens, students may not think of themselves as ready for 4-year colleges even if they are prepared, which represents a loss of social agency. While we recognize that community colleges can provide the first gateway of access (e.g., Voorhees, 2001), students may experience these colleges as a barrier to attaining a 4-year degree. Through the stories examined in subsequent chapters, however, we examine how community colleges can serve as gateways to success in 4-year colleges.

TWENTY-FIRST CENTURY SCHOLARS

One of the key understandings to emerge from the recent research on the Twenty-first Century Scholars Program was the central role family engagement played in academic preparation (Enersen, Servaty-Seib, Pistilli, & Koch, 2008; St. John, Fisher, Lee, Daun-Barnett, & Williams, 2008). Factor analyses of data on student and parent engagement in support services in the 2004 Scholars Cohort (appendix 1), along with analyses of the role of support services in academic preparation, revealed the ways that family engagement can overcome cultural barriers to preparation.[1] The interviews conducted by the Purdue University research team reinforce the central role family engagement plays in taking steps to prepare for college within low-income families.

Population

While the eligibility criteria for Twenty-first Century Scholars—enrolled in sixth to eighth grade in an Indiana public school and eligible for the federal free and reduced cost lunch program—is relatively straightforward, the fact students must sign up and take a pledge complicates research on the program because students who sign up may be more motivated or their parents may be more encouraging than eligible students who do not sign up. Thus, the decision to voluntarily sign up is a self-selection process. After making the decision, students and their parents have access to resources and services to help them prepare for college. As descriptive background on the Scholars population, we present information related to the use of services by Scholars and their parents, then compare the backgrounds of Scholars and other low-income students who make it to college.

Family Engagement in Program Services.   Twenty-first Century Scholars services are provided at regional service centers and at a statewide call-in center. Regional centers provide direct assistance with counseling and homework along with parent groups and campus visits for both students and parents. Whether students and parents make use of these services depends on the initiative of the families, their engagement.

The 5,688 Indiana students on track to graduate from high school in 2005 who took the pledge were eligible to use services under the Scholars Program. The state's information system collected data each time a student or parent used a service. As noted in Table 3.3, most students used the services at one of the regional centers. Only 694 used services like phone-in questions at the state center; 198 used no services; and 2 used services from an unknown regional center. A higher percentage of students who used regional services eventually enrolled in college than did students who did not use services, although the rate differentials were not statistically significant.[2] However, when using services at a center (coded as a dichotomous yes-no variable) was included in a regression analysis, students who used regional services enrolled in college at a significantly higher rate (St. John, Fisher, et al., 2008), so it can be concluded that use of services offered at regional centers was associated with increased odds of college enrollment. This illustrates that making human connections is an important force in large-scale outreach programs.

A large number of service categories were reported in the administrative files. We conducted factor analyses of service use. One factor, *Counseling*, converged for the student data. Students who engaged in greater use of these services were more likely to enroll in college. A regression analysis confirmed this descriptive finding, with a similar 0.1 alpha (St. John, Fisher, et al., 2008), but this does not prove causality.

The role of self-selection in TFCS—students choose whether or not to sign up for the program—complicates efforts to understand factors like service use, and it is not possible to make causal claims. Qualitative research has something to add with respect to increased understanding of how social mechanisms actually work. For example, Levine and Nidiffer (1996) found that both students and service providers in outreach programs spoke to the crucial role of connectivity. We explore these mechanisms. Understanding the ways interventions influence capital formation is an important next step.

Parent Access to Information.   In the literature on college access, the notion of access to information is often conveyed in relation to knowledge of costs and requirements (e.g., King, 2004). No doubt getting information about college costs to students is an important element; indeed, there is substantial evidence that providing information on student aid can create opportunities for parents and children (Hossler et al., 1997). What prior research on college information does not sufficiently convey is the role trusted others play in this process. Written information on requirements may convey facts; however, the verbal and nonverbal messages conveyed by teachers and advisors in schools and colleges and within support networks are crucial to enabling first-generation students to consider college enrollment and success as realistic options.

Three factors converged for parental involvement: *academic preparation* (using services related to learning about high school graduation options); *visits and events* (making campus visits and attending other [including cultural] events hosted by the center); and *career planning* (involvement in events related to learning about employment options). Visits to campuses were significant in enrollment and in the regression analyses. Seeking information about career opportunities was not significantly different for enrolled and nonenrolled students (Table 3.3). However, the mean score for parent involvement in preparation was significantly lower from students who enrolled in the public system than it was for students who did not enroll. In contrast, this factor had a positive association with enrollment in the logistic regression (St. John, Fisher, et al., 2008).

Table 3.3 Descriptive Statistics of Factor Scores for Engagement Activities and Service Center Site Use for Twenty-first Century Scholars in the 2004 Cohort: Breakdown Comparing Enrollment to Non-Enrollment for Fall 2004 (N=5,668)

Activities	Enrollment Status[a]		
	Enrolled (Mean)	Not Enrolled (Mean)	Sig. Diff.
Counseling for the Student (Standardized Factor)[b]	0.03	−0.02	~
Academic Preparation for the Parent (Standardized Factor)[c]	−0.05	0.02	*
Visits and Events for the Parent (Standardized Factor)[d]	0.05	−0.03	**
Career Planning for the Parent (Standardized Factor)[e]	0.03	−0.01	

Support Sites[f]	Total (Count)	Enrolled (%)	Not Enrolled (%)
State Center (Bloomington) ©	694	24.64	75.36
Charlestown	254	37.01	62.99
East Chicago	442	32.81	67.19
Evansville	254	37.01	62.99
Fort Wayne	238	34.87	65.13
Gary	228	44.74	55.26
Indianapolis	567	38.10	61.90
Knox	145	35.17	64.83
Kokomo	243	40.33	59.67
Lafayette	202	37.13	62.87
Muncie	475	36.84	63.16
North Vernon	265	29.81	70.19
Richmond	383	26.37	73.63
South Bend	584	38.18	61.82
Terre Haute	302	31.46	68.54
Unknown ©	2	100.00	0.00
Vincennes	252	38.49	61.51
No Support Site - Student Did Not Engage in Activities	138	30.43	69.57

Note: *** $p<0.001$, ** $p<0.01$, * $p<0.05$, ~ $p<0.1$

a. Enrollment information comes from the SIS database, which contains data only for students who enrolled in Indiana's public institutions of higher education.

b. Continuous variable measuring frequency of personal counseling, academic advising, career advising, and other counseling. Mean = 0, SD = 1

c. Continuous variable measuring frequency of workshop attendance on the following topics: Core 40/Academic Honors, Right Questions, Study Skills/Time Management, and SAT/ACT. Mean = 0, SD = 1

d. Continuous variable measuring frequency of college visits, general events, cultural events, project specific events, and ISTEP workshops. Mean = 0, SD = 1

e. Continuous variable measuring frequency of workshops for study skills, career, and college preparation. Mean = 0, SD = 1

f. Dichotomous variables of participation at this support site or not, with the support site at Bloomington and Unknown support site as comparison

There are several reasons to consider parent involvement in activities related to academic preparation as a positive factor in access. First, the descriptive findings include students who enrolled in private in-state or in out-of-state colleges in the comparison group. Based on research on the 1999 Indiana Cohort, which included information on private college enrollment, we expect that students who sought information on academic preparation would be more likely to enroll in private colleges. The prior study found that Scholars were four times more likely to enroll in private colleges than not to enroll (St. John, Musoba, Simmons, & Chung, 2002). Second, in a logistic regression controlling for other variables, the academic preparation factor was positively associated with enrollment, especially in community colleges (St. John, Fisher, et al., 2008).

Thus, when parents took the steps to learn about preparation, they improved the odds their children would go to college, even though needing this service meant a student had an apparent disadvantage within the public system (i.e., enrolled in public colleges at a lower rate). Each of these factors is informative relative to the goal of building an understanding of academic capital formation.

These findings also reinforce the concept of status maintenance as a pattern of family behavior that values children. Specifically, the fact that children of parents who sought information on careers were less likely to go on to a public 2- or 4-year college implies that these families looked into career options, possibly including trade schools (not part of the public system). We conclude, however, that it is more productive to view status maintenance among working-class parents as a stance that is informed and protective of children's future well-being. In a period of history when college (2- or 4-year) is thought to be a minimum standard for employment, there can be a tendency to view these family patterns negatively. We seek to understand these patterns and therefore try not to assume one type of option is implicitly better than another.[3] While there are some interviews that reinforce this interpretation, we lack the data to test this particular hypothesis in a multivariate or causal model.

Comparison of Enrolled Scholars and Enrolled Pell Recipients.   As is evident in Table 3.3, the majority of students who took the Scholars pledge did not enroll in college. We know from the analyses discussed above that there was a relationship between engagement in services provided by regional centers and the eventual college enrollment of Scholars. The extent of parental involvement seemed to be an important factor for those who made it. In Table 3.4, Scholars who enrolled in college are compared to non-Scholar Pell recipients (Pell also requires that students be eligible for the free and reduced cost lunch program). These comparisons provide interesting insights into the background of the Scholars population, especially when interpreted in relation to the analyses of engagement.

First, there were significant race/ethnicity differences for Scholars compared to non-Scholar Pell recipients. Higher percentages of the Scholars were African American and Hispanic while a higher percentage of non-Scholar Pell recipients were Whites. This could be an artifact of two facts: the centers were in urban areas with higher African American and Hispanic populations and underrepresented students had a greater likelihood of signing up for the program. Since the program does not collect information on race/ethnicity (this information comes from college records), we could not examine engagement with the program broken down by race. However, it is evident that the Scholars Program provides an opportunity for minority students to build academic capital relevant to college enrollment. Thus, while a low number of low-income students were taking advantage of the program, TFCS apparently was a force in the pattern of improving representation of African Americans in college (St. John & Musoba, 2011).

Second, there were SES differences between the two groups. The non-Scholar Pell recipients were more likely to be from families in the low-income quartile of aid applicants[4] (59% of non-Scholar Pell recipients compared to 51% of Scholars). Both groups were clearly lower SES, but non-Scholar Pell recipients had slightly lower incomes, on average, and Scholars had more disadvantages of other types, including being from families that did not provide any financial support (e.g., foster homes, etc.).

Third, there were very substantial differences in the academic preparation of Scholars compared to non-Scholar Pell recipients. While similar percentages of the two groups

Table 3.4 Statistics Comparing Background Characteristics for Twenty-first Century Scholars and Other Pell Recipients Who Enrolled in Indiana's Public Colleges and University, Fall of 2004 (N=8,002)

		Pell Recipient			Twenty-first Century Scholar		
		Count	Col %	Sig.	Count	Col%	Sig..
Gender	Female ©	3569	58.59		1160	60.70	
	Male and unknown	2522	41.41		751	39.30	***
Race/Ethnicity	Native American	20	0.33		11	0.58	***
	Asian/Pacific Islander	93	1.53		28	1.47	
	African American	947	15.55	***	417	21.82	***
	Hispanic	229	3.76	***	106	5.55	***
	White ©	4675	76.75		1314	68.76	
	Missing ©	127	2.09		35	1.83	
Income Quartiles	Low Income	3602	59.14	***	974	50.97	
	Lower-Middle Income ©	2224	36.51	***	660	34.54	
	Upper-Middle Income ©	202	3.32		176	9.21	***
	High Income ©	22	0.36		47	2.46	***
	No reported income (did not apply for financial aid) ©	41	0.67		54	2.81	***
Dependency status	Dependent on parents or indeterminate ©	5769	94.71		1860	97.33	***
	Self-supporting	322	5.29	***	51	2.67	
Completed Core 40	No, Not Applicable, or Undeclared ©	4089	67.13		1175	61.49	
	Yes	2002	32.87	***	736	38.51	***
SAT Verbal score in categories	Low (<=386)	541	8.88		240	12.56	***
	Middle (>386 and <=568) ©	2762	45.35		1000	52.33	***
	High (>568)	654	10.74		194	10.15	
	Missing	2134	35.04	***	477	24.96	

SAT Math score in categories							
	Low (<=389)	556	9.13		243	12.72	***
	Middle (>389 and <=571) ©	2801	45.99		1003	52.49	***
	High (>571)	602	9.88		189	9.89	
	Missing	2132	35.00	***	476	24.91	
Engagement Support Site							
	Bloomington or Unknown Center ©	-	-		169	8.84	
	Regional Center	-	-		1701	89.01	
	No Center: Scholar did not Participate in Activities ©	-	-		41	2.15	
	No Center: Student is Non-Scholar Pell Recipient ©	6091	100.00	***	-	-	
Engagement Activities							
	Scholar did not Participate in Counseling ©	-	-		786	41.13	
	Scholar Participated in Counseling	-	-		1125	58.87	
	Scholar's Parent did not Participate in Academic Preparation ©	-	-		1710	89.48	
	Scholar's Parent Participated in Academic Preparation	-	-		201	10.52	
	Scholar's Parent did not Participate in Visits and Events ©	-	-		1202	62.90	
	Scholar's Parent Participated in Visits and Events	-	-		709	37.10	
	Scholar's Parent did not Participate in Career Planning ©	-	-		1811	94.77	
	Scholar's Parent Participated in Career Planning	-	-		100	5.23	
	No Activity: Non-Scholar Pell Recipient ©	6091	100.00		-	-	
High School Diploma Type							
	Regular ©	1947	31.97		595	31.14	***
	Honors	780	12.81		281	14.70	***
	Core 40	1759	28.88		652	34.12	***
	N/A, Other, GED ©	1605	26.35	***	383	20.04	
Type of College Enrollment							
	Public Four-Year	2798	45.94		965	50.50	***
	Public Two-Year ©	2075	34.07	***	509	26.64	
	Research	1218	20.00		437	22.87	***
Total	8002	6091	76.12		1911	23.88	

~ p < .1; * p < .05; ** p < .01; *** p < .001

(about 10–11%) were in the highest quartile of SAT scores, significantly higher percentages of Scholars took the SAT. In addition, higher percentages of Scholars completed college preparatory diplomas and went on to 4-year colleges and research universities. Thus, Scholars were more likely to take additional steps to prepare for college, a process examined in the next chapter.

Concerns about Costs

There was substantial evidence in the focus group interviews related to the three hypotheses in Table 3.1: (1) low-income families were concerned about college costs, especially before receiving grant notification; (2) receiving information on aid informed choices; and (3) students and their parents took additional steps based on knowing about available aid.

Initial Concerns, Aid Guarantees, and Parental Involvement. The Twenty-first Century Scholars Program asked students to sign up during junior high school, before major concerns about college costs arose. Parents were usually encouraging of the students to follow through and sign up. Some parents reported they got the information in the mail; others reported their children brought them the applications.

One parent reflected, "There wasn't much talk between us, she brought the application home, I filled it out just in time, and at that point did not really understand what we would be getting out of it. I said I want her to go to college and this is going to help us out some way" (Enersen et al., 2008, p. 9). An exchange between three students in a focus group illustrates the students agree:

1. "Actually, it [the paper] was in my backpack; it was crumpled up in my backpack, and my mom saw the paper and joined up for it."
2. "My parents kind of told me to do it. They signed it" (laughter).
3. "Same here. My mom said I had to sign up so I did." (Enersen et al., 2008, p. 9)

This student exchange reinforces the notion that TFCS expanded opportunity through providing information. The parental responses to the information sent home with children is the best example we found of trustworthy information coming from printed material. Yet, as the interviews indicated, parents developed their understanding of college pathways from visiting campuses, getting to know staff in regional centers, and other social behaviors. In this case, we concluded the information was crucial but not sufficient, because the students with more engaged parents were more likely to go to college.

Finding Out about Options. When parents got involved in the program, they learned more about college, a major advantage for first-generation families. One shift is that achievement began to take a priority in families. A parent observed, "They're teenagers and they have sports, and I have to cut the sports out to ensure they get the grades in, and at that school they tell me they can play if they have a D, but I think a D is the same as an F. So I tell them that the lowest grade they can get is a C, but if they can they have to do better" (Enersen et al., 2008, p. 12). Parents learned they can afford college as a result of their engagement in the program. A site coordinator observed, "The college-cost estimator and building relationships between the two of them, you can convince families that they need to go on to higher education and that they can afford to attend" (p. 15).

Taking Additional Steps.   Scholars indicated that college trips expanded their horizons. "When I first joined I was intimidated by people and I made new friends...when I went on college visits. I like doing that stuff with all the people" (Enersen et al., 2008, p. 22). Another student added, "You can live in one area for 17 or 18 years and not go outside of it, and all you know is that region and the people there.... So going to events supplied this you meet gobs of new people" (p. 23). For many of the Scholars, the college support services provided a new social support network.

Networking

In their daily lives, Scholars had many experiences that discouraged preparation and college enrollment. The support services provided by the service centers opened up new possibilities. As a result of college visits and other services, Scholars and their parents could begin to visualize new networks.

Families and Social Communities Can Reinforce Status Quo.   Many of the parents expressed concern their children would face peer pressures that would not reinforce college going. One parent commented: "His friends...they run wild.... Their parents don't care what grades they get and that is very frustrating to me. I can't understand the mindset, and I haven't been with somebody that really wants to help their student" (Enersen et al., 2008, p. 21). Another parent indicated there was "peer pressure from friends to do things that would get him into trouble, alcohol, sex. I haven't heard too much about drugs yet" (Enersen et al., 2008, p. 22).

Through their engagement in Twenty-first Scholars, parents found a way to encourage their children to enroll in college. They engaged in the process of finding out about what it would take for their children to enroll. For example, one parent stated, "If you traced the successful students, I think that you will find that the parental involvement is the key" (Enersen et al., 2008, p. 10).

Support from Service Providers and Parents.   A striking feature of the Twenty-first Century Scholars Program is that service providers in regional centers and parents forged relationships that were cohesive in supporting students. A site coordinator observed, "We have found that a one-to-one relationship with an adult mentor has the biggest impact on students" (Enersen et al., 2008, p. 14). Site personnel clearly tried to build relationships with students, but they were few in number and were reinforced by parental support, enhanced by a peer network of parents.

Parents also found each other to be sources of support. One observed, "And because we are all in the same position, we don't feel alone. There are all these other parents, and the support we get from each other is great." The next parent added, "It's nice, you get to interact with other different parents and find out about their kids with our kids, and they all go to different schools so it's really kind of fun to interact with different people" (Enersen et al., 2008, p. 19).

Parents appreciated the program events which put their children in contact with other children who were motivated. "If you're here, there's a goal. You're around people who, when you get a 13- or 14 year old to come here two weeks before school to do homework or class work, you're focused.... So the program puts them around positive, like-minded people for their age group, which is very tough. So you've sorted out all those who may not be" (p. 20). Parents and service providers became cohesive, reinforcing networks that supported student uplift.

Networking Expands Opportunities. The Scholars site administrators reinforced the importance of relationships in building trust. One stated, "Building relationships with the Scholars and their parents is the number-one key element to building trust with them and keeping them connected" (p. 14). Another commented, "We offer encouragement to students and parents in every interaction we have with them." Parents echoed the importance of having a trusted source of information. One stated, "I like the security of knowing there's people I can call if I have questions. To me it's kind of a foggy thing…knowing all you gotta know and go through to get a kid into college and all the paperwork that's involved and everything" (p. 17). The pathways to college, from filling out paperwork for application through preparation and college enrollment, became known routes that could be traveled rather than mysterious and elusive goals.

Trust

The networks of service providers gave parents trust in the system. They built relationships with staff at the centers, giving them people to call when they had questions. The social network became an important source of trust and encouragement.

Trust of Mentors. In the Twenty-first Century Scholars Program, a pattern of trust was evident between engaged parents and staff in the service centers. They shared responsibility for creating an environment to support academic preparation. For example, a parent commenting on the staff said: "There is a wonderful staff…who always go out of their way to make sure the parents and Scholars receive important information on upcoming events and about their scholarships, their ability to help us whenever needed, and their openness to new suggestions and ideas to make a fantastic program even better" (Enersen et al., 2008, p. 17). This was not an isolated comment, but rather captured the trusting relationship frequently mentioned by the parents interviewed.

Support for Students and Parents. In addition to providing mentoring to students, Twenty-first Century Scholars service personnel provided support to parents. Interviews illustrated the importance of this support for both parents and students.

Site coordinators discussed the importance of parental involvement. One coordinator observed, "Some parents do not participate in programming with their students, so they do not know what Scholars are experiencing. Most of the time these parents are the ones who call too late, wondering why their Scholars missed the deadline for something or how the programs worked" (Enersen et al., 2008, p. 13). Another site coordinator observed, "[I] wish parents would understand the importance of attending events even if there is not food involved." The researchers observed that, "Parental 'buy-in' to the program appears crucial to student involvement in the program [referring to the services provided]" (Enersen et al., 2008, p 13). TFCS was more dependent on parental support, whereas in WSA, teachers reached out to students.

Intermediate Reflection. Parental involvement was a key link in the service component of the Twenty-first Century Scholars Program. Prior research has noted the importance of parents in outreach and support programs (Levine & Nidiffer, 1996). While the link between parents and service providers was not evident in interviews with WSA students, it was definitely a distinctive feature of TFCS students and their parents.[5]

Information

In Indiana, information about the Twenty-first Century Scholars Program has been sent to the homes of students in middle school and high school for nearly two decades (Hossler et al., 1999). The regional service centers provide workshops and facilitate campus visits, promoting learning about college environments and admission requirements. The critical issues, however, are not the delivery of information and mode of delivery, but rather the ways parents and students construct meanings from and act upon the information they receive.

Trustworthy Information. The quality of information was judged by the insights gained by parents and students. The researchers emphasized the idea that through engagement, parents and students come to know about the formerly unknown. They summarize:

> Through participation in events sponsored by various support sites around the state, things that are unknown become known, they become more familiar, easier to enter into and navigate, particularly as the Scholars and parents experience them. There is no substitute for the actual experience. No college brochure can show a Scholar what it will feel like to move about a campus, live in a residence hall, sit in a [college] classroom, do his laundry, or balance her studying and social life. (Enersen et al., 2008, p. 24)

Regardless of social class, most students need to learn about what it is like to live outside their families and to become an engaged learner during college. Children from high- and middle-income families typically know people who have gone to or are in college and are able to visit colleges. On the other hand, students eligible for Twenty-first Century Scholars usually have limited prior connectivity to college in their families and communities, so the opportunities offered by the program for first-hand observation took on great meaning, especially when it was coupled with the many formal communications they received which emphasized students could afford to attend 4-year colleges if they prepared and met admission standards. The visits to campuses seemed to be central to gaining personal insights that could be linked with the vague notion of college as possible.

Realistic Assessment. For many of the Twenty-first Century Scholars and their parents, the challenge was to build an understanding that college was a realistic option. Consider this exchange in a parents' group:

1. "But you know, the other thing too is, it doesn't make it seem like it's so unattainable…like it used to be."
2. "The rites of passage: it just makes it smoother because it is not so much unknown territory."
3. "And it gives them a chance to see the world, it lets them know that the world is bigger than (home town)…It helps a young man say, 'I do care. I do care about my future,' and for a young man that is crucial. (Enersen et al., 2008, p. 27)

In these instances, the knowledge of college opportunity as a realistic goal was evident. Three different images were noted in sequence: College as "attainable," college as a "rite of passage," and college as a "gateway." Learning about college helped in the family transformation from thinking of college as impossible to seeing college as a real possibility.

Financial Opportunity. The key link in the process for Twenty-first Century Scholars is the personal knowledge they can afford to enroll in college and, if they are successful in college, they will have a better quality of life, an opportunity to do better financially than their parents. This sequence of student comments reveals the meanings of the opportunity:

1. "Basically it opened my eyes to all the things you have to do if you want to be successful."
2. "I would say it has given me hope…. It is easier for kids in a resource center, that they offer the different presentations. So every opportunity they had to bring somebody in to give you a glimpse of the outside, so to speak, is just worth its weight in gold."
3. "Not only would it help me afford college, it would help me with the dream, to be able to go to college and get an education." (Enersen et al., 2008, p. 27)

Each of these comments assigns a value to the opportunity and gives insight into the links: between access and eventual success (the first comment); among personal hope, visualizing college as possible, and recognizing an opportunity of great value using gold as a metaphor (second comment); and among college affordability, realizing the dream of going to college and attaining a degree (third comment). In combination, they convey understanding of the opportunity to earn an education as a personal ambition unleashed by access to necessary resources. It is doubtful these students would have been as confident about their future opportunities had they not had the promise of aid and the opportunity to visit colleges.

Cultural Capital

Limited knowledge of college and career pathways narrows the expectations of low-income students and their parents. Even high-achieving, low-income students often have only witnessed medical doctors and a few other professionals first hand, so their aspirations are narrowly focused (evident also among WSA students). This constraining role of cultural capital in low-income families appeared to be in a state of transition among the engaged parents and Scholars.

Transforming Patterns of Discouragement. Looking across their findings, the researchers gained insight into how cultural capital can be transformed from a discouraging force into a form of encouragement. The researchers summarized:

> In many instances, these Scholars are the first generation in their families to attend college. There is no "storyline" of higher education in families. How to think about college—what goes on there, even the ideas of what benefits higher education brings, are all brand new to the scholars and their parents. Without

the role models and support from their families, scholars do not see themselves as college students. The Twenty-first Century Scholars Program opens up new opportunities and possibilities to whole families. (Enersen et al., 2008, p. 25)

This observation links the family narrative to the image of opportunity and possibility of cross-generation uplift. The narrative of the family alters because the possibility of college becomes real; the chance to realize the college dream is suddenly evident. This discovery helps explain the correlation we found between factors related to parent engagement and subsequent outcomes including preparation and college choice, as discussed in the next chapter.

Learning about Options.   Learning about college as a realistic option was apparently the force that changed the family narrative for engaged Scholars and parents. The following comments by parents capture the transformations in expectations along with the altered family narratives:

1. "And it opened the boy's eyes to different kinds of opportunities that are available. It makes a big difference to us."
2. "Well, helps them to succeed in life. They will have skills and a career as opposed to a job at McDonald's (laughs) There is nothing wrong with McDonald's, but it will give them a career...."
3. "But they enjoyed it. You know they really enjoyed it. And, that did make them think on a higher level, because they start thinking like Notre Dame, or I can be an engineer, because some people think they can't be an engineer, you know because they don't have those role models.... I can be a teacher or I can be whatever, you know." (Enersen et al., 2008, p. 26)

These comments illustrate an implicit transformation: from the dead end McDonald's job to a career, a profession; from low expectations to better schools and career options; and from a constrained image of the possible to an expectation of uplift.

Engagement in Civic and Educational Opportunities.   There was only limited emphasis on civic engagement in the Twenty-first Century Scholars Program, and the interviews did not address the topic. So it is not possible to judge whether a commitment to give back or a shared commitment to cross-generation uplift of children in their home communities—the patterns evident in WSA—emerged among students and their parents.

Habitual Patterns

There is often a wide gap between the goal of going to college and expectations of doing so, especially for low-income families. The interviews with engaged parents and Scholars indicated a formation of expectations of going to college.

Developing Expectations.   Parents and children communicated an understanding that college would not be possible without the program and that they must make (and they were willing to make) the effort necessary to make it work. The evidence strongly suggests that students had low expectations before the program, but their parents recognized the potential, creating opportunities to transform family patterns. As noted above, parent interest was a sorting mechanism for most involved families.

Students' comments reinforced the parents' role in the program. One student commented, "My parents had instilled in me that I'm going to college no matter what so I was just, you know, looking for all types of aid that I could find to help me, so why not" (Enersen et al., 2008, p. 9). A parent put it this way, "They know if they do their part, it's there. I can't send them to college, they can't see the total picture, and I can't afford to go, so they are just in school. I have the opportunity to send them now" (Enersen et al., 2008, p. 11). Parents of Scholars expected that college was possible, but realized hard work was necessary.

Supportive Networks and Pattern Transformation. Looking across the analyses of parent and Scholar interviews, it is apparent that a form of social networking emerged among involved parents and Scholars, including parents' decision to have their children take the Scholars pledge; development of trust between parents and service providers in regional centers; and visits to campuses that gave students and their parents an image of college as possible. The multifaceted social networking process engages parents in a process of building a new family narrative that includes communication that college is possible and the formation of grounded expectations among Scholars based on their observations and experience.

Taking Advantage of Options. Parent engagement in the networking services provided by the Twenty-first Century Scholars Program was a critical factor. The researchers described how the families discovered that options might be real and would be facilitated by the program:

> Once the seed of possibility has been sown, there are many questions and some fears. The program uses activities at the sites to introduce scholars and their parents to preparation for, access to, and success in college. The sites offer many activities that range from programs to prepare students for interviews, to build pride in heritage, to make a difference in the world, to spend time on college campuses. Those college visits are, by far, the most mentioned when students and parents are asked about the activities they think are the most meaningful. (Enersen et al., 2008, p. 28)

At one time, cross-generation uplift was part of the American ideal. For low-income families, this hope was lost as the income and education gaps increased between rich and poor (Fogel, 2000; Friedman, 2005). The evidence from Twenty-first Century Scholars indicates that reforming the college dream is facilitated by awareness of college affordability, but is also a result of family engagement, raising expectations through engagement in opportunities to learn.

CONCLUSIONS

Family and community engagement play crucial roles in the initial formation of academic capital among students in low-income families. The two programs (WSA and TFCS) provide contrasting images of family and community engagement as means of forming early academic capital, but both reveal the importance of social networks.

We briefly consider the differences in this capital formation process for the two groups before focusing on the commonalities (Table 3.5).

The selection criteria used in WSA worked in consonance with supportive teachers and counselors who nominated students for the scholarships. Some of these WSA awardees would have gone to college anyway, but most would not have gone to 4-year colleges as is evident in the analyses in the next chapter. For these students, the reaching out of school officials who recognized their talents served as a sorting mechanism that involved, in part, student resilience as measured by the noncognitive variables (Sedlacek & Sheu, 2006) and expressed in student voices in their interviews.[6]

For TFCS, parent engagement played a large role in the process. The quantitative analyses revealed more distinctive patterns of engagement among parents (i.e., the three parental factors in appendix Table A1.1) than students (one factor). The qualitative study of parents and Scholars revealed a pattern of family engagement: Parents played a major role in students' signing up for the program; students and parents engaged in services including college visits; and college expectations were transformed through engagement. For the Scholars, the expectation of attaining a 4-year degree was formed in part through their own and their parents' involvement in the program.

The outreach of and nomination by teachers in WSA was integral to the program design, as was the parent and Scholar engagement and other outreach services were facilitated through the Twenty-first Century Scholars Program. The research on Twenty-first Century Scholars indicates a relationship between involvement in the program and college enrollment, as was evident in prior studies (St. John, Musoba, Simmons, &

Table 3.5 Family and Community Engagement as Academic Capital Formation: Core Process for Washington State Achievers and Twenty-first Century Scholars

Construct	WSA	Twenty-first Century
Easing Concerns about Costs	Students selected late influences engagement late in the preparation process.	Selection by 8th grade maximizes opportunity to influence preparation during middle and high school.
Networking	School personnel—and in some cases parents—provide support and encouragement; churches and other community organizations provide additional support.	Personnel in regional centers support parents and children, enabling them to learn about college; a sense of advocacy becomes evident.
Trust	Students have trusted others in schools and support programs	Parents and students gain confidence from engagement.
Information	Information on college arrives too late in the process to influence preparation	Strong evidence of parent and student engagement in services provided by regional centers.
Cultural Capital	Pattern1: Parents support capital formation. Pattern 2: Students find their way without family support.	Strong commitment of parents and support personnel begins to change culture of the family
Habitual Patterns	Strong individual self-navigation, based on early aspirations, recognized in selection process.	Strong support system enables parents and their students to collaborate on building new knowledge.

Chung, 2002; St. John, Musoba, Simmons, Chung, Schmit, & Peng, 2004). The role of the WSA program in college choice is examined in chapter 5.

There are commonalities between the two programs. Both programs encouraged preparation and college enrollment and provided social support in addition to guarantees of student aid. Based on prior evidence, we assert that social support boosts the impact of aid guarantees. The social mechanisms differed, but both approaches empowered social agency.

Two distinctive patterns of engagement were evident largely as artifacts of design. TFCS motivated students to go to college and their parents to support them to that end; both students and parents became actively engaged in the process. Having decided to get involved when their children were in eighth grade, parents had opportunities to learn about options. In contrast, WSA students were selected later in the preparation process, after they had managed to find their way through most of high school. Mentoring and encouragement during the senior year provided an added boost to students who had already demonstrated self-navigation skills.

4

ACADEMIC PREPARATION

The ability of students to enroll in college preparatory courses is generally viewed as a right in middle-class families, but this is not the case for low-income families (Brantlinger, 1994; Oakes, 2008; Wooden, 2007). Easing concerns about college costs can empower students and their families to consider college as a realistic option, but it is also necessary to have access to advanced courses in high school. Not all families who were awarded Washington State Achievers (WSA) scholarships or who took the pledge for Twenty-first Century Scholars (TFCS) were able to acquire preparatory courses, but as the studies in this chapter reveal, a larger number of these early-aid recipients acquired advanced preparation than did their low-income peers. An investigation into how this prima facie measure of success came about is warranted. This chapter undertakes the difficult task of untangling the effects of school reform and student choice on access to advanced courses.

Many factors can influence whether students gain access to advanced courses. When advanced courses are provided in high schools, prior achievement (i.e., grades and test scores), teacher recommendations, and student preferences have an influence on course placement. Parents also have an influence through advocacy for their children, if they have sufficient knowledge of course offerings and their alignment with college admissions requirements, a form of cultural capital often acquired across generations. Guidance provided by counselors and other advisors may be an important source of information and encouragement if parents lack this knowledge. Both WSA and TFCS provide this type of encouragement and support.

In addition, high schools are in a nearly constant state of reform, tending toward increased access to advanced courses. The WSA program provided grants for the development of small schools within larger high schools and Indiana implemented an ambitious requirement that all schools offer a preparatory curriculum, although neither state had a college preparatory curriculum as a graduation requirement during the period studied. This chapter examines the relationship between high school reform and family engagement as integral aspects of college preparation. The underlying question is: How does involvement in a comprehensive reform—receiving a WSA scholarship or taking the Scholars' pledge—relate to navigating a path toward college preparation during high school? More specifically, does the easing of concerns about costs and participation in support services remove barriers for students to engage in and successfully complete a college preparatory curriculum during high school? The analyses explore how social forces in schools and families along with support provided by the programs empowered students to develop college knowledge and gain access to and success in advanced preparatory courses during high school.

REFRAMING SCHOOL REFORM AND ACADEMIC PREPARATION

High school reform has become one of the major strategies states use to improve college access. The National Governor's Association (Conklin & Curran, 2005) and other groups (e.g., Hoffman, Vargas, Venezia, & Miller, 2007) have advocated for college preparatory curriculum as the minimum standard for all high school graduates. A few states, like Michigan and Indiana, have adopted this new standard for graduation for currently enrolled high school students, but such requirements were not in place at the time the students in these studies graduated from high school. For the next decade or so, most low-income high school students will be enrolled in schools in which advanced courses are an option rather than a requirement. Therefore, examination of how students navigate their way into advanced preparatory courses within schools that offer curriculum options is required. Even when new requirements are implemented, there will still be a struggle for parents and students to get access to the best courses or to teachers whose teaching methods match their student's learning styles. Prior research indicates that low-income students are disadvantaged compared to wealthier students when it comes to securing advocacy (from parents, teachers, and counselors) for participation in advanced courses (Brantlinger, 1994; Oakes, 2008; Tierney & Venegas, 2007; Wooden, 2007). Knowledge of college admission requirements and a perception of an ability to pay for college can, in theory, influence this advocacy.

The quantitative indicators used in this chapter relate to enrollment in advanced courses, measured differently for the two different programs. Receiving an early commitment for aid and encouragement to take advanced courses, features of both of these interventions, can influence completion of advanced courses during high school. In WSA, we used surveys that asked high school students about courses taken or completed to compare the WSA awardees to other groups in WSA schools and comparison schools. The surveys provide self-report data on courses completed. For TFCS, we examined the relationship between variables related to family engagement and high school curriculum for students who went on to college. Although we had no data on high school curriculum completed for students who did not enroll in college, colleges collected and reported on the types of diplomas completed by Indiana residents who enrolled.

We were interested in whether and how students in the two programs gained access to advanced courses in high school. For TFCS, we had data on the extent of parent and student engagement in precollege services, providing a capacity to look at the linkages between student and parent use of services and high school curriculum. Supplementary analyses related to parent and student involvement using factor analyses are to be found in Table A1.1. In WSA, the ongoing school reform process expanded access to advanced courses, and WSA mentors encouraged students to take this step.

Another important question is how the intervention—the awarding of aid and encouragement—empowered the development of new social agency that built college knowledge in the family and resulted in advocacy, if necessary, for access to advanced courses. The six conceptual constructs examined in the qualitative analyses have logical linkages to preparation processes summarized in Table 4.1. The following relationships were hypothesized at the outset of the qualitative analysis:

1. *Easing Concerns about Costs:* We expect that children who do not think they can afford to pay for college will consider a track other than college preparation. On the other hand, providing aid guarantees should increase student expectations of attending college and advocacy among both parents and children for access to advanced courses during high school.
2. *Networks:* It is anticipated that the social networks of low-income children—peers in schools and elders in their families and neighborhoods—will have doubts about college as a realistic expectation. However, students' peers in the engagement programs and the opportunities to visit campuses can create support networks that encourage college enrollment.
3. *Trust:* There is likely to be a breakdown of trust between low-income families and schools, as an artifact of parents' experiences when they went to school (St. John, Griffith, & Allen-Haynes, 1997; Wooden, 2007). In contrast, encouragement can build trust between teachers and students, and outreach services that involve parents can provide opportunities for parents to support students in college planning and visits.
4. *Information:* The social environment can undermine access, creating an unofficial form of knowledge that discredits official and formal information that claims college is accessible and affordable. It was anticipated that engagement programs have the potential to overcome this barrier, creating an inner sense of trust of information about college and that college is possible.
5. *Cultural Capital:* Families with prospective first-generation students typically have limited first-hand experience with colleges and career pathways associated with college degrees. Attaining trustworthy information about college and careers, coupled with taking the steps to prepare and visit campuses, can change the family narrative about college, transforming the impossible to the possible.
6. *Habitual Patterns:* Set patterns within low-income families can reinforce the transition from high school to the workforce, without looking at college as a step toward professional education opportunities. These interventions can help overcome these habitual patterns.

Our findings are consistent with prior research on social capital as a process of engagement (e.g., Oakes, 2005; Stanton-Salazar, 1997). The focus on distinctive constructs provides a new lens through which to explore the ways that the social capital process of networking and mentoring relates to building cultural capital. In these students, we begin to untangle the process of how these mechanisms work together to form academic capital. Clearly, cultural capital is a form of knowledge and learning in a family based on family habits, an orientation toward work or college (habitual patterns), and the willingness to engage in a social networking process to gain knowledge. We continue to explore these linkages.

Table 4.1 Hypothesized Preparation Processes for Basic Patterns Reinforcing No College or Community and Technical Colleges, Low-Income Families Making Transitions (1), and Low-Income Families with Opportunities to Engage in Comprehensive Programs (2)

Concepts	Academic Preparation (Basic Patterns)	Academic Preparation (Alternative Patterns)
Concerns about Costs	Awareness of college costs and failures of student aid system reinforce mistrust of education and pursuit of alternatives	1. Eased concern about paying for college can enhance expectation for college by both parents and children 2. Providing early guarantees of aid can motivate students to prepare and parents to advocate for preparatory courses
Networking	The networks that support preparation can seem distant for children in schools that do not have college preparatory courses and teachers who believe in them	1. Building a capacity for caring reform and in (urban and rural) high schools is necessary 2. Supportive elders in community organizations, churches, and schools build network.
Trust	A breakdown in trust between families in schools leave many adults felling like they are "unwelcome guests" when they talk with teachers	1. Learning to advocate for a child is central to gaining access to the best courses and teachers within schools (becoming worthy of a child's trust as an educational guardian) 2. Mentoring and advocacy by agencies enables parents to advocate for their children
Information	Receive information about vocational options (i.e., tracking); alternatives to high school may be an appeal to parents	1. Take advantage of college preparatory courses; seek information about college options; 2. Take advantage of financial incentives for preparation (merit and/or guaranteed aid programs)
Cultural Capital	Low expectations in the family and community can discourage preparation, encourage alternatives; discouragement can be situated in commonly held concepts of care in the community	1. Community members can provide role models, mentors, and encouragement 2. Cross- and within-generation family support (that is, "giving back") provides addition support for high school students

Concepts	Academic Preparation (Basic Patterns)	Academic Preparation (Alternative Patterns)
Habitual Patterns	Cross-generation patterns or undereducation can persist as an integral part of family culture, even when former employment options disappear	1. Culture of uplift, valuing each generation doing better than the former, should be enacted 2. If families have opportunities to learn about requirements, tests, and their alignment, along with college options, it should be possible to encourage children.

WASHINGTON STATE ACHIEVERS

High school reforms progressed in Washington during the early 2000s, but the pace of change in requirements was slower than in many other states. During the study period, the state had not undertaken reforms in graduation requirements. Washington only required two credits in math and no algebra for graduation. A high school exit exam was required starting in 2008, but this policy was implemented after the students studied in this book had graduated from high school. However, there was evidence in our study that school reforms were underway, including a trend toward increased AP offerings. Thus, during the period when WSA students were in high school, the level of advanced courses available to them was dependent on district-level policy and school-level initiatives.

High School Courses

The students at both WSA and comparison schools had increased access to advanced courses in their high schools. Between 2002 and 2004, the percentage of students in the University of Washington (UW) surveys in WSA comparison schools who took advanced courses—Advanced Placement (AP), Honors, or International Baccalaureate (IB)—increased from 49.3% to 57.1% (Figure 4.1) compared to an overall increase in WSA schools of 41 to 45%. These trends illustrate that the WSA and comparison schools represented different SES strata; the typical student in the comparison school had higher odds of gaining access to advanced courses than the typical student in a WSA school.

Within the WSA schools, students selected for WSA were more heavily represented in AP/IB courses than their peers in school; in 2002, the differential was 14.8 percentage points (55.9% of WSA recipients compared to 41.6% overall). By 2004, the percentage of WSA awardees completing advanced courses had grown to 71.8%, illustrating that most of the WSA students had "gotten the message" to take advanced courses. WSA program officers took this as confirmation their advising had influenced course selection.[1] Program officials considered the trends to be a consequence of their encouragement rather than selection because students were not selected based on curriculum, nor were transcripts considered; instead, students were selected using noncognitive variables. It is likely that the increase in advanced courses by recipients for 2004 is attributable to the encouragement, given the timing of selection before the senior year; students selected in 2002 were selected as seniors, after they had chosen senior year courses.

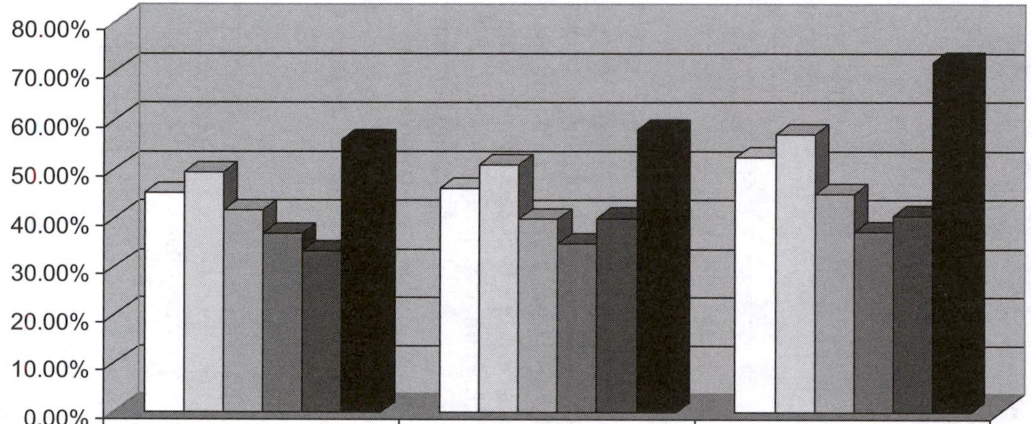

	2002	2003	2004
☐ All Schools	45.30%	46.10%	52.40%
☐ Non-WSA Schools	49.30%	50.80%	57.10%
☐ All WSA Schools	41.60%	39.80%	45.00%
☐ Non-WSA Applicants in WSA Schools	37.00%	34.90%	37.30%
■ Applicants but Non-Awardees in WSA Schools	33.30%	40.00%	40.40%
■ WSA Awardees	55.90%	58.10%	71.80%

Figure 4.1 Trends in percentages of students at Washingotn State Achievers and comparison schools who enrolled in AP/Honors/IB courses.

Concerns about Costs

When we use statistical correlations, most analyses reveal that low-income students are less likely to go to college. Because there is a correlation between low income and lack of parental education, it is easy to conclude parents' lack of education is the problem (e.g., Choy, 2002a, 2002b). Certainly both factors—lacking the money to pay for college and knowledge of college within the family—can impede academic preparation and enrollment. Our analyses focused on the underlying concerns about college costs, along with the implications of removing this barrier. The interviews were conducted long after students had received Achievers awards and experienced college success. Student comments in this section are retrospective and include reflections on situations they faced during high school.

Overcoming Mistrust. Coming into this study, based on critical reading of social theories and research, our hunch was that life circumstances created boundaries of trust: The family and community created a trusted world in which students formed expectations. If social networks conveyed an understanding that college was not affordable, students would think it was out of their reach. By the same token, if teachers and others with whom students interacted implied college was not right for them, such messages would be hard to overcome. It is evident from the analyses in the prior chapter that many students faced these conditions. The receipt of the scholarships changed this, at least in part; however, the culture of concerns about money stayed with students as they made their way through high school and into college. As we dug into the interviews, we found two patterns remarkably similar to patterns of college choice evident in prior quantitative students (Paulsen & St. John, 2002; St. John, Paulsen, & Carter, 2005).

First, a working-class pattern of making choices in relation to work (Paulsen & St. John, 2002) was evident among students. For Leslie, the process of transition to college was grounded in a commitment to work. She commented, "When I graduated from high school I had a good job and so when I started college I kept that job, and then I got two more jobs in college, and so I was always working." Sky Warrior described his life during high school: "The whole time that I was in high school, like I was working. I always had part-time jobs…that's the only reason I never played sports or anything like that. I never had time or money." Neither Leslie nor Sky Warrior probably would have gone on to college full time without the scholarship. Leslie's trajectory suggests she may have become a periodic consumer of college courses, making these locally situated decisions as time and resources permitted. For Sky Warrior, going away to college would not have been possible and even periodic enrollment would have been unlikely. Both examples illustrate a working-class orientation.

Another pattern can be described as situated in poverty, resulting in being dependent on financial support provided by the state, be it from student aid, welfare, foster care, or other forms of assistance to families (Paulsen & St. John, 2002). Consider Missy's story:

> Okay so, being poor, I had lost my belongings several times because we had been evicted before I went to middle school and I lost everything. You know, like pictures, birth certificates, stuffed animals; everything people take for granted…. And, you know, being homeless right before starting middle school…. And just my mom being an alcoholic, not being there, and driving drunk.

Living in difficult situations is not unusual among the students selected as Achievers. As part of the selection process, teachers and service personnel in schools identified and reached out to students who had resilience in spite of difficult life circumstances.

Raising Expectations through Encouragement. Digging deeper into this colorful puzzle of success, WSA students had encouragement from friends as well as educators; students who pushed themselves through tough circumstances seemed to learn from and encourage each other.

Sky Warrior described how one of his friends influenced him to think about college:

> One of my best friends…was always really, really smart. She was always like, she studied a lot, really hard…. And so we actually did some competition as far as our grades and we would teach each other every couple of weeks or whatever, you know? So that actually, that actually encouraged me.

Sky Warrior also credited teachers who took an interest. "I had a lot of teachers that really encouraged me because when it comes to teachers, like, they can recognize a student that has talent and has ability, and is just not using it."

The element of this story that was similar to other stories told by many of the focus group students was the support from school personnel. As illustrated in Sky Warrior's comments, teachers or counselors reached out to students. Beneath the surface of these official networks, peers play a role in the process of coming to understand the potential pathways ahead. The substantial influence of school personnel is evident throughout.

Taking Steps (Role of Guarantees). Most of the case history students received their WSA awards during their senior year in high school, sometimes late in the year. For students who got the scholarship as juniors, WSA provided a boost academically. One focus group interviewee said, "It was a blessing from my junior year. It came out of nowhere…. It was just like, wow, like really changing the game. I am really glad I was going for it." Such comments are congruent with the analyses of UW survey data above: The majority of Achievers who received awards as juniors were exceptional in their schools with respect to taking and completing high level courses. It is highly likely that the awards had a motivating influence on this intermediate outcome, but it is difficult to substantiate this causal link.

Networking

Networking is central to the study of college access (Tierney & Venegas, 2007). Inquiries focusing on strategies for strengthening networks that support educational attainment, including access to and success in advanced high school courses, seem crucial. Based on the reading of the literature, three specific concepts are examined.

Family and Community Networks. It is evident from the examples above that life circumstances often did not reinforce college aspirations. Many students indicated they would have tried to find a job had they not received the scholarship. However, there are also cases of students who faced even more serious circumstances.

A student in a focus group commented: "I wasn't living with my parents. I was living with my older sister in kind of a foster type situation. My sister was my foster mom, which was really bad." She elaborated, "It worked out really bad. But there wasn't any money. There was a lot of dysfunction, fighting and yelling in our family...I really put in my application for the Achievers scholarship way last minute. Then I didn't even apply for college until I had the scholarship." In this instance, it would have been hard for this student to step out of a difficult life circumstance had she not been able to leave home for college.

In some life circumstances there is a deep pull toward replication of dysfunctional patterns, unless there is a transforming force such as the GI Bill, WSA, or TFCS.[2] Compelling features of WSA that made it possible to reach students without benefit of strong family support systems included selection based on recommendations from teachers and support services based in the school that did not require parent involvement.

Caring School Reform. Another question is whether raising requirements for high school graduation is enough to break reproductive cycles that reinforce high school dropout and only modest college attainment. Leslie commented: "Well my cheer advisor was one of my teachers and so I was always her TA. Well, I guess, for example, I have been graduated for 5 years now and I've probably gone back to school every year just to visit with the teachers.... So I had a really good relationship with all of them."[3]

This illustrates a close, trusting relationship between a teacher and a student, a form of advocacy beyond the normal expectations and practices of teachers. This often comes up as we explore other concepts, illustrating how care is conveyed as part of the reform process.

As another example, Monica described the benefits of her access to advanced courses, "I was a smart kid. Like, I started in Honor classes, and then moved on to International Baccalaureate classes." She went on to describe the meaning of one of these classes:

> [In] my English class, my history class...we had oral exams at the end of the year and you're graded on, like, an international basis. And so we had to, it was a really high level of work. Like commentaries and big readings and big papers, and each quarter we had a different stage to it. Like you had a paper once, then you had an oral one quarter, then you had a written exam one quarter. It was pretty intense.

These cases illustrate the commitment to the rigor of the courses and the pride it engendered. This is part of the human aspect of reform, overlooked when analytic models are applied to educational attainment studies. Instead, statistical analyses often use course grades and the types of advanced high school courses completed in analyses of college attainment (e.g., Adelman, 1995, 1999, 2004; St. John, 2006a). As we would expect based on the logic of "success begets success," these variables are always correlated with subsequent success. What these models can't convey is the meaning of the achievement for students, the experience of rigor, and the role of teachers as guides in the process.

Supportive Elders. Recall that Coleman (1988) argues that people in the community function as reinforcing systems. He used the example of Catholic schools as organizations that strongly support educational attainment. He also described a family that moved from a low-income community in the United States to Israel to find a more supportive environment for their child. Coleman's examples can be interpreted as representative of the structural aspects of social capital: (1) schools can provide support structures to improve educational achievement and high school completion; and (2) some community networks provide more support for children than others.[4] These concepts can be applied to the academic capital formation process during high school, focusing on the ways interventions can influence capital formation within existing schools or communities.

In WSA, many examples of teachers reaching out to students have been shown in the analyses, indicating that schools were supportive of Achievers. In another example, Liliya described how she received support from her ESL teaching assistants for the college application process: "There were, like teacher assistants in English as a second language department and they were always, like, helping me with everything. It was, like, 'fill out applications for financial aid' and I didn't even know what financial aid is and they were, well, like, always there for me." These teaching assistants clearly played an active advocacy role for Liliya, providing strong encouragement to apply for the program.

There were, of course, other sources of support in schools and communities. Seth, a student who was "tracked" in negative ways by teachers because of his family background, found other sources of support: "I mean they [support people] really were there for me, you know. It was everything from sports to because I was working. And church, I mean plenty of people that I could always talk to or if I had a problem go to. So I mean I had plenty of people, I just didn't really like high school." Such comments were common among interviewees. These systems of human support were prevalent among the students who made it. Unfortunately, these students may have had potentially high-achieving peers who did not receive this same encouragement.

These examples further illuminate the roles of elders, as people who can support or deter opportunity. In Liliya's case, the support came from teacher's assistants in her ESL class; for Seth, the support came from a broader social network that helped him overcome the negative projections of teachers that could have deterred a less determined student.

Trust

An overall pattern among the WSA interviewees was that teachers and other adults became members of networks of support that helped students overcome the barriers that discouraged academic preparation during high school. Consistent with social capital theory, trust can play many roles. For example, trust in families may pull students back into class reproduction or push them forward in the process of cross-generation uplift. It was important to dig a little deeper into the role of trust in the relationships that emerged between adults and students, both in schools and the community.

Preparation Networks. The idea that family trust could prevent attainment might seem foreign to many readers, but this notion is integral to Coleman's original theory (1988). If you live in a community where there are not many examples of academic success, it is natural to trust the visible evidence around you as a tacit way of knowing, and you might mistrust information that runs counter.

Many of the WSA students had to overcome life circumstances that were trustworthy but not supportive of college going. For some of the students, it would have been difficult to overcome predispositions and behaviors that would have limited college opportunities had it not been for interventions. For example, Missy explained, "I had a couple of teachers take an interest in, you know, tell me I was pretty bright. But I would set myself up. I wouldn't turn in my assignments, or I would, you know, ditch and wouldn't make it to school, where I had the potential and they acknowledged that I had a less-than-stellar work ethic." For Missy, the low-level work ethic in school was congruent with her family culture that was not supportive of education. Her foster family supported development of better work habits, and the support and outreach of teachers helped her overcome a pull from life circumstances to drop out.

In addition, some minority students had to confront prejudice. Monica described her experience dealing with these conditions:

> Some people would just like, oh, [say] "you're getting this because you are a minor-ity"…. Yakima has the Hispanic Achievers Program. And so [if you achieve cer-tain goals]….they award you at a banquet, and I've gotten [that] every year since they started it, since 6th grade…I was pretty proud of myself…. My best friend… she's a minority too and we'd sit in this little patch together, you know, what's the deal with all of this. I don't know, but it didn't hinder me in any way.

Monica had strong support structures through community groups early on, a network of trust which empowered her to overcome problematic social and family barriers.

Peers and Advocates.   There is a long history of viewing college access and success as a function of peer networks (Feldman & Newcomb, 1969/1994a, 1969/1994b; Jackson, 1978; Pascarella & Terenzini, 2005). WSA interviews also showed that peer support was enabling, creating an additional force for uplift in the lives of school children and young adults.

Students learn a great deal from peers, including older students. Seth had not felt strong support from teachers, but he found older peers a source of motivation.

> I come from a small high school, and so…you know some portion of people go to college, and some didn't go to college at all and some of them go to college and then sort of drop out at the end…. A lot of them are either in college or some go on to a 4-year university. So you know, I hang out with a lot of them, so that kind of influenced me a little bit toward getting a 4-year degree.

Sky Warrior found a single peer who was an important source of support through a period of difficult life circumstances. Monica described exchanges with friends about how to deal with overt prejudice. What stands out from these stories is that students who made it into college found people—peers as well as mentors—who helped them envision and move toward goals that uplifted them into new circumstances.

Enabling Parents.   Parents were a source of motivation for some of the WSA students. However, when it came to one of the core components of academic capital formation—strong encouragement and support in rigorous courses and information about college—there was no evidence that parents played a strong role. However, there were few opportunities for parents in the WSA program; few Achievers spoke about parental involvement, and selection came later in their education than did selection for TFCS, which required parental signatures on the applications.

Information

Coleman's (1988) concept of information provides a basis for examining the meaning-making process. We focused on how students constructed meaning from information gained from trusted adults and peers, formal information sources in print and on the web, and observations from experiences in school and college visits as possible components of academic capital formation.

Overcoming Tracking. As noted in the descriptive data, Achievers attended high schools engaged in comprehensive reform. They were selected from among students who all had the opportunity to take advantage of these reforms. Thus, high school tracks that precluded preparation for some students were not evident among this group of WSA students, although tracking was a pattern observed by others (e.g., McDonough, 1997; Oakes, 2008; Wooden, 2007). Other forms of tracking, however, did exist.

Schools sort students into different channels that could be considered diverse pathways to postsecondary education and careers (Oakes, 2008). In the United States, there has been an increased emphasis on preparing more students for 4-year colleges. Oscar, a transfer student from Hong Kong, explains his transition.

> In Hong Kong, they have a slightly different system…. So they don't really have like…just one secondary education, just one chunk. Then you have some sort of precollege, 2 years of precollege before you go into college. And so you have 13 years. The first 6 years are about the same, but then after that is a British system.

Oscar's father had received a technical engineering education in Hong Kong; in his U.S. high school, Oscar had entered a two-plus-two technical program similar to his father's that steered him toward community college, a pathway he eventually changed as a result of doors opening because of the Achievers award.

For students living in difficult circumstances, there can be a stigma of family life that can lead to an unofficial, and sometimes even more troubling, form of tracking. Seth's recollection illustrates the role of family stigma and the withholding of support in school:

> There already were a bunch of teachers who had kids in younger grades and so they would know my brothers and sisters and they would be like, "Oh these people and blah, blah" and so I automatically get them. It's already [a] preconceived notion like, "This kid is going to be a troublemaker." And that really did reflect in some of the teachers' opinions of me…I was actually told once that I was never going to succeed in anything I did.

Because he had keen insights, Seth navigated through the system. He observed about some of his teachers:

> They always had a funny sense of humor. I'd end up kind of like, under their wing because I could get most of their jokes. It'd be over a lot of kids' heads, they kind of, like, shoot them an insult but they wouldn't quite catch it, it'd be over their head, and I would be in the back laughing and they would always notice. Ah, it gets pretty cool. I ended up TAing for a couple of them.

Seth's story illustrates a sophisticated form of insight and cognition for a high school student. Students are tracked—or classified into implicit categories—in the minds of teachers as well as in the official course assignments. These mental classification schemes can be constructed based on the achievement or lack of achievement by older siblings. This finding is not a surprise, but one that teachers need to be aware of and guard against.

Access to Advanced Courses and College Knowledge.   The core concepts in academic preparation as conceptualized in the literature include completing advanced courses in high school and acquisition of college knowledge (see chapter 2). These can be viewed as interrelated concepts, recognizing that students who have college knowledge through the cultural capital of their families are more likely to take advanced courses in high school, students who complete advanced courses get higher test scores, and higher scores are associated with receiving marketing information from colleges which is mailed to high-achieving students each year.

Many WSA students could take advanced courses in high school. Liliya described how the feedback from a computer-based career information program helped her conceptualize her fit in college.

> I had a good GPA and so I was told that, like, with that GPA you can get to whatever program you want. And also, like, I think it was in the end of my junior year, I went to the career center we had and there, like, a program was online that you put your, like, talents and abilities and then it comes out what your profession, what you're supposed to be…. The one I wanted was there, so I was like, okay, that proved one more time that it fits me.

Most students had opportunities to learn about college options in their high schools. For example, Monica described how she learned about her future college when she was a high school student:

> Well, one day we were in class, and I heard this announcement that representatives from Western [Washington] were coming down and talking. And I didn't know where Bellingham was, I didn't know. I had heard about Western but very vaguely…I was going to go to WSU and I went down there and it was a half-an-hour thing and, by the end of it, I was sold. Bellingham was so beautiful.

These examples illustrate ways high school reforms enabled students to learn more about college options. In particular, Monica's comments illustrate the role achievement, as measured by GPA, influences students' perceptions of their options. Even the computer information systems placed in schools to support career planning have assumptions about linkages between grades and success in different fields. In this case, the correlations are embedded in the computer code. This is not necessarily a problem because it is probably based on reliable statistical information. However, there are always exceptions to these common patterns, some of which are explored further below. It is important that educators and other advocates for children be aware of the exceptions–the children who make it in spite of the odds.

Taking Advantage of Financial Incentives.   While most of these students had the opportunity to take advanced courses in high school, most could not have gone to a 4-year college without the scholarship. Examples of the monetary links to academic success are laced through these transcripts. One focus group student put it simply, "If I didn't have this I probably, I definitely would not be going to college because I didn't have the funding."

Students do respond to financial incentives, especially if they are coupled with encouragement. We can state this as an intermediate hypothesis with an important qualification: Money alone cannot lead to student success in college. Students also need to be prepared and to believe they can succeed. However, students have more opportunity to excel if financial barriers are removed.

Cultural Capital

Cultural capital functions as student and family knowledge transmitted through human systems of support and trust. The most natural human system to transmit cultural capital is the family. But if the family is dysfunctional, broken, or lacks role models who have completed college, it is more difficult to acquire this knowledge. Many WSA students were encouraged to consider options other than college.

Alternatives to College. The notion that comes across strongly from the literature is that children whose parents did not go to college are at a disadvantage with respect to both college knowledge and academic preparation. Most of these children were the first in their families to go on to 4-year colleges after high school. The activist role of teachers can provide an uplift mechanism that overcomes family discouragement. Yet it is important to consider the alternatives to college that are communicated to students. Some of the Achievers faced severe conditions that made alternatives to college likely.

WSA students had been strongly encouraged to consider alternatives to 4-year colleges. In an extreme case, consider Sky Warrior's situation before he heard about the WSA: "Looking back at it, because I had spent, like over a month of my last year of high school in jail. So the fact that I had failed, like, a couple of classes from that stuff, there is no way I could have made up. Got really bad grades in most other classes." In another more typical example, one of the focus-group students commented, "I was actually looking at the Army, some other route, and then, hopefully, some kind of school. But this [WSA] came, kind of a surprise." These cases illustrate that without the WSA program, some recipients would have found pathways to prison, the army, or the workforce rather than to college.

The selection process for WSA recognized that some students built a form of social capital through life experiences (Emeka & Hirschman, 2006). Many of the students interviewed were from one-parent families or foster homes; some were immigrants; a few were from two-parent homes; but, whatever the family circumstances, most of these children were the first in their families to aspire to go on to a 4-year college. Very few of the students were from circumstances that would have landed them in college without external support, both social and monetary.

Role Models in Schools and Families. Having role models was an important part of the process of academic capital formation during high school. Three types of role models were evident:

1. *Extended Family*: Monica described how family knowledge about college was conveyed: "I didn't have a lot. I didn't know what to expect, like, nobody in my immediate family had gone to college. And so nobody prepared me for it. My aunt and uncle, the ones that helped me, were kind of, you know, were telling things here and there, but I didn't really grasp the full concept of it."
2. *Mentors in Schools*: For Oscar, one of the teachers took the time to talk about college: "I took physics from him, and also, you know, I talked to him about my own background because he seems to know more, in general, about education systems.... He would just talk to me through a lot of different things."

3. *The Culture of Schools*: The diversity of high schools helped some students build understanding of self during high school. John, a White student, observed: "Lincoln was a diverse school and I think that helped me out much more with my, just, understanding of people in general, society in general." Diversity and other indicators of support of students within schools serve as indicators of a supportive and inclusive school environment.

The idea that extended family or mentors can serve as role models is hardly new. However, the idea that the culture of a high school can help form an inner image that functions like a role model is somewhat more novel. It is an intriguing possibility that supportive cultures can be created in high schools, especially given the challenges of diversity facing education and society.

Family Support.   Some of the WSA students had support for advanced preparation from their families. Oscar's father had received a technical diploma in engineering in Hong Kong. Liliya, another immigrant, noted, "I really like math. And, like, if there was homework from the math class, I was, like, not go to sleep till morning, but I'll do it and my dad really, like, was helping me in this." These are both examples of the classical pattern of support expected in families with high levels of cultural capital.

An array of different patterns of support was evident. Some students had encouraging parents, but they did not know much about college or what is required to prepare for college. About half were from families that were dysfunctional in some form or another. Many children were from foster homes, had single parents, and had experienced severe poverty. However, to be chosen for WSA these students had an inner resilience that was recognized and validated, at least with respect to the noncognitive variables in the selection process (Sedlacek & Sheu, 2006).

Habitual Patterns

Habitual patterns, as examined in this book, are inner personal patterns exhibited by students, forged from personal experiences within and possibly developed through overcoming the social systems in which they live and are educated.

Overcoming the Poverty Cycle.   As noted, there were two major patterns evident among the students: poverty or a working-class background. Both merit attention with respect to the role of habitual patterns.

The main story line above, the theme that emerges from the analysis of interviews, is that the WSA students had developed an inner will to achieve. While many had grown up in poverty, something gave them a capacity to envision a new future. A focus group student put it succinctly, "I was terrified of being stuck in poverty. I had been poor my whole life. And I had, I mean, I had been homeless as a preteen. Like, I was really afraid to be stuck there, but I also didn't think I had the support or the courage to move away from it." Many students told similar stories.

Not all students had opportunities to complete advanced courses in high school and continued to struggle. In a focus group one student observed:

> With math I am still going through it, but I am putting in more study time. I hired a personal tutor. With the financial problem, it is more kind of like, my spending habits that I have learned, you know, I can't go to the mall every weekend any

more you know. I have a friend…who helped me to invest in what's better for the future…instead of spending on random things, you know.

This comment communicates two stories: one academic, the other economic. This student apparently struggled with math in high school and the struggle goes on in college. In addition, she faces the challenge of learning how to manage money, difficult if you have never had any.

Culture of Uplift. The analyses above show that students whose parents did not go to college and who aspire to complete 4-year degrees benefit from families and schools that create a culture that supports uplift. For many WSA students, the process of learning to set new goals involved overcoming patterns learned in the family and community.

In response to a question about the factors that influenced her academic achievement, Monica observed: "I didn't have, like, the best home life and so, like, putting it in school and setting goals for myself and trying to reach them and getting help from people, and reaching out." The process of dreaming, seeking and receiving support, and succeeding seems to be at the core of academic capital formation in high school among students who would become the first generation in their family to go to college.

Several students spoke about the diversity in their high schools as a source of inspiration. Oscar, an immigrant student from Hong Kong, commented:

At first it was kind of awkward when I got into the school [with African Americans, Chinese and other minorities]. Like, ooh, so many different type[s] of people, different ethnicities…. Kind of new to me. And after a while, I actually felt like a fit there, because I started to join different clubs, and know more about teachers and have different conversations with them…. Toward the end of my last year I felt like, you know, it is just like home…. Since the school is small I got a lot of individual attention so I could talk to them one-on-one very easily.

These examples illustrate that cultures of care within schools make a big difference for students who face challenges due to social circumstances at home. The caring attitude of educators was one of the forces that could transform trajectories of students.

Encouragement within Families and Communities. A few of the students were on pathways that might have led them to 4-year colleges even without a scholarship; however, most were not.

The case histories and focus group comments illustrate the difficult paths students traveled to build the inner capital necessary to gain recognition, to be encouraged to apply for and be selected by the Achievers program. Some students, like Sky Warrior, seem to have had a personal fortitude and will that led him through difficult circumstances without family support. Others had emotional support in their families, sometimes even when their homes were "broken" in some way. For example, Monica viewed her mother as a source of inspiration. "She wasn't around a lot but when she was…she was very adamant on going to school, and succeeding, and, you know, helping me. At a certain point in time, she couldn't help me with homework anymore, but she tried, and she did what she could to encourage me."

Teachers were the major source of motivation for most WSA students in the first cohort. Most would not have applied for the Achievers program or gone on to a 4-year college if they had not had the support and encouragement of teachers in their schools.

Their access to opportunity may have been accelerated by the fact that their schools had large grants to enable school restructuring resulting in a greater emphasis on advanced (mostly IB) courses and formation of small schools within larger schools. Certainly the Achievers award made it possible to transition to 4-year colleges.

Distinctive Features of WSA

The WSA program provides a distinctive model that links funding for high school reform with early scholarship awards for low- and moderate-income students selected using noncognitive variable. The analysis of trends illustrates that in 2004 Achievers were more likely than comparison students to take advanced courses. In addition to the promise of student aid, the caring support of teachers and other elders in the WSA schools enabled students to overcome barriers to preparation that would have precluded college enrollment. The caring environment of these schools was evident in the students' voices which captured images of their learning environments. For WSA, it appears this caring environment is a key factor in creating patterns of uplift for students, enabling them to become first-generation college students.

TWENTY-FIRST CENTURY SCHOLARS

During the period studied, the State of Indiana required schools to offer a college preparatory curriculum and provided supplemental funding for high schools based on their success in graduating students with this preparation. The state had three diploma options during this period (Table 4.2): a regular diploma that required a general curriculum; a Core 40 diploma, that required courses necessary for admission to the state's research universities; and an Honors curriculum that required more advanced courses in math, science, and language. Historically, the state provided financial incentives for high schools to graduate more students with Core 40 and Honors diplomas (Theobald, 2003). The actual course requirements in math, science, and language are at a higher level for Honors than for Core 40, and at a higher level for Core 40 than for the regular diploma (Table 4.2). The state does not require students to take the advanced program, a condition that will change starting in 2011.[5]

Comparison of Scholars and Other Low-Income Students

The 2000 cohort provided a database uniquely suited to examining the role of high school context in preparation of low-income students.[6] A longitudinal file was constructed for this cohort that combined SAT questionnaires and data from the State Student Information System (SIS) used for several studies of academic progress (Musoba, 2004; St. John, Carter, Chung, & Musoba, 2006; St. John & Musoba, 2011).

Pell recipients who were not Scholars provide an appropriate comparison group. Both Scholars and other Pell recipients were from mostly low SES families; parents' education and educational aspirations were similar for the two groups. There were a few differences between these populations (Table 4.3):

- There were more African Americans and fewer Whites among the Scholars.
- The majority of both groups were in the low-income quartile, but this was more likely among non-Scholars.

Table 4.2 Minimum Diploma Requirements (in credits) for the Three Indiana Diploma Options in 2000

Subject Area	General Diploma	College Prep. Dip. (Core 40)	Honors Diploma
English/ Language Arts	8	8: Literature, Composition and Speech	8: Literature, Composition and Speech
Mathematics	4: Algebra I or Integrated Math I	6: Algebra I and II and Geometry	8: Algebra I and II, Geometry, and more advanced (e.g. Calculus, Trig., or AP Statistics)
Social Studies	4: US History, US Government, and other	6: US History, US Government, World History or Geography, Economics, and other	6: US History, US Government, and credits in World History, Geography, or Economics
Science	4: More than one area of science represented	6: Laboratory in Biology I, Chemistry I, Physics I or more advanced	6: Laboratory in Biology I, Chemistry I, Physics I or more advanced
Foreign Language		Can be part of the 8 "other areas"	6 -8 credits, must include 6 in one language or 4 each in two languages
Fine Arts		Can be part of the 8 "other areas"	2 credits Visual or Performing Arts
Other areas	2: Above subjects or technology competency	8: Either more courses in above subjects or computers or career/ technical	
PE and Health & Safety	1: In each	1: In each	1: In each
Electives	16	2-4	9
Total Credit Hours	40	40	47
College Access	Eligible for regular admission at 2-year campuses, below requirements for public 4-year campuses	Eligible for regular admission at a 4-year public campuses, recommended for 2-year campuses	Eligible for regular admission at a 4-year or 2-year public campus

Source: St. John & Musoba (2010).

- A higher percentage of non-Scholars were enrolled in schools with a high percentage of low-income students.
- Scholars enrolled in 4-year colleges of all types at higher rates than non-Scholars; about 8.7 percentage points more of the non-Scholars were enrolled in 2-year colleges.

About a third of both groups completed regular diplomas, and similar percentages of Scholars and non-Scholars completed Core 40 and Honors diplomas (Table 4.4). Higher rates of African Americans and Native Americans had regular diplomas, while a larger percentage of Asian Americans had Honors diplomas. About one third of students in

Table 4.3 Comparison of Scholars and Non-Scholars (other Pell Recipients among Freshmen Indiana Residents)

	Not a Scholar	Scholar
Composite Gender		
Male	41.45	40.10
Female	58.55	59.90
Composite Ethnicity		
Native American	0.53	0.48
Asian American Pacific Islander	1.88	0.80
African American	12.63	24.78
Hispanic	2.70	5.77
White	76.07	64.55
Other	1.13	2.33
Missing	5.06	1.28
Composite Student Income Level In 2000		
Below $30,000	60.10	52.85
Missing	0.12	0.00
$70,000 and over	1.35	5.61
$30,000-$70,000	38.43	41.54
Composite Parent Education		
Middle/Jr. High school or Less	2.58	2.97
High school	52.00	51.00
College or beyond	41.18	37.85
Missing	4.24	8.18
SAT Test taker		
No	35.83	33.84
Yes	64.17	66.16
College Destination		
Community College	23.54	14.84
Four-year Public	68.39	78.19
Four-year Private	8.07	6.98
Locale		
City	24.60	42.10
Suburban and Town	41.42	35.93
Rural	26.29	18.77
Missing	7.69	3.21
Percent minority students in school 1= greater than 11.4%		
Missing	7.98	6.09
Less than 11.4%	59.52	44.91
Greater than or Equal to 11.4%	32.51	49.00
Percent free and reduced lunch		
Missing	9.57	5.29
Less than 15.4%	44.80	31.52
Greater than or equal to 15.4%	45.64	63.19
Total	76.89%	23.11%

Source: St. John (2010), p. 33.

Table 4.4 Breakdown of Independent Variables by Diploma Type for Scholars and Comparison Group

	N	Honors Row %	Core 40 Row %	Regular Row %
Composite Gender				
Male	2,220	21.13	41.22	37.66
Female	3,177	28.49	41.14	30.37
Composite Ethnicity				
Native American	28	10.71	46.43	42.86
Asian American Pacific Islander	88	47.73	34.09	18.18
African American	833	12.85	44.90	42.26
Hispanic	184	16.30	52.72	30.98
White	3,962	29.48	41.65	28.87
Other	76	30.26	39.47	30.26
Missing	226	0.44	12.39	87.17
Composite Student Income Level in 2000				
Below $30,000	3,153	21.38	40.79	37.84
$30,000 to $70,000	2,113	31.42	42.31	26.27
$70,000 and over	126	27.78	33.33	38.89
Missing	5	20.00		80.00
Composite Parent Education Level				
Middle/Jr High school or Less	144	20.14	36.11	43.75
High school	2,794	25.02	42.30	32.68
College or beyond	2,181	28.43	41.91	29.67
Missing	278	9.35	26.62	64.03
21st Century Scholar				
Not a Scholar	4,150	25.61	40.75	33.64
Scholar	1,247	24.94	42.58	32.48
SAT Test Taker				
Yes	3,488	33.34	46.27	20.38
No	1,909	7.36	36.20	56.44
College Destination				
Community College	1,162	3.79	26.59	69.62
Four-year Public	3,813	31.08	46.60	22.32
Four-year Private	422	34.36	32.23	33.41
Locale				
City	1,546	22.06	44.76	33.18
Suburban and Town	2,167	28.43	42.87	28.70
Rural	1,325	29.74	41.06	29.21
Missing	359	6.41	15.88	77.72
Percent minority students in school 1 = greater than 11.4%				
Less than 11.4%	3,030	30.10	45.20	24.70
Greater than or equal to 11.4%	1,960	24.01	41.46	34.53
Missing	407	6.14	20.09	68.68
Percent free and reduced lunch				
Less than 15.4%	2,252	30.10	45.20	24.70
Greater than or equal to 15.4%	2,682	24.01	41.46	34.53
Missing	463	11.23	20.09	68.68
Total	5,397	25.46	41.17	33.37

Source: St. John (2010), p. 35.

both low-income and high-minority schools received regular diplomas. In Indiana, students in all types of schools had access to advanced courses, but not all students who enrolled in college had completed college preparatory diplomas.

While TFCS reached only a small percentage of students who were economically eligible, African Americans were well represented. Between 1992 and 2006, African Americans made substantial gains in representation in public 2-year colleges and in private 4-year colleges, reaching equal representation in the state system of higher education (St. John, 2011). There is trend evidence that TFCS helped equalize opportunity for college enrollment in the state.

When we examine the effects of being a Scholar on completion of advanced diplomas controlling for background, aspirations, and school characteristics using the 2004 cohort, we find a significant difference between Scholars and non-Scholars on completing Core 40 diplomas, but not for Honors diplomas. More detailed analyses indicate that for low-income African Americans, being a Scholar was associated with completion of an Honors diploma and completion of calculus (St. John, Fisher, Lee, Daun-Barnett, & Williams, 2008). These analyses provide a basis for concluding that the Twenty-first Century Scholars Program improves access to advanced courses during high school, but it falls short of a causal standard of evidence. The qualitative analyses focus on the services provided by the program that made it easier for students and their parents to make informed choices about high school curriculum and take the steps to prepare for college.

Concerns about Costs

Indiana's Twenty-first Century Scholars Program provides support services to students and their parents along with a guarantee to pay tuition costs. To build an understanding of how the program actually empowered students to build knowledge and prepare, we consider the meaning the promise of the scholarship has for students and their parents.

Overcoming Mistrust.   Many parents who did not have the opportunity to enroll in college themselves harbor doubts that their children will be able to enroll. Not only is it difficult to gain preparatory opportunities, but these parents also doubt they will be able to pay for college. The parent's comment below is illustrative of parent attitudes about the program:

> I know he can go to school. It's such a relief to a working person. It a relief to know he can go to college. Because I've worked all my life you know, I've worked. And to know the system is supporting the working class…. [If] you're in that blue collar, in the middle, and your child is a B student, or maybe a B/C student, which can still go to school and graduate from college. You know not everybody's a straight A student that goes to college. (Enersen, Servaty-Seib, Pistilli, & Koch, 2008, p. 32)

As this comment illustrates, many parents expected their children would receive aid only if they had exceptional grades, a standard that seemed unattainable to them. As this quote also illustrates, parents often viewed opportunity through the lens of social class.

Raising Expectations. When parents begin to think of college as possible for their children, they communicate this message to their children. Students feel grateful for this opportunity, as illustrated from this sequence of quotes by students:

- "My mom thinks it is the best thing that ever happened to me because I can go to college. Basically everything is given to you, you just have to work for it."
- "It has relieved a lot of pressure. You don't have to worry about the future as much."
- "It's a sense of relief."
- "My parents are just excited they don't have to worry about money for college." (Enersen et al., 2008, pp. 32–33)

At the very least, the fear of not being able to pay for college is a psychological barrier to access that can inhibit preparation for college among students who live in low-income families.

Taking Steps. The Scholars Program empowered parents to harbor dreams for their children, to believe in the possibility of cross-generation uplift, an optimism evident in these comments:

- "I want him to go. We have to encourage our children to go to college, to get a better life than we had."
- "My kids want a better future than what we had…I mean they've lived through some pretty rough times and financially they don't want that." (Enersen et al., 2008, p. 49)

These parents express hope for cross-generation educational uplift which has been unleashed because the financial barriers have been removed. Hope for their children may be a major factor motivating parents to get involved in the program and find out more about college opportunities.

Networking

A networking process was evident in the interviews involving staff at service centers, teachers and other school personnel, parents, and Scholars. Scholars and their parents had opportunities to engage in services, from homework support through college visits, providing them with opportunities to learn about college preparation. This process enabled parents and Scholars to make better-informed choices than would have been possible without this monetary and social support.

College Visits. Among the Scholars and their parents, visiting campuses provided the most critical learning opportunities (Enersen et al., 2008). Typical parents' comments, as summarized by the researchers:

- "The school visits have opened our eyes…it has been really helpful to have the experience. It opened doors."
- "It would give her tools that she would need to prepare for college and hopefully assist her through college. She sees what living with other girls would be like…."

- "It helps them in their decision-making processes to where they would like to go, and helps them in their start in life." (Enersen et al., 2008, pp. 28–29)

This process of searching out opportunity would not have happened for most families without the financial aid guarantee provided by the TFCS program. As one parent put it, "It helped me by getting him to as many campuses as possible because I couldn't have done that on my own" (Enersen et al., 2008, p. 30). In their own voices, parents described how the visits and other program support added an element of social agency: As they learned more about college and what it took to prepare for and apply to colleges of choice, parents became advocates for their children, making sure they had the opportunity to prepare appropriately.

Caring School Reform.   While Indiana's high schools were required to offer advanced courses, students were not required to take those courses. In addition, junior and senior high schools are not always supportive environments for low-income children. The structure and support of TFCS provided a viable set of standards to guide performance. Consider this exchange about the pledge:

- "I think it is good because it makes us, you know, we're expected to keep a certain…moral level as well as an academic level. It's like you know it helps you to, you know, think about things more."
- "When I signed that pledge card, I said 'I can do this, I already have the grades, and I can be drug-free and smoke-free'…. So one of the reasons why I never used alcohol was because I wanted to achieve my goal more than anything, and the pledge…I knew what I wanted in my future."
- "I like what you said because my freshman year was a disaster, I ended up getting a D in a class…I thought I really have to buckle down now, I can't get another one of those. I have to get B's and A's to go to college, and that reality does drive a lot of decisions."
- "And kind of giving us a standard and a goal to keep grades up because without our grades we won't graduate." (Enersen et al., 2008, pp. 50–51)

As part of the pledge, students made personal commitments when they received the aid guarantees. These commitments functioned as a set of life and educational standards for students. These students took seriously both the moral and academic aspects of the pledge. With the support provided through the regional centers and the engaged and active interest of their parents, these students had a framework to guide them through high school and into college.

Supportive Elders.   The pledge also provided a guide parents could use, along with the information and support systems provided by the regional centers, as a framework for support. In the exchanges among parents, there was an awareness of the role the pledge played in keeping their children on the pathway toward college. Consider this sequence of comments by parents:

- "I think the first thing, that they have to do the pledge, and when they pledge, you know, say what they are going to do, no drinking, no smoking and all of that, they know they have to stick to that…."

- "I think the guidelines the program sets for students, even just makes them much more able to see themselves as a positive adult. 'I can do this and this.' So the negative aspects that would come into play here would not because they have something at the end to gain...."
- "Yes, and I know it works because my brother's wife's down here as well, and like I said he graduated in '97 and that pledge sticks with him. His friends will ask him to do things and he's like 'nope.' It sticks." (Enersen et al., 2008, pp. 52–53)

The pledge also provided a guide for the students in their interactions with other students, using the image of a Scholar as a guide through the academic challenges in school and moral challenges in their social life. The pledge is a student-centered guide both students and parents buy into as a workable pathway to college.

Trust

Having the pledge as a guiding framework for parents, Scholars, and service personnel in the program provides a basis for building trust. The three dimensions of the trust-building process are examined below.

Preparation Networks.   For students, the opportunity to visit campuses provided a basis for judging whether the information and guidance they received was trustworthy, whether they really would have the opportunity to enroll in college if they followed the guide and took the steps to prepare. The students and parents commonly talked about college visits as a source of information about college life. Consider the following illustrative comments:

- "We also learn stuff we're able to use in future reference about what to do in college."
- "It helped me to see what all college students have to do, like majors, and what campus life is like, the size." (Enersen et al., 2008, p. 31)

High school learning environments differ dramatically from those in college, and colleges vary substantially in what they have to offer students. Many middle-class families journey to campuses so their children who are nearing college age can make an informed choice. This has become a ritual for families with substantial college experience. However, for low-income students and their parents, acquiring this type of college knowledge is more challenging. It is easy to understand, from the comments above, how the personal insights gained from college visits are vital for students in developing a personal vision of themselves as future college students.

Advocates.   The college visits, along with the practical knowledge gained at workshops and other specialized sessions, empowered parents to learn how to be advocates for their children—and what to advocate for. The parent comment below illustrates how parents begin to build the understanding that they can help their children:

You tell your child that their grade average has to be so and so...and then you state there will be mentoring programs to help those that are falling through the cracks, that need your help, so this is the reason why I say Twenty-first Century is one of the better college-informed scholarships out there, but most times those scholarships lean toward those who have 4.0 or 4.2.... But the Twenty-first Century Scholarship, it's like you're behind us, this is what we can help you help your child to achieve his goal. (Enersen et al., 2008, p. 41)

The advocacy for children became a shared commitment among program staff, parents, and students involved in the program, who often banded together. Twenty-first Century Scholars created a community of trust among those who chose to become engaged. Unfortunately, the quantitative analyses show that many students did not take these steps.

Parents as Social Agents.   A pattern of social agency emerged among parents and service providers. In fact, distinctive patterns emerged from the symbiosis of outside support coupled with responsible action by parents. For example, a parent commented: "And just like this young lady...I'm a single parent household, because their daddy is out there but don't give a hoot. But it's just not all that pressure on the mom to keep the male child on the straight path. Somebody else is helping by saying, 'okay, you gotta get your education now, because that is what is required'" (Enersen et al., 2008, p. 41). This comment, along with many others like it, illustrates the cosupport mechanism of parents and service personnel providing a reinforcing message for students. It also demonstrates that parents become agents of support for each other as well as for their children.

Information

A core issue for students is to use trustworthy information to navigate a course through college. By setting the standard at an achievable level academically, the Twenty-first Century Scholars Program creates authentic opportunity to take risks and take advanced courses to prepare for college. Engaged students and their parents take in new information, process it, and make informed choices. The information is not just from official sources, but also comes from trusted peers who share a commitment to the promise.

Overcoming Tracking.   Even in school systems where options are available, low-income students may be tracked or guided by counselors and teachers into lower-quality curricula because of low expectations. Trustworthy information that is encouraging empowers students to overcome low expectations projected on them by teachers and others, illustrated by this exchange:

- "They switched my classes, so I was in the first hour math class, and all the kids were like, 'You're going to hate this class because the bad kids are there.' I hated that class because the teacher was just sitting up there talking, and you like try to raise your hand and ask a question and all the kids are like, 'Be quiet.' So I switched back to my old math class, which was harder, and I got a B in it."
- "What she was saying, about a lot of people don't like math, but sooner or later they have to look at the big picture...you might look like the bum because you didn't care about math and doing well in school."
- "At my school we have a few students who go in there and it takes them 5 minutes to do the test because they mark all of them A. They don't care, they'd be spelling people's name, and that's it." (Enersen et al., pp. 44–45)

Students shared their insights about what it took to overcome low expectations. Raising the bar through encouragement, at least in these cases, involved self-advocacy based on insights gained from parents, college officials, program personnel, and other students. This sense of self-agency was integral to self-navigation skills that are supported through social networks.

Access to Advanced Courses and College Knowledge. The knowledge of college requirements coupled with a sense of being able to enroll creates a context in which students can aim high. In fact, students learn from parents, program service providers, college counselors, and peers in the program that they must advocate for themselves within their schools. Consider these students' comments:

- "I like math, but I am a little slow in math, but I apply myself.... So I kept trying to do harder things in math, and I can do it. And I think the Twenty-first Century Scholars does a good job in encouraging us to do harder math."
- "I don't like math but I am still trying. And you have to pass ISTEP and that's cool. I keep trying."
- "My counselor told me I was not good in math. I just couldn't do it all. So I walked in a year later, and she said 'You did so well.' And I told her. 'You are the one who told me I am not going to do nothing. Well I took summer math and passed it."
- "Like if you set yourself low, you may not have a good teacher, but in the Honors classes, if you set your goals high and take the Honors classes, you have better teachers."(p. 43)

What is conveyed in this exchange is a form of student activism: at the core of the Scholars Program, students learn to become *activist learners*. These students communicate a will to succeed in spite of discouragement.

Taking Advantage of Financial Incentives. The Twenty-first Century Scholars Program provides an implicit guarantee from the state to parents: If parents can support their children through high school and if the students take the steps to prepare, the state of Indiana guarantees financial support equaling tuition in a public college. The state's commitment to children becomes a compelling force for parents, an incentive to act as agents for their children. This comment is illustrative:

> [A] lot of times, and you assume you send your children to school and you assume they are getting what they need. I think parents are not aware of what is required in the college years, like going to the school, what they're short of, what they need in order to come to the schools.... This program in a sense empowers parents to be active for their children, and make sure they get the right classes and everything. I think this parents' program helps them. (Enersen et. al., 2008, p. 39)

In addition to enabling activist learners among high school students, the Twenty-first Century Scholars Program empowers parents to be activists for their children. These are positive indicators of program effects, but we need to remember that not all parents become advocates.

Cultural Capital

It is evident from the stories conveyed above that most Scholars were potential first-generation students. The monetary guarantee, information, and support provided means of engaging students and their parents in pursuit of a pathway to college, an explicit step toward cross-generation uplift. This commitment to uplift represents a cultural change in many families, from working-class patterns of school to work to a new pattern of school to college to new career paths. This support of uplift represents a transition in cultural capital within families.

Alternatives to College.   Most Scholars aimed to attend college, but there were a few exceptions. Based on their review of the data, the researchers observed:

> There were a small number of responses that indicated that some Scholars were not interested in attending a traditional college, others planned to enter the military [and] others were considering taking some time off before deciding. There were a few parents who thought their children were not ready for college. It was outside the parameters of this study to investigate the reasons or to explore what other options of higher education might be more appropriate and meaningful to them. (Enersen et. al., 2008, p. 37)

Students recognized the central role commitment played in the process. For example, one of the students commented: "Some people care about the program and others don't. Some people are in the program because their parents put them in, but they need to choose to be in" (Enersen et al., 2008, p. 55). To the extent these families had reinforced and reproduced patterns of school to work, the parents and Scholars who were interviewed mostly conveyed the alternative image of a culture supporting uplift.

Constructing Images of Success.   Images of college are conveyed to Scholars from their environments and reinforced by parents who have hope for their children's futures. But the Scholars, like most students, construct images from a variety of sources. Consider these comments by students:

- "They've helped me realize what it's gonna be like in college. Now I see like all the little things my mom was telling me, like pick up your clothes…that this is what I'm going to be doing for 4 years whether I'm with a roommate or not. So now I kind of get a feel for what college is gonna be like."
- "All that stuff you see on TV like Duke lacrosse players who had a party and then it got too out of hand, or Michael Vick, remembering all your morals and staying true to yourself…and then bringing that to the real life that you're not there to do all those things. You can have fun but you have to feel in control." (Enersen et. al., p. 36)

These comments convey images of success, one constructed from observations and messages conveyed by parents and other elders, the other conveyed by media, reinterpreted through a lens of resilience. Students construct inner images of their future paths to academic success; information is conveyed—from formal visits and media—and understood based on a desire for college success.

Family Support. The information parents acquire during the program becomes a substitute for the knowledge and experience in families with a history of college, an authentic form of cultural capital. One of the parents described this phenomenon concisely:

> They help us learn about things we didn't know about, that we can go back and look on also and we can get information. So it's like us going to college and getting information also. It helps parents so we can help the students more. It's a real good program. Hands-on is a lot better than reading it in a book. If you explain things hands-on, it speaks a lot for itself. (Enersen et al., 2008, p. 40)

Parents, like their children, interpret information and form expectations based on experience. The college visits and other support provided were sources of information that added to the emergent family narrative of uplift, a realistic and collective appraisal of opportunities that lay ahead.

Habitual Patterns

The story of the Twenty-first Century Scholars Program has unfolded as one of first-generation students taking steps to prepare for college with the advocacy of their parents who are more informed about college as a consequence of their involvement in the program. From this data—interviews with highly engaged groups of parents and Scholars—we did not gain much insight into status maintenance as a family pattern. Instead we found patterns of advocacy, consistent with Alternative 2 (Table 3.1). Below we examine the role of the family patterns.

Overcoming Undereducation. There was substantial evidence from the qualitative study that parents and children actively considered alternatives to college, but instead formed a culture of uplift. There were exceptions to the pattern of expecting children to go on to college and transition from the working class, but even parents who placed an emphasis on their children finding work after high school recognized the role of the Scholars Program and of college. Consider this comment by a parent: "Just getting a better job once he graduates from high school he can look forward to having confidence in himself to get a job, because they like have a job right after high school, even if they want to go to college they still want to have a job" (Enersen et al., 2008, p. 54). While this comment is framed within a working-class outlook, this parent has integrated an emphasis on college-going.

Some regions in Indiana are largely working class. Students go to college part-time and work. In fact, based on a review of research on their students, some Indiana colleges have committed to the redesign of their programs to serve working students (St. John & Musoba, 2010; St. John, McKinney, & Tuttle, 2006). There continues to be a working-class culture in the United States that views college within the frame of work. In these families, having a job takes priority, but college can be integrated into the culture. More attention should be given to the ways support systems in schools and state programs can encourage uplift within the working-class culture.

Hardiness and Resilience. The strong, overwhelming pattern that emerged from the qualitative study was an image of family support for cross-generation uplift. The researchers reached the following conclusion:

Both Scholars and parents exhibit aspects of the concept of hardiness—challenge, commitment, and control…. The attitude appears to be *a priori* to their involvement in the program. However, it is possible that the program has enhanced this aspect of personhood. The program offers to those individuals open to the challenge the opportunity to make a commitment in the future—particularly in connection with the pledge. (Enersen et al., 2008, p. 38)

Thus, a similar phenomenon was observed for Scholars and Achievers, an inner resilience or hardiness that foreshadowed the prospect of future academic success. For WSA, the noncognitive selection criteria sorted for this quality. Twenty-first Century Scholars were empowered to build their inner strength, while similar strengths were recognized through the selection process used by the WSA program.

Residual Concerns. An enabling and supportive culture of uplift was evident among the Scholars and parents interviewed. Comments by parents illustrate their understanding of the changes that lie ahead when their children go on to college and their concern for their children:

- "I think one of the hardest things for my daughter will be to adjust from the high school environment to the campus environment where she is responsible for every aspect of her life at that point"
- "My major concern is having enough money. And if she be wanting a job, how you gonna get a job?"
- "Getting into the habit of studying. High school has been easy for both of them. I think they know the college classes will be harder but I don't think they realize how much more rigorous it will be. It will be an eye opener I think."
- "I worry about her always making wise decisions. She is used to us making a lot of decisions for her or at least being there." (Enersen et. al., 2008, p. 33)

These comments are illustrative of family narratives that support college preparation even though concerns remain. There should be no doubt that site visits and other forms of encouragement supported and strengthened resolve. Attributions of causality are more difficult because of the statistical standards for making such claims, but this research conveys a compelling story.

Key Features of the Twenty-first Century Scholars Program

In the Twenty-first Century Scholars Program, Indiana makes a commitment to students to pay for college if they take preparatory steps. Both parents and students tell stories that indicate that parents were a major motivating force for signing up; students took the pledge, at least in part, because their parents encouraged them to do so. The money may have been a motivator, but the services made a very substantial difference in the lives of parents and their children who became Scholars.

One crucial aspect of the TFCS program was that care and support were provided by parents and service providers rather than school insiders. Students became their own advocates within their high schools, steering their way toward a more challenging curriculum. This evidence portrays a very different image of uplift than is evident in the structural notions of school reform through raising requirements. In fact, Indiana demonstrates that having the courses available was crucial, but parent advocacy was also necessary. Whether or not raising the graduation standard to the level of college preparation (i.e., Core 40) will ease the burden of family advocacy and result in higher enrollment rates will be evident after the new requirements go into effect for the graduating class of 2011.

We conclude that some type of social support is needed to empower children to become their own advocates in schools that do not appear to readily support them. Changing requirements and making teachers teach higher-level courses alone does not change the attitudes they and their administrators hold toward students. The fact that parent and student advocacy were so critical in TFCS is consonant with this conclusion.

A remarkable aspect of the Twenty-first Century Scholars Program, evident in analyses of both interviews and quantitative data, is that an implied contract emerges between engaged parents and service providers. A tacit behavioral support system emerged that empowered parents and children through social support coupled with aid guarantees and opportunities to visit colleges. When parents engaged in these services, their children were more likely to gain access to advanced courses, quantitative findings (St. John & Musoba, 2010) reinforced by the findings of the qualitative research's.

CONCLUSIONS

These studies provide compelling evidence of the impact of aid guarantees and support networks on academic preparation (linkage 3 in Figure 1.2). In addition to encouraging academic preparation, social support, networking, and mentoring empowered academic capital formation as a process of acquiring college knowledge and developing habits that reinforced a commitment to cross-generation educational uplift. Both concepts merit consideration—academic preparation as capital formation and support mechanisms that empower it. The two programs illustrate the linkages between college knowledge and academic success in different ways (Table 4.5). In both programs, awardees were more likely to complete advanced courses during high school than their peers, and their understanding of the linkages between preparation and college knowledge played a role in the process.

In WSA, the case history students and the focus group participants represented different generations of awardees: Students in the case histories had acquired their high school education before they received the award, while the focus group students had received the awards earlier in their high school careers. Students included in the case histories described a caring environment with many elders in their schools who supported their work, but selection into the WSA program itself had little relationship to preparation for the first cohort. College preparation by Achievers in the 2004 cohort was at a higher level, evident in the trend data, because students received the award early enough in their high school career for it to have an impact on improving academic preparation. In addition, some of these students indicated the encouragement they received from WSA support personnel motivated them to take advanced courses.

Twenty-first Century Scholars was a more mature program at the time of these studies. The quantitative evidence indicated that parent engagement in site visits and other events was a major factor in preparation and college access (St. John, Fisher et al., 2008),

Table 4.5 Academic Preparation as Cultural Capital Formation: Summary Findings on Washington State Achievers and Twenty-first Century Scholars

Process	WSA	Twenty-first Century Scholars
Easing Concerns about Costs	Working class and poverty patterns represented; easing concerns changes trajectory	Working class and poverty patterns; easing concerns in junior high school enables parent and student engagement
Networking	Strong networks of supportive teachers and staff reach out to students	Statewide network of service providers support parents and children in building college knowledge
Trust	Trusted peers and support people in school provide network for developing trustworthy information on college	Strong bonds between parents and service center personnel provide extended support network; college visits provide trustworthy information
Information	Students gain college information from trust networks; high school courses experienced as supportive	Students and parents use college knowledge to advocate for high school courses and take other steps to prepare
Cultural Capital	Family capital remains in place, unaltered by intervention	Parents and students develop new college narrative based on college knowledge
Habitual Patterns	Strong individual self-navigation as skills recognized through selection	Family engagement develops new family patterns, including reinforced parent support of college preparation

a conclusion reinforced by the qualitative evidence examined in this chapter. The links between being a Scholar, having involved parents, and completing an advanced curriculum (appendix 2) helped explain themes that emerged in the qualitative data. Parents and service providers formed a bond that supported Scholars. Scholars developed strong internal images of themselves as college students and became activists in pursuing their educational goals within their high schools. Both parents and children exhibited an inner resilience evident in taking assertive steps to prepare.

There is little reason to doubt that organizational changes are necessary to provide access to quality courses for low-income students (Oakes, 2008; Sirotnik & Oakes, 1986). Twenty-first Century Scholars and Washington State Achievers offered very different approaches to school reform. Indiana mandates courses that are offered, which benefited TFCS students; WSA funded school reforms coupled with student encouragement. In Indiana, parents and students in the focus groups confirmed that they had advocated to gain access to high-quality courses. In contrast, in WSA schools, teachers reached out to students. Both mechanisms worked for some students, but many were still left behind.

Cultural capital that supported uplift was evident in the two sets of qualitative studies, but manifested in different ways related to structural differences in the programs. In WSA, elders in schools and program counselors provided school-based support networks which empowered students to make it through high school and go to college even if they had inadequate preparation.[7] In contrast, in the Twenty-first Century

Scholars Program, parents and service providers made up the network of support that empowered students to advocate for themselves within schools. Scholars told stories of having to steer their own paths toward advanced courses, sometimes without strong support from their schools.

5

COLLEGE TRANSITIONS

Navigating their way to a college consonant with their aspirations and talents is complicated for children from low-income families. As the analyses of family engagement and
student preparation illustrated, low-income families lack experiential knowledge of colleges and careers unlike families with prior college experience and knowledge of professional pathways. Gaining access to high quality, challenging courses remains a problem,
as does learning about options for college. Even when students had success learning
about college requirements, gaining access to and completing advanced courses, and
graduating academically prepared, they can still find it difficult to afford 4-year colleges.
Easing concerns about college costs coupled with concerted efforts to provide information on colleges and student aid can encourage preparation and college application. If
the student is successful, the next step is to choose a specific college.

While the college choice process has been widely studied, most prior research has
been framed using economic and social choice theories that do not consider the depth
of the family decision process (e.g., Hossler, Braxton, & Coopersmith, 1989; Hossler &
Gallager, 1987; Jackson, 1978; Leslie & Brinkman, 1988; Manski & Wise, 1983; Paulsen,
1990). A few qualitative studies have examined how family and social networks enable
or undermine efforts by students to gain access to 4-year colleges, especially high-cost,
selective colleges (Hossler, Schmit, & Vesper, 1999; Levine & Nidiffer, 1996; McDonough,
1997). This chapter examines the college choice process, both as an outcome that results
in enrollment in 4-year colleges by prepared students and as a social process integral
to academic capital formation. We initially envisioned this chapter as considering the
effects of aid on college choice as a process. However, the concept of college choice as a
transitional process that includes major choice and transfer became evident, as it did in
another recent study (St. John & Musoba, 2010). The underlying processes of academic
capital formation empower students to find a fit in a 4-year college, sometimes involving
transfers between colleges.

REFRAMING COLLEGE CHOICE AS AN EXTENDED PROCESS

This chapter uses mixed methods to examine the roles of student aid and family engagement in the college transition. The quantitative analyses focus on the question of whether there is a difference in the college choice process for the aid recipients in two programs, Washington State Achievers (WSA) and Gates Millennium Scholars (GMS), compared to similar students. The qualitative analyses delve into the role of social processes in college choices.

Viewing college entrance as a transition rather than a choice creates space to reconcile the tension between two concepts of access. A college-prepared student can find a good fit in a 2-year college if 2-year diplomas fit their prior education and aspirations or the college supports the transfer process both socially and academically. On the other hand, if the goal of the public is to prepare all students for 4-year colleges, then it is crucial in a just society to *expand and equalize opportunity* for equally prepared students to enroll in 4-year colleges (Rawls, 1971; St. John, 2006a).

A substantial body of college choice research treats choice as an outcome rather than as a process. For example, many researchers have examined the influence of student aid programs on whether the offer of aid has an effect on college choice, including whether recipients attend more expensive or higher quality colleges (Heller, 1997; Leslie & Brinkman, 1988; St. John, Asker, & Hu, 2001), an approach we carry forward in appendix 3. Since 4-year colleges are typically more costly than 2-year colleges, the offer of aid can enable students to attend 4-year colleges. Similarly, private colleges cost more than public colleges. Selectivity also correlates with cost, so providing aid can increase opportunities for low-income students to enroll in selective public and private colleges.

This chapter uses descriptive analyses of college choice by students eligible for the two programs to compare selected students to eligible peers. Supplemental multivariate analyses that further examine specific questions related to the roles of aid and engagement in college choice appear in appendix 3. New multinomial analyses of college choice (Table A3.1) inform the chapter's conclusions.

A few pivotal works inform a reframing of college choice and provide a foundation for viewing college choice as part of the academic capital formation process. McDonough (1997) painted a compelling portrait of class differences in college knowledge and the role of habitus in forming expectations about college. She focused on the role of cultural capital and habitus in social reproduction, revealing how social class and family engagement reinforce status. Hossler et al. (1999) focused explicitly on the role of information in expanding college choice. They found that first-generation students had lower odds of college enrollment in spite of preparation and information. Levine and Nidiffer (1996) illuminated the role of teacher outreach and performance in expanding postsecondary opportunity to underrepresented students. The studies in this chapter examine how participation in comprehensive interventions enables and empowers low-income students to engage in social processes that result in entry into 4-year and highly selective colleges.

The examination of interview data from the GMS and WSA programs explores the five social-process dimensions of college choice. In the prior chapters, we learned that when students and parents in low-income families became engaged in seeking out information about college, they were more likely to advocate for access to advanced courses for their children in high school. In particular, quantitative analysis of the Twenty-first Century Scholars Program revealed a strong parental role, facilitated by service provid-

Table 5.1 Academic Capital Formation and College Choice Processes among Low-Income Students: Basic Patterns (B); Families Making Transitions in Most States (1); and Families with Opportunities to Engage in Comprehensive Programs (2)

Concepts	College Choice Processes (B)	College Choice Process (Alternatives)
Concerns about Costs	Concerns about costs limit college options students consider	1. In most states grants are not sufficient to cover need at most public four-year colleges 2. Guarantee of funding can enable low-income students to attend public and private colleges
Networking	Networks for employment and education mostly local; choosing a college close to home is a priority, if college is an option; community colleges often viewed as only option.	1. Counselors, teachers, and outreach professionals provide expanded network of trusted advisors with respect to college choices 2. Professionals enable college visits by parents and children and provide additional actionable information
Trust	Trust networks formed through the family or neighborhoods; local knowledge valued over formal information (which may not be trustworthy)	1. Coaches, teachers, and mentors become part of an expanded network of trust and obligation 2. Advisors and mentors in programs become trusted "others'" by parents and peers
Information	Trustworthy information is shared through school, family, and/or neighborhood groups	1. Trustworthy information about college is both believable and actionable (college knowledge workshops can help) 2. Student follows through on college and aid applications; students may transfer to find fit
Cultural Capital	Knowledge of college options severely constrained to local, visible options, and learning from the experiences of others who have ventured into postsecondary education	1. Knowledge of college opportunities expanded by trusted others 2. Students take the steps to apply 4-year college(s); may learn more about college options during first year, informing transfer decisions
Habitual Patterns	Local knowledge of familiar options prevails in college choice process, other information is mistrusted as not applying to "people like us"	1. Students observe successful others in schools, churches, and community 2. Students develop personal habits that lead to preparation and informed college choice

ers. We did not have focus group interview data on college choice for TFCS, so it was not possible for us to do a qualitative analysis.[1] This data was available for WSA and GMS and results are presented in this chapter.

The qualitative analyses examine the propositions outlined in Table 5.1. These hypotheses are based on the early conceptions of social capital theory (Coleman, 1988) and cultural reproduction (Bourdieu, 1977, 1990) along with the reconstructed theory of human capital to focus on perceptions of costs (see chapter 2). An assumption guiding the formulation of these propositions was that family engagement and aid guarantees made a difference in the college choice process, enabling low-income students to prepare for, apply to, and enroll in 4-year colleges, including those that were highly selective. For each of the five constructs, a basic (B) process is described for families with low expectations of being able to afford college. One alternative is that the college search process is undertaken by engaged, low-income students with a high capacity to achieve and self-navigate (alternative 1). A second alternative is that the processes of choice used by students in low-income families with their concerns about costs removed by aid guarantees have extended opportunities to build college knowledge and transfer, as needed, to find a good college fit (alternative 2).

The first set of propositions focuses on the role of easing concerns about costs. Students in low-income families are often discouraged from applying to 4-year colleges because of cost and the excessive debt that would be required in most instances. High-achieving students and students who are able to self-navigate through early barriers are likely to search for options, overcoming the doubts in their social environment (alternative 1). In contrast, students who have supplemental aid guarantees have already had their concerns about costs eased (alternative 2). Supplemental multivariate analyses examine the role of receiving awards in the type of college chosen (appendix 3), further exploring the role of comprehensive reforms and state grants.

The quantitative analyses of the role of eased concerns about costs used cohort data with supporting multivariate analyses. The exploration of the qualitative dimensions of these choices focused on the ways students described the role of finances—and their families' concerns about costs—in the college choice process. The qualitative analyses consider the timing of awards, since some students in GMS and WSA received awards after their initial college choice. Using this approach, it is possible to inform further the understanding of the role of aid guarantees in college choice.

Second, the analyses of the role of social networks in college choice focus on how families, others in the community, and service providers influenced aspirations, applications, and college choice. WSA students had counselors through the program, while students in GMS did not have this systematic support. We can expect that eased concerns about costs enabled greater opportunities to enroll just as it empowered advocacy for access to advanced courses. WSA and GMS provide different forms of evidence related to the role of social networks:

- The basic proposition (B) focuses on status maintenance: The networks of working-class families support transitions from school to work and other patterns of cross-generation class reproduction. While most GMS and WSA students find their way to 4-year colleges as part of an extended college choice process, their reflections provide insight into the ways families and communities reinforce transitions to drop out, work, or go to a 2-year college.
- Alternative 1 involves making college choices without benefit of encouragement programs and guaranteed student aid. Most GMS students did not have the benefit of comprehensive encouragement programs in high school, so comparisons to students in the WSA program reveal the role of social networks. In addition, some of the GMS students received awards after entering college, so we gain visibility into the ways guarantees for supplemental aid influence college choice as an extended process.
- Alternative 2 explores the role of early aid guarantees and the ways that support services influence self-navigation by students as part of an extended process. When

students build networks that support the choice of a 4-year college, they have to reconstruct the meaning of signals from peers and elders that contradict their aims. If students start out in a 2-year college as a means of accelerating preparation or staying involved in family life, they retain the opportunity to attend 4-year colleges through the transfer process if they have aid guarantees and supportive networks.

Third, because most first-generation college students lack family histories that provide information about college as part of the common narrative, it is important to look at the types of information students consider when they make college choices. It is evident that students gathered and interpreted real life information about college using their life experiences as a filter. In particular, we were interested in college fit and how it related to college choice as an extended process that could include transfers enabled by guaranteed aid. Since both the GMS and WSA interviews were conducted late in the college experience, it was possible to consider transfer as part of the college choice, as an extended process based on building trustworthy information.

Fourth, trusted others, such as parents, peers, and teachers, play a substantial role in initial college choice, while networks developed in college play a role in college choice as an extended process. Trusted others play a crucial role in the process and having mentors in comprehensive programs can help.

Fifth, cultural capital also plays a central role in college choice and transfer and relates to the notion of families as learning systems. Student choices about college are influenced by family expectations, but also inform the family narrative. Older children discuss their college experiences with younger siblings and their parents, and students often consider family expectations as they reflect on their initial college choice. In this chapter, we explore how students constructed meaning from information about college when there was no family narrative, when college and the career pathways associated with college education were more foreign.

Finally, complex issues related to habitual patterns are examined for GMS and WSA using the interview transcripts. Low-income, first-generation students who make it to college demonstrate strong character related to the ability to navigate through high school into college; however, their departure from home for college represents a change in family patterns, leaving parents and children with issues to reconcile as the processes of initial choice, transfer, and persistence evolve.

The emerging concept of college choice, tested in the analyses below, is one that leads to an integration of first- to second-year retention into an extended college choice process (St. John & Musoba, 2011), a stance implicit in alternative 2. Much of the persistence research has focused on students returning to the same campus after the first year of college (Braxton, 2000; Pascarella & Terenzini, 2005). Yet persistence theory uses the same background variables as college choice research (St. John, Paulsen, & Starkey, 1996). As we test this extended notion of college choice, it is also important to consider that the idea of transfer is also part of the process of finding fit. In this chapter we further examine the concept of college choice as a process of finding fit, a student-centered process that involves initial enrollment, major choices and changes, and transfer decisions during a 2-year transition process. Students who transfer may find a better fit, which is a clear departure from the retention literature that views transfer as a negative process—an institution-centric view.

WASHINGTON STATE ACHIEVERS

For the initial WSA cohort, the noncognitive variables were used to select students, but the timing of awards limited their impact on initial college choice. In subsequent years, awards were made before the senior year so they had a more substantial influence on high school courses completed, as documented in chapter 4. This difference in the timing of awards also influenced the timing of student decisions about transfer and major, illuminating the process of finding fit.

Differences in Initial College Choices

The sample of students in the UW studies expanded between 2000 and 2004. In 2000 and 2002, the surveys considered only Tacoma students, while in 2003 and 2004 a larger sample consisted of students from WSA and comparison schools; when reviewing trends (Figure 5.1), it is important to compare 2000 to 2002 and 2003 to 2004. Key indicators include:

- In both 2000 and 2002, college-going rates were higher in non-WSA schools than in WSA schools in Tacoma.
- Within the 2002 WSA schools, students who received WSA awards attended college at a much higher rate than either applicant nonrecipients or other students in their schools.
- Between 2003 and 2004 there were slight improvements in the enrollment rates from both WSA and non-WSA schools, with non-WSA schools continuing to have higher enrollment rates.
- Between 2003 and 2004, the rate of enrollment increased for both WSA awardees and applicant nonrecipients.

Based on these indicators, it is evident that WSA did not substantially expand access during the years studied. During this period, school restructuring had not yet been implemented. In contrast, it is apparent that the percentage of WSA recipients going to 4-year colleges immediately after high school improved across the early years of the program (Figure 5.2). This pattern correlates with the improved access to advanced courses for WSA students (chapter 4).

Two prior studies used Hirschman's UW data to examine college choice by WSA recipients compared to nonrecipients. St. John and Hu (2007) used the data on WSA and comparison schools in a logistic regression to confirm a positive association between receipt of award and enrollment in a public 4-year college, controlling for background and preparation; WSA recipients were also more likely than nonrecipients to enroll in private colleges. In a regression discontinuity study using data on WSA applicants, DesJardins and McCall (2008) found a positive association between selection and college enrollment for students with similar background and scores. This study meets the causal inference standard for studies at the cut point of selection (i.e., students at the margin of inclusion). These studies confirm WSA had a substantial impact on enrollment decisions. The analyses below examine the five dimensions of college choice as an extended social process.

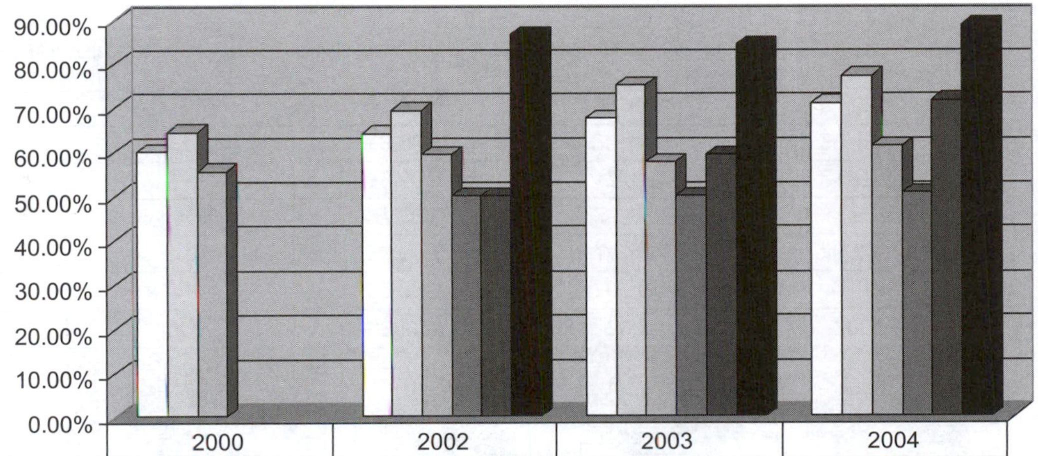

	2000	2002	2003	2004
□ All Schools	59.90%	64.10%	67.60%	71.00%
▤ Non-WSA Schools	64.40%	69.30%	75.00%	77.20%
▧ All WSA Schools	55.50%	59.30%	57.60%	61.30%
▨ Non-WSA Applicants in WSA Schools		50.10%	50.20%	50.70%
■ Applicants but Non-Awardees in WSA Schools		50.00%	59.40%	71.60%
■ WSA Awardees		86.70%	84.40%	88.70%

Figure 5.1 Trends in college enrollment rates for Washington State Achievers and comparison schools. Note: Data for 2000 and 2002 are for Tacoma area schools. Enrollment rates for 2003 and 3004 add additional WSA and comparison schools.
Source: St. John & Hu, 2007, p. 369.

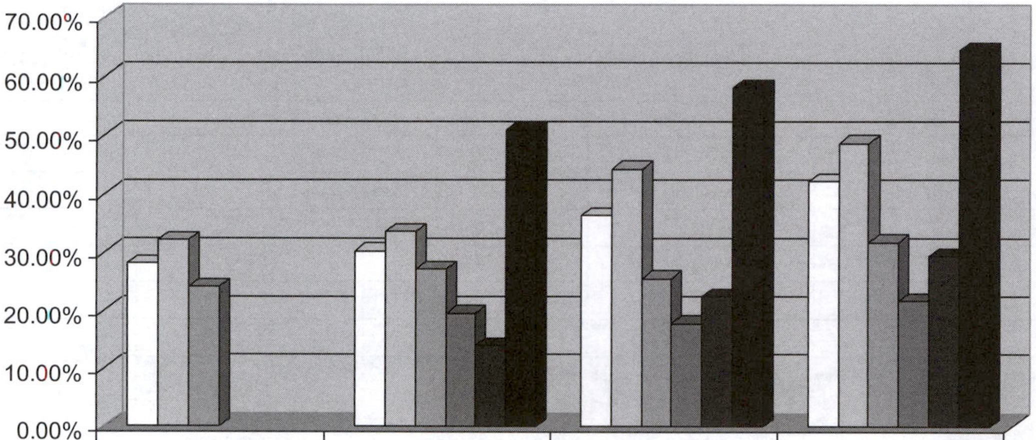

	2000	2002	2003	2004
☐ All Schools	28.10%	30.30%	36.30%	42.10%
☐ Non-WSA Schools	32.10%	33.60%	44.20%	48.70%
☐ All WSA Schools	24.10%	27.10%	25.50%	31.80%
☐ Non-WSA Applicants in WSA Schools		19.50%	17.80%	21.70%
■ Applicants but Non-Awardees of WSA		13.90%	22.40%	29.40%
■ WSA Awardees		51.00%	58.10%	64.60%

Figure 5.2 Trends in enrollment rates in 4-year colleges by seniors from Washington State Achievers and comparison schools.

Easing Concerns about Costs

The interviews with WSA students were retrospective, capturing students' reflections on their college choices. The case history and focus group interviews provided insights into the ways that easing concerns about college costs over an extended period gave students an opportunity to rethink their college and career choices as they progressed through college. We examine the propositions about easing concerns about college costs from this retrospective stance.

Information on Aid Expands Options.   WSA students were required to apply for other types of student aid. In some instances, being awarded the scholarship encouraged students to learn more about the options available. One focus group student explained, "State and government financial aid that was actually pretty good on top of the scholarship...I don't think I would have actually bothered had I not found out about the Achievers Scholarship and went, 'Hey, here is a big pile of cash. I'll take that.' And then, it kind of, it helped me realize that there is more out there than just that, too." This comment and others like it illustrate that some of the WSA students had concerns about costs that had been based on poor information, consonant with the importance of early information about student aid (King, 1999a, 1999b).

The Achievers Scholarships eased financial concerns in multiple ways. As is evident from the analysis of high school cohort surveys, most Achievers enrolled in a 4-year college the year after high school. Guaranteed scholarship aid empowered some of the students who started in 2-year colleges to transfer to 4-year colleges when they were ready, an opportunity that can be denied if students think they can't afford 4-year colleges or if they have been steered away from this trajectory by elders who were trying to be supportive. The guarantee also made it possible for students who enrolled initially in-state to transfer out-of-state after 2 years if they felt that would be better for them. Transportable guarantees enabled students to think of college choice as a sequential process, with a transfer or change to a different college based on their personal experiences with college fit. Having guaranteed scholarship funds available opened doors for students to discover more options than they would have otherwise.

Scholarship Initially Discouraged Out-of-State Choices.   Most state aid is limited to students who enroll within their state, and the Achievers program had a 2-year requirement for in-state enrollment. Thus, both state aid and the Achievers award constrained choice.

Liliya described her initial college choice, "I actually got accepted to schools out-of-state but I know education is cheaper if you are a resident of the state. And also my mom didn't let me go." Not only did the scholarship constrain Liliya's choice, family dynamics were also at work. However, financial constraints were critical: "I come from a low-income family and so I know that I would have financial barriers."

Aid Guarantee Expands Options.   It is important to consider how crucial receiving the aid guarantee can be in creating the opportunity to go to college, to break the basic access barrier. Sky Warrior told how teachers and friends empowered him to learn about college and apply for college and aid:

> Well, I was…a senior in high school. It must have been my last semester…. And when they received the grant there was a large assembly in the school…there was a scholarship available…blah, blah, blah…And I was, like, "all right, fine." They forced the paperwork on me, like, here do this…. And I am like I don't know, I don't know. But I really liked math and science. I really liked engineering. I really liked cars, so I wanted to design cars. So I was like I want to be a technical engineer, and I don't know where I'm going yet, but my girlfriend had decided to come here to WSU…. So I decided to come here.

Even though Sky Warrior heard about the program at the time it was announced, he did not believe it could apply to him. He was encouraged to apply by teachers who were his advocates. Only after receiving the award did he finally realize new doors were opening. At that point, he seems to have realized his interest in math, science, and cars could give him a new vision of the possible, but he did not put a lot of thought into choice of a specific college.

Leslie was one of the students who transferred out-of-state at the start of her junior year. There was some cost for her in making this choice, which she made for personal reasons related to faith and social interaction, but the WSA scholarship made it possible. She explains, "I got the FASFA grants and Pell grants and stuff. And then I got a few scholarships by freshman year and then I guess a couple my sophomore year. But after that, I mean, I didn't have very many other scholarships and I don't…I definitely would have had a lot of loans when I graduated." Leslie took on more debt to make a choice that fit her interests better than her initial college choice. The decision had additional financial costs, but she found what she was looking for. Even this choice may not have been possible had she not had the transportable scholarship aid. Leslie's case illustrates the seriousness of financial concern and how it permeates educational choices.

Networking

A central role in college choice is played by networks within families and communities, along with those in schools that exist naturally or have been created through reform. The retrospective interviews provided further insight into the three conceptions of the role of networking as part of academic capital formation.

Images of Career and Education Options. Prior research shows most students apply to a small number of colleges. Their choice sets are limited by their experiences, but social networks can expand the range of choices. The college choice literature assumes students examine options as a rational process that considers costs and aid offers (Hossler et al., 1989; Jackson, 1978); recent research also raises the idea that social class makes a difference in the way information is processed (Hossler et al., 1999; Paulsen & St. John, 2002). These interviews provide further insights into the ways low-income students develop educational and career expectations.

As noted earlier, the response of health care workers to a family car accident influenced Liliya to aspire to a health-related career. She described how this was integral to her initial decisions about colleges: "Another barrier, like only two schools in Washington State that had my program. And I applied once, didn't get accepted and then I was thinking…I'm just going to give up. And well, that's good I don't quit for, like, after the first time because I did get in." She transferred among three colleges in state—starting in a community college, transferring to a private 4-year college, and finally to Washington State. Along the way she gained entry into her desired program specialization.

Liliya's case illustrates career aims and college choices are intertwined as they unfold over time during the early college years. Also, the aid guarantee—not having to worry about added costs associated with transfer—made it possible to pursue her career dream. In the literature on student persistence,[2] student preferences about careers and majors are seldom emphasized. Social and cultural experiences can limit visibility of professional pathways. Choice of a career could be narrowed as a consequence of a decision to persist in a college that does not have the desired career path or constrains entry to some majors to students with high grades.

Expanded Ideas of College Options and Career Choices. Easing the concerns about costs along with social support from the network provided by the Achievers program encouraged students to consider goals that extended beyond their campuses, a conception of perseverance not normally considered as part of research on student persistence.

Leslie's decision to transfer was informed by her personal learning about opportunities for social engagement. She described efforts to network at her first campus: "There was a Gates thing, [person name] would come over once a month and bring pizza. And everybody would get together…. Okay, I had my friends, and I guess I did not make new friends with that group." She went on to explain that in her church, there were deeper bonds among peers that she missed in college. So when she had the opportunity to transfer out-of-state as a junior, she enrolled in a Church-affiliated college. Leslie described her social engagement at her new school:

> Oh, it was scary at first because I didn't know anybody and it was a new experience for me. I have never actually moved where I had not a clue who anybody was. And so I moved in. That was really heard. I think the guy I was dating just went on a mission to Canada and so, like, my only true, like, friend had gone and I couldn't talk to him…. There was six of us in an apartment and I didn't know any of them and they all, they weren't my type of people, but one girl. And so we kind of study together and found some friends together. So it was slower, a lot slower…but still okay.

Leslie had expressed difficulties at both schools. However, at the second campus she was able to find peers with whom she felt she could bond. For Leslie, the faith-based context did not ease social integration in overt ways, but it seems to have given her confidence to persevere.

The Scholarship program offered programming that gave students opportunities to reflect on career options during college. One focus group student commented that the retreats helped her think about careers and encouraged her to network. Another student elaborated on the importance of the scholarship to career planning: "Without the Scholarship I wouldn't have had the freedom to transfer…to apply to a curriculum that was more towards my goals, what I wanted to do as a profession, so that's exciting. I wouldn't be in social welfare right now if I didn't have that flexibility."

When concerns about the costs are eased, students decide to transfer based on social and academic factors. If we look at Leslie's case using the logic of student fit models (e.g., Bean, 1990; Tinto, 1975), it is possible that the difficulty of social integration caused the transfer. She transferred to a new college—one that was more compatible academically and in terms of faith—but it was no easier socially at the new college; it was only her more positive attitude that made the situation look better to her. The social fit argument does not necessarily apply in conventional ways. In contrast, the focus group student, similar to Liliya, had a career interest that influenced her transfer decision. In these cases, academic commitment to a career aim explains the transfer. The simpler notion of academic fit[3] might apply logically, but it would not explain the path toward academic success. If we hold to the academic fit notion,[4] we would consider these transfers as failures, given the focus on departure as negative rather than part of a journey toward academic success enabled by easing concerns about costs and providing networking support (i.e., mentoring and group meetings) which encourage students to consider their career goals.

Information on Additional Options. The increased emphasis on college preparatory courses in high school seems to have had a high payoff, if we consider the descriptive data analyses. However, providing college prep courses does not fully convey the complexity of college life or the academic demands at most 4-year colleges.

A focus group student put it this way: "Well, I personally thought that my high school didn't really prepare me enough for college." She continued, "Study habits, subject-wise, yes. Yeah, exactly! It was like, easy A, easy B in high school. And once you go to college, like, it really hits you, you're like, 'Okay, oh, wow! I never expected that.'" This comment and others like it should not be interpreted as criticism of school reforms. This student was able to enter college and persevere, like many thousands of other students, partly because reforms allowed access to the necessary preparatory courses. However, students are exposed to different levels of rigor in their high schools. Sometimes they find it easier in college than they expected, especially if they came from a rigorous high school; usually, however, the reverse is true. College generally represents a leap in academic difficulty, and national research indicates grades drop between high school and the first year of college (Pascarella & Terenzini, 2005).

Trust

Based on Coleman's theory of social capital (1988), we examine trust as a complex social process that could involve: (a) students enmeshed in communities with networks of trust that may or may not be supportive of college going; (b) schools enabling or impeding college going depending on the school culture and the particular student's experience in the school; and (c) activist advocacy for and by students within trustworthy networks that support college going. Each of these notions has been supported by the case studies from WSA students. Three aspects of trust within networks are examined further.

Local Networks. The bonds of trust in local networks are complex and may discourage or empower cross-generation uplift, depending on the emphasis on status maintenance or social agency for uplift. Many of the cases reviewed above illustrated how students are advised to go into the military, go to local colleges, or to not go to college at all. However, all of the students who experienced these barriers overcame them through financial support and encouragement from educators and mentors, illustrating the positive influence of trust building within a reform process.

The local push to success, sometimes working against pullback into the community, is illustrated in a complex way in Sky Warrior's case. He explained how his legal obligations contributed to his delayed college enrollment: "I was required to do 2 years of probation and 200 hours of community service…. They required it; it was one of the stipulations in my release and they required I graduate from high school. And then right after I graduated, I had to start paying my restitution or whatever, my court fines and all of that." Sky Warrior was skeptical he would receive one of the awards, but he did apply, received the award late in his senior year of high school, and went on to college. He overcame his legal obligation, one that required high school graduation and providing community service to avoid more serious legal problems. The legal decision itself appears to have recognized the unique circumstances of Sky Warrior's case, providing him a way through the access puzzle, a path he took.

Networks Support College Transitions. Whether students persisted in their initial colleges or transferred, the process of transition was complex because of the altered sequence of choices. Traditional college choice theory is framed as stages of decision making during and immediately after high school, but for students who are acquiring college knowledge during the first few years of college, the search process can be extended.

While we have evidence from the cases that church-affiliated schools can enhance social transition, a finding reinforcing arguments by Durkheim (1951) and Coleman (1988), if students do not share the faith orientation of their school it can add to the difficulty of making the transition to college. Seth attended a church-affiliated college in Washington, but found that students were critical of him because he was different. He described the campus as "overly pious," and he relayed an incident related to commentary on his smoking that troubled him: "I was told on a handful of occasions, just by people walking by, that 'you're going to go to hell for smoking cigarettes.' That's funny, I never saw that in the Bible, you know. I'm glad you're not going to judge me for that." He described other incidents, including being called a "stupid stoner" because he rode a skateboard to class. He had chosen the campus because of the scholarships they offered and decided to stick it out: "I was going to leave after my first semester. I was not having it, but I loved the education so much that I stayed and stuck it out." He went on to describe how he met students from another part of campus who became his "best buddies." So Seth found his fit within the counterculture of his campus.

The process of transfer involves navigating new physical and social terrains, complicating the ways that networks influence college transitions. Consider Liliya's description of these transitions: "And as I went from one college to another, the different environment…[these] people are different but it's just different." She added: "It was my first time that I had lived away from family. So it was kind of hard at first, for months, I think." College involves changing from one form of support—a family and educational system that is known—to a new system that is unknown. Liliya's comments illustrate a theme frequently voiced in the cases and in the focus groups: The changes in social, geographic, cultural, and academic environments between high school and college are major transitions, even for high achievers. Students whose parents went to college probably know better what to expect and how to navigate the complex new systems they encounter.

The processes of college transition are not limited to the decisions to go to a single college and stick with that college. While initial choice is important from an institutional perspective—securing enrollment and retaining students is important to the financial health of a college—it does not necessarily fit with the experiences of students.

Social Agency. One of the strong themes emerging from our studies is that students who received WSA awards developed a sense of civic commitment as a consequence of the financial and social support they were provided. This theme of social agency becomes stronger as we examine engaged learning and academic success as forms of academic capital formation (chapter 6).

Students frequently began to formulate an inner sense of payback as they reflected on what they gained from the support. For example, John talked about a sense of responsibility:

> And the scholarship was amazing and I think I definitely felt that burden that pushed me to go on [to graduate school].... I definitely got a lot of burdens upon me you know, it's just interesting about that, but yeah, and so I think it helped me. This big investment was being made in me, you know, they gave me [a] lot of money from that program. And I worked [staffed] a couple of campus visits they did and stuff over the summer.

Several notions are implicit in this concept. First, there is a sense of commitment to complete the 4-year degree and, in John's case, to go on for a graduate degree, which is beyond the period for the WSA financial subsidy. This feeling of responsibility, as a form of social agency, extends the concept of being given an opportunity to go to college to making the choice to attend graduate school. If we ponder this notion, it is noteworthy that some first-generation students come to feel that attaining a graduate education is their personal responsibility for having received this award. John was also moved to provide payback by supporting other students when they visited his campus. This moves toward the concept of social capital discussed by Coleman (1988). A sense of cross-generation obligation can be formed from having received: (a) financial support, and (b) support services provided through an engaging support network, both of which are provided by WSA.

Information

Students receive multiple forms of information from diverse sources. In families with little prior college experience, students often received the message growing up that college was beyond their potential and financial means, while other students had strong family support from the beginning. Some students had parents that supported advanced education as cross-generation uplift, and even some foster children experienced emotional support that conveyed the idea that college was possible. It is in the context of this lived experience that students interpret information about college options.

Information on Alternatives. Chapter 4 examined how college knowledge developed among WSA students. Many students chose college based on the advice they received from counselors and peers. In this chapter we learned that some students rethought their goals and changed colleges because they learned their campuses did not fit them.

This process of rethinking, based on the informed insights gained from experience during college, also occurred for some students who persisted at their initial college. Some learned they needed to rethink their social engagement strategies. For example, Sky Warrior chose his campus because of his girlfriend, but later reflected on this choice: "Well, I probably wouldn't have come to WSU. I don't think following a girlfriend is a good idea. Other than that, [had] I really thought about it from the beginning, I would have done a lot more research on it." He went on to discuss how his early major choice was not a good one and that he should have assessed his strengths and weaknesses more realistically. He observed, "And my scholarship is going to run out a semester before I graduate. So for that last semester it is on me basically."

Believable Information from Trusted Sources. Successful WSA students gained information pertaining to college choice while in high school. As students made the transition to college they formed new linkages, often with people who had common prior life experiences, which were an important part of building trustworthy personal knowledge of college. Consider the stories told by Sky Warrior and Oscar.

Sky Warrior described his transition experience as being enriched through people who shared his cultural heritage: "I found out about the Multicultural Student Center and the Native American Center. And I started going down there and I started meeting some people down there. Actually, I identified with a couple of my teachers, and was able to talk to some of my teachers and stuff like that. That was definitely helpful." In Sky Warrior's case, trustworthy information was culturally situated in the sense that finding other Native Americans at the university helped him to understand how to navigate through the college.

When Oscar started college he lived at home, but he decided to reconsider this choice. "Since there is a scholarship," he decided to go ahead and live on campus. "It is probably easier for me to live on campus in terms of getting my work done or going to, like, review sessions that are at night, or to professors' hours, so I felt I should probably try it out." He described the cultural transition as a difficult one, "getting to know different ethnic, you know, people is kind of difficult, still feel awkward." He went on to reflect on the troubles with roommates, changing dorm rooms, and so forth. Finally he reflected, "So that was kind of a big barrier for me to, you know, to move from home to the dorm." For Oscar, a native Chinese student, the pursuit of learning opportunities through living on campus involved a detour through learning about diversity in new ways.

There are two compelling issues in these stories: (1) Learning about college involves both social and academic processes that may be intertwined in ways that are not easily deconstructed into different variables; and (2) for students from cultures outside of the pluralist environment of a campus (e.g., American Indian or immigrant Chinese), the process of social integration involves learning about oneself in new ways. Sky Warrior's case reinforces Tierney's (1992) argument that notions of social integration should be reconstructed for Native American students.

Applying to 4-Year Colleges. It is abundantly evident from the data on college choice (Figure 5.2) and the case information that WSA students had enhanced opportunity to choose a 4-year college. In the prior chapter we learned how this option was part of the college knowledge formation process. Some of the cases in this chapter illustrate how the idea of finding a 4-year campus that fits is a process that does not end with initial college choice. For students who start in community colleges, it is important they have support to encourage and empower them to make the transition to 4-year colleges, if they so choose. In addition, as revealed in these cases, students need to make adjustments during the college years to find the fit that works for them. This could be through transfers from one 4-year college to another or through finding new support networks on campus.

Cultural Capital

The concept of cultural capital emerging across these analyses holds two distinctive notions: (1) cultural capital is formed through early student experiences in the family; and (2) during the college years, late adolescence, and early adulthood, students form their own cultural capital.

Local Knowledge. The life experiences of students, especially the ways they construct understanding from family and high school networks, are intertwined with their experiences in the college choice process. Most of the WSA student cases reveal that high school environments were supportive of students making these transitions, but this was not a universal pattern. Consider Seth's case. Seth did not always feel supported in high school: He had to overcome the projections of teachers based on their experiences with his older siblings. He observed, "So, I mean, I had plenty of people, I just really didn't like high school. Don't really plan on revisiting those times too much, you know." Seth seemed to use his own personal observations and insights as a basis for college choice. "I was just kind of on my own. When I got over to visit colleges or whatever—it was my decision. My parents were like, 'You're the one doing it, go on a tour,' I really appreciated that."

When students do not have college knowledge conveyed through their families and communities, they need some means of acquiring that knowledge. In Seth's case, he had an inner desire to learn and a supportive family that gave him the will to overcome negative projections from teachers.

College Knowledge Expanded. For most students from troubled backgrounds, school counselors and mentors were the major sources of information that empowered them to overcome the odds by taking personal responsibility for navigating a life course. Students often learn more about how to navigate their pathways through college from social interactions with more experienced students, staff, and faculty.

Consider Missy's trajectory through the educational system. She had gone to a high-poverty high school, lived in a foster home, and married during her senior year of high school as a way of finding social stability. She described how one of her mentors in high school helped her apply for college: "Honestly, because I heard that it was a good school from [name of counselor] and it is a great school and that you can decide your own programs. It turned out that I needed a lot more structure, but I don't regret the 2 years that I spent there. But I selected Evergreen just based off of...my guidance counselor's recommendation." For Missy, the first college she chose was based on information from a trusted mentor, but as she got to know herself as a student, building authentic college knowledge, she eventually made a transfer decision. However, if she had not had the encouragement in high school she probably would not have gone to college in the first place.

Extended College Search and Transfer. As Leslie's transfer to an out-of-state, church-affiliated college illustrated, the process of finding a campus fit involves acquiring knowledge about one's self in relation to learning about colleges, a difficult form of knowledge to acquire. The fact that WSA students had the freedom to extend the choice process to consider a transfer was critical to their eventual academic success.

A focus group student indicated she had opportunities to attend a 4-year college out of high school, but chose to go to a community college: "I just said I didn't think I was ready, so I ended up going to community college.... I think that is the best thing that ever happened to me." She went on to explain that transferring after attending the community college "was a lot easier for me as far as being able to adjust to the college atmosphere and stuff. So I am glad I went to community college." These comments illustrate an inner understanding of the need to make a college choice as part of a progressive process of personal development.

Initial enrollment in a community college can be empowering, especially when students know they can afford to transfer when they are ready. If the financial and social barriers often implicit in the choice of community colleges are removed, early college experience and additional preparation gained from this choice can have substantial future benefit.

Habitual Patterns

The WSA students had personal habits that were recognized through a selection that involved recommendations from and encouragement by teachers along with a formal selection process that used noncognitive variables. These processes recognized students who had personal habits that could help them to navigate a successful path during college.

Sticking with or Overcoming the Familiar. A big challenge for most of the WSA students was making a social class transition through education, a transition that takes strong personal will. Students whose family experiences did not include college had to do extra research if they wanted to find a college that fit. One first-generation college student put it this way, "I was pretty motivated as an individual, but…I didn't have the experience or exposure because neither one of my parents were college graduates…I had to do research on my own and get my information that way." The "familiar" for this and other students, that which is learned through early experience, was not college. The process of going to college involved overcoming the familiar and learning about environments that were different, a process linked to personal will and habit.

Role Models Influence Images of the Possible. Where do students gain this inner will and sense of self? For some, the concept of cross-generation uplift, integral in the African American tradition (Siddle Walker, 1996; Wooden, 2007), played a central role. Consider this comment by a focus group student:

> In growing up I was a member of the Black Achievers Program. And it's basically a career development program for students of minority backgrounds. And I just, like, see what my parents went through and they already, they always instilled in us go to school, get an education be the best you can be. And that was my motivation, you know, of, like, I want to do this and, like even seeing as much as my parents have done without any college experience, like, they owned their own business, they are successful.

This comment illustrates the complex pattern evident in Emeka and Hirschman's (2006) analysis of selection for WSA. WSA students were from low-income circumstances and many were minorities but, on average, they had more social capital than comparison students. Whether these inner habits were formed through systems of support, as illustrated in the comments above, or through personal perseverance, as illustrated by the cases of Sky Warrior and Seth, the inner sense of self seems to be one of the qualities sought by the use of noncognitive measures in the selection process.

Social Agency Reinforces Success. The inner will to succeed, manifest in personal habits that reinforce traveling the path toward academic success, seems to be a key ingredient of overcoming the odds and breaking through the barriers to access. Sky Warrior told a compelling story of navigating a course to beat the odds:

> Well, everybody else from my graduating class went to school that very next fall, and I didn't. I had to take a semester off to work because there was no way I could make it. I had to get money just to get down there, just to get all my stuff ready...I had to help my family for the winter time so I had to go cut a bunch of firewood and stuff like that to help, because I'm going to be gone for the winter or whatever. So, I mean, I had to take the summer and that semester off to work.

We learned earlier that Sky Warrior also had legal problems holding him back from college during the fall term after high school. Consider how he dealt with the family obligations: In spite of being from a family that was not supportive of his educational aims and personally having run into legal problems, Sky Warrior took responsibility for fulfilling family obligations—cutting firewood for the winter—so that he could leave home and go on to college.

The underlying sense of social agency and self-navigation come through in many of the life narratives of WSA students. In the early years of WSA, teacher nominations played a large role in indentifying students who had navigation skills. The financial and social support provided by the program fostered the inner sense of self-agency that resulted in compelling stories of discovery of pathways to educational success.

Key Features of WSA

It is apparent that WSA created supportive networks that facilitated college transitions through direct support by program officials who became part of a caring community of trust; mentorships within college; and engagement of enrolled Achievers in providing support for younger students visiting and enrolling at their campuses. This social support structure seems to be an important part of the success of the program in enabling students to enroll in 4-year colleges, either as an initial or transfer choice.

As these cases portray, the process of finding a good college fit is part of both transfer and persistence as extended processes of college choice. This is not inconsistent with the logic of research on first- to second-year persistence (Braxton, 2000); however, we shift our interpretive stance to a consideration of college transition as an extended process, focusing on how students find better pathways to their own academic success. The persistence literature is motivated by the institutional intent of retaining students and revenue (Bean, 1990), an institution-centric view. At the very least, transfer should be viewed as a successful alternative to dropout, even among researchers who focus on retention.

GATES MILLENNIUM SCHOLARS

The GMS program provided awards to high school students, college students, and graduate students. In the initial year, the awards were made late in the college choice process. Over the years, the GMS program has tried to improve the timing of the awards so that students know they have a scholarship in advance of college choice decisions. The surveys included samples of awardees along with students who were qualified academically but were not selected for the program. The quantitative analyses below examine college choice for freshmen in the first three cohorts and include comparison students. In the 2005 focus group interviews, students from each of the cohorts were included, since many new and current students in the 2000 cohort were still enrolled.

Comparison of College Choices

The descriptive statistics (Table 5.2) for the three freshmen cohorts indicate that both recipients and nonrecipients were more likely to enroll in 4-year colleges. GMS students enrolled in selective colleges at higher rates:

Table 5.2 Comparison of GMS Recipients and Non-Recipients in the Combined Sample of 2000, 2001, and 2002 Freshmen

Variable	Value	All (%)	GMS Recipients (%)	Non-Recipients (%)
Institutional Type	Public Two-Year	4.5	2.6	5.4
	Private	36.2	42.1	33.4
	Public Four-Year	59.3	55.3	61.2
Institutional Selectivity	Low Selectivity	15.4	13.3	16.4
	High Selectivity	38.1	42.4	36.0
	Middle Selectivity	46.6	44.3	47.6
College Major Fields	Mathematics & Science	25.8	25.7	25.9
	Engineering	14.2	13.5	14.5
	Education	4.4	4.3	4.5
	Library & Information Science	0.7	0.6	0.7
	All Others	55.0	55.9	54.5
Gender	Female	70.1	69.2	70.5
	Male	29.9	30.8	29.5
Father's Education Attainment	Bachelor or Higher	28.4	21.4	31.9
	Other	71.6	78.6	68.1
SAT-ACT Crosswalk Score Group	Lowest quartile	29.0	28.9	29.0
	Highest quartile	21.6	20.7	22.0
	Middle quartiles	49.4	50.4	49.0
Reason select school low expenses	Very important	49.7	46.4	51.3
	Other	50.3	53.6	48.7
Reason select school strong reputation	Very important	77.3	79.8	76.1
	Other	22.7	20.2	23.9
Parents contributing college finances	Parents are contributing college finances	52.3	35.9	60.3
	No	47.7	64.1	39.7
Cohort	2001 Freshmen	38.0	29.0	42.4
	2002 Freshmen	28.7	29.3	28.4
	2000 Freshmen	33.3	41.7	29.2
N		5,264	1,727	3,537
% of All		100	32.8	67.2

- More than one-third (38.1%) of all students in the sample attended high-selective institutions (in the top third of selectivity); however, 42.4% of GMS recipients enrolled in selective colleges compared to 33.4% of nonrecipients.
- About one-third of African Americans and Hispanics attended high-selective institutions (31.95% and 37.8% respectively), compared to a higher percentage of Asian Americans (52%) and a lower percentage of American Indians (16.2%).

The analyses in appendix 3 examine how student background, preparation, GMS award, and state funding for grants influenced enrollment in high-selective and low-selective colleges compared to mid-selective colleges. The analyses reveal that both GMS awards and state funding for need-based and non-need-based grants were associated with enrollment in high-selective colleges by high-achieving, low-income students of color. A causal analysis of environmental outcomes of GMS students has yet to be published or reported. While there is a statistical association between the monetary award and college, causality cannot be claimed.

The interviews with GMS students provided a wealth of qualitative data to explore further the reconstructed understanding of college choice as a process that extends over time. Students who received GMS awards and attended focus groups in 2006 had received awards at various stages of their educational careers. In the initial selection process in 2000, the pipeline was filled with new undergraduates, continuing undergraduates, and graduate students. Some interviewees received awards in this initial cohort. In subsequent years, efforts were made to award students early enough to influence the initial college choice, but this did not always happen. Given the changes over time in the GMS award process, along with the ethnic and geographic diversity of students, the focus group interviews with GMS students provided an excellent resource for examining the relationships between relieving serious concerns about costs and college choices.

Easing Concerns about Costs

All of the GMS awardees were Pell eligible, so they had high financial need. They were chosen based on a combination of academic and noncognitive criteria, so they were high-achievers in terms of both academic and social capital as measured by the ability to navigate systems and act with social responsibility.

Limited Options Considered. Some GMS students commented about being unable to afford college without the program. For example, an Asian American student said, "We're a family of five, so my sister is in college also and she was making less than $30,000 a year. I wouldn't have been able to come to college if it wasn't for the GMS Scholarship." Other students would have had limited college choices, at least partly due to perceptions of costs. For example, consider this sequence in a focus group of Native American females:

Mary: I know that I would have to take a student loan if I didn't have the scholarship, and I would have to pay those back later. My parents might have to take out a loan to help me.… So I would probably be in great debt right now if it weren't for this.

Kerry: My parents told me that I couldn't come to OU [University of Oklahoma] at all if I didn't get a scholarship, so I probably wouldn't be at OU without it. I would be at maybe a regional Oklahoma college instead.

Jen: Same with me. I think I went to…[a college-information] program when I was in high school and they…stressed loans and how they were bad…. So, thank goodness the scholarship came around and I was able to get it because if not, I would probably have ended up at some local or regional college.

This exchange illustrates the central role of finances in initial college choice and how that choice may be limited for students from low-income families. It also appears there was a strong message conveyed to Native American high school students to avoid debt if at all possible. Not surprisingly, this message is conveyed in other cultural groups as well. Similar stories were told by Hispanic, African American, and Asian students in focus groups; these same sentiments were also evident among the case histories of WSA students.

Since some of the interviewees received awards after initial enrollment decisions, there were many comments about the ways limited resources had actually constrained college choice, and that choices expanded after receiving the award. For example, one student observed: "Once I got the Gates scholarship I was actually able to quit…work and go to school full time." Another student followed up: "Yeah, it's made a huge impact for me, because…it just makes it easier so that I can go to school full time and not have to work. And so I can really concentrate on my studies." There were a plethora of examples of students who altered their college choices or extended their goals to include graduate education after receiving GMS awards.

Guaranteed Aid Expands Options in College.   Having money available made it possible for students to take advantage of educational opportunities that are typically part of college life. A female in a mixed-race group commented, "I've been having a half-time assistantship, which is equivalent to 20 hours a week…I do that for experience but there is also a stipend with that." She continued that, since tuition was paid by her scholarship, she was able to use the stipend for travel so she could interview for internships.

This expansion of opportunity opened up avenues to learning not previously envisioned by low-income students. A student in a Hispanic focus group commented, "It… gave me the opportunity to get an internship. It is a little less money but…I didn't have the pressure of having to make money to pay for school because I had the scholarship." Another student in a mixed-race group indicated she decided to take out a loan so she could take a summer course, but added, "A reason why I decided to work was to save money, you know, paying back the loan or whatnot that I did take out for summer school. But that's because, you know, I chose to." An African American student commented, "One other thing that Gates helped me with, in addition to paying for school, I actually took a course in England, a research course, and they helped me pay for that." These comments are illustrative of many stories about the ways educational opportunities expanded as a result of easing concerns about college costs.

Networking

The GMS students consistently demonstrated a high resiliency, an ability to navigate pathways toward academic success in spite of barriers encountered along the way. In sharp contrast to the WSA students, most of the GMS interviewees did not have supportive communities or mentors in their schools that provided extra encouragement.

Locally Situated Images of Options.   Many GMS students expressed an early desire to be a lawyer or medical doctor, professions they had some familiarity with. When they made it to college, their horizons expanded. While the GMS students were high achievers in their high schools and might have expected to go to college without the scholarships, many came from schools that seemed to be in different worlds than the colleges they attended.

Consider this reflection by a Native American student, "I was in a really small high school so I knew everyone. I'm not used to, you know, 30,000 people, not knowing everyone." She continued, "I felt like a closeness, even though appearances may be deceiving, I felt a closeness because we could, like talk about things that we received from our tribe and different events that we got to attend." This student had a deep sense of community, and she experienced feelings of loss when she left for the large university community.

The concepts of care and images of engagement that students held when they entered college were related to their experiences before college. Their engagement during college was often constructed through this lens of prior experience. GMS opened doors to new images through their conferences, but the process of choosing educational and career pathways is complicated.

Expanded Ideas of Career Choices and College Options.   Having the discretionary choice about working and borrowing to supplement education empowered many students to explore new career options in ways that would not have been possible if they had to work longer hours to pay for college. For example, a Hispanic student at UC Berkeley observed, "The only reason I worked during the summer was because of my professional development, for my own career, for internships." Many students commented with pride that, after receiving the scholarship, they could make choices about education that would lead toward their desired career such as taking internships that provided experience but little money, a type of opportunity those students might not otherwise have had. The theme of having a choice about whether to work was mentioned in the focus groups. Further, a regression discontinuity study confirmed a causal link between being a GMS scholar and working fewer hours (DesJardins & McCall, 2008).

Information on Additional Options.   Like the WSA students, there were many stories told by GMS students who discovered additional educational and career options after arriving at college. There was some added complexity for GMS students because they could receive funding through graduate school in only a limited range of fields. They had opportunities to learn about the preferred majors at the leadership conferences, which took place in the first year of the program. For most students, this occurred before the process of changing majors, so it may not have been an optimal time to provide information about alternative career paths. However, there was evidence these programs opened students' eyes about alternative pathways. Evidence related to leadership conferences and career pathways is reviewed below and in the next two chapters.

Trust

Concepts of trust, images of leadership, and visions of pathways to success were often culturally situated. Below we explore the three aspects of trust within culturally situated networks.

Local Networks.   Students in low-income families grow up in a complex network of family and community. There was a great deal of variation in the contexts of family life in which students were reared. An exchange in a focus group illustrates this. An African American student observed, "Luckily I've been blessed with a grandfather who is relatively well-off. And I needed to buy a computer recently, so he sent me a couple of grand for that." The next student commented, "I rarely got money from my family. I've been living on my own for a while now, so yeah, I take care of myself." Such variation in life contexts was evident across groups.

Expanded Networks Support College Transitions.   The GMS program provided workshops for all Scholars that introduced them to different pathways. Most students praised the conferences. The following exchange, from a focus group of Asian/Pacific Islanders at UCLA, is illustrative:

- "It was, yeah, well they taught us like leadership activities. But it's like for two days I think. I don't really remember."
- "I remember the conference…I had a lot of fun at the conference and I got to learn a lot about the Gates Millennium Scholarship Program. But as a freshman, honestly, I didn't know anything, really…. So I grew in college—what I did get from the conference was a lot of inspiration, because there were a lot of charismatic characters and a lot of leader personalities in the group which really inspired me and kind of let me see potential for, you know, young students to be really strong."

While some students had only a vague sense of the value of the leadership workshop (e.g., the first comment), others felt empowered. The points made by the second participant were echoed throughout the focus groups: Although inspirational, the leadership conference came too early in the college choice process for her; she was empowered to find out more about options later, when she was ready. A sense of empowerment, "to be really strong," was evident.

Indeed, exchanges that combined critiques of the GMS leadership program with reflections on its intrinsic value were numerous. There were extended conversations about the need for more networking among GMS students during college, and some wanted the GMS program to provide more web links. It was evident throughout these interviews that while GMS students were on trajectories toward college success, they still sought ways of learning more about colleges, majors, and careers. Many expressed hope that the GMS program could provide more support of this type in the future.

Student Follow-Through.   One of the themes that had emerged in early studies was that GMS students felt an obligation to provide support for their families, which often lacked the resources needed for survival and financial well-being (Allen, Bonous-Hammarth, & Suh, 2004; St. John, 2006b). In the second round of interviews, questions were asked related to this challenge.

Several students chose to work on top of their scholarship awards so they could help the family. For example, an Hispanic student commented, "Realistically, like my parents up to this day are still struggling to make ends meet like with their own wages and their own expenses." He said he would have had to ask them for money for rent if he had not worked, adding: "So that is why last year was hardest for me. And, I mean, I was able to manage…. Like the $2,000 that's supposed to be my parents…to cover." In another group, a student commented, "Mostly I work so, you know, so I don't have to ask my dad and my mom for money. And secondly, my older sister goes to school here. Actually she just graduated but she's really…in debt so I've been sending money over to her." These were not unusual cases. Many students, who appreciated the opportunities they had been given, took steps to provide support for their families who were still struggling.

Information

While GMS students were not asked about the college choice process per se, they were asked questions about their financial navigation of the educational enterprise and their experiences. From these interviews it was possible to get an idea of the ways students used information, conveyed in various forms, to navigate through college choice which evolved over time as students built college knowledge and cultural capital.

Funding Information.   Once GMS students entered college, they had a commitment for funding, but this information was conveyed to them, not their campuses. Given the legal issues related to racial preference in higher education and the targeting of aid on minority students in GMS, the program did not maintain a direct relationship with colleges. As a result, students became the conveyors of information about the aid award to the colleges, thus extending the role of finances in the college choice process into the first year of college. The GMS program made awards copayable to students and their institutions as a means of ensuring that institutions would coordinate the aid package. Students were obligated to take the money to campus, creating some complexities in the management of student aid.

This process could cause problems for students. A student at Howard described a problem during her freshman year: "I didn't get my check on time, but all my classes were purged." At first she turned to her mom, but the extended family came through: "My brother lives in the area, so he came up and he went to the financial aid with me and we got everything straightened out and had the Gates people call or whatever." The next speaker in the focus group added, "My freshman year it was a little difficult because I guess Gates wasn't aware of the deadlines for Howard and Howard was set with their deadlines and whatnot." She added, "After the first year I kind of knew what to do so it wasn't a problem after the freshman year." The second speaker confirmed that she too had the problem her first year, illustrating that it was a problem with the ways the two systems interfaced with respect to information and monetary exchange. In both of these cases, an intervention was required to resolve the problem and establish a workable procedure. The agency exhibited by these students is critical, because some students can give up when they encounter system problems of this nature.

This exchange within a focus group was between students who experienced a common problem: The GMS program required they play a role in reconciling aid, tuition payment, and course enrollment. The copayable check created a system problem during the freshman year, extending the college choice process for students enrolling at Howard. In this case, the first student relied on a trusted family network to resolve the problem when it emerged.

Believable Information from Trusted Sources.   The process of building trusted human networks continues through college. Using information conveyed through social exchange can be essential to persistence in the college of choice as part of an extended college choice process.

Academic problems are a common reason for departure during the first 2 years of college (Pascarella & Terenzini, 2005). But students can navigate their way through these challenges if they have information as support. Consider the following example: "The first time my GPA ran below [requirements] because of my family obligations but I brought it back up and I was able, I took a semester off and I worked where I had been a work study [student]. They gave me a full-time job for a semester and then I came back to school this summer...I didn't want it to happen again, where I was asked to take a semester off." A compelling aspect of this case is that a human network was in place that empowered this student to make adaptations. The student had the insight to use this information to inform persistence as an extended process rather than see it as discouragement and drop out.

Applying to 4-Year Colleges. Like the WSA students, many GMS students came from circumstances that did not support college going. Consider this comment in response to a question on leadership by a student in a mixed-race focus group at the University of Oklahoma:

> I am Mexican and Catholic.... We tend to be naïve and don't look at things from both perspectives and not be open-minded. I think a lot of people from my culture just don't want to take a step forward or a step farther than a lot of people do, and they just get stuck with what they see, what meets the eye, and don't look beyond that. So I think I am able—I thank God to be able...not to be so naïve as a lot of Hispanics are.

This reflection illustrates an inner courage that relates to the student's self-understanding of the Hispanic culture. Just going to college and leaving a community that was known required the student to transcend the family culture by moving from a system that did not support uplift to 4-year college to a new environment that required new forms of capital. Many GMS students who lacked examples of people who went to college found ways to navigate through college transitions.

Cultural Capital

Many students experience a tension between knowledge gained from family culture and lived experiences when they have aspirations to achieve educational uplift. Personal navigation skills are crucial in overcoming this tension, implicit in the process of enrolling in 4-year colleges for first-generation students. Below, we explore how this transition relates to the concept of cultural capital acquisition.

Local Knowledge Conveyed. GMS students in the focus groups often reflected together about the information and encouragement they received as high school students. As was evident from prior chapters, processes can be organized to encourage and empower high school students to learn about college options. In contrast to this type of supportive pattern, most of the GMS students indicated a lack of information about college in their high schools. An exchange among students in the UCLA focus group of mixed-gender Hispanic students provides an example. A participant described her high school experience: "They didn't care about you getting into college, they didn't care about you doing anything after that. As long as you get your degree, or your high school diploma, you can get out." Later, the participant elaborated, "the only reason I knew about college was because of people I kind of followed that had already gone on to college…. Nine out of my 10 friends didn't go on to college and that's just kind of how it goes."

The group went on to have an extended conversation about what a mentoring program for high school students should be like. A student reflected:

> I think a barrier…was the lack of knowing someone, having a mentor. I did not. I was the first child in my immediate family and in my cousins and aunts and uncles that went to college. So, the lack of having someone there as a family or friend to ask all of the questions about college and about high school, so the lack of a person had already done it [was a barrier].

Many first-generation college students who acquired the academic capital needed to meet the screening criteria for GMS (i.e., at least B+ average and college preparatory curriculum) lacked supportive high school environments. The second level of screening, the use of noncognitive variables, selected students with demonstrated ability to navigate the system, a form of social capital that overcomes these systemic and cultural barriers.

College Knowledge Expanded.   Many of the GMS interviewees received their awards after they enrolled in college. Their reflections on the reasons for the awards provided visibility into their reasoning about their capabilities, the social capital they had acquired that made them distinctive. Consider the following exchange:

Simone: I think part of the reason I got it [the scholarship], I was involved in my community and that didn't change.
Camille: I'll ditto that. I came in, I got involved, I was all about my grades, too, and so that is why I got it. So my attitude was great, but I was able to be involved and be all about grades at the same time. So it was a nice balance, mix, doing both.
Simone: If anything, for me, it just…solidified what my parents were saying to me or what people I love were saying to me, "You're doing great. You're making your grades. You're active. These are the things you should be focusing on."

This sequence of comments illustrates how students coconstruct understanding of cultural capital acquired through engagement and service. Simone reflected that her community engagement had been recognized in her selection. As follow-up, Camille observed that here selection was based on both social and academic achievement. Simone acknowledged that it was both and added a comment that this was reinforced by feedback in her family and community. This brief exchange also illustrates how cultural capital derived through community engagement helps build college knowledge.

Extended Choices and Transfer.   There were multiple examples in the focus groups of students whose horizons were expanded as a consequence of receiving these awards while in college. Consider these two examples:

> Jack, a student in a mixed-race focus group, commented, "I wouldn't be here if it wasn't for the scholarship. I actually attended another school that was closer to me and commuted for one year. I did not know that I received the scholarship

until the summer after I graduated (high school), and by that time I had already committed to another school. So I put in for a transfer to come here after that, you know, everything's been paid for."

A student in another mixed-race group explained that he was enrolled in a community college when he first received an award in the base year of the program (2000), then explained, "but then I transferred to Cal Tech...I wouldn't have thought about going to Cal Tech if I didn't have the scholarship because the tuition was so high. And now I am a master's student here [Stanford]."

Both examples illustrate that: (1) many low-income, high-achieving students choose local colleges for financial reasons; and (2) removing financial obstacles opens new possibilities outside options previously considered. They reinforce the argument that a free market does not exist in higher education: Able students are constrained by financial circumstance. Whether financial constraints were real or perceived—and the analyses in appendix 3 suggest they were real—the constraints functioned within the lived circumstances of these students and many others who received GMS awards.

Habitual Patterns

There is a strong tendency in social science research to seek out the universal pattern, which is evident in both attainment theory (Blau & Duncan, 1967) and social capital theory (Coleman, 1988), at least in their original iterations. But habitual patterns are culturally situated. The GMS interviews provide a resource for examining the role of race in this social construction of habitual patterns. The three hypothesized patterns (from Table 5.1) are explored further below, with an explicit focus on racial/ethnic group differences.

Sticking with the Familiar.   Identity within a cultural group is an important part of academic capital formation. Identification and bonding with a community can both keep students home for college and reinforce their pursuit of college. Consider the following examples.

A Native American student from a small town explained how she felt pulled back to her community. She reflected, "When I took my year off I moved back to my town and I worked for this large research foundation down there. But we were also very involved in the community and I had the chance to go to all the area high schools [to speak]." She had a chance to share her experiences in college and was asked a number of questions about scholarships and college. "I really thought, you know, I was, like, yes, I'm going to get some kids into college now. So I really felt good about that and I got to go to like seven schools in the area and really tell them about my experience in college and stuff, because they really didn't have any experience like that."

Strong community connectivity can be a force pulling the student back to the local community, a phenomenon evident in the case of the Native American student who reflected on how the closeness of her home community differed from her college experience. The same sentiment of community connectivity is seen in this example, but in this instance the student's return to the community, as a stop to work with other high school students, became a motivating force for returning to college and encouraging other students from her community to go on to college. This illustrates that the uplift of one student can become a motivating force for others.

Asian Americans also lived within close-knit communities, but they shared an expectation of uplift, not only within the community, but also projected by outsiders. In a focus group conversation among Asian American students, a female Asian student discussed how she had played a necessary role in the family, making it hard to leave: "My parents speak English, but not very well, I guess, so when you're younger you find yourself in a very funny situation, being the child and trying to teach—not teach, but show your parents or explain something to your parents." Reflecting on this, another student described an incident when, as a 9-year-old, a friend with whom she had "hung out" confronted her: "I knew her and she came up to me one day and she said, 'I figured out why you are so smart and why you make As,' And I'm like 'Why?' And she said 'Because you are Asian, and my uncle said, 'All Asians do that." And I was like 'Oh!' Okay. I didn't know what to say to that."

While this exchange provides two different examples, they have some similar elements: (1) the expectation of achievement was integral to the experience of these students; (2) the interaction with external groups provided visibility into differences with respect to expectations around achievement; and (3) families reinforced these notions of distinctiveness. These patterns are consistent with the strong expectation of achievement in the Asian American families observed in earlier research on GMS students (Hune & Gomez, 2008).

Role Models Influence Images of the Possible. In addition to group differences with respect to patterns supporting uplift, there were also differences within groups, especially related to gender. A Black woman in a female focus group observed:

> As far as I can see within the black community it's a lot easier for a black woman to be actually in a position of power or leadership. That's what I see.... Like growing up, the Black mother, the Black female is the dominant figure which I think is good and is empowering for Black women.

The difference in educational attainment for men and women among African Americans is now a well-documented pattern (Loury, 2004; Perna, 2004; Reynolds & Burge, 2008; Walpole, 2007) that goes back even to aspirations (Wood, Kaplan, & McLoyd, 2007). This comment illustrates the differences in images of leadership by gender within the African American community. Perhaps with the election of Barack Obama as President of the United States, the image of African American males as leaders and high achievers will gain more recognition and become more of a force in the lives of African American families.

Social Agency Reinforced Success. The cases provide many compelling examples of the agency of students and the roles of family and culture in supporting or inhibiting uplift through college choice. However, not all GMS students were of traditional age, especially during the initial award year.

Referring to a prior comment by a student who was working to pay for a car, an older GMS student observed: "My situation is very different. My mother is 84 years old. She is living on social security and plus what I can send her. I pay for her house related expenses, I pay for her health, I pay for her insurance, all of the taxes keeping her going." This was an older graduate student speaking of being able to pursue her educational dreams, to get a doctoral degree in library science, while also fulfilling her cross-generation obligation by providing support for her elderly mother. This example serves to further reinforce the ways family and community obligations can complicate efforts to attain a college education, especially for low-income students who take their family responsibilities seriously.

CONCLUSIONS

The analyses in this chapter have examined two interrelated factors with an influence on college choice: guaranteed scholarships and other forms of aid and academic capital formation. Findings related to both topics are summarized below.

College Choice as Uplift into a 4-Year College

The descriptive indicators and supporting regression analyses for these programs add to the research on the impact of comprehensive interventions on college choice.

Gates Millennium Scholars.   The descriptive data indicate that GMS students enroll in selective colleges at higher rates than comparably prepared nonawardees. The supplemental hierarchical multinomial analyses found that, controlling for background and prior preparation, receipt of GMS increased the odds of enrolling in a high-selective college compared to a mid- or low-selective college. In addition, the state level analyses in the model show that state funding for need-based grants, non-need-based grants, and average public tuition charges[5] were positively associated with enrollment in high-selective colleges.

Washington State Achievers.   The descriptive analyses of college choice indicated that WSA students were more likely to enroll in public 4-year colleges than comparison students. Multinomial logistic regression analyses controlling for background and preparation confirm these findings: WSA improved the odds of enrollment in both public and private 4-year colleges (St. John & Hu, 2007). Further, the impact on enrollment in 4-year colleges increased when awards were given in the junior rather than senior year, and students were encouraged to take advanced courses in high school. The findings indicate that support services, along with Scholarship dollars, were associated with the choice of a 4-year college.

Academic Capital Formation

College choice is appropriately viewed as a process of academic capital formation using college knowledge along with the advantages gained from academic success in high school to make informed choices about college, including choosing a 4-year college. WSA and GMS offer contrasting images of this extended process of college choice because of the focus on strong academic preparation for GMS students (Trent et al., 2008) compared to the focus on support systems for WSA students. However, the selection process used for both WSA and GMS provided opportunities for students to develop the personal habits that reinforced academic success and empowered them to navigate pathways to 4-year colleges, many of them highly selective colleges in the case of the GMS program.

A problem for many of the students who apply for WSA and GMS is that they do not have family members who have attained 4-degrees who can convey what it takes to make

Table 5.3 College Choice as an Academic Capital Formation Process: An Examination of GMS and WSA Students

Process	WSA	GMS
Easing Concerns about Costs	WSA students selected during senior year for first cohort, during junior year for subsequent cohorts; selection for all cohorts in time to influence college choice.	GMS students selected during college for first cohort (after college choice for all but freshmen) and during college choice process for subsequent cohorts; could influence college choice.
Networks	Program staff and school personnel provided support network to supplement family support; funding influenced enrollment in 4-year colleges.	GMS students were high-achieving, low-income students who navigated pathways to scholarships and 4-year colleges; funding influenced choice of selective colleges.
Trust	WSA students had trusted relationships with peers, family members, and support networks; experienced contradictory messages about college.	Strong trust of self-navigation distinguished GMS students; many lacked the support systems in high school normally associated with going to college.
Information	Aid guarantee enabled WSA students to learn from experience in an extended college choice process.	Aid guarantees enabled students to choose selective colleges; fit of college with aspirations played a role in college choice as an extended process.
Cultural Capital	Support of transition to 4-year college facilitated by support network, easing difficulty of process.	College transition involved living in two worlds, with expectations of continuation of role in the family.
Habitual Patterns	Self-navigation skills enhanced by network support and new college knowledge acquired during college.	Self-navigation skills enhanced by early college experiences; race-based patterns evident.

it. Families with a strong commitment to uplift can adapt and support their children (see chapters 3 and 4), but for the WSA program this was not always the case. Instead, WSA students found support from schools, community organizations, and other sources. The encouragement provided by WSA itself also had an enabling influence on the college choice process. Students often chose a college because of recommendations by teachers and service providers who encouraged them. Having the opportunity to visit campuses before making a college choice, encouraged by the program, was considered an important factor by many students. For the most part, GMS students navigated their way to selective colleges through outstanding academic achievement, most without a support network, although some spoke of family and community members having an influence on college choice.

Many WSA and GMS students made college choices that would not have been possible without the scholarship. Some students in both programs actually changed colleges after learning about other opportunities, exhibiting an ability to learn about college fit from their own experiences. For GMS, a few students described a decision to transfer to a better college after receiving the award. WSA students found they could pursue their desired career and educational pathways, like specialized programs or out-of-state colleges, as a result of having the guarantee of support.

Student financial aid played a large role in the college transition process. After the award, students described the increased freedom to choose the college they wanted to attend. When controlling for background and gains in preparation attributable to the program, WSA had a significant association with enrollment in private and public 4-year colleges (St. John & Hu, 2007) while for GMS both receipt of state grants and the GMS award had a positive statistical association with enrollment in high-selective colleges (appendix 3).

Low-income families were often described as needing their children to be sources of family support. In WSA and GMS, some students described choosing colleges close to home so they could contribute to their families. There was a pattern of students providing both monetary and emotional support, a pattern even more evident in the next two chapters.

6

ENGAGED LEARNING

The concept of engaged learning is widely accepted and advocated in higher education (Kuh, 1995, 1996; Kuh & Hu, 2001; Kuh, Kinzie, Schuh, Whitt et al., 2005). Academic engagement typically includes working with peers and faculty inside and outside of classes along with other forms of engagement that involve active learning. Social engagement during college—involvement in civic and social groups—can be considered vital to the formation of social capital. If low-income students have to work long hours to pay for college or must study excessively to keep up academically, finding the time for engagement in academic and civic activities outside of class is difficult. First-generation students often lack the knowledge of the college environment needed for academic and social engagement; guaranteed aid eases the difficulty of acquiring this knowledge about system navigation.

The theory of academic capital formation as a process important to academic attainment is further developed in this chapter by testing the idea that engaged learning is a social process related to academic and civic involvement. Viewing engaged learning as situated in the lives of students provides a lens for examining how students from low-income families choose engaged approaches to learning as part of their college experience. We also explore the role of financial resources, including the ability to pay for college, as a means of overcoming barriers to engagement as traditionally measured. The surveys and interviews with GMS and WSA students provide an opportunity to explore how engaged learning is related to academic and civic engagement.

Once first-generation college students leave home for college, they enter social environments that are mostly unknown to their families. Through extended networks and campus visits, they are able to enter college with some understanding of what to expect; without these opportunities, they have to learn the fundamentals of college knowledge as part of their transition to college, which may seem akin to entering a foreign culture. The process of integrating into this culture merits study from the vantage of our sample of mostly first-generation students, especially with respect to the cultural transitions associated with college engagement (Tierney, 1992).

REFRAMING ENGAGEMENT

The literature treats academic and civic engagement as intermediate outcomes on which colleges are now being evaluated (Kuh et al., 2005). The theories in research on engagement controlled for social class but overlooked how financial and other policy variables enable engagement; this research has informed theorizing about strategies for engaging diverse students in academic and civic activities in college (Harper & Quaye, 2008). There is a growing body of research on African American males that extends the engagement tradition (Harper, 2008). While the theories and measures of engagement as traditionally framed were used in the questionnaires examined in this chapter, we use the framework for this book to analyze both the surveys and interviews. While the survey questions we examine relate to the social aspects of the college experience, some also have a civic aspect. The traditional notions of student engagement do not always capture the voices of students who overcame very substantial barriers as they navigated their way through college, nor does it incorporate the idea of uplift as a central aim of academic capital formation. So we used discretion to examine responses to questions in surveys and interviews in ways that *both* respected the researchers who posed the questions *and* the experiences communicated by respondents, using the concepts in the theories as a guide for seeing what emerges as new, expected, or unexpected.

Previously, we have examined the links between receipt of grants through GMS or WSA and student engagement (Hu, 2008; St. John, 2008; St. John & Hu, 2004, 2007). In this chapter, we situate this approach in theory that considers the role of race and culture in academic and social engagement.

The African American tradition of education (e.g., Allen-Haynes, St. John, & Cadray, 2003; Freeman, 2005; Siddle Walker, 1996; Siddle Walker & Snarey, 2004; Wooden, 2007) is integral to reframing engagement as part of academic capital formation. In this tradition, engagement and support of parents and community play a substantial role in the uplift process, enabling children to aspire beyond the educational attainment of their parents and persevere in spite of prejudice. There is evidence of this in prior chapters, but it is critical to extend this frame to include college engagement. The GMS survey data were examined in relation to patterns of engagement, finding elements of the African American tradition of uplift (St. John, Rowley, & Hu, 2009) while exploring academic and civic engagement as intermediate collegiate outcomes. In this chapter, we extend this frame by examining academic and civic engagement as related to the six processes associated with academic capital formation (Table 6.1).

First, logic suggests there is a direct link between easing concerns about college costs and opportunities to engage academically, socially, and civically during college. Students from low-income and working-class families often choose colleges that are close to home and work (Paulsen & St. John, 2002). Many students who leave home for college have obligations to their families which increase their financial burden, leading students to work to send money home as well as to pay for college, as was evident in the prior chapter. It is crucial to examine the ways in which students describe these challenges as they relate to engagement processes.

Second, networking during college includes, for example, supportive relationships with peers, faculty, and service personnel, represents an extension of the concept of community support consistent with the uplift tradition. Students who are successful in preparing for college often had such support (chapter 4). Similarly, we should expect

Table 6.1 Learning through Academic and Social Engagement: Hypothesized Patterns among Students in Comprehensive Intervention Programs

Concepts	Academic	Social/Civic
Concerns about Costs	Easing concerns about costs enables students to engage academically	Easing financial concerns enables students to engage in civic activities and to be supportive of their families and communities
Networking	Education mentors help students make informed educational choices; students learn with each other	Students engage in collegiate organizations; students support community initiatives
Trust	Students build trustworthy relationships with professors and academic support personnel	Students develop trustworthy relationships with peers and communities of interest
Information	Students learn from mentors and seek out information from new sources at their campuses	Students build skills through engagement with family, school and community
Cultural Capital	Students build personal knowledge of college; reflects in relation to family circumstances	Students social and civic engagement builds self understanding
Habitual Patterns	Students develop learning habits that enable academic progress	Students develop work and social habits that build social capital

that: (a) students seek out mentors and peers to learn about educational pathways; and (b) they find community organizations that provide opportunities for civic engagement, acquiring along the way a personal commitment to support the uplift process for others.

Third, it is likely that trustworthy relationships underlie this personal engagement process. Building trustworthy relationships with professors and academic support personnel is crucial with respect to the academic side, while peers and others within academic communities can provide support in the civic and social domains. These concepts are similar to the literature on engagement, but our focus is on how a sense of trust emerges in the engagement process as an integral part of academic capital formation rather than the link between engagement and persistence.

Fourth, information acquired as a result of navigating pathways through college builds college and career knowledge through interactions with mentors, teachers, and others who provide support in colleges. Such knowledge is reinterpreted through experiences and can be passed along to others. We look at the ways low-income students develop a commitment for uplift using information from students who talked about this in the focus groups. Our contention is that students build knowledge of college, community, and society as a consequence of engaged learning, and this forms the foundation for a commitment to cross-generation uplift.

Fifth, cultural capital of students and families changes as a consequence of engaged learning during college. In addition to personal learning, students often translate lessons learned into messages shared with siblings and parents, increasing family college knowledge by constructing a new family narrative. We can expect students to gain a better understanding of self through social and civic engagement processes, providing a strengthened inner capacity to support uplift for the next generation.

Finally, these processes of social engagement can enhance the student's strength of character, the qualities examined in research on the use of noncognitive variables to select students for WSA and GMS (Sedlacek & Sheu, 2004, 2006). In particular, we focus on how self-navigation as a habitual pattern intersects with commitments to family and community. We are interested in the ways students describe their own habitual patterns in relation to engaged learning during college.

WSA STUDENTS

The WSA program, unlike GMS or Twenty-first Century Scholars (TFCS), provides support services during college, including mentors and ongoing support by program personnel at the College Success Foundation. In addition, a few campuses with relatively large numbers of WSA students provide additional support services. Combined, these services comprise a unique support process for WSA students. Below we examine the quantitative evidence of engagement from student surveys along with the six dimensions of academic capital formation.

Patterns of Engagement

Prior research using regression discontinuity with applicants to WSA has established a causal link between receipt of WSA and college enrollment by students near the selection cut point (DesJardins & McCall, 2009). This illustrates that differences are not solely attributable to selection. Analyses here confirm differences, but we do not establish causality.

Our analyses use the National Opinion Research Center (NORC) surveys. A total of 427 recipients and 245 nonrecipients responded to the Cohort III baseline survey, but there was a drop when students who had never enrolled in any college were deleted (Table 6.2). This was the first year for which there was a large enough number of applicants who applied but did not receive aid to compare with students who received aid (as noted in the prior chapter, the number of applicant nonrecipients in Cohorts I and II was quite small). The descriptive and inferential statistics were calculated with the application of relative weights provided by NORC. The actual numbers of responses analyzed were 334 WSA recipients and 234 nonrecipients.[1] The descriptive statistics (Table 6.2) compare the two groups on variables related to student background, college attended, and composite measures of academic and community engagement. Significant differences are not reported because readers should be cautious about reaching conclusions about the meaning of differences from mean comparisons. While about two-thirds of nonrecipients went to community colleges, only about one-third of recipients did. These differences in college opportunity as a form of access should be considered when interpreting the results of the comparisons of student engagement.

WSA recipients were more involved in leadership: 14.4% of WSA students reported being involved compared to only 8.1% of nonrecipients. In addition to asking a specific question about leadership, the 2004–2005 follow-up survey asked questions on social and academic engagement from the National Survey of Student Engagement (NSSE). These questions used a Likert-type scale with responses ranging from 1 to 4.

Effect size analyses indicate that WSA recipients had statistically higher scores on composite measures of academic engagement than nonrecipients, including significantly more engagement in: (1) working with other students outside the classroom; and (2)

Table 6.2 Descriptive Statistics of Sample of WSA Applicants in Cohort III

Variables	Value	All Sample	WSA Recipients	Non-Recipients
Institutional Type	Private Colleges	20.8%	25.6%	14.0%
	Public Two-Year Colleges	47.0%	33.7%	65.9%
	(Public Four-Year Colleges)	32.2%	40.7%	20.1%
Full-Time Enrollment	Full-Time Enrollment	75.9%	86.3%	61.1%
	Part-Time Enrollment	24.1%	13.7%	38.9%
Work for Pay in College	Work For Pay	50.0%	47.6%	53.5%
	No	50.0%	52.4%	46.5%
Debt Load	Total Loans For The Current Academic Year/1000	1.721	1.472	2.097
Self Concept	Self-Concept Score	49.952	50.465	49.149
Academic Engagement	Academic Engagement Score	14.538	14.833	14.113
Community Engagement	Community Engagement Score	12.684	13.137	12.032
Persistence	Persist	89.9%	94.8%	82.9%
	No	10.1%	5.2%	17.1%
Leadership Involvement	Holding Leadership Position	11.8%	14.4%	8.1%
	No	88.2%	85.6%	91.9%
Academic Progress	Academic Progress	7.859	7.874	7.838
WSA Scholarship	WSA Recipients	58.9%		
	Non WSA Recipient	41.1%		
Gender	Male	42.4%	39.6%	46.4%
	Female	57.6%	60.4%	53.6%
Ethnicity	African American	18.2%	20.0%	15.5%
	Asian American	21.4%	17.5%	27.0%
	Hispanic	12.2%	12.0%	12.5%
	Other	8.1%	10.8%	4.2%
	(White)	40.1%	39.7%	40.8%
Reason select school low expenses	Very important	47.3%	42.9%	53.5%
	Other	52.7%	57.1%	46.5%
Reason select school strong reputation	Very important	47.2%	52.3%	40.1%
	Other	52.8%	47.7%	59.9%
N		568	334	234

discussion of readings outside of class. In addition, WSA students reported significantly more community engagement (based on composite scores), participation in residence hall activities, participation in tutoring sessions, and that at least one faculty member had taken an interest in them. WSA students did not take as much advantage of support networks as non-WSA students, probably an artifact of their higher levels of preparation. Significant effect-size differences reported (Table 6.3) are the mean difference for the two groups, divided by the pooled standard deviation.

The WSA recipients were significantly different from nonrecipients on the composite measure of *academic engagement* and two of the related items (see Table 6.3):

- The composite (sum score across all items) was significantly higher (0.05 alpha), with a 0.17 effect size difference (and means of 14.8 for WSA and 14.1 for non-WSA).

- Students with WSA reported more frequent "work with other students on school work outside of class": an effect size difference of .20 with means of 3.11 for WSA recipients and 2.86 for nonrecipients.
- Students with WSA awards reported higher engagement on responses to "discuss ideas from your readings or classes with students outside of class": an effect size difference of 0.33 and means of 3.29 for WSA recipients and 2.86 for nonrecipients.

The WSA students also differed significantly on the composite score and two variables related to *social engagement*:

- WSA students had a higher composite score on community engagement, with an effect size of 0.22 and means of 13.1 for WSA recipients and 12.0 for nonrecipients.

Table 6.3 Effect Size of the Differences between WSA Recipients and Non-Recipients on Key Indicators for Cohort III

Scale	Item	All Sample	WSA Recipients	Non-Recipients	Effect Size	Sig.
Academic Engagement	Composite Score	14.538	14.833	14.113	0.17	*
	Work with other students on school work outside of class	3.01	3.11	2.86	0.20	* ***
	Discuss ideas from your readings or classes with students outside of class	3.13	3.29	2.89	0.33	
	Discuss ideas from your readings or classes with faculty outside of class	2.39	2.46	2.29	0.15	
	Work harder than you thought you could to meet an instructor's expectations	3.42	3.41	3.42	-0.01	
	Work on creative projects that you help design (research or artistic)	2.60	2.55	2.68	-0.10	
Community Engagement	Composite Score	12.684	13.137	12.032	0.22	*
	Participation in events sponsored by a fraternity or sorority	1.58	1.62	1.52	0.10	
	Participation in residence hall activities	2.10	2.36	1.72	0.53	***
	Participation in events or activities sponsored by groups reflecting your own cultural heritage	2.14	2.19	2.07	0.09	
	Participation in tutoring sessions where you received help for specific courses	2.41	2.53	2.24	0.22	*
	Participation in community service activities	2.26	2.24	2.29	-0.04	
	Participation in religious or spiritual activities	2.21	2.21	2.21	0.00	
N		568	334	234		

Note: Effect Size = (Mean of WSA Recipients-Mean of Non-Recipients)/Pooled Standard Deviation; *** $p<0.001$, ** $p<0.01$, * $p<0.05$

- WSA students self-reported higher, on average, than nonrecipients on "participation in residence hall activities": an effect size of 0.53 and mean of 2.36 for WSA students compared to 1.72 for nonrecipients.
- WSA students had a higher affirmative score in response to "at least one faculty member has taken an interest in my development": an effect size[2] of 0.31 and means of 2.91 for WSA compared to 2.63 for nonrecipients.

These analyses reveal that Achievers were more engaged in college life, both academically and civically, than were their peers who did not receive the awards. There were a number of factors that could explain these differences for WSA students including the higher rates of enrollment in 4-year colleges, having financial aid that eased concerns about costs, having mentors who encouraged involvement and provided information on navigating a path through college, and inner strengths recognized through the process of selection (i.e., teacher nominations for the initial group and the noncognitive selection process for subsequent groups). It is increasingly evident that social skills alone are not enough, a finding consistent with prior empirical studies (St. John et al., 2009).

Students must have enough time to take advantage of opportunities that arise for engagement, consistent with our analyses. Once considered a necessity of the college experience, student engagement in the academic and social aspects of college has become a luxury afforded students who do not have excessive work-loan burdens. Below we examine how reducing the work-loan burden allows social and academic engagement as forms of academic capital formation during college. We also examine how engagement in the learning process came about for WSA recipients, along with the meanings they attribute to this process of engagement in the academic and social aspects of college life.

Easing Concerns about Costs

Given the rising cost of college and the decline in income for poor families coupled with the decline in federal grants, paying for college is complicated for low-income children, even when they have scholarships. It appears that low-income students use available student aid and work to minimize contributions from their families as they pursue their education. In years past, higher education researchers argued that if students mentioned finances as a reason for college departure, it was an excuse for their failure to integrate socially and academically (Tinto, 1987). Given the very real financial constraints for many low-income students, this position now seems ludicrous.

Academic Engagement.   Having scholarship funding made it possible for the WSA students to get involved in academic organizations. Liliya said, "Since I don't have to worry about the financial part, it allowed me to use my talents in developing new ones, to pursue my future goals." After mentioning time for academic work she added, "And I have joined a number of organizations…such as Professional Pharmacy…and Kappa Phi Pharmacy Fraternity. And this semester, the past, I was able to volunteer for those organizations during Pharmacy week." She seized the opportunity, a pattern also reflected in the stories below. The time acquired from not having to work enabled most of these students to become part of their academic communities, to live the life of a student rather than the life of a worker who may attend college part-time.

Social Engagement.   When low-income students go to college, their families may lose their financial support, a situation that can be very problematic for families that already struggle to survive economically. While the middle class often assume parents should pay their share, this may no longer be possible even for middle-class families struggling in the conditions of the New Recession. A more appropriate truism might be: It takes a family to support one. Consider these examples:

- Oscar said he worked in addition to the scholarship as a means of providing family support: "So it goes to my family, just to support my family for house mortgage, and all those things, and beyond that…. Sometimes you just go out with friends."
- Consider John's story: "My parents borrowed my first 2 years. Then I took everything on the rest of my time here…. I was very active about applying for scholarships…I think I did the math when I got done…[it was] about $120,000, $130,000 for 4 years. Then I think I ended up owing about $15,000 to $16,000."

These are two variations on a theme: Student support is necessary for family well-being in low-income families, as is fending for oneself rather than drawing from family resources.

Most low-income students have at least some expected family contribution (an amount to be paid by the family determined through financial aid worksheets) and very often it is difficult for parents to pay these costs. When economic conditions are unusually difficult, it is little wonder that older children from low-income households feel an obligation either to contribute directly (e.g., Oscar's work) or to ease the family burden (e.g., John's decision to take on loans). John averaged about $8,000 in debt for those 2 years, an amount substantially greater than the allowable borrowing limit for subsidized loans. In fact, both low- and middle-income families now face difficult decisions about borrowing for college, especially given the decline in lending on lines of credit for homes since 2008.

Networking

Social capital theory argues for networking as a mechanism that supports student engagement in college (Coleman, 1988). We find support for this argument in the interviews with WSA students.

Academic Engagement.   In the WSA program, students have opportunities and encouragement to work with mentors. Liliya (who was from Ukraine) developed a relationship with a professor with a similar ethnic background: "I met one professor and his parents came from Ukraine, and he is my friend now too." For Oscar, having a professor as mentor made a big difference given the many cultural transitions he experienced during college. He commented, "I chose the professor just because…he's in a more general area, he handles the undergrad programs a lot." He went on to explain, "I can talk to him about different ideas and see where, you know, I should go exactly after, you know, after a while." These comments illustrate that the personal connection with mentors is a crucial part of the educational process. While it is not easy for all students to build these relationships, the encouragement provided through the WSA program seemed to make it easier.

Social/Civic Engagement.   Research indicates that social integration can be both a positive and a negative force in the college attainment process (Pascarella & Terenzini, 2005). For low-income students entering 4-year colleges, these transitions can be more complicated than for middle-class students who expect to make this transition as a rite of passage, as a form of capital expected as part of the family narrative.

Social networking with college peers was a complex process for many of the WSA students. Consider these two cases:

- Missy described how she "felt isolated" when she first went to college. Social integration was constrained by her personal reaction to the social climate. She described the social pressure to take drugs and commented, "I just don't do them [drugs] because my mental health is so tenuous." She reflected, "So that was bad, which is why I moved out of the dorm." After changing colleges and integrating into a new college, she reflected: "And we have a lot of friends now, whereas the first couple of years in Olympia we did not."
- Monica also discussed how the social pressure of dorm life conflicted with her priorities: "The social pressures...living in dorms during freshman year was a killer on me because so many people did not want to go to class."

These WSA students were often more concerned about finding their way academically, as illustrated by these comments; some avoided social interaction that could deter them from their goals. Monica and Missy illustrate a pattern evident among most of the WSA students: They took the academic part of schooling very seriously. They faced difficulties at home, so integrating into social environments that valued socializing over academics was troubling.

Of course, most of the students found ways to integrate socially during college, and they found peers with whom they shared values. Some of this peer engagement came through the WSA program. Oscar described his own involvement in mentoring other students through the Achievers program: "I kind of know, have some experience.... So that makes me, you know, feel more comfortable when I host other programs or host other students." He went on to explain, "I feel like I help out a lot with new students in terms of transitioning.... So, I help out with a lot of, like, for example, the scholarship program. I help out with tours or...talking about the college." As is evident from his unfolding story, Oscar at first lived at home and continuously contributed to the family financially while in college. Given this strong draw to the family, the peer connectivity provided through WSA was an important part of the relationship-building process for him.

Trust

Not only does social capital theory provide a lens for viewing the way students build trusting relationships that enable them to make transitions into college culture, but it also focuses on the role of trustworthy information.

Academic Engagement. The WSA students entered college with an understanding of their own abilities situated in their high school experiences. When describing his transition to college, Sky Warrior commented on his interest in science and math (quoted in chapter 5), but he found his math preparation had not been sufficient. He had received A grades for math in high school, but in college, "I ended up taking it [calculus] twice and then dropping it. And taking it a third time and I got like a C- in it." So he reflected on his situation and made changes: "I switched to business and once I got into business college, my GPA shot up and I started to like the professors. People seemed much more friendly, much more outgoing. My advisor was much more helpful. I actually got to, like, meet my advisor and talk to him and stuff." Sky Warrior was able to deal with his transition in expectations about math and science by connecting with both the subject matter and faculty who taught in business.

Finding subject matter of interest and people who are supportive are important factors in college success. Do not overlook Sky Warrior's comment, "I actually got to, like, *meet my advisor.*" Creating a culture within an academic program that includes the connectivity and encouragement to master difficult subject matter may be important forces. Regardless of causal attributions, the story of changing majors and securing trustworthy information from faculty advisors, professors, and others in the system recurs as a critical element in students' efforts to find pathways that work.

Social/Civic Engagement. The process of providing programming that helps students make personal connections and acquire information that is trustworthy relative to their own educational experience is not a simple issue. Strategies that work for one student may not work for another. It is not easy to predict how interventions might be received and experienced by students. Consider the following examples:

- Missy described her reactions to requirements placed on her when her mother was dying: "And when my mom was dying, I mean they were compassionate, but they still docked me a lot after telling me I didn't need to do that work…. They wanted us to journal part of our childhood, and I was like 'I can't do this right now.'" Given the difficulties of her childhood (discussed in prior chapters), this requirement was not trust building, as it seems to have been intended, but alienating.
- Monica described how her mentor helped her make the transitions, indicating she visited "every week." She also reflected "My RA [resident advisor] was really…a lifesaver. She had her doors open always and every time I needed to talk or needed help she was there. I became involved in my dorm's hall government, I guess. And so, like, I made friends with the advisors and stuff. You know, if I needed help I could always go to them."

Both students were from poor families, but the personal trauma that Missy faced was more severe than the challenges of social integration Monica faced. Missy felt a compassionate response from instructors, but this did not ease the pain or the pressures. In spite of these challenges, Missy made it: She transferred and entered a college culture that was more supportive of her core values. Ironically, this move led to marriage and dropout with a prospect of returning, rather than to completing college (see the next chapter).

In contrast, Monica found social networks that enabled social integration within the initial college of choice. For her, a resident advisor in the dorm provided an ear, a shoulder, a person who cared. That connectivity seemed to help make it easier to overcome what had been uncomfortable social pressures and to integrate into student life. The community of the college became a form of social support akin to the way functional families support their members, as a force supporting academic success (see next chapter).

Information

While there is a literature about the information on college and how it is used in decisions about college-going, less attention has been given to the ways in which students process information in learning to navigate during college.

Academic Engagement. There is a great deal of literature showing that one of the components of student academic engagement involves studying with peers. There is evidence from the quantitative analyses above that WSA students were more likely to discuss readings with peers and to meet with other students outside of class. Studying together is a form of information exchange that builds academic capital through social interaction.

This engagement process is not always easy, especially for students who live off campus like Seth. He explains, "There is a lot of reading in certain classes and…things are more difficult. So it is like, more time-consuming getting homework done and just understanding materials. And, like, you know in high school things are easier or you know, they don't push you hard." He learned finding peers to study with was important, but not easy: "So sometimes it was really hard to find a study group, or just to find people…to get homework done." He continued, "I had a certain group of friends that I commute with, carpool with. So there are certain times I had to leave…. So sometimes it is hard to get things done."

One of the strong features of WSA was that through mentoring and other means the program encouraged students to focus on academics, to find peers who shared their interests, and to study with them. As noted previously, Oscar moved to campus so it would be easier. Seth's story is similar, but he needed to stay close to home because of the demands of his family: His father was ill and he was needed to fill in, providing leadership and mentorship for his siblings.

Social/Civic Engagement. The case studies revealed that social interaction during college provided a basis for learning about social issues. For Sky Warrior, meaningful social engagement started with involvement in the Multicultural Center. He started going for free printing services and comradeship. Over time, his engagement in the Center became central to his emerging sense of social responsibility. Consider Sky Warrior's reflections on and interpretation of his university's efforts to deal with litigation over discrimination:

> There have been a couple of discrimination cases recently. I guess last semester maybe, there was an incident with a couple of…basketball players who were walking by the Multicultural Student Center…. They were walking by making faces or something like that at one of the girls working down there. She reported that they said something…. But mostly it seems like it's WSU policy to just brush and sweep it under the rug…. So I don't know, it seems like since then they are reforming the policies towards discrimination and stuff like that. So we'll see how it changes, if it changes.

As a result of Sky Warrior's involvement in the Center and the opportunities for social networking created by this gateway for involvement, he was in the process of considering a run for student government president. He reflected, "I am really into advocating for students and I think that we're paying a lot of money to go to school here…I think they're [administrators] pretty much see[ing] dollar signs. So I'm, like, pushing for student rights." After describing some other incidents, he summed up: "So one of the things that I'm for sure going to be doing is advocating for students' rights and student awareness, and making sure that the people that are in the positions of authority here…are actually being forced to listen to the students that they're serving."

Sky Warrior's story illustrates how he learned from observation and experience, developing a critical attitude about issues of student rights. He links issues related to the treatment of students to rising costs, arguing that the university should be more responsive to students because they charge students a high price. While a compelling case can be made for this, his critique per se is not our focus. Rather, we focus on his learning about the system through experience, developing new interpretations of how the system works. Sky Warrior's story illustrates some of the ways information is embedded in experience and how advocacy for socially just practice can emerge from reflections on experience.

Cultural Capital

Cultural capital, according to the concepts emerging in this book, is acquired knowledge of college and community transmitted through lived experience. As students gain knowledge of education from navigating educational systems, they can convey it back on a cross-generation basis, building cultural capital in the family. Below we examine how academic and social forms of cultural capital form during college.

Academic. In the theory of occupational attainment it has been argued that knowledge of the professions is conveyed from one generation to the next (Blau & Duncan, 1967). Cultural capital explores an aspect of the cross-generation conveyance of knowledge as a cultural process, but does not overlook the role of reproduction of professional class from one generation to the next. How is knowledge of professional pathways conveyed to students who lack this culture?

Monica described her transition from focusing on learning the "basics" in high school to learning how to apply knowledge in college: "I had a professor who told me college isn't about learning, it was about retaining…and applying." She reflected on how expectations of college changed her orientation toward learning: "I guess I didn't anticipate the reading, so much reading and stuff like that. But you get used to it. I mean, you do it because that's what you have to do." Learning in this new mode was critical for Monica, as she refined her focus on preparing for law school: "It took me a long time to…get the prelaw advising that I wanted. And so I kind of got a late start when it came to majoring in political science and stuff like that."

The unfolding of Monica's life story illustrates another pathway toward learning about the types of knowledge that are useful, trustworthy, and enable people to acquire academic knowledge that illuminates a professional pathway. Monica described how she had to view learning differently, from mastery of facts to learning in ways that created useful knowledge. Since Monica had been a student government president in high school, it may not be surprising that she chose political science and prelaw. What is interesting to note is that she did not understand this commonly traveled academic pathway when she graduated from high school; instead she had to discover it during college, at which time it became a personally empowering insight. Had Monica been in a family of professionals, she probably would have had ways to learn about these linkages among academic fields and professions earlier in life. It is part of the college knowledge passed along at the dinner table and in other settings where people talk about life experiences. This is not to argue that political science is the only link to law school, but it is a logical one, like studying biology and applying to medical school.

Social Aspects of Cultural Capital. There were many examples of engagement as an empowering process during college in the life stories of WSA students. Very often, students' choices about engagement in civic groups related their cultural orientation and sense of social class when they entered college. For example, a focus group student who indicated she had benefited from being engaged in a local Black Achievers program growing up commented on her commitment to give back: "When I go back…I volunteer for the Black Achievers Program and they work in conjunction with other programs, like the United Way…I participated in giving time back." Reflecting on the support she received growing up, she observed: "I just want to be that kind of person for someone else growing up."

It is striking how so much of the time related to social engagement was spent working through complex issues within families. For example, Missy observed, "So when my mom died…I almost quit then. And then a year later I had this huge depression thing. There's two points I really thought about quitting school…. And I was kind of, [there's] something waiting on the other side for me to keep persevering through." This comment adds substance to Missy's story, which unfolds across these vignettes. She had the inner strength to envision a new personal path through the crisis of losing her mother. This inner strength was part of what compelled her to persevere.

Seth described how his family encouraged him to stay in college. He indicated that he partied a lot. He reflected, "I know they were very worried about that. Like, 'we don't want you to drop out.' I won't, I can handle it." He described his family involvement during his college years: "There's a lot of times where I had to step up and be the leader while my father was [sick]…I was kind of thrust into this position where I had to be the head of the house type thing." Given this social pressure to be a source of emotional support for a family in a time of need, it is remarkable that Seth made it and that he was pondering graduate school.

These cases demonstrate some of the ways strength of character emerges from life experiences that include social giveback during college. In each case, the student's culture had been shaped by life experience and became a source of strength for building the personal knowledge about making it through college, with building college knowledge taking an empowering form during college. These cases provide different vantages of the ways family culture supports cross-generation uplift even when the families do not have or transmit knowledge of educational pathways to professional success. They illustrate that college knowledge is built through life experience during college; it is a form of knowledge that is not bounded by precollege experience, but rather it is integral to maintaining a personal orientation toward navigation of social systems.

Habitual Patterns

WSA students frequently told stories of finding the inner strength to succeed, a process encouraged through the recognition brought by receiving the scholarship. For example, Liliya indicated: "I had doubts about my abilities but receiving [the] scholarship helped me to realize that I can and will succeed." This inner strength was a manifestation of habitual patterns illustrated by students in their interviews.

Academic Engagement. The intermediate understanding that emerges from the experiences of WSA students is that they have inner strength as an habitual pattern that propels them toward success in college and life. When reflecting on finding the way in college in the face of the social pressures of dorm life, Monica reflected: "It's just that it all reverts back to, like, the foundations. So if you have this foundation of being a hard worker, setting a goal for yourself and then getting it done, then you'll get it done, but there is always, like, peer pressure." She explained how she looked inside herself for strength: "But you always have to revert back to where you started.... All that doesn't matter, you just have to do what you have to do." This illustrates Monica's inner strength—a personal will to make it through education and life—on which she drew when she was confronted by crises that could throw her off path. Her habitual pattern, as she expressed it was "setting a goal yourself and then getting it done."

Piecing together these stories we see a combination of habits—setting goals and pursuing them, finding strong anchors in their new communities and relying on them, and seeking areas of interest linked to long term goals—that appear to empower students to overcome social and cultural barriers to college access and success. This process of taking charge, of steering toward goals that were personally constructed, is an empowering process of self-navigation that continues to develop during college. It involves hard work, but also setting goals, navigating a course, and finding others who can be trusted and relied upon.

Social/Civic Engagement.   Students from poor families who attend high schools with other low-income students, the schools targeted by the Gates Foundation and the WSA program, are confronted by a new culture when they enter residential, 4-year colleges. Consider these cases:

- Missy commented, "It was a culture shock. One thing was that a lot of students... had a lot of money. And that was difficult for me. It was just.... You've got to realize being lost into poverty. You've got to be able to deal with all people and all economic areas of the world here. But it's just a different culture when you grow up with a lot of money.... And even on my poorest day I realized that I was richer than two-thirds of the world anyhow. So I'm just thankful for what I have."
- Oscar described how he supported his family while in college: "In my family...my parents have only a high school education and so their English is getting better but it's not good. So I have to handle a lot of stuff with the family, doing tax returns, you know, sometimes writing letters, or reading some things." He summed up, "So basically, I'm the main person in the entire household for, you know, for them to rely on."

Both Missy and Oscar illustrate an inner strength of character based on understanding of self in the family and the external world. Missy chose to appreciate what she had rather than to lament what she did not have. She confronted the challenge of class transition and found inner strength. For Oscar, the challenge was basic and immediate. He not only worked to help pay the family's mortgage, as we learned above, but served as a family guide, using the education he had gained to help his family navigate life in a new land.

Intermediate Understanding.   Navigating a course through college was a process that involved setting personal goals, navigating the academic system, and dealing with family and social issues in new ways. Acquiring self-navigation skills became, for WSA students, an extended process that had been encouraged by their high school teachers.

As students they demonstrated the ability to both handle complex social issues, often related to family experiences, and to engage with faculty and others during college to acquire the additional knowledge needed to navigate the education system. WSA provided the money that gave them time to engage and the social support that enabled self-empowering strategies of navigation to emerge during college.

GATES MILLENNIUM SCHOLARS

The GMS program selects students with the intent of encouraging engagement, including forms of social and civic engagement to enable a new generation of leadership. The program also fosters academic involvement in high-demand fields, such as STEM fields, in which minorities have been historically underrepresented. The concept of engaged learning is, therefore, integral to the program design. Below, we examine evidence from the GMS freshman surveys about student engagement, followed by an analysis of the constructs related to human capital, social capital, and social reproduction as they contribute to the idea of academic capital formation.

Freshmen Surveys

The GMS surveys included a battery of questions about civic and academic engagement. Our analyses compared GMS recipients and nonrecipients to build an understanding of the academic and social dimensions of engaged learning as intermediate outcomes in higher education. We used an effect size analysis to determine whether the indicators of engagement and self-reported student aid awards were significantly different (St. John et al., 2009). This involved dividing the sum of the difference of means for the two groups by the standard deviation for the measure. All of the variables related to academic engagement, social/civic engagement, support networks, and financial awards differed significantly using this method (Table 6.4), similar to findings from a study using regression discontinuity (DesJardins & McCall, 2008).

The questions related to academic engagement asked students the extent of their involvement in working with other students outside of class; discussing ideas from readings or classes with students outside of class; discussing ideas from readings or classes with faculty outside of class; working harder than they thought they could to meet an instructor's expectations; and working on creative projects they helped design. The fact that Scholars were significantly more engaged along all of these dimensions indicates a substantial difference attributable to the program.

The social/civic engagement variables included participation in events sponsored by a fraternity or sorority, residence hall activities, events or activities sponsored by groups referencing a student's cultural heritage, tutoring sessions for specific courses, community service activities, and religious or spiritual activities. Over this diverse range of activities, it is apparent that GMS scholars had more opportunity to engage in activities of their choice.

GMS students were more engaged in networking, including relying on racial/cultural groups as a main support group on campus, working with faculty, feeling like a part of the campus community, turning to faculty for support, turning to a resident advisor for support, and turning to other students for support. The ability to network and engage is clearly recognized in the use of noncognitive variables in the selection process, so it is very difficult to untangle the effects of selection and student aid awards.

Table 6.4 Effect Size of the Differences between GMS Recipients and Non-Recipients on Key Indicators (Continuous Variables)

Scale	Item	All Sample	GMS Recipients	Non-Recipients	Effect Size	Sig.
Academic Engagement	Composite Score	19.290	20.074	18.904	.212	***
	Work with other students on school work outside of class	4.296	4.491	4.200	.191	***
	Discuss ideas from your readings or classes with students outside of class	4.341	4.535	4.245	.197	***
	Discuss ideas from your readings or classes with faculty outside of class	3.157	3.353	3.059	.190	***
	Work harder than you thought you could to meet an instructor's expectations	4.468	4.554	4.426	.087	**
	Work on creative projects that you help design (research or artistic)	3.027	3.139	2.972	.096	***
Community Engagement	Composite Score	16.908	17.832	16.457	.211	***
	Participation in events sponsored by a fraternity or sorority	2.220	2.260	2.200	.039	
	Participation in residence hall activities	2.790	2.930	2.730	.134	***
	Participation in events or activities sponsored by groups reflecting your own cultural heritage	3.110	3.340	3.000	.225	***
	Participation in tutoring sessions where you received help for specific courses	2.720	2.880	2.650	.154	***
	Participation in community service activities	3.090	3.330	2.970	.252	***
	Participation in religious or spiritual activities	2.980	3.090	2.920	.103	***
Supportive Network	Relying on racial/cultural groups as main support group on campus	2.309	2.4242	2.253	.148	***
	At least one faculty member has taken an interest in development	3.063	3.1786	3.006	.152	***
	Feeling like being part of the campus community	3.231	3.283	3.206	.100	***
	Turning to one or more faculty members for support and encouragement	2.449	2.574	2.388	.193	***
	Turning to a resident advisor for support and encouragement	1.918	1.945	1.905	.041	
	Turning to other students for support and encouragement	3.264	3.301	3.246	.065	*
Debt Load	Total Loans For The Current Academic Year/1000	3.406	1.611	4.282	-.382	***
Grant	Current Grant/1000	10.117	14.208	8.119	.532	***
N		5,264	1,727	3,537		

Note: Effect Size = (Mean of GMS Recipients-Mean of Non-Recipients)/Pooled Standard Deviation; *** $p<0.001$, ** $p<0.01$, * $p<0.05$

Source: St. John, Rowley, & Hu, 2009, p. 23.

Grant awards students received differed significantly. The GMS students reported receiving higher grant amounts allowing for less borrowing than their peers. This difference is attributable to the GMS program because it provided additional grants to minimize debt.

These findings do not rise to a standard of causality. They are, however, consistent with findings from a discontinuity analysis using these data: "We find…GMS recipients' loan debt and work during college, and parental contributions toward college are lower for GMS recipients than non-recipients" (DesJardins & McCall, 2008, p. 1). Thus the observed differences *really are different* for the core financial variables. The more interesting questions in our view are how students experience the process of navigating college.

Easing Concerns about Costs

The concept of easing concerns about costs illuminates both the financial and social consequences of receiving aid. Money alone would not enable greater engagement if it were not for the extra time students gained from not having to work and if students were not predisposed or interested in engagement in learning and social activities. GMS student accounts of the advantages gained—academically and socially—from the time freed up by the program were common.

Academic Engagement. There were many different ways that receiving additional aid enabled students to take advantage of learning opportunities. One form of engagement not normally considered in survey questions related to owning a computer. Many students said they had never owned a computer before, and they were able to purchase their first one as a result of the award. There were, of course, many indicators that reducing concerns about costs enabled greater academic engagement.

In most of the focus groups, some students who worked indicated they did so as a means of gaining experience in their preferred fields rather than to earn money to pay the costs of attending college. For example, an Asian American student gave this reason for working: "It's more like an internship position, but fortunately I got paid for it." Later in the dialogue, this student explained, "So I'm in one professional business fraternity… there are dues there, so the amount of money I received [from GMS], it helped me a lot, to pay for dues for the organization and I have time to volunteer once a week." The economic support was especially valuable for graduate students who had the time to engage in scholarly pursuits. One graduate student said, "Most of my matriculation with Gates has been in graduate education…. There are some activities you can be involved in, but most of your concentration is focused on getting a degree."

In addition, some students worked or borrowed to extend their educational options. A participant in a mixed-race group observed, "I take some loans for summer school, like the first year I went to summer school GMS covered it, but like after that they didn't do it, so I went the next year, so I have loans for summer school." Another student in the same group commented, "I am also working, but it is just part-time and it is an internship, so it's for experience. I don't really have to work for money…. I kind of feel like I have to have this backup money a little bit." While students did not have to work as part of their award package, working and borrowing enabled many of them to take greater advantage of their learning environments.

Social/Civic Engagement. There were also many stories of increased opportunity to engage in social and civic activities because of the student aid. Consider this exchange in a mixed-race group:

- "For me...I wasn't forced to like to leave classes and go to work. You know, it's hard to be like the vice president...and you're in all Honors programs and different community services that I did through my undergraduate experience, just because I wasn't forced to go to work anyplace."
- **Moderator:** "Someone else with that experience?"
- "I also agree with her. Just not having to work, you know, just I guess gave me the time to pursue things besides school. And...you just feel more inclined to be involved on campus."

This exchange demonstrates a shared and socially constructed understanding of the advantages gained from the aid, including freedom to engage in campus activities rather than concentrating on working to pay for college. Easing financial concerns provided fuller opportunities for academic citizenship during college. These vignettes also illustrate the ways low-income students build a sense of civic responsibility.

Networking

GMS national conferences, held each year in Virginia and California, provide students with visibility into national networks. They meet with peers from around the nation. They learn about leadership in communities of color and are introduced to career pathways in college. These conferences provide encouragement to explore options on campus, but GMS does not have a follow-up process to encourage networking among Scholars.

Academic Engagement. A Hispanic student described how her experiences at the conference enabled her to learn about Native American values and encouraged her to reach out to others from this cultural tradition through her academic work:

In my cohort group there were five Native American students that were extraordinary people and I will never forget them. The energy that they brought to the conference, that's something I've attempted to bring with me.... One of our professors is a Native American woman. She's inscribed in one of the tribes.... Nobody can see what she's doing, but I guess I had the opportunity to meet these people and I can recognize what's she's doing and that there's a creation of community unlike any that exists in this campus and I can see it. So I feel like I gained that insight from that group and it's phenomenal.

In this case, a student came to know and understand a concept differently because of her experience with a different ethnic group at the conference and was able to transfer this understanding into the learning process at her home campus. She was able to understand her professor differently because of the networking experience.

Students make choices about engaging in activities on their own campuses that relate to their academic and career interests. An example of local networking that supported academic and career development was described by a female in a Hispanic group:

> I remember attending like a small, one-day math conference here at UCLA…. I was interested in talking to a teacher and I told her I was interested in teaching in her district, and gave her kind of like a business card. And on it I put I was a Gates Millennium Scholar, and she said "Oh, I helped my student to get this scholarship." So I think it was something very nice for her to know that I was a [GMS] Scholar.

These examples are illustrative of many stories that emerged from the transcripts. Students took advantage of opportunities to network, using insights gained to make contacts that promoted learning and career opportunities.

Social/Civic Engagement. Networking is both local and national. While GMS leadership conferences expose students to social-action opportunities and national movements, especially related to cultural issues, there are similar opportunities on campuses.

In most instances, the networks that enabled learning about social and civic engagement were local and evolved over the years during college. For example, a student in a Hispanic focus group explained that her involvement started as a freshman, as a result of living in a thematic dorm. "By default you have to be, like, involved with Raza Recruitment and Retention Center. So I was like, because I was living there, I was able to do that." The involvement extended across years: "My second year I also became an intern at the Raza Recruitment and Retention Center…. [T]hey have a lot of events…like they bring in like kindergarteners from Oakland district to Berkeley." She went on to explain that in her third year she collaborated on a Latino/a youth leadership conference and drive to "promote Latino literacy." This was local activism within a group that was part of a national organization.[3]

Later in this same focus group, other students reflected on the Gates Leadership Conference:

- "I mean, the conference was very empowering and, sure, I think some influence…. It [GMS] gives you time to commit to a leadership role."
- "I was going to agree…I don't think there's necessarily, you know, a connection that leads you to be more involved or you to be a leader, but I think the conference I went to was also very empowering…I came back and I was like, oh, I'm going to do this and that, you know. I'm going to be a leader in the community."

This exchange illustrates how students learned from their peers' reflections on the leadership conference. The first comment demonstrates two aspects of the award: the conference adds to the vision and the financial aid provides the time to engage. The second student made the link explicit, recalling how the conference added to an inner image of leadership, which in turn led to action.

There were also examples of social networking that involved using new technologies. In a mixed-race group at Chapel Hill, a student described how a network evolved from the conference: "Like our group out of Los Angeles, a little Yahoo! We really were proactive among ourselves to do something. As years go by, kind of like we're off and Facebook has struck every campus in the country. That happens, like there is a little Facebook group in Chapel Hill and other schools." In this case, students used computers to bring their networks, created at the national conference, home to be actively used to continue the exchange.

Trust

Social capital, according to Coleman (1988), is built on trust. Below, we consider a few examples of how trust emerged as a force for uplift for GMS students.

Academic Engagement.   One form of trust as a function of uplift involved learning about options and trusting in the process of academic engagement. An Asian American student described the meaning of the scholarship and leadership conference:

> When I first got the scholarship and I went to the conference, it really boosts up my confidence. And you know, to see, wow, what such a great group that I'm in right now because I was able to see like all the Scholars, like a lot of universities, like different background, different, you know, colleges, different majors, everything.

This comment illustrates how the GMS conferences led to an increased trust in self as a result of being part of a group that was so inspiring. Trustworthiness is conveyed through mentoring relationships as well, seeking out help as well as providing help to others. For example, an African American female commented, "I think the majority of my mentorship on campus came through being an RA.... So they ask you, 'Have you pledged?'...or, 'What classes should I take?' or 'When do I enroll?' So you are kind of like a 24-hour mentor, in that aspect." This comment conveys understanding of the importance of having a trustworthy source of information for others navigating a course through college.

Social/Civic Engagement.   The Leadership Conferences and other support services through the GMS program have the potential of developing a national network supporting social and civic engagement, but students noted there were no mechanisms for follow through on networking. A participant in an Hispanic male group commented, "And those conferences are great for motivating and for bringing people together, but I don't think the communication after the conferences was really maintaining to a lot of the members because there weren't other events to attend, there weren't other planned events."

The issue of building trust within and across cultural groups was often a topic for reflection in the focus groups. Consider this exchange:

- An Hispanic student explained some of the differences in social interactions inside and outside of classes: "I think for the most part the students get along well with each other, especially if you're in like a class environment. We tend to group into cultural distinction, though, once we're outside of the class environment, you know, like Asians have their own subgroups, and the Hispanics have their own.... We tend to stay in one area."
- The next student to speak reflected, "I guess I agree...[but] I have not interacted with the Hispanic community on campus very much. I feel like everybody is doing their own thing. It is diverse and there's a lot of like different interest groups.... All of my friends are Anglo, probably because I started in a field where...a majority of the people were Anglo."

It is easier to engage socially with culturally similar peers in spite of espousing multicultural values, a point made by the first student. The second student agreed with the notion, but added she had built networks with Anglos because they were her peers in class.

Information

While information plays an important role in gaining educational opportunities, the ways students learn about possible pathways are complex and varied. The academic and social/civic dimensions of the role of information are examined below.

Academic Engagement.   Some of the original awardees in the GMS program were selected because of their academic engagement in high school. Many of the students who were in the first group of awardees indicated their teachers had reached out to them. For example, one student commented, "My English teacher received the packet in the mail and she gave it to me and just told me I should go for it." Malisa Lee (2008), a GMS recipient, recalled her own experience as a student at UC Santa Barbara, where a professor gave her the information and nominated her. Students who are nominated for and receive GMS awards have social skills that help them navigate, and the demonstration of those skills, their becoming visible in educational settings, is one of the ways students found out about and gained entry into GMS.

As GMS students became engaged academically in college, they experienced the freedom to make choices based on their interests, rather than economic considerations.

- In a Hispanic focus group, a woman commented: "Like I came into UT studying engineering because that's what's acceptable in my family, but I ended up switching…. I'm a linguistics and foreign language student."
- Another student in the same group explained how she came to her major choice: "So being Hispanic and speaking Spanish and coming from a different culture has allowed me to adapt a lot easier and fit into an anthropology perspective. The students who are in the anthropology division are all, you know, culturally marginalized [people]."
- A third student added, "I felt underestimated in another field…. It had to do with family pressure to study a certain thing. So I switched. I found something I really liked and I had more opportunities to do, to show what I really had to give."

College is unlike high school because of the range of educational choices available. It can be difficult to navigate personal educational pathways through these labyrinths of choices. Family tradition and expectation, understanding of self, and information gained in educational experiences are all sources of insight for navigating through the college experience and choosing a major.

Social/Civic Engagement.   The GMS leadership program enabled the type of exchange of cultural information that informs understanding of self in a broader context. Consider this exchange between two Native American students in a mixed-race focus group in Texas:

- "Growing up in my situation, one thing the program has done for me, and I think it was 2001 or 2002 when we had the big—our first meeting in California—it introduced me to so many other Indian tribes that I never had a connection with before."

- "And one thing I noticed is we had a lot of similarities in our problems, and you know, our problems were unified. A lot of reservations have poverty. A lot of reservations have subpar education, have social issues of alcoholism, suicides, murders, those types of things."

In the case of Native Americans, maintaining culture is often hampered by isolation from other tribes, especially tribes concentrated in different parts of the country. Strikingly, the GMS leadership conferences provided an opportunity for Native American college students to meet in a cross-tribal setting, a process that enabled them to gain a multitribal perspective of their own traditions and come to see similarities. This insight seemed to not only reveal causes of problems but also potential avenues for transformation.

Providing information to enable other students to make informed choices was another aim frequently expressed in GMS groups. In a mixed-race group, for example, a student commented:

> Right now, I work in the multicultural information center and so I come across all different types of students. Like they're having trouble academically. They need scholarship help. They're having just a lot of cultural, even identity issues. That's one of the things that brought me to the center…. You get a lot of leadership roles like, you know, helping out with Explore UT is a big huge event where people come from all over the Austin community…. You show them the university.

This commitment to helping others by providing information about educational options was a theme running through the interviews. Students wanted to give back as part of finding their own ways forward, a process that contributes to building new forms of academic capital in their communities as well as in their colleges.

Cultural Capital

Cultural capital can be a force that reinforces social class across generations, a force that must be overcome to expand access. At the same time, a family's cultural capital enables opportunity and provides support and uplift. However, unlike social capital, which has mechanisms that can be tools for uplift (i.e., information, trust, and networks), cultural capital must be built during the process of becoming the first generation to obtain a college degree is the life history of a family. The emergent concept of college knowledge as a form of cultural capital that can be acquired during college takes further shape from analyses of focus groups interviews with GMS students. Below, we explore the academic and social/civic aspects of cultural capital inclusive of building college knowledge as an activist process during college.

Academic Engagement. While research indicates that GMS students had more access to AP and advanced courses than most minority high school students (Trent, Gong, & Owens-Nicholson, 2004) and while GMS students came from some of the better schools serving minorities, students frequently indicated that their schools lacked the quality of preparation they needed, even when they had advanced courses. Even when they had the advantage of advanced courses, many faced challenges in navigating and contending with the rigor of the collegiate academic system.

A Hispanic student at Berkeley commented, "My school had mainly two AP courses and that was it…. My physics teacher was teaching without a, you know, teaching credential, like underqualified teachers. Just like not having…a high school that didn't really prepare you to write well, concise. A high school that didn't tell you every paper needs to have a thesis." This is a troubling aspect of the cultural capital being conveyed within low-income communities. Once they arrive at college, many of these high-achieving low-income students still had to overcome academic barriers created by deficiencies in their preparatory education during high school and earlier.

Yet many GMS students also realized they were creating new images of the possible for their communities. In another example, Carl, a student in a mixed-race group, commented, "A lot of my friends are not very motivated and they think that, you know, well, 'I'm just going to do this and I'll be OK.' And I guess what we need is somebody to come in and show people that there is something better out there, and they can have it if they want it enough." The message conveyed, often both culturally and academically, is to use what is available to bust through the educational barriers embedded in an unequal educational system. Carl's sense of personal empowerment was essential in overcoming deficit thinking. His message of overcoming barriers and inequality is an important one for first-generation students who remain in communication with their communities. It can become part of a within-generation pull-up process.

These comments get at the core of a very serious problem. Frequently the educational barriers for entering first-generation college students are related to their prior education. Even students who acquired some accelerated opportunities during high school felt some disadvantages. The frame of academic capital formation emerging here is one that places value on taking advantage of opportunities to break through educational barriers and pull others up in the process. Unfortunately, K-12 education may never be equal for lower income families compared to wealthy ones.

Social/Civic Engagement.　Some students experience the class struggle as transnational, especially new immigrants. A Mexican American student who had been involved in political action in Mexico City, commented, "Being politically active, I think the cultural values are very important." Describing political events and protests organized in Mexico, he commented, "The mayor of Mexico City was basically almost impeached and, having grown up in Mexico City and being in a public university there, basically all that organized the protest…were from the same background." He added: "I was one of the leaders for that stuff."

The forces for cultural reproduction are not necessarily easy to overcome. In Hispanic families, for example, young males often share responsibility for supporting the family, creating dilemmas about college-going. Consider this story:

> I think what happens is a lot of times in low-income communities as younger individuals in your family start to get to the age where they're finishing high school, they start to assume a leadership role in the family. And it's this transition period…. You're being able to take control of either things like finance or things like just keeping the family together, personal issues. And for me, reaching that age in my family and being able to kind of take control and sort of assume a position of leadership in the family is an entirely different direction from going off to college…. And for me I know I was in the position where I had to make that decision whether to leave home and go to college or really continue to hold things together for my family at home.

For some students, however, going away to college did not mean leaving the family and community behind; rather, it meant reconstructing their role in their families and communities. The experiences of the struggles for uplift and dedication to social change were in the conversation among GMS students. What became clear was a commitment to uplift across and within generations that extended beyond community boundaries.

Other stories of culture and uplift come from focus groups. The complexities of uplift as a process that engages one in reflection on community and culture were evident in the stories told by students in all types of groups. Some cultural groups tended to be more supportive of education—Asian Americans often indicated that academic success was projected upon them by both family and community even when they lived in multicultural communities. The processes of uplift and reaching a personal understanding of self within a culture and family are not simple for students from any racial/ethnic group.

Habitual Patterns

In families with a history of higher education, college is an expectation conveyed across generations along with knowledge of college. First-generation college students are faced with the challenge of learning about college as they go, a condition they face whether or not their families seem supportive of the transition. While cultural capital can function as a force for change—acquiring cultural capital is to educational attainment what making money is to financial well-being—the goal is not to alter cultural capital but to add to it through college knowledge. What emerges in this book is an understanding that college and professional knowledge are specialized forms of cultural capital that add to a family's capabilities.

Academic Patterns.   One aspect of the uplift process relates to the value placed on education within families, communities, and cultures. Many low-income students live in communities with poor-quality schools. Even when advanced courses are available in their high schools, they frequently are not similar in quality to courses taught in wealthier schools.

Chelsea, a student in a mixed-race group commented, "Some of the barriers that I faced is like I said, I'm the first one to go to college in my family, so no one in my family really knew how to guide me through college. So I've had to learn from myself or by observing other people, or my friends, asking around. I ask more questions than probably anybody I know because I don't know a lot of things." Chelsea struggled more than her wealthier peers, but she described a self-reflective form of engaged learning as a means of acquiring necessary knowledge.

Other students came from families that supported and valued education, especially students from Asian American families. One student commented, "My family really values education…. My parents really expect that, you know, my brother and I should get a degree." This student may face the challenges of learning about new environments with support from her family, but also faces strong family expectations.

Inferior preparation creates a barrier to educational opportunities for many students, constraining their ability to realize some of their academic dreams. Some of the major changes students experience are attributable to prior preparation. For example, a Native American woman described her experience:

> When I got here I had to take zero level math classes.... The science classes I, that I took I did well in but I'd always kind of wanted to do things that had more of a science edge to them. When I got here I realized that it probably wasn't going to be possible for me, just because my previous experience hadn't prepared me well enough.

The condition of low-quality preparatory education is one told and retold by many of the GMS students. In this case, the student learned about options and changed directions during college rather than dropping out.

Native Americans face an especially difficult challenge in conveying and maintaining their culture in their new institutions (Tierney, 1992). It is not only a matter of fitting in, it is also a matter of making a cultural transition that involves explaining one's culture. The cross-cultural experience was a factor for many Native Americans. A student commented:

> Sometimes I forget how small the native population is, if you look at it overall. So I think a lot of my professors are kind of shocked when they see me in class sometimes. I think that when I talk to them after class it's especially shocking because I think they've always thought, "Oh, they're quiet people".... They have a lot of questions and they all really enjoy learning and hearing different things that I have to say.

Underrepresented minority (URM) students are often able to speak to empowerment issues for their racial/ethnic groups. This Native American conveyed a personal understanding of self and of overcoming projections of the group on self, a part of the process of academic engagement for many URM students during college. It was spoken with the patience and wisdom of a person who understood what it took to preserve a culture within an institution and among a faculty that misunderstood her culture.

URM students face extreme barriers during the college years. In many elite universities, Hispanics, Blacks, and Native Americans are rarely over 5% of the enrolled students. Even if one of these groups were 5% of all entering students and if all students persisted equally, which too often is not the case, there would be on average only one URM student in the average classroom of 25 upper division students. In such a context, it is difficult to have inclusive "intergroup dialogue" and to overcome group projections onto the individual. In these universities, academic engagement in the classroom benefits from an inner sense of self as a form of personal empowerment. Engagement in social and civic groups can reinforce this inner sense of self as an empowering process during college.

Social/Civic Patterns.   Many students from low-income families also experience greater problems during college because their families expect them to contribute to the family well-being. The concept of expected family contribution, a financial obligation of parents to support children in college, may be counterintuitive when families need and expect children to contribute financially (i.e., wages) and socially (i.e., child care and sibling support).

A Hispanic student reflected on how hard his parents had to work: "My dad works a good 12 hours a day and see he's old already and they shouldn't be working as much.... I want to retire my parents as soon as I start making money. I don't want to see them

keep working, you know. I want to serve as a role model for other women in my family."
Another female in the same group added this comment:

> But I think one of the hardest things for me as a woman coming to college was
> that my parents were very ambivalent about me moving away from home because
> they thought that, you know, the cycle of women in our family was you go to
> school, you graduate from high school and then after that you start working and
> then eventually you get married.

In addition to having an obligation to family, students derived images of leadership
from their communities that they could internalize. Two comments in a conversation
about leadership in a mixed-race group illustrate ways students may reflect on their
experiences in envisioning their future:

- An African American student commented, "I can speak for me, personally. My
  vision to see improvements in the social and economic problems in the community pushes me to be a leader, because if I have a vision, if I feel like I can help make
  a difference in my community, that is what I need to do…It gives me the inner
  drive to continue to do what they do."
- Later in the group, a woman added, "Me being Asian American, I really feel that
  has given me a sort of passion…. I really think coming from a cultural background
  as culturally diverse as the one I have, it's really given me a passion for learning
  about cultures and participating in international activities on campus."

Through their own academic and social engagement during college, students learn
about themselves as members of changing families. The case of the African American
student above is consistent with the image of women as leaders in the African American community, as noted in the prior chapter, a pattern that reinforces the idea of
promoting change. As students construct new meaning from their experiences during
college, they discover new ways to contribute to their families and give back to their
communities.

Intermediate Reconstruction. A personal sense of empowerment is crucial to
academic navigation during college for URM students. Even when they have had some
advanced college preparatory courses, which is the case for many GMS students, they
face an unequal educational environment in the nation's top universities, the sites where
most of the GMS focus groups were conducted and where most enroll. They face the
challenges of being less well prepared than most of their peers and underrepresented in
college classrooms.

These challenges of navigation should not be overlooked by proponents of diversity. It is crucial to provide opportunities for empowerment: the academic support that
accelerates learning and the social support that empowers navigation of educational
systems. GMS students had sufficient academic preparation to persist on a par with
the college peers, but their stories reveal they had a sense of overcoming inequality.
In addition, the social network support provided by the GMS leadership workshops
and social organizations in college provided opportunities to learn about self and to
continue building the navigation skills needed to persevere through college and pull
others up in the process.

ENGAGED LEARNING AS ACADEMIC CAPITAL

It is evident from the analysis of survey data from WSA and GMS that students who received the scholarships were more engaged academically and socially than similar students who did not receive the same financial support. These differences are due to the type of students who were selected based on noncognitive criteria and the influences of financial aid awards make academic and social engagement possible. Since engaged learning represents a desirable intermediate outcome of the academic capital formation process, it is important to explore the meaning of the process from the vantage of students.

The interviews provided further evidence of the meanings of the core constructs of academic capital, derived from the theories of human capital (easing concerns about costs), social capital (networking, trust, and information), and reproduction theory (cultural capital and habitual patterns). The analysis further illuminated the role engaged learning plays in academic capital formation, viewed through the uplift lens. Key understandings reached are summarized in Table 6.5.

During the college years, the forms of engaged learning as social processes were similar for WSA and GMS students. Both groups matured through a process of self-navigation coupled with social engagement. There were differences in personal capacity for the two programs at the point of college entry: GMS students were selected for high academic achievement in high school along with noncognitive scores, and WSA students were selected for noncognitive scores alone. This led to differences in the extent of academic struggles during college, but individuals in both groups were able to navigate through these problems. In fact, there was a strong image of pathways to success emerging from the ways students spoke about their college experiences.

The fact that high-achieving students from underrepresented backgrounds seek academic support to accelerate their learning should not be a shock to educators. The inequalities of K-12 education abundantly evident have not been overcome by efforts to raise standards for all students. Rather, even students who were high achievers in high schools that offered advanced courses were faced with challenges to acquire the skills to navigate academically during college. The support of faculty, student affairs personnel and mentors all played important roles in this process of academic empowerment, as students built the college knowledge they needed to navigate through educational barriers.

A strong sense of social and civic responsibility was evident within both groups. Socially, this was clear in their commitments to their families. Civic responsibility was demonstrated in commitments to social groups, with both GMS and WSA students working on issues of diversity and social justice. Within the race-specific focus groups for GMS, many students voiced images of justice and caring situated in an understanding of their racial/ethnic groups. While the group-specific aspects of this commitment merit further exploration, it appears that the commitment to one's own group is a commonality, situated in family and culture.

It was evident from interviews with both WSA and GMS students that active engagement in social and civic groups, including groups of students with similar backgrounds, was central to the empowerment process. While students spoke of social integration with majority students, most also spoke of their own identity in terms of race or social class. Four-year colleges continue to be comprised mostly of students from families with college experience. The majority of students come to college with personal understand-

Table 6.5 Engaged Learning as Academic Capital Formation: Lessons from WSA and GMS Students

Processes	Academic	Civic/Social
Easing Concerns about Costs	Scholarship funding enabled students to engage academically by: • Taking internships to learn rather than working for pay • Working to support families • Borrowing to support families.	Scholarship funding—and time gained from not having to work long hours—enabled students to engage in social and civic activities and build a sense of pay-back that has implications for cross-generation uplift.
Networking	Social networks in college, including advisors and teachers, provide support along with supplemental program support • WSA mentors and staff provide guidance • GMS conferences provide inspiration and vision for academic pathways.	Social organizations, peers, and cultural groups provide inspiration and support along with supplemental program support • WSA students provide mentoring to the next generation of students • GMS students seek more national networking.
Trust	Relationships with faculty, advisors, and peers enable connection with academic programs.	Relationships with peers, advisors, families and community groups build commitment to making a difference.
Information	College and career knowledge build as a consequence of academic engagement.	Civic, social, and family responsibility become stronger personal values based on experience with self navigation.
Cultural Capital	A divide in college knowledge between students and parents emerges; efforts made to transmit knowledge in the family, especially through cross-generation uplift.	Social activism and responsibility emerge and take varied forms as students learn from personal experience in college, community, and family.
Habitual Patterns	Inner strength as a self-navigator enables students to steer a path through college.	Moral consciousness of self in relation to community begins to emerge.

ing of educational pathways. The underrepresented low-income students got to college because they had already acquired some college knowledge and they progressed during college because they had the ability to acquire knowledge. Finding trusted others among peers and college personnel served as a key to unlocking some of the mysteries of advanced college knowledge for these students, the personal knowledge needed to navigate college as a social and academic system.

Scholarship funding appears to have enabled academic capital to build for many of the GMS and WSA students during college. Because of the necessity to work to pay an excessive share of college costs, many low-income students cannot afford the time to engage in academic activities outside the classroom like study groups. Yet engaged learning is integral to academic capital formation. Given the opportunity—the chance to attend a high-quality college and the aid to pay for it—low-income, high-achieving students have higher odds of engaging in the academic culture of their colleges as active learners and civic activists.

7

COLLEGE SUCCESS AND COMMITMENT TO UPLIFT

The goal of improving degree attainment in the United States is closely linked to the nation's economic goals; for example, the aim of improving the science, technology, engineering, and math (STEM) educated workforce is widely advocated (e.g., Commission on the Skills of the American Workforce, 2007; Conklin & Curran, 2005). The common argument is that the workforce of the future will require a higher percentage of technically educated college graduates than is now the case. In addition, the Bill and Melinda Gates Foundation has dedicated substantial resources to doubling the percentage of low-income students who graduate from college in the next 3 decades (Hoffman, Vargas, Venezia, & Miller, 2007). In this context, it is important to learn more about the factors that promote degree attainment.

The reasoning behind improvement in educational attainment is not solely economic. After decades of improving social equality in college enrollment, which culminated in near equality among racial groups in the middle 1970s, the United States has seen inequalities in educational opportunity reemerge in the decades since 1980. Social class differences have become more accentuated and the patterns of class reproduction more entrenched. It is crucial we reverse this pattern by extending opportunities to attain college degrees and enter high-paying professions to the children of low-income families. To make this transformation, it is necessary to identify the patterns of cross-generation uplift that can be reinforced and enhanced through social interventions, educational reforms, and student aid. The nation is at greater risk of a continuing decline in equality than it was when *A Nation at Risk* (U.S. Department of Education, 1983) was published over 25 years ago.

REFRAMING COLLEGE SUCCESS

The theory of persistence widely used in research in higher education offers an alternative to viewing degree attainment as a function of high school preparation. This body of theory and research treats attainment from the lens of social integration theory, focusing on both academic and social integration as social processes of engagement (Braxton,

2000; Tinto, 1975, 2000). In the prior chapter, we reframed the idea of social processes in educational attainment to provide a refined view of access to and attainment of higher education as an uplift process involving academic capital formation. This reframed view reinforces the role of engaged learning, but situates the process within the financial constraints of being poor in America. This chapter extends the frame of uplift to consider college success both as a process of degree attainment and of the social process that supports cross-generation uplift.

Of course, the measurable aspects of college success are persistence and degree attainment. We examine evidence related to persistence and degree attainment by students in the three programs, Washington State Achievers (WSA), Gates Millennium Scholars (GMS), and Twenty-first Century Scholars (TFCS). A minimum *equity standard* for judging the academic success of these comprehensive programs should be: If interventions raise the odds that low-income students gain entry to college, and these students have at least the same chance for attaining a degree as other students who make it to college without the financial support, then the interventions have improved degree attainment. While intuitively it seems desirable that comprehensive programs improve the chances that students will attain degrees compared to other students with similar characteristics, achieving this higher standard would likely result from additional funding for support services during college. Two of the early interventions studied—TFCS and WSA—provided precollege support and raised the odds of enrolling in 4-year colleges (as discussed in chapters 3 and 4). WSA and GMS provided supplemental aid along with support services during college and could be expected to raise attainment rates (chapters 5 and 6). However, as the evidence in this chapter reveals, it is difficult to raise attainment rates above those that would be predicted based on academic preparation before college. The three sections that follow consider evidence of degree attainment for awardees and comparable students in TFCS, WSA, and GMS.

In addition to enhancing the opportunity to attain degrees, comprehensive interventions that provide supplemental and support services during college (i.e., WSA and GMS) can increase commitment to uplift. An aim of this chapter is to build an understanding of this social aspect of college success. We examine whether WSA and GMS open pathways to new career opportunities and enable a new generation of students to support uplift in their communities. Our argument is that academic success is not limited to degree attainment and economic productivity through professional employment, but should also emphasize a commitment to cross-generational uplift, to enable subsequent generations to have the opportunity to achieve academic and career success. This image is a fundamental reversal of the narrow image of private interest and economic development that has been the focus in the literature on educational investments (Pasque, 2007).

The six components of academic capital formation as a social process are examined in this chapter, with an explicit focus on the academic and civic aspects of capital formation (Table 7.1). Specifically, the propositions examined relate to:

1. *Easing concerns about costs*: By reducing the necessity of working and borrowing to pay for college, the WSA, GMS, and TFCS programs should increase aspirations to attain degrees and, because students will have no or little debt, make it easier to build life structures after college (e.g., marry, purchase homes and cars, and so forth).

Table 7.1 College Success: Academic and Social/Civic Capabilities as Students make Transitions after College

Concepts	Academic	Social/Civic
Concerns about Costs	Concerns about college debt can influence decisions about careers and graduate education.	Financial concerns can constrain choices about marriage, housing, and transportation.
Networking	Students learn about education and career options through networks	Students consider social good as part of personal, educational, and career choices.
Trust	Mentors can enable new network s to facilitate transition from local perspectives (of home and college).	Ability to build trusting relationships supporting social transformation
Information	Ability to communicate about academic experiences within educational and career networks.	Ability to communicate about social concerns within local and/or national networks.
Cultural Capital	Acquire college knowledge to support siblings and community.	Active support networks of care, as "giving back".
Habitual Patterns	Develop capacity for self steering, addressing professional challenges using self understanding.	Build life structures to support communities and enable cross-generation uplift.

2. *Social networking*: Students learn about educational and career opportunities through academic networks formed in college and consider social uplift as a viable goal as a result of social and civic engagement during college.

3. *Trust*: Mentors enable students to make judgments of trustworthiness of academic information, while peers and community members enable students to develop a personal commitment to uplift.

4. *Information*: Students communicate about academic experiences and career pathways within networks; they also develop skills associated with communicating about social concerns and acting upon them.

5. *Cultural capital*: Students develop college knowledge that is shared with their families, extending the family narrative to include college; they begin to engage in networks of care that promote giving back.

6. *Habitual patterns*: Through their college experiences, students build their capacity for self-navigating educational and career systems, and they build commitments to cross-generation uplift that become part of a new life pattern.

TWENTY-FIRST CENTURY SCHOLARS

The analysis of TFCS in this chapter is limited to assessing whether students attain college degrees or persist as well as other students in similar family and financial circumstances who make it to college as an equity standard. From initial studies, it was evident that receipt of aid improved the odds students would enroll in college (St. John, Musoba, Simmons, & Chung, 2002).

The 1999 cohort combines two databases: a survey of eighth grade students in Indiana high schools who would graduate in 1999 if they made normal progress; and the Indiana Commission for Higher Education (ICHE) student information system (SIS) data on students enrolled in public colleges[1] (these data do not include information on students who enrolled in private colleges in the state or in out-of-state colleges). The problem with

Table 7.2   Indicators for Twenty-first Century Scholars in the1999 Cohort Tracking

Tracking Numbers of Scholars	Number	Source
1999 Scholars Cohort (Took Pledge and Enrolled by Fall 1999)	2,590	From: SSACI, Table 1, 2002 report, p. 8
Responded to Survey	2,097	From: Table 3.1 2002 Report, p. 33
% Enrolled in public colleges in IN	64%	From: Table 8, 2002 Report, p.17
Number enrolled in public colleges IN	1342	From: 64% of survey respondents
Number with reported aid (included in 2004 report)	855	From: 2004 Report, also as published in *Readings on Equal Education*
Number of Scholars used in earlier draft of 2004 report.	5,487	From: SIS Scholars Indicators as reported[1]
Number of Scholars who completed survey and enrolled in public colleges	1,300	From 1999 tracking files
Number of Scholars in persistence analyses (Subsection 5.2)	1,224	From: Analyses of survey responses plus tracking data
Number of Scholars with Sufficient information for Propensity Score Matching (PSM)	1,255	From: Analysis of survey responses plus tracking data

Note: 1. This Twenty-first Century Scholar Identifier (from the SIS format) stated: "If the student is known to be a Twenty-First Century Scholar, enter a "1" in this field, otherwise enter a zero. This is in order to consistently identify students from the program even in the event that they do not receive an award amount under the program in the given year."

Sources: 1. St. John, E. P., Musoba, G. D., Simmons, A. B., & Chung, C. G. (2002). *Meeting the Access Challenge: Indiana's Twenty-first Century Scholars Program.* New Agenda Series, vol. 4, no. 4. Indianapolis: Lumina Foundation for Education.
2. St. John, Fisher, Lee, Daun-Barnett, & Williams, 2008.

finding the appropriate number of students is complicated by different indicators which have been used for being a Twenty-first Century Scholar.[2] Table 7.2 illustrates the tracking of Scholars across databases used for the 1999 cohort.

According to the numbers reported by the State Student Assistance Commission of Indiana for the 2002 report (St. John, Musoba, Simmons, & Chung, 2002), there were 2,590 students in middle school who became Twenty-first Century Scholars. In the 2005 report (St. John, Gross, & Chung, 2005), a total of 1,342 TFCS students enrolled in public colleges. Using the designation for Scholars from the 2002 report as a base group, these updated analyses found 1,224 students with the SIS information needed to complete the persistence analyses; these students were used in our analyses. In the analyses using propensity score matching, we found one additional case (1,225).

As documented in Table 7.3, the percentage of Scholars attaining 4-year and 2-year degrees was lower than that of the non-Scholars. Of the students who started in 4-year colleges, 30.6% of Scholars received 4-year degrees compared to 48.0% of non-Scholars. In addition, some students who started in 4-year colleges attained 2-year degrees as their highest degree.[3] Of the students who started in 4-year colleges, 5.9% of Scholars received 2-year degrees as their highest degree compared to 5.2% of the non-Scholars. More than half of the Scholars starting in 4-year colleges departed without degrees (51.7%), and more than two-thirds of the Scholars starting in 2-year colleges had dropped out with no degree by the sixth year after college entry (69.5%). In contrast, slightly over one-third of non-Scholars had dropped out of 4-year colleges (36.7%) and nearly two-thirds had departed from 2-year colleges (61.7%).

Table 7.3 1999 Cohort Degree Attainment: Based on Original Enrollment

Original Enrollment	n	Attainment				
		Four-Year Degree	Two-Year Degree	Persister, No Degree	Non-Persister, No Degree	Total
Four-Year						
Scholar	1008	30.56%	5.85%	11.90%	51.69%	100.00%
Non-Scholar	20825	47.96%	5.18%	10.19%	36.67%	100.00%
Two-Year						
Scholar	292	3.77%	11.99%	14.73%	69.52%	100.00%
Non-Scholar	3727	4.11%	23.53%	10.68%	61.69%	100.00%
Total	**25852**					

Source: St. John, Fisher, Lee, Daun-Barnett, & Williams (2008), p. 59.

When we compare the percentage of Scholars and non-Scholars in the original survey population who had attained degrees or some college (Table 7.4), we find that substantially more Scholars than non-Scholars attained at least some college. A slightly higher percentage of non-Scholars than Scholars had attained 4-year degrees in the public system (16.9% of non-Scholars compared to 15.4% of Scholars); however, a slightly higher percentage of Scholars than non-Scholars had attained 2-year degrees (4.7% for Scholars compared to 4.5% for non-Scholars). There are clearly some gains in attainment among the population attributable to the Scholars Program. Yet there is also reason to argue for further improvement in degree attainment.

To provide a statistical test of the influence of background on degree attainment

Table 7.4 1999 Cohort: Attainment Based on Enrollment Decisions for Twenty-first Century Scholars in Study Sample using Percentages from 2002 Lumina Report

Part A. Attainment by Institution Level

Original Enrollment	Four-Year Degree	Two-Year Degree	Persister, No Degree	Some College, No Degree
Four Year				
Scholar	14.78%	2.83%	5.76%	25.00%
Non-Scholar	16.64%	1.80%	3.54%	5.76%
Two-Year				
Scholar	0.59%	1.88%	2.31%	10.92%
Non-Scholar	0.29%	1.67%	0.76%	4.39%
Total				

Part B. Total Attainment

Original Enrollment	Four-Year Degree	Two-Year Degree	Persister, No Degree	Some College, No Degree
Scholar	15.37%	4.71%	8.07%	35.92%
Non-Scholar	16.93%	3.47%	4.30%	10.15%
Total				

Source: St. John, Fisher, Lee, Daun-Barnett, & Williams, 2008, p. 60; St. John, Musoba, Simmons, & Chung, 2008.

among low-income, Pell-eligible students, we conducted a propensity match for Scholars and non-Scholars from among Pell recipients in the longitudinal file for the 1999 Cohort (appendix 4). The analysis verifies there was not a statistically significant difference in degree attainment once students had enrolled in college; there was no advantage for Scholars compared to other low-income students once they arrived at college. This is not a particularly surprising finding given that there were no additional support services available to Scholars in public colleges once they enrolled. In sum, the Twenty-first Century Scholars Program improved the odds of enrollment by students who signed up for the program; Scholars who enrolled had similar odds of completing their degrees or continuing their enrollment as comparable students.

The large number of low-income students in the 1999 cohort who found their way to college without support of the Scholars Program is far in excess of the number who signed up for the program and matriculated, so the TCFS program did not reach most prospective students. Further, degree completion rates were similar for the two groups. There is evidence that a large percentage of Scholars made it into college but did not complete degrees. We conclude better academic support during college is needed (see also Lumina, 2008; St. John & Musoba, 2010).

WASHINGTON STATE ACHIEVERS

Since selection of WSA awardees was not based on academic achievement, students were typical of the majority of low- and middle-income students who attend high-poverty high schools. The analyses in this section will examine both persistence outcomes and the six social processes related to academic success.

Equity Standard

The College Success Foundation tracks college completion rates for Achievers. Loraine Solaegui (2008), a program administrator at the foundation, reported the 4-year retention/graduation rate for Cohort 1 was 53%, and the rate for Cohort 2 was 58%. The goal was that by the 10th cohort of Achievers the target of 67% earning bachelor's degrees would be achieved. It is now argued that, with current supports provided by the Foundation, a 75% rate is possible. The success rate for the first cohort of WSA is modestly higher than the rate for the Twenty-first Century Scholars Program 1999 cohort (if we combine all persistence categories for TFCS). The rate for the second year appears to have improved for WSA, when students received their aid award early enough to have an impact on preparation.

The persistence rates for WSA include private colleges, which usually have higher persistence rates than public colleges. Also, the College Success Foundation followed students who enrolled in public and private colleges both within and out of state; only data on in-state public college students was available for the Twenty-first Century Scholars.

The College Success Foundation does not track students who do not receive awards, but the Gates Foundation contracted with the National Opinion Research Center (NORC) for surveys of all students who applied for the WSA program, asking questions about social networking, a set of indicators that provides information about the social aspects of academic capital formation. Effect size analyses[4] of key social indicators reveals Achievers report a significantly higher rating (on a Likert scale) on the variables asking if one or more faculty were interested in their work or whether they felt part of

Table 7.5 Effect Size of the Differences between WSA Recipients and Non-Recipients on Support Networks

Scale	Item	All Sample	WSA Recipients	Non-Recipients	Effect Size	Sig.
Supportive Network	Relying on racial/cultural groups as main support group on campus	1.88	1.88	1.88	0.00	
	At least one faculty member has taken an interest in development	2.80	2.91	2.63	0.31	***
	Feeling like being part of the campus community	2.73	2.80	2.65	0.18	*
	Turning to one or more faculty members for support and encouragement	2.67	2.58	2.80	-0.24	**
	Turning to a resident advisor for support and encouragement	3.15	3.12	3.18	-0.06	
	Turning to other students for support and encouragement	2.08	1.99	2.19	-0.19	*
N		568	334	234		

the campus community (Table 7.5), which indicates greater skills at social networking. In addition, Achievers reported lower rates of turning to others for support regardless of group referenced (faculty, advisors, other students), indicating higher self-reliance. Both sets of findings could be related to the use of noncognitive variables in the selection process that were related to strong personal habits supporting success. It is also possible that those who enroll in 4-year colleges are more self-reliant overall. However, having mentors as part of the WSA program may also be a major factor promoting engagement and success (Hu, 2009).

Concerns about Cost

Concerns about costs, navigating a course in life, and making life transitions are central to decisions in low-income families. Many students described working long hours so they could pay costs beyond grants and avoid debt. Many researchers have considered the ways costs influence college choice and degree attainment (Chen, 2008; Heller, 1997; Hossler, Ziskin, Kim, Cedric, & Gross, 2009; Leslie & Brinkman, 1988; Manski & Wise, 1983), but the social aspects of academic and social outcomes related to academic success have not been previously examined. In the analysis of WSA students' interviews below, we consider how easing concerns about costs relates to the formation of academic and social capital.

Academic Low-income families are more likely to make decisions in context, acknowledging the constraints. Many students from low- and lower-middle income families have higher odds of choosing a college close to home than do upper-middle-income students (Paulsen & St. John, 2002). The prior chapters examined how easing concerns about costs enabled low-income students to attend 4-year colleges and reduce debt.

For example, Monica explained that her scholarship minus tuition "translates to about $1,500 a quarter that I personally get in my pocket. My rent...bill is probably about $600 [a month]." Even after the WSA award, Monica had to work to pay rent. She said she worked "till eleven or twelve and then go to class afterwards. And then I'll come home from class and then I'll go to sleep because I am so tired. I did that for a long time." While not all students had this strong an attitude toward debt avoidance, many did. For these students, the deep personal concerns about costs also influenced cautious attitudes about future possibilities. These interview comments reveal how cultural preferences about work and debt impact educational choices.

Social Capital.   The roles situated preferences and constraints play in educational and career choices are complex and deeply intertwined with religious and social values. For some, the formation of social capital—the ability to have stability in life consistent with their values—took preference over the academic aspects of choice. The ability to make these choices can be enabled by easing concerns about costs, just as academic and career success are outcomes of educational attainment.

Leslie's case exemplifies some of the ways that locally situated conditions and personal values constrain and inform life choices. She had chosen a small, out-of-state, religious-affiliated college for transfer. Social interaction with peers had been challenging for her at the larger public university, and she found the new college compatible with her values. She had also married a man who shared her values, and he had helped her build a new life structure, which became more important to her than pursuit of her academic interests. She said, "Actually, last semester I was kind of thinking, I thought it would be fun... to go on and look into occupational therapy. But with the position that I am [in] right now, my husband is a farmer. We are farmers in Idaho. There is no occupation therapy school around here." Her deep, personal religious convictions enabled her to venture to a new college out of state, but the local bonding became a constraint on her choices. Readers should not overlook the difficult personal barriers Leslie overcame, including a broken home and other serious family problems. It is a sign of inner strength that she valued social stability. By centering herself in her faith tradition, Leslie had found the inner strength to make educational choices and found a relationship and life goals that enabled her to envision a future consonant with her own values.

Networking

Social networks are considered integral to social capital formation and thought to have an influence on academic and career opportunity (Coleman, 1988), a proposition supported by the analyses of educational choices by WSA students in prior chapters. Below, we explore how networking is intertwined with the academic and social aspects of capital formation in the transition after college.

Academic.   Engaged learning was enabled by the scholarships and support services provided through WSA (chapter 6). WSA students had more opportunities to engage academically because of opportunities to enroll in 4-year colleges and a reduced work-loan burden.

The opportunity to have work experiences related to a student's personal interests during college spurred Leslie's professional and academic interests: "I worked with disabled kids.... And we just kind of helped them learn new things, work on their skills, work on phone skills. We just did therapy and this is what I would want to go into." Leslie went on to explain that while she might not be able to go on in therapy, her real interest, she could find career options that involved working with children, if she needed to work. Although Leslie gave preference to social goals over academic and career aspirations, the work-learn opportunities during college enabled her to envision herself in the world of work. Martha Nussbaum (1999) has found that education to a level high enough to support a family is a necessary human capability, a threshold Leslie had realized. If she were to encounter serious challenges, like the loss of her husband, she would have the educational foundation to support her children, a capability her mother did not have.

Oscar had delayed moving to campus and provided financial support for his family even after he made the move. Becoming integrated academically had been his goal when he moved on campus, but he found some of the aspects of social life on campus to be difficult. Yet he continued to emphasize social networking as a means of developing academically:

> I tried to get out more in 5 years. So…I applied to internship, and I got internship before, so I worked in the industry for the summer. I've done summer research, and done research on a regular basis and I kind of exposed myself in the particular area and at the same time I've been a TA and I actually talk to a lot of [people]….[I've] done a lot of volunteer work just to kind of recruit people so that's nice.

These cases illustrate some of the ways academic engagement in learning opportunities during college enabled students to discover and realize life aims, whether social or academic values took preference.

Social. Another aspect of networking during college involves building capital for social engagement. For some of the students, this involved maintaining connections with their communities. Two students' stories illustrate how social activism became central to life goals after college.

Sky Warrior had to overcome legal problems before college. His engagement in multicultural groups became an inspiration and a locus of personal learning, as discussed in the prior chapter. In his interview he reflected on his education:

> Well, the education has brought like, completely new ideas. And had really changed a lot about my personality and the things that I want to do; obviously my goals for the future. It's also provided me with tools, just by having the knowledge, the power, and…also the connections with people that I've met, the other people…I got a bunch of friends to vote to pass a law to stop smoking in public places…. So I felt really, really good about that. So definitely just by meeting people and by getting educated I am learning the avenues and how to combat the obstacles.

John's experience illustrates how support by mentors can empower students to engage in social action:

> I was talking to my mentor, a teacher, and he said there's a guy who substitute teaches at Thomas Jefferson, who's a state…legislator. I think that's the coolest job in the world. I'd love to do something like that. But, ideal job, my ideal job

would probably [be] to be a city council person, the mayor, and then be a teacher on the side too.

The experiences of John and Sky Warrior illustrate how engaged learning as a social process led to a different way of thinking. Social engagement with mentors and peers provides vital learning opportunities that allow students to envision future pathways that include a commitment to social justice and civic good.

Trust

In their transitions from high school to college, many of the WSA students benefited from advice from teachers and other advisors who encouraged them to apply for the scholarship program and even recommended colleges (chapters 5 and 6). In college, the process of finding trustworthy information about majors and careers proved more complex. Most of the students processed information they received from advisors to build an inner understanding of which information and people proved to be trustworthy.

Academic.   Building trust of professors and mentors was central to choosing a pathway through college that made sense personally, given the students' self-understandings and personal goals. For example, Monica indicated, "It took a long time to figure that out and get the prelaw advising I wanted. And so I got kind of a late start when it came to majoring in political science and stuff like that...I wish sometimes I had been more focused." She communicates both the inner and outer aspects of discovering trustworthy information on educational and career choices. For Monica, the inner aspect was related to the long-term aim to be a lawyer, the outer to the discovery of political science as the major that worked for her.

Reflecting on the advice one might give others based on college experiences, Sky Warrior commented:

> Everybody's got a different definition of success. For some people it is money, for some people it's fame. I mean, it depends on the person. So figure that out, figure out what your strengths and weaknesses are. I mean, if there's something you really like to do, that's what you should do as, like, a career, because a career is basically what you are going to do the rest of your life. So, if you can find something you really enjoy doing, you're going to be a much happier person.

Sky Warrior was telling aspiring students that the journey to academic success involves finding educational and career pathways that correspond to values and interests uncovered through an inner understanding of self.

Social.   The WSA students used their peers and work experiences to create an understanding of their social aims in relation to their college experiences. Students found social support networks to meet social needs and used their emerging concerns about social contributions to make career choices, providing two contrasting vantages of trustworthiness of expectations.

Students who experience personal traumas while growing up can gain new images of social relations during college. For example, Missy explained how her friends helped her understand the role of support:

I would have liked to have my family supporting me. I would have liked to have had a home to go to for holidays. But because I didn't, I met a lot of wonderful people who supported me more that I could have ever imagined. It worked out, I have a family, but they're not just biological.

Having grown up in foster homes, Missy found an experience of family through building trusting relationships with friends.

Students who develop strong social values during college can internalize them as they ponder their career pathways. Liliya explained, "Well, pharmacy is all about helping people and that's why I am in pharmacy." She added, "I want to see the difference I am making. And what to give good coworkers, so that [I] can be, like, friends with them." Then she summarized "And I am now biased toward hospital pharmacy because you can actually, like, see patients recover." Liliya's maturation from a youngster in a bad accident with her family, receiving care from an inspirational team of professionals, to a committed future health professional was evident.

Information

Information about educational, career, and life pathway options and strategies has been interlaced in the stories of both academic and social aspirations. However, there was an authentic awareness in the interviews about barriers that lay ahead with respect to both career and personal pathways. Persevering in spite of the odds was a strong characteristic of many of these students. Consider these illustrative examples:

- *Academic/Career*: Monica learned about educational pathways to a legal career more slowly than she would have liked, but she also exercised caution when pondering the future: "some of my older friends have graduated, they don't have jobs in their fields and they work, you know, in an Office Depot or something, but they are not giving up. They understand that just, like, a glitch they have to keep going until they can find what they like to do, you know."
- *Social/Civic*: In a focus group, a young Latina commented, "I think that for us, you know, that our women…we want to get our master's and we want to get our bachelor's. We want to prove to other people that we can do it, you know. If they have lower expectations of, you know, your gender or lower expectations of your ethnicity, then that proves to them that more Hispanics in my case, they are attending college and they are getting a degree. So it proves to people that we can do it, you know."

In both the academic and social domains of action, most of the students demonstrated an ability to filter through information that could be discouraging and find the inner strength to pursue their goals in spite of the barriers they encountered.

Cultural Capital

In high school, many WSA students did not have the college knowledge to make informed choices about college and, in fact, they continued to reappraise their college choices as they gained more practical knowledge during college. However, unlike their attitudes toward the future when they graduated from high school, when they graduated from college most students had a strong sense of direction

Academic.   Consistently across the case studies these young scholars demonstrated an understanding of their educational and career trajectories. They knew where they were headed and the options open to them in the future. Consider these examples:

- **Oscar:** "Right now, my immediate goal is trying to get into grad school, get into a doctoral program…. But, you know, for me it's just hard, again just because there are, like, you know, there's the GRE and other things, so not so, not sure if I will get in or not, just like back in high school, so we'll see…. Unlike high school…I have options I can choose from."
- John's career interests were locally situated: "I would love to teach in Tacoma. I would love to teach in my high school. But other than that, I just would like to stay [here]." Continuing his education was also critical: "I love history. I could really see myself going on in that…I could see myself going on in education degree-wise and staying in high school education, but I think I will get my master's in history no matter what…. Now whether I get a PhD in history or a PhD in something else, that's the decision to be made."

Bourdieu (1990) argued that cultural capital was produced through a relationship between the family and the educational system. Using this lens of reproduction to view educational attainment, it is easy to see why it is difficult for first-generation students to transcend the family's collective knowledge gained from interactions in the educational systems without an intervention capable of transforming the individual's understanding of the pathways ahead. This extends the concept of college knowledge to include personal understanding of the linkage between academic majors and alternative career pathways. In their comments, Oscar and John illustrate an understanding of pathways ahead that transcend the probable trajectories evident from their commentary on their lives before receiving the scholarships.

Giving Back.   It seems especially important in the United States to rebuild a social ethos of giving back—through social support and taxes—rather than merely getting all one can for oneself. Many of the WSA students expressed a sense of commitment to the social good.

Missy was acutely aware that she gained from the support—financial and social—given to her by others:

> Somebody took a chance on me, invested in me, some pretty risky investment with long-term gains. There's not short-term getting return here. And that means somebody believed in me even though I didn't consider myself worthy…. And that's kind of inspiring. It's easier to believe in yourself when you know somebody else believes in you.

This sense that others believed in her not only enabled Missy to overcome great odds, it also gave her an inner sense of her own obligations: "It's like you get a check but you know somewhere there's all these faces who contributed to it, and that kind of, never really get a chance to thank them, other than just being a good part of society."

However, in spite of their hopes, students still had to deal with inner despair about the world around them. Seth observed, "I'm not very happy with the politics of this nation. I don't want to get into a big thing, but for the most part, just because every-thing in this nation…doesn't work. I really want to go live in Sweden. I like the social aspect of everything up there. They really take care of their people." At other points in his interview, however, Seth also talked of his commitment to social action in the United States.

Habitual Patterns

The selection of WSA Achievers was based on noncognitive variables related to their ability to navigate the system and to deal with prejudice and racism. This approach to selection recognizes the inner strengths of individuals that enable them not only to per-severe through hardships, but also to build strength of personal character to discover new vistas of knowledge. These inner strengths have been evident throughout, and it is important to consider some examples of habits that reinforce this inner strength.

Academic. Some of the WSA students developed commitments to learning that extended beyond the boundaries of college per se.

- Seth reflected, "Most of my friends [from high school] aren't going to college…. They're just kind of working and getting married and all of that stuff right now. I don't need to have those things in my life. I'm pretty much, out of most of my bud-dies in college, I'm the only one who went on to get my master's."
- John expressed a similar sentiment as a reflected on his own "self-description" in the concluding portion of this interview: "I guess my identity is the constant student…. And more now that I've gotten out of college and got an education and thought about education and of my identity as a teacher. But just to be, always be the student. I think that in any situation where I go, I try to learn everything. From every person I meet, from every conversation I have, from every book I read, from every situation I enter, I'm always trying to learn."

Seth and John illustrate an inner commitment to learning that transcends formal education. It is an inner sense that may have been enhanced during the college years, but it also must have resided within them long before college and will probably continue for many years into the future. Similarly, our concept of academic capital includes an inner sense of navigating education and career as well as a commitment to within-generation pullup and cross-generation uplift.

Social. The life stories of the WSA Scholars convey the development of an understanding of the social aspects of their life journeys.

Leslie's decision to delay advanced education was related to self-image which was situated in her family plans: "I hope that my husband and I are able to build a house by then. That he is graduated from the school and able to go on his own [as a farmer]." When asked to describe herself she commented, "Happy, content, I guess, with life… probably successful. I've had goals in my life and even though I have kind of strayed from the path of my goals, I have been able to get back on and to achieve the goals I've had." This image of self is congruent with and even helps explain some of the choices she made previously, from choosing a new college that was more comfortable socially to integrating socially and marrying a husband with similar values.

In contrast, Liliya explained, "I actually didn't like moving place to place [when younger]. But now, I kind of like [it].... So I probably won't be in Pullman, or in Western Washington where my family lives. I want to be something different, to have, like, a new experience and to meet new people." Liliya has also traveled through personal hardship to a new discovery of self. She acquired an ability to see herself in new circumstances, learning from and with new people that she met along the way.

Key Features of WSA

Compared to the Twenty-first Century Scholars Program, Achievers in WSA appear to excel more in college. They persisted and graduated at higher rates, although the statistical significance of difference in persistence has not been confirmed. Unlike TFCS, WSA provides support services through college, including mentors at their campuses and support services by the College Success Foundation. This is at least prima facie evidence that combining student aid with social support has some advantages over student aid when persistence and degree completion are considered.

The selection process and support services of the WSA program distinguished it from the Twenty-first Century Scholars Program, the other comprehensive reform that included an emphasis on precollege services. TFCS provided support that fostered more substantial family engagement enabling more students to enroll and create a new family narrative about college. However, the support mechanisms dropped off after high school. Twenty-first Century Scholars, like other low-income students, were left to navigate their own ways through college. The system of support provided by WSA appears to enhance opportunity beyond that which would be otherwise possible.

GATES MILLENNIUM SCHOLARS

The first three cohorts of GMS scholars represent a generation of low-income students who have become engaged learners and proceeded through college and into graduate school. The statistical comparison of student engagement by GMS recipients and nonrecipients revealed that Scholars were more engaged academically and in civic activities during college; the students attributed this increased opportunity to engage to the GMS award. With this summative background, it is interesting to compare GMS recipients and nonrecipients on long-term indicators of academic success.

The Equity Standard

The college completion rates were higher for GMS recipients, although both recipients and nonrecipients persisted at very high rates (unweighted); 98.8% for GMS recipients compared to 97.3% for nonrecipients (Table 7.6). The nonrecipients had higher test scores and a higher percentage of their fathers had college degrees, variables positively associated with persistence. In the regression model that controls for background and preparation, there is a positive association between GMS and persistence (St. John, 2008; St. John & Chung, 2004b). However, given the small margin of difference, it is appropriate to conclude that most students who qualify academically for GMS persist through college whether or not they get the award. When differences in graduation rates were examined for students in Cohorts II and III using regression discontinuity, DesJardins and McCall (2008) found there was no relationship between GMS award and undergraduate comple-

Table 7.6 Descriptive Statistics for Variables in Persistence of 2000 Freshmen Follow-Up Sample with Variables Imported from Baseline Sample

Variable	Value	All (% or Mean)	Gates Recipients (% or Mean)	Non Gates Recipients (% or Mean)
Persistence	Yes	97.9	98.8	97.3
	No	2.1	1.2	2.7
Gates Scholarship	Gates Recipient	38.0		
	Non Gates Recipient	62.0		
Gender	Male	32.8	32.2	33.1
	Female	67.2	67.8	66.9
Ethnicity	African Americans	33.5	29.8	35.8
	American Indians	5.5	5.1	5.8
	Hispanic Americans	25.8	33.1	21.4
	Asian/Pacific Islanders	35.2	32.0	37.0
Father's Education Attainment	Bachelor or Higher	36.6	21.7	45.7
	Other	63.4	78.3	54.3
SAT-ACT Crosswalk Score Group	Lowest quartile	27.2	34.6	22.6
	Highest quartile	23.9	17.3	27.9
	Middle quartiles	48.9	48.1	49.5
Reason select school low expenses	Very important	44.9	43.9	45.5
	Other	55.1	56.1	54.5
Reason select school strong reputation	Very important	78.9	80.2	78.2
	Other	21.1	19.8	21.8
Parents contributing college finances	Yes	40.9	26.3	49.9
	No	59.1	73.7	50.1
Loan Burden	Annual Loan/1,000	2.406	1,286	3.094
N		1,226	466	760

Note: Percentages are unweighted.

tion rates. However, they did find some variables were positively related to persistence (lower debt, working fewer hours, and lower parental contribution), identical to findings from prior logistic regressions (e.g., St. John & Chung, 2004a, 2004b). They also found a positive causal impact on graduate enrollment, an important new finding. This confirms a modest quantifiable impact of GMS on long-term outcomes although a causal link to undergraduate completion does not hold up with available evidence to date.

The National Opinion Research Center (NORC) has imputed weighted persistence rates for the first two GMS cohorts based on the survey results.[5] The 6-year bachelor's degree completion rates (Cohort I) are 88.3% for Scholars and 85.2% for nonrecipients; the 5-year rates (Cohort II) are 67.2% for Scholars and 59.8% for nonrecipients. These data show that Scholars were significantly more likely to complete college than nonrecipients, especially Cohort II (.05 t-test).

The majority of both recipients and nonrecipients worked in jobs related to their majors; however, this was somewhat more likely among recipients (Table 7.7). In a supplemental regression, there was a positive association between GMS and students taking jobs congruent with majors. With the substantial differences between GMS recipients and nonrecipients in engaged learning (chapter 6), both academic and social/civic, and the modest differences in educational outcomes, it important to consider the academic

Table 7.7 Descriptive Statistics for Variables in Debt Load, Employment, and Congruence of 2000 Freshmen Follow-Up Sample with Variables Imported from Baseline Sample

Variable	Value	All (% or Mean)	Gates Recipients (% or Mean)	Non Gates Recipients (% or Mean)
Loan Burden	Annual Loan/1,000	2,384	1,283	3,066
Work for Pay	Yes	61.2	57.9	63.4
	No	38.8	42.1	36.6
Congruence between Work and Major Fields	Yes	52.0	52.3	51.2
	No	48.0	47.7	48.8
Gates Scholarship	Gates Recipient	38.0		
	Non Gates Recipient	62.0		
Gender	Male	32.6	30.4	32.9
	Female	67.4	69.6	67.1
Ethnicity	African Americans	33.3	28.9	35.8
	American Indians	5.6	3.7	5.9
	Hispanic Americans	25.7	33.1	20.8
	Asian/Pacific Islanders	45.4	34.3	37.5
N		1,060	598	462

Note: Percentages are unweighted.

capital formation process among GMS scholars, including the ways they view their futures in higher education and beyond.

Easing Concerns about Costs

GMS provides subsidies through graduate school, but only in a restricted set of fields: education, library science, computer science, math, public health, and engineering. A substantial number of GMS students go on to graduate school, and some of the students funded in 2000 were already in graduate school when selected. There was a modest positive association between GMS and choosing majors in education (St. John & Chung, 2004b), which may be a result of the program. It is important to consider how the promise of aid influences decisions about graduate education, especially the field of study, but it is also important to recognize the social forces that influence educational and career decisions.

Academic Choices. The GMS program can influence students to consider going on in a subsidized field. Consider these comments by students in an Asian American focus group:

- "Like I've seen some of the funding for the graduate schools and I actually don't personally know if I am going to go to graduate school but there isn't any funding for like literary arts or the fine arts or any of those things."
- "For me, like I was always a science person so like Gates really worked out for me. And I hope to pursue either public health or like grad school for neuroscience."

As will be illustrated in the commentary below, some students are persuaded to go on to graduate school because costs are eased. Most GMS students followed their interests and sorted among fields related to those interests; however, GMS sometimes influenced decisions at the margins when students were choosing among possible fields of study or whether to go on to graduate school.

GMS eased concerns about costs during graduate school, enabling students to choose courses and jobs based on interest. For example, in a mixed race and gender group, a graduate student observed, "I do have a half-time assistantship, but that's also because of the experience that you get with an assistantship that I choose to do that." In fact, the program has encouraged students to take graduate assistantships out of recognition of the importance of collaboration between students and faculty in graduate school as critical to early career formation.

Social Forces.   As noted in the comparative statistics (Table 7.7), GMS students were less likely to take funding from their families than nonrecipients. GMS students are committed to supporting their families and carrying out their responsibilities as family members while in college. These patterns were most frequently evident among Hispanics, but similar comments were made in most focus groups. Two major causes for student contributions to families are parents with financial needs and siblings in college.

The comments below, made in response to a question about whether students provided financial support for their families, illustrate the types of reasoning evident.

> My mom, she tries to get into the business of flipping houses, real estate. For 2 years we were struggling, because she couldn't flip our house as quickly as she thought she could, so I had to send money to her a lot, so I always helped her out…. With all my siblings….none of them have completed college yet. So it is a real struggle for them. So I send money out to them all the time.

Some students' commitments to their families influenced their future goals. For example, a Michigan State student:

> I guess like one of my biggest fears is that, you know, my older sister just graduated 2 weeks ago and she has $150,000 in loans from undergraduate and so she needs to start paying that off. And my little sister will be starting college when I graduate with my BA. So I guess at this point like pressure to get a job immediately, you know, when I get out of, get my undergraduate degree, as opposed to going directly into a master's program.

Some students feel obligations to the family that keep them working during college and cause them to reflect on going to work after college, forgoing available economic support for graduate education. This inner commitment to family represents a cultural strength, part of the connectivity that holds families together across generations, even though it may constrain personal educational achievement.

Networking

GMS students had high levels of connectivity to families and communities, an experiential background that added to their skills to navigate the academic system in college, a skill set recognized in the use of noncognitive variables for selection. However, as also is evident, the connectivity to family can be a force that constrains future opportunities. Students need to build support systems within their colleges, especially in graduate school. Below, we further examine the social and academic dimensions of networks as a force that enables and limits choices.

Academic Networking in Graduate School.   As undergraduates, GMS students had many opportunities to make connections with social and academic programs. There were many examples of engaged learning, where students took advantage of cocurricular learning opportunities that might not otherwise have been possible, as noted in the prior chapter. How do the processes of academic connectivity manifest in graduate education?

The graduate students in the GMS program conveyed an understanding of the pathways through education and how to expand them for others. For example, one graduate student worked on a university initiative to increase opportunities for underrepresented students in graduate programs:

> I was asked to participate in a Pathways, it's Career Pathways, but it is done by graduate division here…I am basically on a board with all the deans of each college…. Right now, as we see it, high school seniors are now finally starting to think about going to college. They're getting that connection…. But then once the undergrad is done…they are not connecting to either grad school or a profession of some sort. What we are trying to do is make that connection.

This GMS graduate student was invited into a university-wide exchange about strategies for encouraging students to make the transition from undergraduate education to graduate school. The comment illustrates both the student's recognition of the importance of smoothing transitions to graduate education and the initiatives within the university to enable these transitions.

For graduate students, one of the most important forms of networking was with their faculty, gaining a sense of membership in the academic community. An African American graduate student said, "I have a different relationship with faculty, you know, it's not so much the hierarchy…. It's kind of interesting being on their level and kind of seeing how much respect they have…I can say I have authority to say anything, because I'm an expert at what I do, too." The connections between graduate students and their faculty are central to success in graduate school and to early career development (Walker, Golde, Jones, Bueschel, & Hutchings, 2008). Making these connections represents a social and cultural transition for many first-generation college students because they lack images of how to engage in professional action.

Social Forces.   The process of making choices about careers is part of the social expectations of families. One of the complexities of attaining a degree for students from low-income families is that their relationships with family and community change. Two comments made by students in a group of Hispanic males at MIT:

- **Jerry:** "Because I come from a lower income background and most of my family isn't as educated, they don't understand the decisions I'm making at this point at all. They just have no idea what's factoring into my decisions on where to go and what to do…. So the main thing is they want to get me back home. They'd like for me to take a job as close to home as possible and there's just so much more that goes into my decision."
- Another participant (in response to a probe about decisions): "It's interesting just

because it's reinforced in terms of just helping people out. It's not necessarily just to—it's more than just being part of a group or an association that helps people out…. I'm a student at Sloan [MIT's business school], so I mean there's people there that are obviously very money hungry, especially the MBAs. With me, it's more, I'm definitely more curious as to what kind of company I want to work for. Obviously it would be great if it's involved with the community, that's a big focus; also what do you want to get out of it."

These comments illustrate the complexity of negotiating the personal role in the family in relation to career choices. The first comment expressed the pullback to the community as a constraint that complicates choices about majors and other educational options in relation to family expectations. The second comment illustrates connectivity to the community and the desire to give back, to engage in work that has a social and civic value. If students are away from the community, it seems important to them to find a means of being a contributing member of the community. Recognition of these issues of connectivity and community seems critical in efforts to engineer pathways through undergraduate and graduate education and can inform institutional efforts to design new educational pathways for underrepresented students.

Trust

To have trusted others within the community is a crucial component of social capital that can both constrain and enable (Coleman, 1988). Trusted others can discourage uplift, as evident in the discussion above. Building new trusted relationships can also be a force enabling uplift. The academic and social roles of trust are explored further below.

Academic Dimension. The issues of trust are complex and can influence choices throughout the college process. It was often the case that faculty and communities had low expectations for students and lacked a collective knowledge of educational opportunities outside the community. Consider the following comment by an African American student at UCLA:

I had no idea where any of these colleges were…. Growing up in Pasadena, you know, they play at the Rose Bowl. So I had heard of them, and so that's why everyone was pushing me, pushing me to go to UCLA, because that was the only one everyone had heard of…. And then my first year here, I swore, I swore that like somebody was going to walk into my dorm and tell me that they were up late and that they didn't really mean to let me in, it was a mistake, and that my admission was going to get rescinded. In my first year I would really think of that, because I had no idea how I got here.

Pasadena and UCLA are in the same metropolitan area, but this student had virtually no image of this or other colleges, other than knowledge that football games were played at the local stadium; she chose her college based on that. After making the choice, she had great self-doubt; she felt unworthy, that her admission had been a mistake. This illustrates both a trust of networked information in the community and a distrust of the unfamiliar. This was a common theme in GMS focus groups and reinforces the importance of early outreach.

Students can also feel challenged if they lack a sense of trust of their institution. These personal challenges and self-doubts can be the result of not having people in their communities with whom they can communicate about issues related to the inner transitions embedded in the college experience, especially for first-generation college students. Finding those people and social organizations that feel trustworthy is crucial.

Students grow and gain college knowledge from exchange of and reflection on experiences with peers, a pattern evident in many of the focus groups. In an African American focus group, a student observed:

> I just realized I needed to be around other people who were like me. So, I took Afro-M as a minor, and I think that really helped in terms of support network. I was in classes with people who looked like me, professors who looked like me, and you, talking and discussion about issues that we collectively, you know, sort of have all dealt with. I think that was one of the ways I reached out for support.

This comment illustrates the inner resilience evident among many GMS students. When they needed it, most found people with whom they could relate and share experiences. One common manifestation is social—students frequently hang out with students of similar races—but it can also be academic; students can make academic choices based on the need for connectivity and trust. These forces merit consideration in efforts to construct pathways to educational opportunity for underrepresented students.

Social Dimension.   When social environments were discussed, students in most of the focus groups indicated their campuses were supportive of diversity, or that they could find people to connect with. However, students of color are aware of various forms of prejudice in society and their colleges. These forces influence their sense of safety and strategies for navigating through campus social systems. Consider this exchange in an African American focus group:

- "Just recently, over the past year, there's been several hate crimes that have occurred on this campus. A couple of individuals who were LGBT community were killed.... I think a lot of things sort of get swept under the rug, like it's not a big deal.... Especially when you're White, you want to minimize the fact that there's like racist people that exist and they're very much working to make sure that minority students get as little respect and support as possible on this campus."
- "I think that last part is most important, the fact that you see there is so little support for people of color. And they only look at the incoming students, and the numbers are dropping.... You know, people are definitely not so all that open.... But you know, just kind of look from the outside looking in, you just see it."

This ability to contend with racism is a necessary part of the lived experience of African Americans who navigate predominantly White colleges in the United States. The African American tradition has combined a commitment to cross-generation uplift with an awareness of prejudice (Siddle Walker, 1996). Intergroup dialogue can reduce fear, adding to and enhancing trust (Locks, 2008). Building trust through open exchange still seems to be missing on many of the nation's campuses, so the challenge remains.

Information

GMS students, predominantly first generation, frequently have problems associated with lack of information about college. The cultural capital typically conveyed in families with multiple generations of college attainment is not accessible. So it is necessary to discover and build college knowledge through alternative means.

Academic Dimension. Students frequently lack information about academic and career pathways, a barrier that artificially limits choices. When discussing barriers, a student in a UCLA African American focus group observed:

> I think another personal challenge…[was] finding purpose.…I felt going to college was, I was on the same track of everyone who was a doctor or lawyer. Those were [the] only two jobs that pretty much exist, and so I came to college thinking I wanted to be a lawyer. And then…I just realized this wasn't what I wanted, and so then I was very much floundering in terms of my purpose and what I wanted to do.

The lack of role models and other information on career pathways narrows choice. Searching for alternatives once in college was not unique to GMS students; it was also evident among WSA students in the analysis above. The GMS focus groups included graduate students and the next student to speak, Peter, provided a graduate student perspective on this challenge.

> For me the biggest thing has been the…PhD. That's a multifaceted issue. Just about, you know, anything you can think of, it's an issue, it's a problem with the PhD. You're trying to balance your life, and like you're a student but then you're really not a student…. You don't have anyone to really tell you what these issues are ahead of time, until you're dropped in there.

Making it into graduate school overcame a barrier but, as Peter notes, the information void continues as students progress. Later in the conversation, Peter observed, "I've been fortunate because some of my Morehouse brothers are also out here doing PhDs, so they kind of serve as my support group, you know. And so I kind of deal with undergraduates too, kind of helping them out." This illustrates the role social networking, including peer support and mentoring, plays in overcoming the information barrier.

Social Dimension. As Peter's comment above illustrates, social networks play a role in overcoming barriers worsened by an absence of trustworthy information. This process can begin by seeking out opportunities to engage. Consider the reflection by an undergraduate:

> I started tutoring early in college, and through the community service commission here…I joined their administrative staff and just got to learn so much…I feel like it helped me so much. You know, you learn a lot from administration. And to know that it's something you don't have to do, just makes the experience so much richer. You're just there for the experience and you know it, and so it has helped out a lot.

This illustrates how the pathways opened by not having to work for money create opportunities to engage in activities of interest, which can lead to new experiences and learning about the unexpected.

The social commitment of GMS scholars came through as they talked about seeking opportunities after college as well. For example, in an Asian American focus group, a student observed, "Like I just tried to go into the Peace Corps and I'm definitely going to do that afterwards. And then, I don't know, something related to doing things for other people." GMS students exhibited an ability to seek out information related to their interests and personal commitments, a skill that enabled many to find new educational pathways.

Cultural Capital

The theme of giving back to the community comes across very strongly in most of the focus groups. Certainly many of the comments above illustrate this underlying theme. It is as though by acquiring education, many of these students felt they had an obligation to try to pass this gift along, a process that can be characterized as contributing to cultural capital as a community resource. The academic and social dimensions of this process are examined below.

Academic Dimension of Giving Back to Community. Late in their undergraduate careers, many students began to think seriously about the fields subsidized by GMS for graduate study. Simone, an African American interested in business, shared this reflection: "I probably would have never thought about receiving a PhD in education, but I am tweaking those to where I can look at finance or development or organizational behavior and it is in education instead of an MBA." A bit later in the dialogue she commented, "I want to be in my community and continue to be active and I think that just kind of, sometimes there are people like us who do so much for their communities and it's like no one ever cares. And this is almost kind of like saying, 'we see that and we appreciate you.'"

In a group of Hispanic students, a participant commented: "In my family it's always been a big thing to, like give back to the people that have kind of helped you along and things like that. And my parents have always instilled, like, giving back to people who are less fortunate." He went on to describe his experience working in Costa Rica as part of a summer program run by an international medical foundation. He reflected on how the experience had influenced his future plans: "And that's actually made its way into my long-term goals, because now, like after medical school and everything I plan to do—I plan to go back to countries like that, that have absolutely nothing. They have no clinic. With this foundation they try to raise money to build a clinic."

Giving Back to the Community. The process of integrating social commitments with career decisions was illustrated by the comment by the Hispanic student at MIT's Sloan School. The process of integrating social commitments into postcollege goals was a complex process that was culturally situated, creating distinctive forms of cultural capital.

In an exchange among students in a focus group of Native Americans, two students responded to a question about how the scholarship shaped their future:

Mary: I actually have had this kind of conversation with Jen before in another class. We had talked about how, as Native American people, we always like to give back to our people and our tribe…I don't know if there's going to be an opportunity but, ideally, maybe not right after I graduate but later on I'd like to go back.

Jen: I've always been pushed to do different and put myself after, but to me, I would be perfectly fine with going back to my community. I think that being raised a Native American you are taught not to just think of yourself and just go by what you want to do because you have your family to worry about.

Both students reflected on their inner commitments to their communities and tribes, as an integral part of their understanding of self. Having the opportunity to share both reinforced the commitment and enabled consideration of alternative paths, as evident in Mary's comments about making an eventual return to the community.

Habitual Patterns

The stories above illustrate how patterns of lived lives for most of the GMS students had been situated in their families and their communities. Frequently, personal identities as racially or ethnically situated self-understanding were integral to the issues and challenges students confronted, as was evident in exchanges among students within the different groups.

Academic Patterns. While the linkages between social patterns within groups are often evident, there is also substantial variation within groups. Consider this exchange within an Asian American student group, in response to a question about the influence of the scholarship on educational and career choices:

- "I guess it's just more of a practical perspective for where my parents come from and where certain people from my community come from. But then for me, it actually gives me more of a drive to say, you know, that's not all I want from myself and that there's a great need to satisfy a certain, you know, yearning or like a goal that I have for myself, which is beyond that."
- "My whole family, my dad's side, basically everyone is in business and that's all…I guess growing up in Vietnam my grandfather had a store and my dad and my aunts and uncles all worked in the store…. I think with that type of low expectations I kind of felt that, you know, why not just go and do something else and not go into business and not do what they expect. And so that's where I kind of looked into science and you know now they're actually happy that I've taken that route. They're all pretty much supportive about it."
- "I don't think [of] meeting my family's expectations or, you know, people around me, like representing them. I don't really feel that way, to be honest. I just do my thing. But it'll be good if I…win a prize or something and then these people who had said, 'Oh, this Korean' or whatever, I mean it'll be good, it'll be rewarding."

All three students reflected in ways that reveal the tension between discovery of self and one's own interests in relation to social expectations, the habitual patterns of community in which they were raised.

Social Patterns. A tension was evident between the push toward opportunities for uplift and pullback to community and known patterns, as evident from the text above. The engagement in social and academic opportunities provides means of moving toward uplift with values consonant with communities of origin. One of the big challenges during college is to discover one's self in the midst of external expectations.

Some of the GMS students emphasized their social commitments to family expectations over other interests pulling them toward engagement. These students were more likely to experience problems with discovering self along the way. Consider the following examples:

- A student who earlier commented on sending "a lot of money home" observed, "It helped me being an overachiever. I have worked pretty much anywhere from 20 to 40 hours, depending on how much free time I have with my semester. But I wish I could have not worked so I could have spent more time on campus, getting involved in other…. But I felt like I really needed to work, so I didn't free up too much time."
- "I haven't really been involved in too much. Now here in my senior year I am involved in an emerging leaders program. I had done an internship for a law firm…I think being married at a young age kind of took me out of that. I am not necessarily the young student anymore."

Both students had social commitments that constrained engagement. As they sat in their group hearing others talk about their engagement during college, both reflected on their choices. Finding academic pathways to engaged learning seems a critical link in the process of building new patterns that both support family and community and take advantage of opportunities for uplift.

Key Features of GMS

The first round of the GMS selection process identifies students with high academic achievement in their high schools. The second round of the process uses validated non-cognitive variables (Sedlacek & Sheu, 2004, 2006), such as the ability to contend with racism and social commitments. When we analyze interviews with GMS students, it is important to recognize the inner strengths observed from the narratives of students that are related to selection. In fact, the analysis of interviews further validates that the selection process found resilient, self-navigating students. These inner strengths of the GMS students are extremely compelling.

In addition, the real value of the monetary guarantees provided by the GMS award is understood in deeper ways as students navigate through the education system. Most of the students selected for the program would probably have gotten college degrees without GMS, but would probably have been less likely to go on to graduate school. There is evidence from the interviews that the limited number of fields subsidized for graduate studies did influence choices. However, within those limitations, students seemed to steer toward choices related to their own interests. The skills of self-navigation integral to program selection also seemed to mitigate excessive influence of these limitations on choice.

CONCLUSIONS

Academic capital formation provided a compelling lens from which to view college success, broadening the frame to include formation of postcollege aspirations and social and cultural capital to support cross-generation uplift. While it is too early to judge long-term outcomes for WSA or GMS students, it appears both programs provided advantages with respect to attainment and capital formation processes.

An Equity Standard

Funders of programs naturally want the students they fund to do better academically than others. There is evidence that both WSA and GMS, as programs that provide precollege services, influenced an expansion of enrollment in 4-year and high-selective colleges. Both the monetary and support services had an influence on enrollment, as noted in chapter 5. The process of improving outcomes during college is more complex. Yielding better persistence rates may be an elusive goal for student aid programs that only supplement available need-based aid, but there were significant differences for GMS students compared to the control group. The difference is one of quality of life, relieving the burden of having to work and borrow to pay for college leading to improved family and personal well-being. The GMS and WSA programs enhanced engaged learning during college by providing both funding and encouragement (chapter 6). Before considering how this engagement leads to gains in the social aspect of academic capital, we must consider the academic side, the attainment of degrees and persistence during college. The minimum standard is one of equity: Do these programs equalize opportunity for their students comparable to similar students? This is a reasonable minimum threshold of success met or exceeded by all three programs.

For the two programs for the general high school population of low-income students (TFCS and WSA), the persistence rates were nearly equal and about what would be expected for groups of mostly low-income, first-generation college students. The WSA students had slightly higher persistence rates than Twenty-first Century Scholars, probably an artifact of higher levels of grant aid and support services during college. The GMS students met high academic standards and had higher persistence rates than Twenty-first Century Scholars, WSA, and comparable students. Based on the statistics available, it appears GMS not only increased enrollment in high-selective 4-year colleges (chapter 5), but also enhanced persistence, meeting the equity standard. Thus, TFCS and WSA met the standard of equalizing opportunity, and GMS exceeded this standard.

The Social Aspects of Academic Capital

Both GMS and WSA provided support services during college: leadership conferences run by the program for GMS and mentoring and additional support services by the College Success Foundation for WSA. Students often mentioned these services as they discussed social networking and trustworthy information during college.

However, the most compelling finding from this chapter, especially when examined in relation to the other chapters in part I, is that the social aspects of academic capital formation are integral to the academic success of college students in both GMS and WSA. Students accepted responsibility as members of their families during college (chapters 6 and 7) and had a strong sense of contributing to younger siblings. The commitment to giving back to communities was strong for students in both programs, but was especially strong among students engaged in focus group interviews for GMS.

Recent research on GMS students has shown a pattern of relationships between student engagement during college and earnings after college (Hu & Wolniak, in press). In particular, the composite measure of social engagement during college had a positive association on early-career earnings, especially for students in STEM fields. But an examination of the variables related to engagement revealed a complex pattern. Community service activities had a positive association with earnings for non-STEM graduates and a negative association for STEM graduates. Engagement in activities in one's own culture had a positive association with earnings for STEM fields and provided a possible explanation for these patterns. Understanding one's own culture might enable easier integration into diverse workforces providing an advantage for STEM graduates. In contrast, community service is directly linked to many non-STEM jobs. Clearly the academic capital formed in college has an impact during early career.

Academic capital formation, a social process which enables academic success and builds commitments to cross-generation uplift, is multifaceted and facilitated in different ways by GMS, TFCS, and WSA. For first-generation students, navigating through college involves building personal knowledge of education and careers not generally available within their families and communities. Gaining this personal knowledge involves more than attending and doing well in college classes. It also involves networking to find peers, faculty, and support personnel who can become sources of trustworthy information. The inner transformation that is essential to acquiring the knowledge to navigate through college is a challenging process that involves taking risks and trusting there will be support. It is in this sense that the traditions of liberal education and student support services must adapt to enable new generations of students to attain college.

Part II

Informing Public Policy

8

ACADEMIC CAPITAL FORMATION

The privatization of public higher education, a shift away from public subsidies to institutions and college students to using loans to fund college costs, has eroded public funding of higher education since 1980 (Heller, 2006; Parsons & St. John, 2004; Slaughter & Leslie, 1997; St. John, 2003). This has been accompanied by, or perhaps been a cause of, growing inequality in educational opportunity to enroll in college (St. John, Piñeda, & Moronski, 2009) and an apparent decline in the public commitment to social good as a rationale for funding (Pasque, 2007). Some scholars characterize this as a neoliberal shift in public policy, from valuing equity to valuing individual liberties (Henry, 2005), a philosophy that rationalizes the use of student loans as a means of funding colleges (Henry, Lingard, Rizvi, & Taylor, 2001; Levidow, 2005). The social ethos of modern societies is put at risk when graduates are burdened with excessive debt before they start their professional careers. In this new world of loans, low-income students who manage to graduate from college have substantially greater debt, on average, than middle-income students. While in college, low-income students often have more limited opportunities to engage in social and academic processes that build understanding of and commitment to uplift because they face greater demands to work while in college, which can also ultimately lessen the desire to give back to society through taxes or charity.

We used a critical-empirical approach to examine the social processes embedded in educational transitions culminating in degrees. The resulting theory reconstruction addresses the specific problems in preparing for the college transition and academic success for first-generation college students, an objective more focused than prior efforts to reconstruct social and critical theory (e.g., Lin, 2001; Lynn, Yusso, Solorzano, & Parker, 2002).

Critical theory can refer to a wide range of theories that take a critical view of society to guide human action aimed at social transformation (Macey, 2000). Rather than focusing just on critiques, the critical-empirical approach also seeks evidence in relation to claims that emerge from critiques. This book has focused on examining quantitative and qualitative evidence about the role of social processes within educational transitions that are central to improving educational attainment by low-income residents of the

United States. Examination of educational transitions relied on quantitative data tracking students, while analyses of social processes relied on evidence from interviews.

This chapter discusses the reconstructed theory of academic formation in two parts. First, we discuss educational transitions that integrate an understanding of ACF processes. Second, we focus on the processes of ACF using insights about transitions to illuminate the process. We hope the related theory is informative for social and policy research and the education of activists who seek to expand educational opportunities for low-income students.

ACADEMIC CAPITAL FORMATION (ACF) AS TRANSITION

The studies of students in the three comprehensive reforms—Washington State Achievers (WSA), Gates Millennium Scholars (GMS), and Twenty-first Century Scholars (TFCS) illuminated alternative pathways to academic success for low-income students, breaking through a series of obstacles that comprise barriers to access to college, especially to 4-year degrees. Given the new academic standard of college preparation as a goal for all high school students, the barriers to access must be broken through to provide opportunities for degree attainment for all college-prepared high school graduates. The guaranteed funding coupled with support services provided through the GMS, WSA, and TFCS programs enabled students to build college and career knowledge they needed to navigate through undergraduate education, find career pathways and, for some, enroll in graduate school. These pathways to academic success are being traveled by a new generation of academic pioneers aware of the potential of giving back in support of new generations of students in their families and communities through academic capital formation.

The studies of ACF (the chapters in part I) systematically examined constructs from human capital, social capital, and social reproduction theories, using evidence from the studies to illuminate the core processes of family/community engagement, academic preparation, college choice, engaged learning, and academic success. Based on these analyses (see Figure 1.2), it appears ACF is a process that can be refined to enable first-generation students and their parents to develop knowledge of college and career pathways to academic success, inclusive of degree attainment and a commitment to give back to future generations.

Academic Capital Formation in Low-SES Families

Economic, social, and educational theories address the access challenge using different assumptions based on an orientation toward educational uplift. The studies of ACF focused on students from low-SES families who were eligible for exemplary, comprehensive interventions that included both aid guarantees and support services. These programs have evidence of success, but causal studies have not confirmed claims related to all of the intended outcomes. Students who were eligible for the programs were studied in the quantitative analyses, both recipients and nonrecipients, which provided a basis for comparing these programs and developing a cross-cutting theory. In addition, analysis of individual interviews and focus group transcripts provided opportunities to examine key social constructs that either hold back or enable students to break through obstacles to access. It is important to reconsider how these studies inform the underlying theories used to frame policy and social research on access for low-income students.

Financial Fears.   Economic theory provides a basis for economic studies of educational attainment. Gary Becker's (1964) human capital theory made progressive assumptions about educational opportunity—implicitly recognizing cross-generation uplift was possible—largely because of the period in which the logic was constructed. Given the relatively low cost of public college at the time, it was possible for most middle-income families to send their children to public 4-year colleges, desirable based on an assessment of costs and benefits, without federal student aid.[1] Becker (1975) considered the role of financial aid in enabling low-income students to attend college. At the time, the United States was in a sustained period of social uplift, which resulted in a massive middle class comprised of factory workers and professionals. Federal programs were created in the middle 1960s to extend opportunity to low-income families.

In the early 21st century, federal and state need-based grant aid is not sufficient to insure low-income students the opportunity to enroll in public 4-year colleges, at least in most states. Of course, some low-income students make it through, especially if they receive philanthropic aid or supplemental aid for merit from their campus, so it is difficult to prove the claim that need-based aid is not sufficient. Rather, we can learn from economic studies about the effects of funding. For example, DesJardins and McCall (2009) found Washington State Achievers scholarships increased the probability that low-income students would enroll by 40 percentage points.

Even middle-income families struggle to borrow sufficient funds to pay for college given what parents are expected to contribute based on the federal need analysis necessary to obtain aid. Access to 4-year colleges has been a challenge for low-income families for 3 decades (St. John, 1994), which means that many parents of today's first-generation college students often were denied access for financial reasons. Cross-generational denial of access can create a predisposition to mistrust that must be overcome to break through the access barrier. In such circumstances, caring parents may caution their children about having high expectations, often reinforced by trustworthy sources within their communities such as teachers and extended family.

Thus, concerns about college costs are a major factor inhibiting engagement in preparation among low-income students in middle and high schools. Students have substantial evidence from life experience that college is not affordable, a conclusion evident in the studies of students and parents (chapters 4 and 5). There were many good reasons for low-income students and their parents to be concerned about college costs and to harbor doubts that student aid would meet their financial needs if they did take the steps to prepare. The notion that providing information on loans would solve this problem (e.g., King, 1999a, 2004) did not take into account the inadequacy of subsidized loans in covering costs (Advisory Committee on Student Financial Assistance, 2001, 2002, 2004; Hartle, Simmons, & Timmons, 2005) or family culture regarding debt.

Easing concerns about costs by guaranteeing student aid played a transformative role for GMS, WSA, and TFCS Scholars (policy linkage 1 in Figure 1.2). The promise of aid encouraged preparation, while the delivery of aid enabled prepared students to enroll in 4-year colleges. Students were able to make college choices and to transfer, if necessary, based on finding the right fit, unfettered by family concerns about costs.

Social Engagement.   Social capital theory (Coleman, 1988) focuses on social processes that can enable uplift through engagement, including information, networks, and trust. These mechanisms are central to the success of services provided to low-income families as they break through obstacles encountered in preparing for college and finding a college that fits. A serious limitation of the original social capital theory is that it overlooked the role of finances, including family concerns about costs; in fact, many sociological attainment theories overlooked the role of finances for decades. The theory of attainment (Blau & Duncan, 1967) focused on parents' occupations and educations rather than the ability to pay for college. Coleman (1965) did not adequately consider financial factors related to moving out of cities in his work on White flight, an issue illuminated by Jencks and colleagues in *Inequality* (1972). By the 1980s, it became evident that African Americans also migrated to suburbs when they entered the middle class, leaving the cities mostly to underclass and minority people (Jencks & Peterson, 1991). These developments influenced social science research by rethinking the relationships between class and race as they relate to the role of social capital in cross-generation uplift, and critical race theory emerged (e.g., Lynn et al., 2002).

Recent efforts to adapt social capital concepts which carry forward the notion that social progress results from breaking through the access barriers have considered the role of legitimate family concerns about costs. For example, Tierney and Venegas (2007) adapted social capital theory to examine ways that low-income students gain access to information about colleges and student aid, part of the process of building college knowledge. The concept of social enablement as an outcome of student aid guarantees emerged in this study, a process that can build cultural capital in families.

Family Hope and Social Action.   Hope is created by providing aid guarantees and support services to families with students in high school or middle school. The WSA and TFCS programs combined precollege support services with student aid guarantees. It is apparent that parental engagement in finding out about college preparation and visiting colleges (chapters 4 and 5) played a substantial role in advocacy for preparation among TFCS students; this engagement was motivated, at least in part, by aid guarantees. Students and parents in TFCS gave testimony to the value of support services, especially college visits. Washington State Achievers students experienced benefits from the additional monetary support and gained also from school reforms and mentoring; teachers made a big difference for WSA students.

Breaking Patterns of Reproduction

Cultural capital can reinforce cross-generation replication of school to work and other transitions that do not include preparing for and enrolling in 4-year colleges. Discouragement as part of the cultural reproduction process is reinforced by social environments and, more recently, by economic conditions and educational policy. Social enablement and a cross-generation commitment to uplift can overcome these barriers.

The period from the end of World War II through about 1980 saw a sustained expansion of the middle class. It was in this social context that theories of human capital (Becker, 1964) and educational attainment (Blau & Duncan, 1967; Turner & Berry, 2000) were formulated. For these theorists, there was little reason to focus on cultural and social reproduction of class—and the Cold War created an ideology that discouraged such critical thought (Marcuse, 1964/1991). However, Europeans used and adapted Marxist theories throughout this period (Wolin, 2006), providing a theory base for the study of class reproduction. As inequality accelerated in the United States in the 1980s and 1990s, neo-Marxist theories provided compelling explanations for unequal access to education (McDonough, 1997). Of the social reproduction theories, Bourdieu's (1977, 1990) has been the most widely used in research on college students (Walpole, 2007).

The studies of students (part I) provided strong evidence of reproductive forces among the underclass as a dominant pattern students had to break through. We can also think of this as a process of status maintenance. In a period when downward mobility is in evidence, families in the working class may struggle just to maintain well-being across generations. Aid guarantees and support services open up possibilities by helping students and parents overcome barriers, yet other forces pull students back, including an orientation toward work, expectations of living close to and contributing financially to the family, and connectivity with local values and culture. In the analyses of GMS focus groups, it was evident that race and ethnicity played roles in cultural capital, both as a focus for uplift and status maintenance. Two key processes from Bourdieu's work— cultural capital and habitual patterns—also contribute to both status maintenance and uplift. In particular, students' habitual patterns—their ability to self-navigate toward goals related to educational and professional success—are crucial forces in overcoming class reproduction across generations.

Commitment to Uplift. The process of supporting cross-generation gains in educational attainment within the culture of families builds college knowledge. The African American tradition of education serves as an historical exemplar of the process of cultural capital that builds college knowledge. Parental involvement in TFCS serves as a contemporary exemplar (chapters 4 and 5); active engagement of parents was a major force in accelerating preparation and enrollment among TFCS students.

Family and Community Engagement

In research on college students, it has long been known that peers and locales as well as parents have a large influence on college going (Feldman & Newcomb, 1969/1994a, 1969/1994b; Jackson, 1978; Pascarella & Terenzini, 1991; Paulsen, 1990). Parents act within a community context. Parent engagement in learning about college has been largely overlooked except by a few researchers (e.g., McDonough, 1997; Hossler, Schmit, & Vesper, 1999). Even the early research on educational attainment processes and human capital theory largely overlooked the role of engagement. Social capital and social reproduction theories have provided a lens for viewing these processes. In addition, the concept of easing family concerns about college costs enables them to overcome fear, suspend disbelief, engage in precollege services, and seek preparatory opportunities.

Easing Concerns about Costs and Family Engagement. Economic theory has assumed that families rationally assess costs of college. Unfortunately, a realistic assessment of costs by low-income families can result in a conclusion that enrollment in a 4-year college would not be affordable without extreme hardship for the family. When parents and grandparents experienced 4-year colleges as inaccessible, it is easy to see how they believe their children cannot afford college, especially when costs of college are climbing faster than student aid.

Further, many families encourage their children to make transitions from school to work, a process that maintains working-class status. These perceptions and patterns of behavior were abundantly evident among the parent interviews discussed in chapters 4 and 5. For many parents who had not gone to college, seizing the opportunity to have their children's college education paid for functioned as a *trigger event*. Both students and parents in TFCS described how parents had encouraged and even demanded that their children take the Scholars pledge, an indication of the conclusion within families that the guarantee could make a difference and enable children to overcome financial barriers that had constrained opportunities for generations.

For students in WSA schools, teachers were a major force for change. They recommended students for the WSA program as it got started in the schools, a form of outreach that was enabling. Teachers were aware that the program was for low- and middle-income students who could self-navigate through educational systems (determined through the noncognitive variables used in selection). The students selected for WSA showed resiliency and an ability to navigate through difficult times. Student engagement in schools can be a force in creating postsecondary opportunities for low-income students when the financial barrier is removed, as was the case with WSA students.

In addition, there was extensive commentary among GMS students in focus groups about their community engagement during high school. Students applying for the GMS program were screened based on academic criteria before the noncognitive selection method was applied. Students who had the grades and who sought out the opportunity had an ability to navigate educational systems, by virtue of making it through the initial noncognitive screening. About 1,000 students were selected each year from thousands who applied, so selected students stood out academically and with respect to the noncognitive variables. Very often, as expressed in the interviews (chapters 5 through 7), these students were actively engaged in social, community, and civic activities during college.

Support Services and Commitment to Uplift.　Networks play a central role in social capital theory; they provide information and people who become sources of trustworthy information. The educational reform literature focuses on advanced courses as the primary mechanism for improving college access (Adelman, 2004; Conklin & Curran, 2004; Perna, 2005b). In addition, support services play a role (Perna 2005a). One of the challenges addressed in this book was to examine how support services became trustworthy networks. The WSA and TFCS programs provided insight into this question.

The support services provided by TFCS served an *enabling function* for students and their parents.[2] College visits—along with opportunities to use college cost calculators and attend other events related to college going—encouraged students and parents to plan for college. Parents engaged in these programs became social agents acting on behalf of their children. Many of the parents commented on their reliance on and trust of service providers in TFCS regional centers. Parent involvement in college visits and events, as a measure of use of services, was significantly associated with students' completion of advanced courses in high school and with college going, even after controlling for program selection. In fact, the engagement of parents—their taking advantage of the opportunities and support services provided by the programs—was a strong force in both preparation and college going.

The commitment to uplift, as an habitual pattern of self-navigation toward educational goals, can be actualized by low-income students. Mentoring of students by external staff was a major factor cited by students in WSA and TFCS interviews. Students exhibited strong self-advocacy in TFCS, using their own college knowledge to steer themselves into advanced preparatory courses (chapter 5). In addition, both WSA and

TFCS selected students, in part, because of their ability to self-navigate toward goals and contend with racism, noncognitive measures that became manifest in the profiles of students.

Family culture underlies their commitment to educational uplift and their engagement in support services. The studies in this volume examined two concepts of family and individual engagement: cultural capital and habitual patterns. Cultural capital is a valuable concept of family knowledge of education, work, and society, conveyed through experience in the family and community. Networks of trust enabled within-generation gains in college knowledge, as evidenced by parental engagement in TFCS services (chapters 3 and 4). Parental and student engagement can change the family narrative, building shared college knowledge. In addition, habitual patterns of individuals in families, as behaviors that can reproduce social class or support social and educational uplift across generations, continue to strengthen and mature during the high school and college years.

Academic Preparation

Academic preparation for college has frequently been framed and studied as a process of taking advanced high school courses which is statistically linked to success in college (Adelman, 2004; Perna, 2005b; St. John, 2006a). The studies (part I) examined the social aspects of access to advanced courses and the meaning of this access, revealing that both academic achievement as measured by test scores and social navigation skills as measured by noncognitive variables are indicators of capacity for academic success. Yet neither type of measure, by itself, provides a complete and appropriate indicator of preparedness as a predictor of academic success, especially of success that includes a commitment to giveback and cross-generation uplift.[3] In addition to access to advanced courses, parents' and students' college knowledge plays a role in gaining access and achieving success in college preparation courses.

For parents to advocate for children, they need some knowledge of what college requires. Below we examine the roles of college knowledge and access to advanced courses as social processes before addressing issues related to measurement of college preparedness, a key issue in efforts to achieve an equitable and fair admissions process in selective colleges and universities. Specifically, the educational environment in schools (policy linkage 2, Figure 1.2) and the program support services provided by WSA and GMS (policy linkage 3, Figure 1.2) enabled families to build college knowledge and to navigate a path toward academic preparation.

Building College Knowledge (as Cultural Capital Reformation).   Logically, if parents and their children have knowledge of what college requires, they will advocate for these opportunities. While the process of advocacy and the strategies for overcoming barriers to preparation are not as simple as is often implied in some of the literature on college networking services, the evidence from analyses of WSA and TFCS[4] indicate college knowledge does inform advocacy, and that access to quality courses and caring teachers also contributes to understanding of college as part of the family narrative.

Gaining access to advanced courses and other preparatory activities requires active engagement, if not advocacy, by parents and students. The studies of parents and children in the TFCS program found that parents encouraged their children to take the Scholars pledge. Once children gained access to the program, active parental engagement in precollege activities played a central role in gaining access to advanced courses and in enrolling in research universities. Parents spoke about how relationships with TFCS service providers and college visits enabled them to learn about college and envision their children as students. They also gained an understanding of the transitions their students would have to make, like taking responsibility for doing laundry, perhaps finding part-time jobs, choosing a major, and so forth. Parents who had taken advantage of these visits and events had an understanding of what to expect and could help prepare themselves and their children for the transition. TFCS students frequently spoke of having to advocate for access to advanced courses and the best teachers within their schools. While Indiana high schools were required to offer a preparatory curriculum, not all students gained access to the courses or to teachers that could facilitate their learning.

Complex social and economic issues underlie the argument that low-income families should focus on college preparation and college knowledge. For generations, children in working-class families transitioned from high school to work. In Gary, Indiana, for example, there were jobs which did not require a college education that provided a middle-class standard of living (i.e., the steel industry). Now, not only have these well-paying jobs been lost from the local economy, but schools are also changing: High schools had offered general and technical tracks along with college preparatory education, but now require college preparation for all; and Indiana's technical college system underwent a transformation into community colleges that emphasized courses transferrable to 4-year colleges. The orientation of the entire education system has shifted from emphasizing transitions from high school to work to completion of 4-year degrees as the level of educational attainment required to maintain middle-class status. Gary is not the only city facing these conditions. Working-class families across the United States are faced with the challenge of advocating for their children in transforming educational systems within which they have no personal experience.

Access to Advanced Courses (with Rigor and Care).   When viewed as a social process, gaining access to advanced high school courses takes on different dimensions than merely being a predictive correlate of eventual college success, although the evidence here and elsewhere confirms that correlation. Access to advanced high school courses is unequal in the United States, so advocacy still plays a critical role for low-income and minority families. In the research on attainment of advanced math courses among students in the high school class of 1992, it is evident that: (a) minority status reduces the odds of completing calculus or trigonometry compared to algebra II or less in U.S. high schools; and (b) middle-income students have benefited more substantially from policies requiring advanced courses than low-income students (St. John, 2006a).

Fortunately, there is also recent research that indicates that: (a) for the 2004 high school senior cohort, state policies were positively associated with access to advanced courses for African Americans, but they remained significantly underrepresented in these courses (Daun-Barnett, 2008); and (b) requiring four or more years of math for high school graduation had a more positive association on rates of African Americans in public 4-year colleges than did requiring two or fewer courses (Williams, Penida, & St. John, 2009). In combination, these findings suggest that barriers to advanced courses still exist for low-income and minority high school students, although there is evidence of progress.

Opportunities to enroll in advanced high school courses were enhanced by involvement in comprehensive programs during middle and high school. Statistical analyses indicated that both WSA and TFCS students enrolled in advanced courses at higher rates than comparison students (chapter 4). Comments by personnel at the College Success Foundation indicated they strongly encouraged WSA students to take advanced courses. However, in interviews, some TFCS students indicated that it took personal and family advocacy to gain access to advanced courses. In both cases, trustworthy information, in the case of WSA by program personnel, provided encouragement, but it took extra effort by students to gain access. While a few states are now requiring algebra II for high school graduation (e.g., Michigan), even this level of math is not sufficient to prepare students for collegiate work in the science, technology, engineering, and mathematics (STEM) fields, so advocacy remains an important factor in ensuring more low-income and minority students gain access to the level of preparation they need to ensure college success.

Advanced high school courses should be rigorous and engaging. Some of the WSA students described their IB courses as challenging and their teachers as supportive of learning. They described both oral and written examinations. However, testing alone does not support comprehension in the same way as multiple forms of learning that stress relevance and aligning content with applications students can understand. In particular, students from first-generation families may need to see and experience relevance in order to persevere, and often their parents cannot help with homework in advanced courses. The relevance of curriculum can be communicated within the family, creating a deeper understanding of its importance and adding to the family narrative.[5]

A major difference in the reconceptualized academic capital formation model (Figure 1.2) is the focus on welcoming, rigorous, engaging, and equitable high schools rather than K-16 policy. Study findings indicate that the environment of the high school, possibly enhanced by external support services, is a major factor in providing access to advanced curriculum. One of the most troubling findings of the quantitative studies of TFCS is that in schools with low percentages of low-income students, college-bound low-income students found it more difficult to gain access to advanced courses than their peers in predominantly low-income high schools. This confirms a long history of research on tracking (Oakes, 2008). The low-income high schools apparently were better able to provide support than the schools focused on serving higher-income students. It is little wonder that in interviews TFCS students indicated they had to advocate for themselves in their schools.

Many of the students in GMS and WSA who took advanced courses in high school indicated their college courses were more difficult than those in high school, and that they were often forced to change majors because of a lack of preparation. Sky Warrior, a Native American WSA student, indicated he had done well in high school math, but had to repeat math courses in college. Clearly the poor alignment in the rigor of high school and college courses represents a challenge for students, an issue that should be given more serious consideration in collegiate programs that aim to support underrepresented students. In addition, while many students found good advisors during college, some described how their initial college advisors had not met with them or given them good advice. Finding trustworthy sources of information in college was a challenge after having relied on mentors from the intervention programs during high school.

There was evidence from the comparison of persistence rates across programs that high achievement in high school is associated with academic success during college. Specifically, the college completion rates were higher for GMS students than TFCS or WSA; GMS students were selected first based on their achievement in high school and then noncognitive variables were considered. There is strong evidence that both access to and achievement in advanced courses in high school can improve subsequent success. Engaged and relevant approaches to teaching are important because they can improve learning and achievement in these courses, but the burden of achievement in high school courses ultimately rests with the students.

Care and support from teachers is not only important within the curriculum, but also outside of class and after courses are completed. The WSA schools were engaged in the process of comprehensive school reform. Many of the interviewed students commented on the support provided by their teachers, including recommendation for the WSA program. They also spoke of the importance of mentoring relationships during high school. Further, parents, students, and service providers in the TFCS program spoke about the importance of relationships between advisors and students. Having strong, reliable, and supportive relationships with adults helps students gain trustworthy college knowledge and also provides guidance along the path to success during high school.

Personal habits, along with academic preparation and college knowledge, are important indicators of success during college. In the WSA, TFCS, and GMS programs, the use of noncognitive variables in the selection process yielded resilient students capable of persevering, navigating through majors and social experiences toward their own paths to success. While high academic achievement and quality educational opportunities that enable students to succeed are both important factors, academic preparation alone is not the only, and possibly not even the most important, indicator of future success. While many of the students interviewed experienced difficulties at some point during college, they found ways through and around problems, altering living arrangements, changing majors, and even transferring to a different college to find the pathway that fit them best. This process of personal navigation enables students to work through problems that could become barriers to academic success.

College Transitions

Research on college choice has focused on the roles of student aid and high school courses, while research on retention has tended to overlook student aid. Yet when viewed as a social process involving low-income students, college choice extends over time to include concepts of fit not normally considered in retention theory and research. Before considering the role of student aid in college choice among low-income students eligible for comprehensive programs, we reconsider the theory of college choice as centered in the experiences of low-income, first-generation students. It is abundantly clear that both the external support services of comprehensive programs (linkage 3, Figure 1.2) and the constancy of financial support (linkage 4) enabled students to navigate their way to 4-year colleges that fit their academic interests and socialization capacity (linkage 4).

An Extended Process of Finding Fit.   Most theory and research on college choice ends with entry into the initial college as the outcome. College choice theories assume a cognitive process of scanning options, choosing colleges to apply to, and selecting a college from those to which the student was accepted. The notion that initial choice terminates the process does not appropriately characterize the college choice process. In addition, most research on persistence focuses on returning to the initial college after completing the freshman year as an outcome influenced by social and academic integration as intermediate processes. The argument follows that colleges can create, alter, and otherwise manipulate engagement as a means of retaining students. The notion that college academic and social programs can fit students is a central premise of the theory. Findings on student experiences resulted in an alternative conception of college choice, a reconstruction that conceives of the process as extended, with engaged students finding a college and major that fit their interests and aspirations. Student aid guarantees eased concerns about costs, enabling students to seek out trustworthy information to inform their decisions in this extended process.

For the first-generation college students interviewed, colleges that were known within the family were often limited, unlike families with college knowledge that has been shared. Students had heard about colleges because of the football teams, officials from campuses visiting their schools, or their counselors and teachers recommending a college. Having relatives who had attended colleges of choice, frequently a significant factor among African Americans attending historically black colleges (McDonough, Antonio, & Trent, 1997), was not part of the narratives of most of these families. College support programs that provide opportunities can expand choice, especially with respect to enrollment away from home. However, the colleges that are seriously considered, even in these circumstances, are usually constrained by state boundaries. Both WSA and TFCS limited initial choices to colleges in the state; in contrast, the GMS program expanded choice by providing the opportunity to enroll in any college or university.

Students in both GMS and WSA, the two programs for which we had interviews about the college choice process (chapter 5), transferred if they discovered their college did not fit their interests and aims. These findings are logically consistent with persistence theory, but view the process of finding a fit from the perspective of students, rather than from the institutional revenue aims implicit in retention theory (Bean, 1990). When we are concerned about institutional revenue, the focus on retention makes sense. Indeed, institutions can focus on retention—and specifically on raising the odds that at-risk students will return—viewed through a cost-benefit perspective, with the revenue from returning students who would have otherwise departed being treated as an economic benefit. However, if our concern is the educational attainment of low-income students, then viewing the process of finding a good fit from the perspective of the student is more important.

In the studies of college choice and persistence, it became apparent that finding social connectivity, a major, and a college that fit were interrelated in college choice as an extended process (chapters 4 and 6). For example, Monica found a good fit after deciding on a political science major, while Liliya transferred to gain entry to her major program. In contrast, Missy transferred to find a college that fit better with her values, while Sky Warrior found a community at his initial campus after getting involved with diversity groups.

Some students enter college with sufficient college knowledge and understanding of self to stick to a major. However, most students change majors or transfer at least once. If educators and policymakers were concerned about improving degree attainment rather than focusing on retention in the institution of initial choice, it would be easier to craft policies that supported and enabled increased attainment.

The Role of Student Aid. There has been extensive research examining the impact of student aid on initial college choice. One study found that state grant funding and GMS were both associated with initial enrollment in high-selective colleges by high-achieving, low-income minority students (appendix 3). The other study provided insight into the roles of the aid guarantee and support services for enrollment in 4-year colleges by TFCS Scholars; for example, parent involvement in events, a key indicator of engagement in program services, was associated with enrollment in 4-year colleges and research universities (St. John, Fisher, Lee, Daun-Barnett, & Williams, 2008).[6] In combination, these findings illustrate the importance of aid in initial college choice and the role of parental engagement in the college preparation and choice processes among low-income students.

Research on degree attainment indicates that 6 years after initial enrollment, low-income students were more likely to still be enrolled than to have dropped out, but were no more likely to have attained college degrees than to have dropped out (St. John, 2006a). In contrast, middle-income students were more likely to have attained college degrees than to have dropped out after 6 years, but less likely to still be enrolled. Looking at college choice as an extended process of finding fit may help explain this finding. If low-income students transfer to find better situations—for academic, economic, or social reasons—the student aid system is unlikely to be as supportive in the second college. Most institutions package their own aid to support initial enrollment rather than to subsidize transfers. Many transfer students are either funded by their families or work extensively and enroll part-time. The portable aid guarantees lifted these constraints for low-income students.

The interviews with GMS and WSA students revealed that the aid guarantees turned the extended process of choice into something constructive. Students were not worried about losing funding when they considered options. This benefit of aid guarantees is crucial relative to the public aim of improving degree attainment rates within states and nationally. If students cannot afford to transfer to another 4-year college, their choice could be constrained to a local 2-year college unless their personal earnings rise to a level that would allow them to pay part-time tuition at a more expensive 4-year college. Yet not having a degree makes it more difficult to get a job that pays enough to afford part-time enrollment in most public 4-year colleges. The finding that aid guarantees enabled a better fit in college and in major choice was unexpected. The concluding chapter considers the implications of this new insight.

Engaged Learning

The analyses in part I provide further confirmation of arguments about the importance of engagement in college life (Kuh & Hu, 2001; Kuh, Kinzie, Schuh, Whitt, & Associates, 2005). Earlier analyses of GMS Scholars found that the social background and financial aid variables associated with engagement were also associated with persistence, but that engagement variables were not significantly associated with persistence when background and financial aid were controlled (St. John, 2008). The analyses suggest it is important to consider how financial aid and social background relate to academic and social engagement. Two forces were evident: having sufficient need-based aid enabled students to limit work hours, leaving time for involvement (linkage 5, Figure 1.2); and the availability of academic and support services that aligned with students' interests (linkage 7) was associated with engagement.

Financial Aid Enables Academic and Social/Civic Engagement. Interviewees explained how student aid enabled their engagement in academic programs and civic processes. The additional funding expanded options by providing discretional time. Both WSA and GMS students who received aid after choosing their initial college explained how they had more time and opportunities to get involved and study with peers. Students explained with apparent pride that they did not have to work, that they could take internships as learning opportunities instead of for money, and that they had time to participate in study groups.

For many of the WSA students interviewed, the process of integrating into college involved finding ways to interact with faculty and peers. Oscar, a Chinese immigrant, explained that he lived at home when he first entered college, but he chose to move to campus so he would have more time to work with study groups. He also explained that his mentors had helped him figure out his major, and his academic advisors helped him think about possible graduate programs. Another student explained that she had gotten engaged in dorm life and later developed strong social commitments on campus. Several students had initial trouble integrating socially and finding academic programs that fit, but their mentors played a key role in changing that.

The GMS students did not have a similar mentoring support system, but they too found ways to connect socially and academically. Not only was time a factor, but many students interviewed in race-based groups spoke about the difficulty of integrating into a White campus culture. Finding students who were like them was important for most students, although some socialized mostly with Whites when there were few people of their own race in their college courses. Group identity played a role in the academic integration process as well, with several students commenting on the importance of ethnic study groups and campus organizations as safe places to talk about and process their experiences. For example, an African American GMS student explained that she feared someone would come into her room and tell her it had been a mistake and that she did not qualify for UCLA after all. Social integration and involvement were closely related phenomena, as students expressed a need to overcome fears.

While having money to pay for college made it possible to integrate socially and get involved in activities, it did not ease the difficulty of learning about a new culture. Students had academic difficulties, changed majors and colleges, and struggled to find the social and academic environment that worked for them. While engagement in campus activities helped with this process, it created complex relations within extended families as students made cultural transitions.

Underlying Social Forces. Largely overlooked in the literature on social integration and student engagement, two areas of research that are closely related to notions of involvement, is the role of the social transition from interdependence in families to engagement in college that changes the student's role in the family. Most of the students interviewed were from families that expected them to play a role in keeping the families together: Some worked to support siblings; many would not take financial support from their families if they could afford not to; and most expressed commitments to their families that continued as they transitioned into college life. These family roles are not only an artifact of tight cultures, but are also related to the reality in low-income households that it takes the family to support the family; everyone is expected to play a role.

Nussbaum (1999, 2000, 2004) advocates a human capabilities standard: Women should have sufficient education to support their families. This standard suggests that the minimum education for *all* students should be sufficient for them to be able to support their families (St. John, 2006, 2009b). However, most of the students interviewed were from home situations that did not meet such a standard of education and living. It took everyone in their family to earn enough to support the family as a unit. The nature of this tightly engaged process of collaborative family support was related to family culture and ethnicity; specific patterns varied, but financial need was a major factor. Hispanic students in particular spoke of the importance of their leadership role in their families, their obligations to siblings and relatives, and the ways these commitments complicated decisions to leave home for college or to choose jobs or graduate programs that would keep them away from their communities. African Americans tended to frame the problem relative to their mothers' financial needs.

This pullback to home and community was a form of social connectivity valued by students. They did not want to give up this sense of belonging when they became college students, so they found ways to keep this connectivity as a part of their life during college. The complication was that their families and communities often did not have a history of collegiate education, so they had to explain themselves in new ways to build an understanding of their lives and learning away from home. Sometimes when they visited home, their neighbors and relatives would express the pride their parents felt about their having made it, important indicators of academic success conveyed through social networks. This process of bringing the college story back to the community seems a critical element of creating a commitment to cross-generation educational uplift in communities with little prior experience in classical collegiate environments, changing family and community narratives to indicate that "people like us" belong in college. Communication about engagement in college life can contribute to creating a cultural capital of uplift, a process that seemed evident in some of the stories told by students (chapters 6 and 7).

Of course, not all students had grown up in supportive families. A few WSA students had lived in foster homes, had lost parents, or had unsupportive parents. There were stories of the struggle to grow up without strong family support, while at the same time recalling early memories that emphasized education. Missy recalled that her father had encouraged her to read before he died, a memory that seemed to be motivating to her over time. Sky Warrior explained that he loved to read from a young age, he was the first in his family to read, and his parents laughed when he said he wanted to go to college. Like the other students in the focus groups and interviews, these students found ways to integrate socially and academically. For students with weak family ties, the social connectivity of college took on great importance. Students spoke of new friends as the family they never had.

Academic Success

In the early 21st century, policy makers have placed a great deal of emphasis on improving rates of high school graduation and attainment of college degrees. While gains in attainment represent an appropriate policy objective, balancing the private gains of attainment with social responsibility for giving back is also important. The academic success of students was related to capital formation from prior experiences and was enabled by financial aid (linkage 6, Figure 1.2) and academic and student support programs that aligned with students' interests and abilities (linkage 8).

Attaining Degrees. Comprehensive reforms can improve degree attainment through expanding enrollment opportunity and equalizing persistence opportunity. If a program improves the rate of enrollment by x percent and the students influenced by the program persist and attain degrees at the same rate as other students, then degree attainment is also improved by x percent, raising more people up into the college-educated population.

For TFCS and WSA, gains in degree attainment have not been confirmed by causal studies, but there was evidence (chapter 7) of improved persistence as well as higher rates of enrollment in 4-year colleges. Students whose entry was marginal in the first place needed support to persist at the same rate as similarly prepared students who entered college with multigenerational knowledge of college and family capacity to fund their study; at least this appears to be the case. The pressures on low-income students to become wage earners are greater because they do not have the implicit family guarantee of support.

Merit programs such as GMS have less influence on initial enrollment in 4-year colleges than do programs based on financial need. GMS applicants were first screened based on academic ability. Students who made it through the academic screen and were not selected for the program did not always attend colleges with high prestige, but most had the capacity to do so and did enroll in 4-year colleges (chapter 5). GMS students and comparison students persisted at a slightly higher rate than comparison students, but the impact was not confirmed in DesJardins and McCall's regression discontinuity study (2009). There were also differences in the types of colleges they attended and their experiences in college. Gates Millennium Scholars graduate with greater cultural capital (ability to support uplift in their own families) and greater social capital (ability to outreach and network to support others pursuing social goals, including cross-generation uplift). GMS students are also more likely to go on to graduate school, a claim confirmed by DesJardins and McCall (2009).

From the social perspective, first-generation students face cultural transitions that are more complex than assumed in theory and research focused on traditional college students. Traditional students from middle-class families usually have a history of college or a family culture that supports preparation, college search, and college going. First-generation college students from low-income families must build this capital, breaking through barriers to access created by family traditions of moving from education to work. Support services provided by colleges and intervention programs like WSA and GMS also enable the formation of this capacity to support cross-generation uplift.

Finding Careers.   First-generation college students enter college with limited images of college and career pathways. Very often medicine, law, science, and engineering are emphasized because they are among the best known and most respected professions. The stories that unfolded among GMS and WSA students is that they navigated through majors to pursue their original professional goals, often transitioning to new majors and professional goals based on college experiences. Some students spoke of trouble with math courses as the barrier to achieving their original goals. Others stuck to their goals, but found better majors to fit their goals; for example, to become a lawyer. In the process of navigating through educational choices in college, their understanding of the multiple processes necessary for success broadened.

The GMS program emphasizes science, math, engineering, computer and library science, public health, and education by providing graduate scholarships for these fields. The program may attract applicants with interests in these fields, but funding only has a modest effect on undergraduate choice of major. Prior quantitative research on undergraduate major choice indicated that the interventions increased the odds undergraduates would choose majors in education compared to one of the nonprofit fields, but did not influence other choices. The interviews examined in this volume indicated that the program had some influence on plans for graduate education (chapter 7). Some students who had other fields of interest expressed disappointment that their fields were not funded, while a few students indicated they chose graduate fields because of the funding. In combination, these findings provide moderate support for arguments that scholarships can influence major and graduate program choices.

Social Giveback.   Social responsibility also played a role in the choice of majors and careers among WSA, TFCS, and GMS students. Monica, John, and Sky Warrior were examples of WSA students who were on trajectories toward careers in public service. Monica had been a student body president so it was not a surprise she ended up choosing political science as a major and was headed toward law school. John was moving to teaching and possibly local politics, a trajectory that seemed related to his reflections on the WSA program. Sky Warrior had entered college interested in engineering, but ended up a social activist. Whether or not these trajectories would have been different had they not received the aid is not known, but reading their cases suggests that their commitment to give back was related to their experience in the program, a sentiment echoed in many of the GMS and WSA interviews.

Many students were introspective about their career choices, reflecting on how to reconcile their career interests with social responsibility and family commitment. As students in a Hispanic group discussed the tension between family expectations and personal career interests, one participant explained how his career choice was seen: "Because I'm from a lower-income background and most of my family isn't educated, they don't understand the decisions I am making at this point at all."

A compelling question is: Will the thousands of graduates enabled by TFCS, GMS, and WSA be able to contribute to the next generation of uplift? Of course, this is an unanswered question and will remain so for decades. But the evidence from interviews was that many WSA and GMS students reflected on the scholarship funding as a gift that was life altering, giving them a sense of responsibility to the next generation. This commitment to giving back is a critical part of the American culture that, for generations, somehow got lost.

RECONSTRUCTING ACF

With this background on the ACF process, we can return to the core constructs of ACF as originally hypothesized to examine whether and how they were altered by the evidence from the studies. While the preceding summary examined ACF as a sequential process relevant to policy, the analysis below examines the social processes as cross-cutting social mechanisms that enable or inhibit ACF and develops a new set of understandings that can inform and guide future research.

- The first hypothesis was: For low-income families in most states, the costs of public 4-year colleges place them out of reach without institutional, state, and federal aid. Awareness of financial constraints represents an informed position.

The first hypothesis was a policy-oriented and state-situated proposition. Our assumption was that the dramatic differences across states would be a determining factor relative to easing concerns about costs. The qualitative studies provided evidence from students engaged in two programs that gave aid guarantees during high school (TFCS and WSA) compared to national focus groups with students who received their aid guarantees after high school (GMS). In retrospect, this assumption was overly simplistic. It was evident from the qualitative studies that:

1. *Concerns about cost were integral to the social construction of schooling for the low-income students.* The social understandings of college—and of preparation for college—held by students and parents in these studies were constructed within a reality that colleges were not affordable without guaranteed aid. Concerns about costs were not just related to college choice, but instead part of family knowledge that carried across the ACF processes. Parents and students had to persevere through educational and social systems with an understanding they were at risk of not being able to pay for college even if they prepared and borrowed. These concerns pervaded the social systems of families, communities, work, schools, and colleges.

2. *Easing concerns about costs by providing aid guarantees enhanced the social dimension of academic capital formation across the sequence.* There was also evidence that providing aid guarantees eases these concerns in ways that enable academic capital to form. The trustworthy nature of the aid guarantees enabled students and families to engage in learning differently—finding out about how high school curriculum relates to college admission and postgraduate opportunities—than would have been possible without the guarantee and the funding. The trustworthiness of the guarantees coupled with support enabled students and parents to alter their trajectories and transform their understandings of college affordability.

This helps illustrate the social aspect of economic class. For nearly 30 years there has been inadequate student financial aid relative to college costs. In fact, there was only a brief period of about 8 years (1972–1980) when there was adequate need-based aid to equalize opportunity (St. John, 2003). Contemporary students and their parents have grown up and become adults during a period of history in which there have been and continue to be substantial and real financial barriers to college.

It is doubtful a temporary increase in funding for student aid—such as the increase in Pell grants in President Obama's stimulus package—will alter ACF among low-income families. To the extent the increases in college costs do not offset the increased grant aid, such a stimulus could improve enrollment rates among students who apply anyway and improve persistence rates for those who are enrolled. However, a more stable commitment or "guarantee" is needed to alter ACF. Even the proposal to shift funding from loan subsidies to grant aid may not be sustained over time because of the politics of decisions on student aid (Baum & McPherson, 2009).

- The second hypothesis was: Family networks situated in schools and work settings provide limited exposure to college learning environments; parents and children may have high aspirations but low expectations.

There was abundant evidence from the interviews with WSA and TFCS students and the TFCS parents that families acquired knowledge about college in part from within their families, a finding that reinforces conclusions reached by others (Hossler et al.,

1999; McDonough, 1997). The findings about parent engagement from both the quantitative and qualitative studies indicate that parent engagement plays an important role in transforming aspirations into a reality beyond predisposed expectations. Based on the studies, we can reach three additional understandings:

1. Families, schools, and social networks can either reinforce (support) or undermine (pullback) college aspirations, depending on the perceptions of college affordability. Throughout their educational process, low-income students must deal with networks that can reinforce or undermine college-going. Many students must contend with family pullback to the home and community as they navigate their pathways through college. Such pullback forces were related to care and support in the family and community and merit value as such. These complex social forces defy overly simplistic remedies to the college access challenge.

2. Parental engagement in learning networks that support college going alters the trajectory of college preparation. The insights gained about parent engagement in the networks provided by the TFCS program represent a new insight not previously evident in the literature. Both the multivariate studies and interviews with parents demonstrated that active parent engagement in the supplemental network of support provided by the program made a difference in preparation. In multivariate studies, parental engagement was shown to create opportunities to learn about college, enabled children to enroll in a preparatory curriculum, and increased the odds of enrollment in a 4-year college (St. John, Fisher, et al., 2008). These quantitative findings were supported by strong evidence from interviews that a family narrative about college was generated from parent engagement in support services.

3. During college, support networks can enable students to navigate a course toward academic success while sometimes maintaining family ties could undermine this process. It was evident that supplemental support services enhanced engaged learning during college: WSA students found mentors and other support services and necessary guidance for achieving aims in college; GMS students found their network meetings and campus support services helped them navigate through college. These findings show that providing preparation and aid alone are not sufficient to break the access barrier; support services during college are also crucial to academic success.

   • The third hypothesis was: Trust is framed by cross-generation experiences of families within communities. Depending on context, there may be school and community support for uplift.

Trust proved an important concept. Our approach involved speculating about trustworthiness from a broad range of interview topics related to trust, since trust per se was not a topic for interviews. Two understandings emerged:

1. *A bond of trust between parents and support personnel enabled preparation and eased difficult transitions to college.* One of the most compelling findings from the qualitative study of TFCS parents was the strong bonds that developed between parents and staff in the regional centers (Enersen, Servaty-Seib, Pistilli, & Koch,

2008). This was in contrast to the WSA schools, where parental engagement was less evident. Further inquiry into parental engagement is definitely merited as part of studies of college access and other aspects of academic capital formation.

2. *Students who successfully navigated their pathways into college frequently built new networks of trust during college.* There was a great deal of evidence that students sought networks of trust; people with whom they could identify and bond. Many WSA students spoke of the importance of finding trustworthy people for information about educational options. The GMS students described many ways in which trusted relationships developed during college enabled them to steer a course through college. There was evidence that culture and ethnicity played a role in the formation of trust, a topic that merits further exploration and study including group comparisons.

- The fourth hypothesis was: Information from family and friends may be viewed as more trustworthy than information from educators. Trustworthy and accessible information on opportunities can raise expectations; new information technologies provide a potential basis for building trust and accessing information that informs educational choices.

The roles of information and trust were intertwined in these studies. In fact, the value of information transmitted outside of trusted relationships may be questionable given the study findings. Two key understanding were evident:

1. Supportive adults outside the family played a key role in overcoming doubt about the trustworthiness of information about college options. From an examination of evidence across the chapters, it is clear that information providers—from networks outside of schools, teachers in schools, and support personnel and faculty in colleges—played critical roles in navigating pathways into and through college, consistent with prior qualitative studies of 4-year college students (Levin & Nidiffer, 1996; Stanton-Salazar, 1997). Student comments about information that mattered were almost exclusively made in relation to people providing the information, rather than printed information about college, college costs, or other official information.

2. Information on college majors was gained through early experiences during college. The integrated concept of college choice and finding an educational fit, a pattern abundantly evident in the studies, alters our understanding of college majors. Before college, many of these students had limited trustworthy information on major options and chose majors based on people and events in their experience. Once students got to college, they could filter through additional information sources to make informed choices about college majors and transfer. In most instances, when information was discussed as something that mattered, usually some form of human interaction was involved. Students were not making rational choices about majors based on expected earnings per se, but rather they: (a) filtered through observed experiences when developing a major choice before college; and (b) processed information based on inner experiences and reactions to critical situations when making major choices in college.

- The fifth hypothesis was: First-generation families lack the knowledge of college that can be passed along across generations; most visible signs of education are embedded in local patterns of success among people who are familiar (e.g., doctors, lawyers, teachers).

This initial hypothesis about cultural capital was not only confirmed, but the mechanism of trustworthy information seems to explain these observed phenomena, as noted above. This hypothesis was based on a narrow conception of college knowledge, which was somewhat limiting given the richness of the evidence. A couple of understandings emerged to extend this narrow conception:

1. In many low-income, first-generation college families, both limited knowledge of college and family expectations other than college can constrain student academic success even when financial constraints are minimized. The understanding of aspirations that emerged from the qualitative analyses was different from the original supposition that there would be a gap between achievement and expectations. The starting proposition was informed by research indicating high postsecondary aspirations among many low-income and minority students (Carter, 1999; St. John, 1991). However, interviews with WSA students indicated that many students who made it to college had received messages to consider alternatives other than college. In addition, the qualitative study of TFCS students and parents found a reconstruction of understanding within families (Enersen et al., 2008). When these parents signed up for TFCS, they were seizing an opportunity, one that interviews revealed they did not think their children would otherwise have had. It was apparent that participation in the precollege services could alter expectations, but we should keep in mind that a relatively small number of eligible students actually signed up for the program for the cohorts studied.

2. College knowledge of the family can be enhanced and transformed through parental engagement in precollege programs and student sharing of their college experiences with their families. It was also evident that family knowledge of college could be enhanced. Both mechanisms above were evident: engagement by parents in precollege services altered family knowledge as did students sharing their college experiences with families and networks. This second mechanism appeared to influence younger siblings, relatives, and community members to consider college. This social giveback was an important force for many of the students.

- The sixth of the original hypotheses was: The routines of families, including attitudes toward education and work expressed in daily actions, are conveyed and reinforced as part of family life. Some students develop the capacity to navigate educational and social systems.

This initial statement was merely a restatement of the ideas of habitus, adapted from Bourdieu (1990), along with an idea linking to the concept of self-navigation as a process related to the noncognitive variables. These concepts held up very well in depicting the two mechanisms of a pattern of reinforcement. In addition, we explored concepts of uplift through the analytic chapters. It is clear there were differences across families in patterns of supporting reproduction of social class as well as patterns of supporting uplift. Three understandings emerge relative to these mechanisms:

1. Patterns of both class maintenance and cross-generation uplift are evident within families of low-income, first-generation college students. Not only were the two patterns—maintenance of class (e.g., family ethos of "school to work") and of cross-generation uplift (i.e., support of navigation through obstacles to education)—evident among the students and families studied, but they could be evident within the same families. For example, in the parent interviews people spoke of encouraging their students to find jobs as a cultural value independent from income for college. In addition, many of the GMS students were from families with a tradition of all family members sharing responsibility to support the family. When these students left their families to go to college, they did not abdicate this responsibility. Many students in WSA and GMS worked to send money home, made efforts to provide money to less fortunate siblings, and played other family roles that exhibited taking responsibility. These patterns of family interdependency not only complicate college going but defy the logic of student aid programs that assume parents give to children but do not assume students give back to families.[7]

2. Low-income students from families without college who make it to college exhibit personal navigation skills that enable individual uplift. The noncognitive variables used in GMS and WSA appeared to select students with strong skills of self-navigation, self-understanding, and resiliency skills. These inner strengths were vital to success in college, as the theory in this area posits (e.g., Sedlacek, 2004). These personal patterns, or habits, of individual students are not only important in their academic success, but relate to their social responsibility within their families. The skill set that motivates students to care for and give back to their families also enables them to network in college, find support structures, and interpret experiences in ways that result in informed choices about academic majors.

3. As students communicate their self-understanding within their families, they describe differences in patterns in ways that reconcile uplift within the family narratives. Through the process of self-navigation into and through college, the GMS and WSA students found ways to reconcile their own uplift with the values of their families. Specifically, supporting siblings was closely linked to personal values and an ability to come to terms with their privilege in relation to the less fortunate circumstances of their family. This does not mean that family problems were solved by students' success. Rather, students' success became part of the lore of the families, caused changes in family narratives, and caused changes in the families' cultural capital.

Finally, it is crucial to recognize that the members of the three populations studied were all exceptional students because they took steps to make it educationally in the face of odds to the contrary. The contention made throughout this book of care within families was based on earlier research (St. John, Griffith, & Allen-Haynes, 1997) and was reinforced in many different ways. However, the context in which students navigated was complex and often troublesome because even many of these exceptional, strong, and resilient young people had to transcend difficult barriers and overcome problematic circumstances.

CONCLUSIONS

This chapter has summarized the findings from part I as part of a theory rebuilding process that can provide a foundation for future research that has implications for public policy. The findings demonstrate that social processes are integral to educational decisions and collegiate learning. Students with strong navigation skills and prior college knowledge have advantages in college. It is crucial that educators and policy makers consider how their interventions enable students to build their social skills and form academic capital as part of the educational process.

The transition to strategies of college finance that emphasized tuition and loans over public subsidies altered the public ethos of higher education. This policy shift was rationalized based on arguments that individuals benefit economically from education so they should pay for it. Whether or not one accepts this rationale as valid, the change from public funding to student and family funding transforms the tax burden and also transforms society from one committed to cross-generation uplift to one that values individual earnings. What is most compelling about the studies of students who received aid guarantees is that a commitment to social giveback became an outcome. For nearly a century, there was progress in educational attainment in the United States. Yet the inequality in opportunity has developed and persisted over the past 3 decades has come at a high cost to society.

Clearly, academic capital builds as a consequence of investing in college students, including family learning about higher education and careers. The work-loan burden for the typical low-income college student has become excessive, undermining some of the crucial aspects of higher education. Even if students can manage these costs, their experience of college is altered if they have to work excessively: They end up with fewer opportunities to engage academically and socially during college, which slows the process of building academic capital, an accumulation of personal and social knowledge that incorporates a commitment to cross-generation uplift in families (as a form of cultural capital) and to social giveback through networks and caring for children within communities (as a form of social capital). Diverse opportunities to actively engage in the social and academic environments are offered by America's high-quality, 4-year colleges; the development of academic capital can be impaired if students do not have the time to take advantage of the opportunities.

The consequences of failure to invest in people are social inequality and community disintegration. The resistance to taxation in the United States since the early 1980s is only prima facie evidence of a deeper problem. There is a huge economic and cultural shift underway in the United States and globally. Advanced education, to the level of at least some collegiate education if not a 4-year degree, is now considered a requisite for quality employment and the ability to support a family. When adults do not have this level of attainment, it can become necessary for both parents and older children to work to support the family. It is extremely difficult for children in these working families to break out of their commitments and leave home to go to college.

The alternative—choosing low-cost colleges close to home so individuals can work as they gradually consume education as they can afford it—can undermine uplift. People who have navigated a course to collegiate education in this model often lack the knowledge and skills necessary to change the family narrative. Many of the TFCS, WSA, and GMS students—along with the comparison students studied—come from such families. The extra funding, along with the support services that enabled preparation and persistence, brought more than marginal increases in the number of students attaining degrees due both to improved enrollment and persistence. It also contributed to academic capital as a force that can break the new poverty cycle of attaining just some education, enough for employment but not enough to support a family in a way that insures low-income children will grow up with equal odds of attaining an advanced education.

For the system to change, the decision to create a more just and caring system of education must take place at multiple levels—in federal and state governments, in schools and colleges, and in the hearts of people. It requires new forms of human action along with policies and programs that support uplift. The Twenty-first Century Scholars, Washington State Achievers, and Gates Millennium Scholars Programs demonstrate that such transformations are possible, but that they occur within systems that are not always supportive of uplift. The final chapter considers how policy, as the formulation of decisions and the will to act, might be changed in schools, colleges, states, and at the federal level to achieve a greater emphasis on academic capital formation as an enabling force in economic and social change.

9

INFORMING PUBLIC POLICY

It is time to change the trajectory of public policy on education. Since the early 1980s, federal policy has emphasized outcomes without considering their effects on students from families without college knowledge (Advisory Committee on Student Financial Assistance, 2002, 2008; Fitzgerald, 2004; St. John, 1994, 2003, 2006a). The educational reform movement of the 1980s shifted the focus of federal policy from trying to equalize inputs (e.g., equalizing opportunities) to promoting improvement in outputs, including test scores (Finn, 1990). The current policy trajectory has remained on track for 3 decades, emphasizing tightly linked standards, curriculum, and testing within linked accountability schemes, as epitomized by No Child Left Behind (2001). In K-12 education, problems with high school dropout rates and urban schools are illustrative of the ways that the proponents of this strategy have misconstrued the problems with education. The human side of the educational system has been overlooked and low-income families have been seriously impacted (Mirón & St. John, 2003). Focusing educational policy on academic capital formation along with cognitive outcomes can bring balance back by emphasizing processes along with both inputs and outputs. Policy should focus on the whole system—the human aspect along with the systemic components—to bring balance to the system and the way it is experienced by those most in need of opportunity.

This chapter considers the ways that policy at the federal, state, and institutional (school/university) levels can be reformed to place an emphasis on academic capital formation by adapting systemic improvement strategies to place more emphasis on the human dimension of reform. We consider how ACF can inform the reconstruction of the logic of education reforms. We identify program features of policy initiatives that should be emphasized in systemic reforms and provide guidance for the development of comprehensive and cohesive reform strategies, based on the lessons learned from the three comprehensive reforms studied in this book—Washington State Achievers (WSA), Gates Millennium Scholars (GMS), and Twenty-first Century Scholars (TFCS).

RECONSTRUCTING THE LOGIC OF REFORM

Since publication of *A Nation at Risk* (U.S. Department of Education, 1983) educational reforms have been developed under the assumption that the system was in trouble. Yet, nearly 3 decades of reform have resulted in a lower percentage of students graduating from high school and unimproved rates of college graduation (Bowen & McPherson, 2009). Part of the problem is that strategies that focus on tinkering with practice but ignore the funding needed to accompany reform have not worked. This shift was explicit in the administration of President Reagan. Leaders in the Department of Education argued for focusing on scores as outputs of education rather than the money as inputs, an argument Chester Finn, Jr., (1990) summarized in "The Biggest Reform of All." Subsequent presidents followed this trajectory, even Clinton, because of limited federal tax dollars.

The new emphasis on spending in the American Recovery and Reinvestment Act of 2009 (ARRA) alters the funding part of the puzzle, at least temporarily, but the logic of the policy trajectory that started in the early 1980s remains largely unaltered. The persistent idea is that a scientific approach based on examining what worked in the past can guide the future through the replication of successful programs to change the system. The problem is that after 3 decades of policy using this logic, the reform model itself has become the logic of the federal and state systems of education. Increasingly, arguments have extended this logic to state and federal policy in higher education (e.g. Conklin & Curran, 2005; U.S. Department of Education, 2006). The emergence of academic capital formation (ACF) as a new conception of the ways policies link to uplift of formerly underrepresented groups provides an opportunity to reconsider this dominant reform logic.

Finding a Just Approach

John Rawls's theory of justice (1971, 2001) has stood up well over time as an underlying logic for progressive reforms in education. Rawls's theory focuses on three principles: a *distribution principle* emphasizing fair treatment of all with respect to basic rights; a *difference principle* which maintains that if social and economic inequalities exist, solutions should be targeted at the least advantaged; and the *just savings principle* which emphasizes the use of public funding for cross-generation uplift (Fisher, 2007; St. John, 2006a). It is important to reconsider how the understanding of ACF might inform ongoing reconstruction of the three principles.

Martha Nussbaum (1999, 2000, 2004) developed a compelling argument about the reconstruction of basic rights to education. She argues that women need education to a level that enables them to support their families as a basic right. There have been dramatic shifts in the international economy and the standards of education needed to support a family (Commission on the Skills of the American Workforce, 2007). This new logic of education for the workforce is parallel to arguments for raising the basic educational standard for all to 2 years of college (Hoffman, Vargas, Venezia, & Miller, 2007). If we accept this new standard as a level of education for men and women to be able to support their families, even in homes with two earners, then both high school graduation and academic success through at least 2 years of college are crucial. Yet, huge gaps remain in achieving this aim in the United States as a new basic standard and a right for all.

There has been a persistent acceptance of social inequality (Alejandro, 1998) based upon the limitations of justice in practice. The tolerance for inequality in access to education, health care, and social services has been a serious problem, especially during the past 3 decades of regress (St. John, 2009b). Raising the standard to education for all through 2 years of college provides an opportunity to focus on education for groups that historically have been underrepresented. The theory of ACF provides a basis for thinking through the current policy trajectory of education accountability informed by a new science of education.

The insights about ACF, as summarized in the previous chapter, provide a lens for reframing logic from consideration of whether to extend the right to education to how to reform it. The logic used in arguments to raise standards has focused on the historic correlation between high school courses and colleges. The studies of students and parents in high schools and colleges (part I) provide evidence that raising standards alone does not address the core issue. There is clearly a need to rethink social connectivity in both high schools and colleges.

Raising the standards has influenced a cultural change within families of underrepresented students during the high school years. For more than a century, high schools provided a gateway to working-class jobs. In the middle of the 20th century, the working class became part of the middle class in the United States, a population that was able to maintain cross-generation status by going from high school to work. The stories of students and parents in chapters 3 and 4 illustrate that comprehensive interventions created opportunities for families to reconstruct their logic, forming new cultural capital as college knowledge in families. The human connections created through support from regional service providers in TFCS and by teachers and mentors in WSA provided new, trustworthy information that enabled students and parents to advocate for advanced courses and navigate their ways through them, getting necessary academic support (e.g., help with homework and counseling) along the way. Thus, at least through the period of transforming high schools from being conduits to work to becoming preparatory for a new type of workforce and college access, the social aspects of school reform will remain crucial. The Indiana case illustrates that in 20 years some progress can be made (St. John & Musoba, 2011). It could take another 50 years to substantially improve the percentage of students graduating from high school and entering college.

John Rawls's third principle is the just savings principle, which refers to cross-generation uplift (1971, 2001). Critics of Rawls on the political right have argued for market-oriented systems in education, including vouchers (e.g., Walzer, 1983). The market is abundantly evident in education, especially in higher education. The rising tuition and increased use of loans create additional barriers to college. A key challenge is to encourage and support ACF within underrepresented families with prospective first-generation college students. In particular, the market condition means it is important for policy makers to consider both the financial and social aspects of easing concern about college costs as integral aspects of ACF during high school and college. Below we consider the underlying ideological questions related to altering the trajectory of education reform.

Political Ideologies in the New Global Period

Perhaps the biggest complexity in moving from the ideal of policy to the practicality of it is that political ideologies have substantial influence on political decisions, including decisions about the use of research (Parsons, 2004). The shift to a neoliberal social policy parallels the development of the new trajectory in education, originating internationally with the elections and leadership of Margret Thatcher in Britain and Ronald Reagan in the United States (Harvey, 2005). This ideology values individual rights over social good, providing a new logic used to rationalize cutting back on government funding of social welfare, a pattern evident across developed countries (Huber & Stephens, 2001). In higher education, the trend internationally has been toward increased use of loans and accountability (Henry, Lingard, Rizvi, & Taylor, 2001). This has been accompanied by increased privatization of public colleges, as evident in rising tuition and declining government support for education of students in public colleges (Fisher, 2007; Rizvi, 2004; St. John, Kim, & Yang, in press).

The substantial federal investment in education resulting from ARRA only appears to be slowing this trend, possibly just for the 2 years that funds go to states to support education. In most states, returning state funding of institutions to the 2006 level would result in a real tuition increase if spending on aid remained constant. At the other extreme, California is experiencing dramatic cuts in funding for college coupled with substantial tuition increases (St. John & Moronski, 2010). The trajectory toward privatization seems part of a larger global pattern. It is simply easier for governments to expand access to higher education by increased tuition than by increased taxation and funding, an approach recommended by the World Bank for more than a decade (Gilpin, 2001).

The election of the new progressive majority in Congress in 2008 did not substantially alter the overall trajectory in public finance or in education. The new egalitarian goals of expanding college access and attainment of 2 years of college must be constructed within the new economic reality. Public 2-year colleges cost substantially less for governments and students than 4-year colleges (Voorhees, 2001). Within the U.S. educational system, opportunities for access are increasingly attainable for 2-year colleges, but access to 4-year colleges is more elusive due in large part to cost (Advisory Committee, 2004; St. John, 2006a). Within this context, access takes on complex contextualized meanings in families with potential first-generation students.

The family construction of college knowledge is difficult but possible, as is abundantly evident in chapters 3 and 4. It took professionals reaching out—regional service providers, teachers, and mentors—to communicate the trustworthiness of information about opportunities to attend 4-year colleges. However, without a visible and dependable financial guarantee that their children will be able to pay for 4-year colleges if they qualify, most low-income families will probably continue to have limited expectations, even if they have high hopes. Controlling for preparation, low-income students in the high school class of 1992 who had enrolled in college were more likely to still be enrolled 6 years later than to have dropped out, but were not more likely to have attained degrees than to have dropped out (St. John, 2006a).

ACF Informing Policy Development

The central question is: Can knowledge of academic capital formation inform the development of public policies that make it possible for more low-income students to prepare for and attain 4-year degrees? This is the real threshold of equal access. Whether or not students start 2- or 4-year colleges, the opportunity to attain a 4-year degree is implicit in the new educational standard (e.g., algebra II and other advanced courses). Will raising this standard increase fairness in access to 4-year colleges, or will low-income, college-prepared students still have unequal opportunity?

The conceptualization of ACF helps build an understanding of the depth of the policy problem. Preparing more students for college is not merely a matter of raising graduation requirements or even providing aid. Families must understand, through trustworthy sources, that the implied promise of opportunity is real and achievable. Otherwise, inequalities will be reproduced over and over across generations. The shift to higher costs for attending public 4-year colleges does not have to preclude opportunity for prepared low-income students to enroll and persist. It is a complex problem, but it can be solved.

TRANSFORMING THE TRAJECTORY OF EDUCATION REFORM

The components of a systemic approach to promoting access include high school reforms, coordinated financial aid and guarantees, encouragement of students in middle and high schools, fair measures of preparedness, and college support services. These components were identified in the revised model of academic capital formation (Figure 1.2). The question addressed in this section is: How can the trajectory of education reform be transformed to enable more students and families to build the academic capital needed to enhance their odds of academic success? We explore the ways that each of these systemic strategies can be rethought relative to the roles they play in academic capital formation.

High School Reforms

A great deal of attention has been given to standards for high school graduation, but these reform efforts too seldom consider the social processes in schools that are needed to support teachers and students engaged in realizing the intent of these changes. There is a difference between changing requirements and changing the culture of schools. If the culture is ignored, it is more likely that the aims of reforms will continue to be elusive for too many schools and students.

Contrast the findings on the two comprehensive reforms for precollege support, TFCS and WSA. In Indiana, the state required all high schools to offer college preparatory curriculum, yet TFCS students frequently reported they had to advocate for access to these courses. However, both parents and students reported that support from TFCS service personnel, along with the opportunity to visit campuses, helped them figure out what they needed for college. In contrast, WSA students indicated that teachers reached out to them, inviting them to apply for the program. For both programs, students who participated acquired more advanced courses (and in TFCS they were more likely to have a college-preparatory diploma).

From the perspective of academic capital formation, both the aid guarantee and the human support were crucial. In fact, once students signed up for TFCS, the extent of student and parent involvement in services became positive predictors of college preparation and enrollment. In WSA, the key finding was that caring, supportive behavior by teachers and support personnel, in addition to higher standards, were essential to building student and parent knowledge of the way the system worked. This type of knowledge is prevalent among families with a history of college attainment, but not within families that lack this history.

It is essential that the process of building academic capital begin as early as possible.

Successful early reading reforms often include programs that send books home and encourage parents to read with their children, an approach that works especially well in schools serving low-income students (St. John, Loescher, & Bardzell, 2003). Reforms that integrate parental involvement in reading reduce failure rates and improve test scores. There is no less need to build academic capital in families as students' progress through school. In fact, as the studies in chapters 4 and 5 documented, parental engagement in learning about the curriculum required for college, where their children can get support with homework, and what the college living environment would be like contributed to their children's academic success (i.e., completing advanced courses in high school and enrolling in 4-year colleges).

It is incumbent on universities and other groups that collaborate on high school reforms to try out new approaches to encourage parental engagement. The WSA high schools illustrated how involved and committed teachers influenced students to build college navigation skills through challenging courses, mentoring, and recommendations for scholarships. The WSA intervention combined grants to schools for reform along with scholarship aid for students. This, of course, improved access to advanced high school courses for all students, not just those who received scholarships. There is evidence that increasing requirements is associated with improved opportunities for underrepresented minorities to enroll in public 4-year colleges (Daun-Barnett, 2008; St. John, Pineda, & Moronski, 2009), and academic reforms without financial reforms made a difference for some students. However, it is necessary to solve the financial aspect of the access challenges for the education reforms now underway to have their intended effect.

Coordinated Financial Aid and Guarantees

Providing guarantees of aid seem to have been critical to the early success of the TFCS and WSA programs. The WSA students described how the grants made college possible, while the parents and students in the TFCS interviews testified to the liberating impact of these early awards. Placing greater emphasis on need-based grants does not necessarily cost states more money. Prices rose in the 1990s and college enrollment rates climbed, but inequalities persisted, including increasing high school dropout rates and growing disparities in college enrollment across racial/ethnic groups (St. John, Pineda, et al., 2009). These disparities can be reduced by increasing state funding for need-based grants when tuition increases. As a practical matter, this involves increasing state funding for grants by about one-quarter of the tuition increase, which drives tuition up further if states have to redistribute funding from colleges to students to achieve this balance. The balance, however, is crucial. If citizens vote against taxes, there are still good reasons for states to distribute funding in ways that equalize opportunity. It is an economically prudent approach; when more students can go to college and attain degrees, there will be more taxpaying citizens in the future.

Guarantees of financial aid not only enable preparation for college, they also make it possible to navigate a course through college choice as an extended process which might include transfer. For all three programs, the aid guarantees were viewed as trustworthy, enabling students to make college choices that were in their own interest. If they found their initial choice of college did not fit them—academically or socially—they could navigate to other campuses with the assurance that their aid would follow them.

Encouragement of Students in Middle and High School through Outreach

The external support services for students in middle and high school and in college were an important part of the success of these programs. In fact, the definition of comprehensive interventions used in this book has been programs that provide both student aid *and* support services. The TFCS program provided support services from middle school through high school, giving families time to build college knowledge and use it. For most of the WSA students interviewed, the information about the award came too late to have as much impact on preparation, but had a very substantial impact on college choice. In case studies and focus groups, WSA students frequently recalled the roles that teachers played in their gaining access to the program and the role program advisors played in supporting them through the process.

When support is provided early, by middle school, it helps build family knowledge, creating new narratives that influence cultural capital in families. For high school students, engagement services provide social networks and trustworthy information that build social capital which, in turn, enables college choice. In both programs, the aid guarantees were treated as trustworthy information by students and their parents. If students and parents receive information on college, but they know from experience that college is not affordable for people in their circumstance, the information is less likely to be heeded.

In addition, many colleges and universities have begun to provide outreach services to local high schools as means of expanding opportunities for underrepresented students (e.g., Oakes, 2003). At the University of Michigan and universities in other states affected by the ban on Affirmative Action, outreach has become a means of expanding the pipeline. It is also a socially responsible approach, if it is coupled with research on high school reform. Universities have an important role to play in improving high school curriculum alignment with college admissions. This can be achieved by coordination with high school reforms, as noted in the revised model of academic capital formation (Figure 1.2). Federal agencies and foundations may provide support for these reform initiatives if they are research-based.

Public colleges should become more engaged in actively promoting math education as a career path for high-achieving students. A closer collaboration between high schools and public universities can enable an increased focus on teacher education for urban schools. It is essential that a greater emphasis be placed on this policy goal in states such as the Great Lakes states,[1] where African Americans are concentrated in cities and underrepresented in 4-year colleges. It is incumbent on universities located in regions with great disparities in access to engage in collaborative reforms if they are to maintain the robust dialogues now considered necessary for the education of all students.

Fair Measures of Academic Preparedness

From the perspective of colleges, universities, and state agencies that play coordinating roles in higher education, regulation of admissions standards is a crucial issue, especially during this period of transition from reliance on affirmative action. The issues of selection for student aid and college admissions are important from the perspective of academic capital formation in low-income families. Students who attend schools that do not have the most advanced courses are at a disadvantage on college entrance exams. There are two generic types of solutions to the problem that can be coordinated in cohesive ways: the adjustment of cognitive measures to take into account unequal opportunity to prepare; and the use of noncognitive measures as part of the selection process for students who do not meet the cognitive criteria.

The first issue is to modify the use of merit measures to improve fairness for students who do not have access to advanced courses in their high school. It is possible to adjust test scores and other measures of merit based on high school context. The simplest way to do this is to use high school rank as, for example, in the Top 10% plan in Texas and the Top 20% plan in Florida. SAT scores can also be adjusted for school context, yielding more diversity and students equally capable of college success (St. John, Hu, Simmons, & Musoba, 2001; St. John, Simmons, & Musoba, 2000). Score adjustments based on high school courses completed can be made based on inequalities among high schools: There is a strong relationship between high school courses and test scores. Table 9.1 summarizes the point score differentials attributable to course variations, as estimated for national and Indiana databases on SAT takers. These analyses controlled for background, school characteristics, and high school grades to examine the point differentials attributable to specific courses. Completing calculus adds about 100 points to the total score (109 points in the national population and 96 points in Indiana) compared to completing algebra II or less, while trigonometry added slightly more than 50 points. Most other advanced courses examined also improved test scores. These advanced courses are not available in many of the nation's high schools. For example, Michigan only recently required all high schools to offer algebra II. Point differentials can be used to adjust scores for the sake of fairness in the admissions process.

Second, as the analyses in part I demonstrate, it is possible to select highly resilient, self-navigating students using noncognitive variables. The variables and their definitions are listed in Table 9.2. In GMS, these criteria were applied after an academic screen; for

Table 9.1 Average Predicted Point Differentials on SATs Associated with Taking Advanced High School Courses in Indiana and the U.S., Controlling for Background and Achievement Variables

Courses	Comparison	SAT Differential Controlling for Background	
		U.S.	IN
Pre-calculus/Trigonometry	Algebra II or less	55	54
Calculus	Algebra II or less	109	96
Physics	No physics	25	26
1 Honors history	No honors history	32	30
2+ Honors history	No honors history	42	36
Honors English	No honors English	38	40
Literature/Historical period	No historical lit.	32	29
4+ yrs of foreign/Classical language	1-3 yrs. Study	38	20
No foreign/Classical language	1-3 yrs. Study	-61	-59
No response on language	1-3 yrs. Study	31	12
Latin	No Latin	31	8
No response on Latin	No Latin	4	NS
R^2 for full model		0.53	0.41

Source: St. John & Musoba, 2010

Table 9.2 Description of Noncognitive Variables Used in Selection for WSA and GMS

Variable #	Variable Name
1	Positive Self-Concept • Demonstrates confidence, strength of character, determination, and independence.
2	Realistic Self-Appraisal • Recognizes and accepts any strengths and deficiencies, especially academic, and works hard at self-development. Recognizes need to broaden his/her individuality.
3	Understands and Knows How to Handle Racism (the System) • Exhibits a realistic view of the system based upon personal experience of racism. Committed to improving the existing system. Takes an assertive approach to dealing with existing wrongs, but is not hostile to society, nor is a "cop-out." Able to handle racist system.
4	Prefers Long-Range to Short-Term or Immediate Needs • Able to respond to deferred gratification; plans ahead and sets goals.
5	Availability of Strong Support Person • Seeks and takes advantage of a strong support network or has someone to turn to in a crisis for encouragement.
6	Successful Leadership Experience • Demonstrates strong leadership in any area of his/her background (e.g., church, sports, non-educational groups, gang leader, etc.).
7	Demonstrated Community Service • Participates and is involved in his/her community.
8	Knowledge Acquired in or about a Field • Acquires knowledge in sustained and/or culturally related ways in any field.

Source: Adapted from Sedlacek, 2004

WSA, the criteria were applied without an academic screen. The evidence illustrates that this approach works for selecting talented students with strong chances of academic success. The method appears to select students with the habitual patterns that lead to academic success. Using these measures or others that evaluate social navigation skills can add fairness to selection.

College Support Services

Student academic and social engagement—their involvement in academic programs, student organizations, and civic organizations—are undoubtedly important parts of the college experience. Ironically, while there is an extensive literature on college students and persistence (Braxton, 2000; Pascarella & Terenzini, 2005), surprisingly few studies examine the impact of interventions on this outcome (Braxton, McKinney, & Reynolds, 2006; Patton, Morelon, Whitehead, & Hossler, 2006). Learning communities and other interventions aimed at improving retention merit study (Musoba, 2006). In addition, the studies in part I suggest it is important for campuses to consider how their student aid programs, student services, and academic support services influence involvement and achievement by low-income and first-generation college students.

GUIDANCE FOR DESIGN OF POLICY REMEDIES

This concluding section considers ways of refining and modifying policies and programs to enable academic capital formation (ACF). The focus of K-16 policy on promoting access and academic success is appropriate, but should be broadened to include an emphasis on ACF, focusing on the social processes that make educational attainment possible. It is time for policy to emphasize cross-generation uplift in families that lack access to the knowledge and skills necessary to enable children to prepare for and enroll in 4-year colleges. Our assumption is that research can inform policy if there is alignment of the research process with the policy decision process.

We make this assumption with an understanding that the policy research literature on higher education makes it very clear that the social aspects of policymaking, including the politics of lobbying, have greater influence than rational research (Hearn, 1993; Parsons, 2004). The history of education reform in past decades illustrates this reality: Policies pushing standards and accountability have prevailed in spite of evidence these policies are associated with increased dropout (St. John, 2006a). Given the tendency for social process to influence policy, it is important to rethink the ways policy researchers can work with policymakers to use research in strategic ways. The alternative is to use an inquiry-based approach with state and administrative data systems as a basis for informing policy development (e.g., St. John & Wilkerson, 2006). This approach appears to be viable (St. John & Musoba, 2011), but it does not solve the greater problem of irrationality and overemphasis on advocacy within policy decisions in government and on campuses.

Federal Policy

K-12 reform emphasizes tight alignment of standards, curriculum, and tests, but leaves little time or resources for schools to promote uplift as an integral part of the reform process. U.S. high schools are in the midst of a massive structural transformation from being comprehensive high schools with multiple pathways, to schools that emphasize academic preparation for a 4-year college. The absolute failure to even consider the human side of the transformation—the fact that teachers suddenly have new jobs and parents find their children in schools that are unlike the ones they attended—is not even considered as part of the policy process. The correlation between courses completed and college success—the historical artifact of comprehensive high schools that provided preparatory courses to only some students—has been used to rationalize a new set of requirements. The research has overlooked the structural aspects of the finding—that, in fact, structural features of schools explained the findings—resulting in serious statistical errors in multivariate models that took a methodological step beyond correlation (Becker, 2004; Fitzgerald, 2004; Heller, 2004; Lee, 2004).

The decision to transform high schools may have been appropriate, but the failure to consider the human side of the structural transformation was astounding. For a half-century, the limitations of experimental methods have been well-documented (McGregor, 1960). Yet, the education reforms of the last 3 decades have repeated over and over again the error of scientific management. Reformers assumed that experiments could be transported with the same effect as the original, ignoring the human process of learning and adaptation. This glaring oversight has demoralized a generation of teachers and stimulated increases in dropout (St. John, 2006a). This is not an argument against improving high schools; rather, it is recognition of the necessity of integrating an emphasis on human learning and adaptation into the reform process.

The human side of the transformation of high schools starts with recognition of the state's role in education. In the U.S. system, states have constitutional authority over education and provide a major source of funding, but local agencies (school boards, charter boards, etc.) have organizational control over schools. Government-mandated reforms are hegemonic and repressive in that the government has financial levers but lacks organizational control or means of authentic human interaction in the delivery of services. The challenge is to encourage, enable, and promote learning and adaptation within schools, school districts, and charter organizations, and among teachers. Further, administrators and teachers face the challenge of learning with parents and students about the best ways to adapt their local systems to reduce dropout and improve preparation. There are at least three different challenges facing community-based learning systems undergoing the transformation from being comprehensive with diverse educational pathways to being flexible with an advanced curriculum that reduces dropout while improving preparation:

- *Advanced Knowledge and Skills in Literacy*: Students need to develop the ability to communicate (read and write) at a level demanded by college and work environments. These skills are, of course, essential for completing high school, especially when high schools focus on preparation for college.
- *Advanced Knowledge and Skills in Math*: Reform advocates consistently argue that middle school children require algebra and that high school students require geometry, algebra II, and other advanced courses (trigonometry, precalculus, and calculus). Unfortunately, the historic methods used to teach these subjects have resulted in the failure of the majority while documenting the success of the few. New, more engaging methods are needed along with rigor in key math concepts (Moses & Cobb, 2001).
- *Family Engagement in Building College Knowledge*: For at least a generation or more it will probably be necessary to develop approaches that engage families in learning about preparation and college. Parents who lack college experience and who were not prepared for college lack the skills to help their children with homework, the knowledge of college necessary to encourage application, and the resources to pay for a 4-year college if their children find a way to prepare and apply.

These are local challenges because educational systems are organizations that serve the needs of the community, including businesses and government agencies that employ graduates of schools and colleges. Requiring a new set of math courses or mailing home information about federal aid programs will not solve these problems. Suburban communities represent an American success story with respect to the organization of schools on a large scale that provide collegiate preparation. But these communities are made up of predominantly middle-income families with high aspirations for their children. As the studies in part I illustrate, schools in low-income communities too often are unable to provide access to advanced courses (St. John, 2006a). It is important that federal education programs encourage collaborations between universities and schools to solve problems locally and provide incentives for states to balance need-based grants with other public finance strategies, both of which are outlined below.

Projects Promoting Local Reforms. There should be a major federal program to support collaborations between universities and high school districts to build the underlying social process of academic capital formation using locally constructed strategies. The process should encourage adaptive learning, focusing on sustainable projects to promote advanced literacy, advanced math, and family engagement. An action inquiry approach to this challenge is depicted in Figure 9.1.

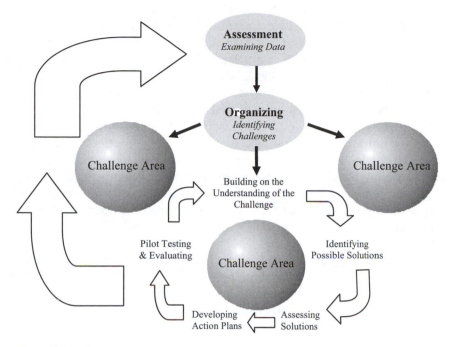

Figure 9.1 Action inquiry model.

Project teams comprised of educators at both levels can collaborate on addressing challenges:

- They can build a locally situated understanding of the challenge, including an assessment of parent information needs, the knowledge and skills of teachers, and student skills and learning styles.
- They can look internally and externally for possible solutions, including approaches that have already been tried locally, the experience of university faculty and staff, and reviews of projects that have been successful elsewhere. This builds an understanding of what might work locally and who could be involved.
- They can realistically assess alternatives, including the development of a plan for funding. Initial grants could be made for planning, but final grants could be based on coherence and viability of options.
- They can develop realistic action plans to pilot-test solutions, including whether the schools and colleges have the skills and will commit the necessary resources, along with evaluation plans that demonstrate how the project met or did not meet the locally defined aim (e.g., related to improved graduation rates, engagement in learning, and so forth).
- They can pilot-test the project for a defined period of time (say, 3 to 5 years) and require both the school and the college to develop plans for evaluating and integrating the project, if successful, into their operating budget. Transition grants could be given to districts and universities dedicated to taking the next step.

An inquiry-based approach differs fundamentally from the assumptions of education science and normal practice. Education science assumes that exemplary practices identified through "experiments" can be replicated and will achieve similar results. Using this model, once reforms cross the threshold of being labeled "successful" or "best" the prescriptive implementation of the practice implicitly treats teachers like factory workers and children like widgets. The tendency of professionals is to adapt practices based on their own professional expertise, a pattern that demonstrates more maturity than strictly following rules (St. John, 2009a, 2009b).

Yet, there can also be a problem with normal practice, including widespread adaptation of reforms thought to be best or successful. Educators, like other professionals, tend to adapt parts of a model to fit local circumstance. Over time, the model changes substantially. An emphasis on integrating inquiry into local practices—using assessment research to identify local challenges, design programs to address challenges, and evaluation to test whether the intervention worked and how it might be improved—provides an alternative. The project-based approach provides a way for government involvement in reform to engage education professionals and focuses on their development as an integral part of the reform process.

Coordinated Public Finance. Currently, federal student aid programs are disjointed, incoherent, and underfunded. Coordination requires a few simple criteria be met: (1) the combined state and federal maximum grant award should equal the average public tuition charge for low-income students; (2) the federal government and states should share the burden, with a basic federal grant and a state need-based grant; and (3) the federal government should fund one-third of the state grant if the state coordinates the maximum award with public tuition. Loans could still be used to supplement costs to supplement grants.

This approach would raise the total cost of federal grants, but it would cost less than many of the current proposals, including proposals to fully fund Pell grants, the current major federal program (http://www.collegeboard.com/press/releases/20790.html). Our argument is that we can economize on the federal cost of student aid through the use of expanded grants and targeting the lowest-income students for both state and federal grants. Given current income levels, if Pell grants were increased to the total amount necessary to ensure that low-income students have access to public 4-year colleges, a substantial amount of money would also go to middle-income families who already have financial access because of state grants, federal grants, subsidized loans, and parental contributions. In contrast, low-income students in most states cannot afford to attend 4-year colleges even after federal grants, state grants, and subsidized loans. By targeting both state grants and Pell grants on the neediest students, the distribution of grants would have an equalizing impact, much as it did in the 1970s. In addition, the requirement that states coordinate their public finance strategies with college costs makes it possible for states to provide authentic guarantees of meeting costs for the lowest-income students, which is the threshold set in the Twenty-first Century Scholars Program.

State Policy and Coordination

States have the opportunity to coordinate K-12 and higher education policy and finance, as well as to develop cohesive programs like the Twenty-first Century Scholars that enable more students to prepare for and enroll in college. Based on the review of the three comprehensive reforms in this book, it is possible to suggest strategies that states can use to promote preparation, access to 4-year colleges, and academic success for low-income students formerly denied these opportunities. Our argument is that state reforms should be both:

- *Comprehensive*: Provide the range of financial and support services that enable more students to prepare for, gain access to, and be successful in public 4-year colleges, either as direct transitions after high school or as part of an extended college choice process; and
- *Cohesive*: Include sound linkages within comprehensive reforms that ensure different components work together to provide pathways to success and enable the coordination of financial strategies in ways that will control public costs.

Guidance for the development of comprehensive and cohesive state programs and policies that are coordinated with public finance strategies are outlined in Table 9.3. The components of a comprehensive reform, from high school reform through encouragement and outreach, are illustrated by the TFCS program. Another comprehensive

Table 9.3 Guidance for the Development of Comprehensive and Cohesive State Policies, Programs, and Financing to Insure Equal Access to and Opportunities for Academic Success

Features	Comprehensive	Cohesive
School Reform	• Align graduation requirement with college entry standards. • Require all high schools to offer a college preparatory curriculum and provide necessary funding. • Take steps to promote teacher education in math and science.	• Aid guarantees for low-income students who graduate from high school prepared for college. • Build collaborative approaches to school reform, possibly through state grant programs. • Build approaches to assessment that include targeted noncognitive measures of engaged learning along with achievement indicators.
Guarantees and Aid	• Provide a guarantee to lowest-income students that grants will equal public college tuition charges.	• Establish budget processes that coordinate subsidies to public colleges with tuition charges and fund need-based grants to fulfill commitments for grant guarantees.
Encouragement/ Outreach	• Use state and federal funds to provide a comprehensive state-wide network that supports students and parents as they learn about college.	• Provide information to networks about high school requirements. • Coordinate supplemental support services with school districts to ensure a safety net for families
Selection	• Encourage colleges to coordinate selection to ensure alignment of preparation, achievement, and adjustment factors. • Explore use of noncognitive measures of achievement linked to specific content areas.	• Engage collegiate and high school educators in the development of content-related noncognitive indicators of success (e.g., math engagement). • Encourage coordinated polling to identify strivers (using noncognitive and merit-aware measure).

(continued)

Table 9.3 Continued

Features	Comprehensive	Cohesive
Academic Support	• Develop targeted programs to provide supplemental support services in college aligned with student preparation. • Build alignment into the budget process through state appropriations to colleges or project grant competitions. • Develop academic support programs that enable students to select and design majors that fit their learning needs and career aims.	• Encourage public colleges to develop student 'contracts' that identify components of success for colleges and students based on an assessment of interests, achievement, and engagement skills on entry. • Facilitate deep alignment of indicators for school success, college admissions and program support for admitted students. • Encourage a social networking approach to learning including service learning that enables students to develop skills in civic engagement.
Student Support	• Encourage colleges to provide coaches and peer mentors for students facing difficult transitions. • Provide community networking and mentoring services, engaging college students in providing support to high school students.	• Align student support services with academic programs that promote academic achievement and civic engagement as criteria for eligibility for state guaranteed aid programs.
Communication	• States officials should emphasize methods used to ensure financial access as part of the annual evaluation process, communications with the press, and dissemination of information to low-income households.	• It is crucial to coordinate public messages about mainlining state commitments to aid guarantees, even in the midst of public debates about college costs and public tuition charges.

approach to reform that combines aid guarantees, enlightened selection processes, and support services for college students was illustrated by the Washington State Achievers. The GMS program clearly illustrates the importance of easing concerns about college costs through guaranteed grants. However, none of these programs individually provides both a comprehensive and cohesive framework that states can replicate to ensure educational opportunity for prepared low-income students.

All three of the comprehensive reforms have strengths, but lack features critical in a comprehensive approach: TFCS was exceptional as a program that encouraged families, eased concerns about costs, and enabled students to prepare for and enroll in 4-year colleges, public and private, but it was not well coordinated with the high school reform process in the state and did not provide support services during college. WSA provided a model of how to coordinate caring high school reform with the support of students through the college access and success process, but the aid guarantees were not provided to all students with financial need. The GMS program illuminated the importance of meeting financial need as a means of enabling academic capital formation for high-achieving low-income students, but it is very expensive.

The human side of reform, including the capacity to create reforms that are trustworthy and supportive of student and family learning, require that the components of reform be cohesive as well as comprehensive. To be trustworthy for low-income families, the parts of a program need to work together to remove barriers to access. For example, the encouragement provided to students and parents by TFCS personnel was trustworthy, in part because high schools were required to offer advanced courses and, after looking into the realities of college costs and student aid, parents found they really could afford to pay for college in state. What was less evident was whether there would be human support—networks of caring peers, professors, and coaches—in the college of choice, which were features of WSA.

Underlying the concept of cohesiveness is the challenge of building social support in high schools and colleges that enable academic capital formation. Our arguments are that states must: (1) pay greater attention to the development of noncognitive measures of social development; and (2) investigate and invest in methods that build academic capital (i.e., the social skills of engaged learning) in high school and college. Balancing the aims of promoting social development as evidenced by noncognitive indicators of academic capital formation could provide a means of enabling more students to break through the access barriers and be successful in college. Sedlacek's noncognitive measures (2004) are a starting point to building state strategies, as illustrated by WSA and GMS, but a transformation of logic and application is needed: Rather than treating the noncognitive measures as sorting criteria, these measures should provide the basis for developing goals for educational systems at both the K-12 and undergraduate levels.

Universities

Public universities are situated at the intersection of policies and practices that can reinforce access barriers to higher education for low-income students. If colleges use traditional selection methods within state systems that advantage some groups of students (i.e., middle-income, suburban, White) over others (i.e., low-income, urban, and minority), then higher education reinforces the discriminatory features of a state's K-12 education system. It is too easy to blame K-12 education and continue with current practices under the assumption they are fair. This elitist position has made it exceedingly easy for public universities to abdicate their responsibility to maintain fair and equitable access for all children in a state.

In states with K-12 systems that are unequal, it is simply unjust for a state university to ignore these underlying inequalities without reinforcing social inequality. Universities in the states of California, Washington, Texas, and Michigan have made efforts to address the underlying problems in systemic ways. These universities were essentially obligated to take action when they could no longer use Affirmative Action as a partial remedy to inequality. Various models of outreach to high schools and financial aid are being tested and merit further study.

Based on experience using action research to support and inform initiatives in colleges and universities that promote equity in college opportunity (St. John 2009a, 2009b; St. John & Wilkerson, 2006), it is possible to provide guidance to college administrators and faculty interested in promoting systemic change. Change in universities evolves from strategic initiatives and, therefore, it is crucial they have a commitment to remedying inequalities. The fact that inequalities in K-12 systems render conventional academic strategy ineffective in promoting equity is not well understood by many college faculty members. It is often argued that all students must meet the same standards. But if the standards are unfair as a result of systemic inequalities, it is necessary to rethink this practice and to consider balancing what John Rawls (1971) calls "the difference principle," which permits inequalities if they benefit the disadvantaged (i.e., the least advantaged should have the first opportunity) with these conventional arguments.

As noted in Table 9.4, building an institutional commitment to equity that also promotes academic excellence requires a deep restructuring. It may not be possible to implement new approaches to partnerships with schools, ease concerns about costs, and revise admissions and support services unless institutions that are unwilling to rethink the meaning of having a public mission in a 21st century global society. For those that are planning to restructure, the University of Michigan may one day provide a model for systemic reform. Certainly, maintaining opposition all the way to the Supreme Court in the 2002 *Gratz* and *Grutter* cases has had an influence on the ethos of the university, evidenced by creation of the National Center for Institutional Diversity (www.ncid.umich.edu) following these Supreme Court cases and, more recently, the creation of the Center for Educational Outreach (http://www.ceo.umich.edu/index.html). However, while such organizational entities may illustrate structural commitment to change, making change happen through partnerships with schools, student aid, admissions, and so forth requires a concerted effort over years. It remains a question whether even the University of Michigan can transform in all of these ways.

A more recent, excellent national example of a comprehensive approach to providing aid guarantees is the exemplary University of North Carolina's Carolina Covenant® (see http://www.unc.edu/carolinacovenant/ and http://www.unc.edu/chan/chancellors/moeser_james/). This program ensures low-income students (with family income indexed to the federal poverty level) will have grants enabling them to pay for UNC if they are admitted. The UNC model includes features of the three comprehensive models described earlier in the book:

- A guarantee of aid for low-income students (from in-state or out-of-state);
- Outreach and support services including affiliated counselors in North Carolina High Schools;
- Summer bridge programs that provide academic support;
- Counselors and peer advisors to support student transition;
- Work opportunities on campus that further support academic and social engagement.

As this illustrates, it is possible for a public university campus to make a transition that moves it toward becoming more equitable in its approach to the recruitment, funding, and support of underrepresented students. Further, the evaluation report on the Carolina Covenant (Ort & Williford, personal communication, 2009) documented that the intervention reduced the gap in degree completion for low-income students compared to students with less need in a study that compared cohorts and controlled for eligibility (see also St. John & Musoba, 2011). The aid commitment made by UNC has been widely replicated, but most of the more than 90 universities[2] adopting this aid policy have not adopted the connected support services our research indicates are so vital.

It can be argued that UNC followed an inquiry cycle in developing and refining their design. Shirley Ort, Associate Provost for Student Financial Assistance, worked closely with a team of administrators to design the program and consult with experts nationally. In spite of all the favorable press, UNC has continued to adapt and evolve the support services in the program, trying new approaches as "pilot tests" and adapting them to maximize results. In addition, UNC has funded a formal external evaluation of the

Table 9.4 Guidance for the Development of Comprehensive and Cohesive Programs and Financing to Insure Equal Access to and Opportunities for Academic Success in Public Universities

Features	Comprehensive	Cohesive
School Reform	• Build partnerships with high-need high schools that support teachers, students and parents in the preparation and college search processes.	• Coordinate high school partnerships with student aid guarantees, outreach and selection to ease family concerns about costs and encourage preparation.
Guarantees and Aid	• Communicate criteria for award of need-based aid and packaging strategies to prospective students. • Commit to meeting financial needs, if possible, for all students.	• Link commitment to supplemental student aid award grants to programs that align with support services. • Coordinate commitments to grant aid with pricing through annual budgeting process.
Encouragement/ Outreach	• Provide consistent, high quality and trustworthy information on aid packages and grants. • Market programs that build bridges to admission and provide comprehensive support once admitted.	• Build strong partnering organizations to provide academic support for students and teachers. • Design and develop support for parents (linked to high school partnerships and outreach services).
Selection	• Adapt selection process for fairness in cognitive and noncognitive measures. • Coordinate use of refined selection measures with support services within major academic programs.	• Promote success indicators—the qualities emphasized in noncognitive measures—as part of the marketing strategy. • Build reliable articulation strategies with high schools and junior colleges to ensure diverse pathways.
Academic Support	• Acknowledge tacit contract on admission, indicating the services accessible to students to ensure their success. • Target program support—cognitive, noncognitive, and financial—to the individual and group needs.	• Integrate opportunities for service learning, engagement in outreach programs, and high school partnerships providing opportunities for give back. • Encourage development of students and professionals.
Student Support	• Provide coaches and peer mentors for students facing difficult transitions, especially first-generation students.	• Align student support services with programs that promote academic achievement and civic engagement.
Communication	• Emphasize development of human networks that support student development. • Use public relations to emphasize community and diversity (if information is authentic).	• Encourage development of mentoring and coaching skills among students, especially upper division and graduate students.

program, which will soon be reported nationally. The process at UNC illustrates how a local innovation can have a substantial national impact on practice even before a formal evaluation has been completed.

Researchers

When developing new reforms at the campus and state level, it is crucial that local planning groups think through how the various program features of the models they adopt and adapt fit together. Just because a program has worked in one locale, it will not necessarily work the same way elsewhere. For example, as mentioned above, over 90 universities have adopted the aid guarantee seen in the Carolina Covenant, but there is no evidence that these adaptations included the Carolina Covenant's academic support. If a program did not include this support, it would be unreasonable to expect this partial replication to have the same effects as the original program. In addition, local conditions vary substantially across high schools, colleges, and states. Even when a full model is adopted, it is possible the program will have a different effect because the context—the students, faculty, and so forth—differs from the original context.

An alternative approach to educational reform at the state and institutional levels requires a new generation of working partnerships between researchers and educational organizations engaged in reform. Current logic emphasizes experiments and replication as a method for reforming education. However, this approach overlooks the adaptive nature of human behavior and professional expertise, especially in colleges and universities (St. John, 2009a). The alternative is to engage researchers as partners within the reform process (Figure 9.2).

In 2005, Lumina Foundation funded the Indiana Project on Academic Success to use a state database to inform reform on public and private campuses across the state of Indiana (St. John & Wilkerson, 2006). Over the 3 years of the project, studies of educational outcomes and various forms of collaborations between researchers and university teams evolved (Hossler, Gross, & Ziskin, 2009). Campus teams used the statewide assessment as a basis for engaging in efforts to initiate new reforms and evaluate and strengthen existing ones. This process illustrates the potential of a collaborative approach to reform

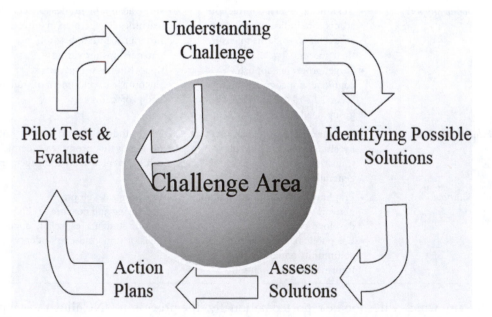

Figure 9.2 Technical support for using AIM to address critical challenges: Change team and technical support. *Source:* St. John, McKinney, & Tuttle, 2006

that focuses on developing new strategies for improving access and retention (St. John, 2009a, 2009b; St. John & Musoba, 2011).

Reflection on Policy and Research

Researchers and policymakers can and should work together to solve the challenges they face. Collaboration on problem solving involves providing research at critical points in the decision-making process. It also requires an altered attitude on the part of policymakers and researchers. Policymakers need to maintain an open mind, to consider alternative arguments in relation to the evidence. It is also important to treat new policies and programs as pilot tests and be willing to make adaptations if results are not what were expected. For researchers, becoming engaged means conducting analyses in timely ways to identify challenges, coconstructing alternatives that might address the challenges, and evaluating the programs, feeding research back into the policy process. If researchers and policymakers are willing to make these changes in attitudes and assumptions about policy and research, it is possible to alter the social processes and use research to inform the trajectory of policy decisions.

CONCLUSIONS

The process of transforming educational systems to value both equal opportunity and academic excellence necessitates a focus on academic capital formation (ACF), which provides a means of viewing academic achievement in relation to social processes that enable new groups to gain access to quality education. Two serious problems face public education: (1) a massive structural transformation of high schools is now underway that changes comprehensive educational systems into college-preparatory systems, the first such national system change of this nature in global history; and (2) families that have a history of transitioning from school to work are faced with a new set of cultural and structural barriers in this new system.

The concept of *breaking through the access barriers* is appropriately conceptualized as a massive system of transformation accompanied by human learning processes that result in human capital formation in families with potential first-generation college students. The many small pieces of policies and programs that comprise the barriers to access have both systemic and human aspects. Efforts to transform the system without giving sufficient attention to methods and means of enabling human culture and social process to evolve rapidly, the method of system change used for the past 3 decades, fail to accommodate social and cultural change. ACF provides a new conceptual lens for viewing this problem. From the industrial age of the late 19th century through the economic boom of the 1960s, educational systems expanded as means of improving social mobility. In the new world of education, there has been a widespread image that all American school children can become college educated or at least prepared for college (e.g. Conklin & Curran, 2005). Arguments for a new American workforce posit that this new educational standard is necessary (Commission on the Skills of the American Workforce, 2007).

By integrating an emphasis on development of social skills through engaged methods of teaching and outreach along with encouraging excellence, a dominant concern at all levels of the public educational system, both schools and colleges can enable more students and families to break through the access barriers by acquiring the knowledge and skills, both academic and social, necessary to support families in this complicated global society. The American emphasis on educational excellence using private markets (e.g., charter schools and vouchers in K-12 education and private loans in higher education), coupled with neglect of the human aspects of systemic reform, has come at a high cost, undermining social equity and helping to destroy the national economy. An alternative to the top-down, accountability-based approach to reform is to integrate more emphasis on human development and learning into the reform process. This is not an argument that existing reforms have the wrong intent; rather, that they took an unbalanced approach that increased inequality.

The three comprehensive reforms—WSA, TFCS, and GMS—provide examples that can be adapted by state education systems and public universities as they seek to integrate an emphasis on social equity into their reform strategies. Given the rapid pace of social economic change evident in the recent past, these reform models merit careful review. States and public universities can adapt features from these reforms. However, we encourage educational reformers at all levels of the educational system to build comprehensive, cohesive, locally based reform strategies that enable low-income families to build college knowledge and advocate for themselves. This requires a humanistic approach rather than an assumption that systemic changes are the only way to solve inequality and promote economic development.

APPENDIX 1

FACTOR ANALYSIS FOR FAMILY ENGAGEMENT IN TWENTY-FIRST CENTURY SCHOLARS PROGRAM

Factor analysis requires the use of continuous variables; therefore, only variables that counted the number of parent and student activities were included in the creation of the factors. Because the support activities could be related to each other conceptually in a variety of combinations, all count variables were entered into an exploratory factor analysis. The exploratory factor analysis yielded four potential factors based on both statistical and conceptual strength; the broader concepts presented by each factor reflect access to social and cultural forms of capital. The next step, confirmatory factor analysis for each potential factor, indicated that each factor stood on its own. For a list of each factor, the variables contributing to it, and the factor loadings, see Table 3.3; the Cronbach's alpha serves as a measure of reliability. The numeric score, which can range from 0 to 1, represents "the mean of the correlations between all of the different possible splits of the scale into two halves" (Cohen, Cohen, West, & Aiken, 2002, p. 129). Each factor was divided into whether or not a student or parent participated in that factor, creating four dichotomous variables.

The factor analyses of involvement in student engagement activities found four factors related to the frequency of student engagement activities between eighth grade (in 2000) and spring of their senior year for students in the 2004 cohort (Table A1.1). The factors were:

- *Student Engagement in Counseling Services.* Frequency of involvement in career advising, academic advising, personal counseling, and other counseling services provided by regional centers (converged with a Cronbach's Alpha of .623).
- *Parental Involvement in Academic Preparation.* Frequencies for activities related to asking the right questions, high school curriculum (Core 40/Honors), SAT/ACT Workshops, and Study Skills workshops (converged with a Cronbach's Alpha of .925).
- *Parental Involvement with Events and Visits.* Parental involvement with campus visits, general events, project specific events, and ISTEP workshops (the state exit exam) (converged into a factor with a Cronbach's Alpha of .623).[1]

Table A1.1 Factor Analysis of Engagement in Outreach Activities between 2000 and 2004 for Twenty-first Century Scholars and Their Parents, Cohort Eligible for College in Fall 2004

Counseling (Student)	Cronbach's Alpha (reliability) = .623	
Variables in Factor	**Factor Loading**	**Factor Score**
Count of Career Advising (Student)	0.837	0.376
Count of Academic Advising (Student)	0.823	0.370
Count of Personal Counseling (Student)	0.778	0.350
Count of Other Counseling (Student)	0.489	0.220
Academic Preparation (Parent)	**Cronbach's Alpha (reliability) = .925**	
Variables in Factor	**Factor Loading**	**Factor Score**
Count of Right Questions Workshops (Parent)	0.932	0.284
Count of Core 40/Academic Honors Workshops (Parent)	0.912	0.278
Count of SAT/ACT Workshops (Parent)	0.910	0.277
Count of Study Skills/Time Management Workshops (Parent)	0.869	0.265
Events and Visits (Parent)	**Cronbach's Alpha (reliability) = .623**	
Variables in Factor	**Factor Loading**	**Factor Score**
Count of College Visits (Parent)	0.810	0.340
Count of General Events (Parent)	0.693	0.291
Count of Project Specific Events (Parent)	0.680	0.285
Count of Cultural Events (Parent)	0.628	0.263
Count of ISTEP Workshops (Parent)	0.625	0.262
Career Planning (Parent)	**Cronbach's Alpha (reliability) = .756**	
Variables in Factor	**Factor Loading**	**Factor Score**
Count of Study Skills Workshops (Parent)	0.846	0.404
Count of Career Workshops (Parent)	0.843	0.402
Count of College Prep Workshops (Parent)	0.818	0.391

- *Parental Involvement in Planning Activities.* Frequency of parental involvement in study skills workshops, career workshops, and college preparation workshops (converged with a Cronbach's Alpha of .756).

These factors provide indicators *of patterns of engagement by students and their parents* that hold together conceptually. The only student activities that converged were related to counseling: Students using these services had a perceived need for counseling they did not receive through the school or home, and they followed through on acquiring these services through their regional centers. Other student engagement activities did not converge into a factor. On the other hand, several parental activities converged. The academic preparation for parents factor represents parental engagement in activities that inform them about the expectations for their students relative to college preparation. Parent activities related to preparation indicate active parental involvement in building an understanding of college, a form of family academic capital. Finally, the parent activities related to planning for college (e.g., attending workshops) are also logically aligned.

APPENDIX 2

PREPARATION BY TWENTY-FIRST CENTURY SCHOLARS IN THE CLASS OF 2004

The multinomial logistic regression for academic preparation compared students who had completed the two types of preparatory curricula (Core 40 or Honors) to students with regular diplomas or with no indicator of diploma type. Indiana's Student Information System database was used, so it was possible to control for the effects of student background and school context. The descriptive data for variables in these models are presented in Table A2.1. A sequence of four logistic regression models was used (Table A2.2):

- Model 1 examines the association between taking the Scholars pledge (comparing Scholars to non-Scholars) and the high school curriculum completed.
- Model 2 adds gender (comparing males to females) and race (with Hispanics, Asian Americans, African Americans, and Native Americans compared to Whites/others).
- Model 3 adds income (with lowest income quartile compared to higher income groups).
- Model 4 adds engagement variables.

FINDINGS

Taking the Scholars pledge was positively associated with completion of college preparatory diplomas, both Core 40 and Honors, compared to regular diplomas in Models 1, 2, and 3 but not Model 4 which added engagement. This finding strongly indicates that it is the extent of engagement in scholar support services rather than opting into the program per se that empowers students to complete preparatory courses. While becoming a Scholar gives both students and their parents' opportunities to secure more support services and build the academic capital for college, not all students take advantage of these services.

Males were more likely than females to complete the Honors diploma than the regular diploma, but males and females did not significantly differ in completion of Core 40.

245

Table A2.1   2004 Cohort Descriptive Statistics Comparing Enrolled Scholars to Pell Recipients (N=8002)

		Pell Recipient			Twenty-first Century Scholar		
		Count	Col %	Sig.	Count	Col%	Sig.
Gender	Female ©	3569	58.59		1160	60.70	
	Male and unknown	2522	41.41		751	39.30	
Race/ Ethnicity	Native American	20	0.33		11	0.58	***
	Asian/Pacific Islander	93	1.53		28	1.47	
	African American	947	15.55		417	21.82	***
	Hispanic	229	3.76		106	5.55	***
	White ©	4675	76.75	***	1314	68.76	
	Missing ©	127	2.09	***	35	1.83	
Income Quartiles	Low Income	3602	59.14	***	974	50.97	
	Lower-Middle Income ©	2224	36.51	***	660	34.54	
	Upper-Middle Income ©	202	3.32		176	9.21	***
	High Income ©	22	0.36		47	2.46	***
	No reported income (did not apply for financial aid) ©	41	0.67		54	2.81	***
Engagement Support Site	Bloomington or Unknown Center ©	-	-		169	8.84	
	Regional Center	-	-		1701	89.01	
	No Center: Scholar did not Participate in Activities ©	-	-		41	2.15	
	No Center: Student is Non-Scholar Pell Recipient ©	6091	100.00		-	-	
Engagement Activities	Scholar did not Participate in Counseling ©	-	-		786	41.13	
	Scholar Participated in Counseling	-	-		1125	58.87	
	Scholar's Parent did not Participate in Academic Preparation ©	-	-		1710	89.48	
	Scholar's Parent Participated in Academic Preparation	-	-		201	10.52	
	Scholar's Parent did not Participate in Visits and Events ©	-	-		1202	62.90	
	Scholar's Parent Participated in Visits and Events	-	-		709	37.10	
	Scholar's Parent did not Participate in Career Planning ©	-	-		1811	94.77	
	Scholar's Parent Participated in Career Planning	-	-		100	5.23	
	No Activity: Non-Scholar Pell Recipient ©	6091	100.00		-	-	

		Pell Recipient			Twenty-first Century Scholar		
		Count	**Col %**	**Sig.**	**Count**	**Col%**	**Sig.**
High School	Regular ©	1947	31.97		595	31.14	
Diploma	Honors	780	12.81		281	14.70	***
Type	Core 40	1759	28.88		652	34.12	***
	N/A, Other, GED ©	1605	26.35	***	383	20.04	
Total	8002	6091	76.12		1911	23.88	

~ p < .1; * p < .05; ** p < .01; *** p < .001

This could be attributable to a difference in access to advanced math and science courses for women compared to men.

Asian Americans were more likely than Whites to complete a Core 40 than a regular diploma, while other minorities (African Americans, Hispanics, and Asian Americans) were less likely. Hispanics were less likely than Whites to attain an Honors diploma. The within-group analysis of the 2000 cohort found that taking the Scholars pledge had a positive association with completion of an Honors diploma and advanced math among African Americans (St. John, Fisher, Lee, Daun-Barnett, & Williams, 2008). This pattern is supported by this analysis: African Americans did not differ significantly from Whites in obtaining an Honors diploma.

Table A2.2 Multinomial Regression Comparing Receipt of Core 40 and Honors Diplomas to Regular Diplomas for the 2004 Cohort of Twenty-first Century Scholars and Other Pell Recipients Enrolled in Public Colleges and Universities

Part I. Honors

	Model 1		Model 2		Model 3		Model 4	
	Odds Ratio	**Sig**	**Odds Ratio**	**Sig**	**Odds Ratio**	**Sig.**	**Odds Ratio**	**Sig**
Scholars Pledge	1.308	**	1.440	***	1.361	***	0.985	
Male			0.935		0.916		0.914	
Native American			0.397		0.409		0.405	
Asian/Pacific Islander			2.540	***	2.590	***	2.580	***
African American			0.213	***	0.240	***	0.242	***
Hispanic			0.311	***	0.305	***	0.309	***
Low Income (<$31,555)					0.513	***	0.513	***
Student Participated in Counseling Activities							1.145	
Parent Participated in Academic Preparation							0.747	
Parent Partcipated in Visits and Events							1.299	~
Parent Participated in Career Planning							1.072	
Regional Center							1.198	

(continued)

Table A2.2 Continued

Part II. Core 40

	Model 1		Model 2		Model 3		Model 4	
	Odds Ratio	Sig	Odds Ratio	Sig	Odds Ratio	Sig	Odds Ratio	Sig
Scholars Pledge	1.346	***	1.372	***	1.309	***	1.005	
Male			1.201	***	1.178	**	1.178	**
Native American			1.240		1.275		1.282	
Asian/Pacific Islander			1.367		1.390		1.395	
African American			0.881	~	0.973		0.960	
Hispanic			0.778	*	0.762	*	0.755	*
Low Income (<$31,555)					0.574	***	0.576	***
Student Participated in Counseling Activities							0.960	
Parent Participated in Academic Preparation							0.942	
Parent Participated in Visits and Events							1.020	
Parent Participated in Career Planning							1.351	
Regional Center							1.355	~
Log Likelihood	-7598.447		-7482.446		-7401.199		-7396.001	
LR Chi-Square	30.14	***	262.14	***	424.64	***	435.03	***
Psuedo R-Square	0.002		0.0172		0.0279		0.0286	

Note: Compared to Regular, N/A, Other, and GED
~ p < .1; * p < .05; ** p < .01; *** p < .001

Engagement in support services has an influence on preparation. Not only does engagement appear to explain the effects of taking the Scholars pledge (this variable ceases to be significant), but the amount of explained variance improves (increase in R^2). In addition, taking advantage of services at a regional center had a slight positive association (.1 alpha) with completion of an Honors diploma compared to completing a regular diploma, and parental engagement in planning events was positively associated (.1 alpha) with completion of Core 40.

In combination, these findings further confirm the relationship between being a Twenty-first Century Scholar and completing an advanced preparatory curriculum, a finding consistent with the studies of the 2000 cohort. This analysis supplements prior findings by illustrating that engagement in support services rather than signing up for the Scholars Program per se seems to be the most critical force behind the gains in preparation.

APPENDIX 3

ANALYSIS OF COLLEGE DESTINATIONS OF GATES MILLENNIUM SCHOLARS AND COMPARISON STUDENTS

The multinomial analysis was conducted to see if, controlling for other factors, the Gates Millenium Scholar (GMS) Program was associated with enrollment in high-selective colleges (Table A3.1). This analysis included variables related to gender, ethnicity, test scores,[1] reasons for choosing a college, and the sample year, and also controlled for these influences when assessing the association between GMS and college choice. Key findings[2] from analyses of all groups were:

- GMS students were more likely to attend high-selective institutions (1.6 odds ratio) than to attend institutions in the midrange of selectivity.
- African Americans, American Indians, and Hispanics were more likely than Asians/Pacific Islanders to attend low-selective colleges than mid-selective institutions.
- American Indians, African Americans, and Hispanics were less likely than Asians/Pacific Islanders to attend high-selective institutions.
- Students with test scores in the lowest quartile (among the sample) were less likely to attend high-selective colleges than mid-selective colleges and were more likely to attend low-selective colleges.
- Students with high test scores were substantially more likely to enroll in high-selective colleges than in midselective colleges.
- Students who chose a college because of low costs were less likely to enroll in high-selective colleges than in mid-selective colleges.
- Students who chose a college because of a strong reputation were substantially more likely to enroll in high-selective colleges (2.1 odds ratio).
- Students whose parents contributed financially to their educations were more likely to enroll in high-selective colleges and less likely to enroll in low-selective colleges.

Table A3.1 Hierarchical Linear Modeling for All Groups on Choice of Institutional Selectivity with the Combined 2000, 2001, and 2002 Freshmen

Variable		Low Selective		High Selective	
		Odds Ratio	Sig.	Odds Ratio	Sig.
Individual Level					
Gates Scholarship	Gates Recipient	.760	*	1.406	***
	Non Gates Recipient				
Gender	Male	.676	*	.993	
	Female				
Ethnicity	African Americans	2.181	**	.752	*
	American Indians	2.601	***	.699	
	Hispanic Americans	1.866	**	.753	*
	Asian/Pacific Islanders				
Father's Education Attainment	Bachelor or Higher	.922		1.373	***
	Other				
SAT-ACT Crosswalk Score Group	Lowest quartile	1.778	***	.535	***
	Highest quartile	.591	*	2.696	***
	Middle quartiles				
Reason select school low expenses	Very important	1.220		.757	**
	Other				
Reason select school strong reputation	Very important	.566	***	1.626	*
	Other				
Parents contributing college finances	Yes	.772	**	1.453	***
	No				
Cohort	2001 Freshmen	1.385	**	.738	
	2002 Freshmen	.963		.772	
	2000 Freshmen				
State-Level (On Level-1 Intercept)					
Per FTE Need-Based Undergraduate State Grant in the Amount of $1,000		.191	**	7.446	*
Per FTE Non-Need-Based Undergraduate State Grant in the Amount of $1,000		1.753		13.279	**
Undergraduate In-State Tuition and Fees for Public Colleges in the Amount of $1,000		.908		2.016	*

Note: *** $p<.001$, ** $p<.01$, * $p<.05$

APPENDIX 4

PROPENSITY SCORE MATCHING COMPARING PELL RECIPIENT TWENTY-FIRST CENTURY SCHOLARS WITH OTHER PELL RECIPIENTS[1]

The population for the possible match included 754 Scholars and 3,970 other students who received Pell grants (Table A4.1). The propensity score matching (PSM) procedure yielded 723 matched Scholars and non-Scholars (Table A4.2). Not only do the percentages comparing matched Scholars and non-Scholars appear to be very close, they are not statistically different from each other based on a logistic regression using participation in the program as the outcome. This lack of significance suggests a good match, since a student had an equal chance of participating in the Twenty-first Century Scholars Program based on these characteristics. In other words, this matching procedure approximates random selection into the program.

The overall model is not significant, as evidenced by the LR Chi-square statistic. However, significance of the model does change when observable control variables are included, as indicated in Table A4.3. Finally, the logistic regression including the selection variables does not alter the findings on differences (Table A4.4). Consistent with the analyses above, among comparable students who received Pell there were no significant differences in degree attainment.

Table A4.1 Comparing Pell Recipient Scholars to Pell Recipient Non-Scholars on Attainment after 6 Years, Prior to Matching Procedure

	Four Year Degree Earned	Two Year Degree Earned	Persist, No Degree	Non-Persister, No Degree	Total
Non-Scholar	1,099	377	457	2,037	**3,970**
Scholar	175	53	103	423	754
Total	**1,274**	**430**	**560**	**2,460**	**4,724**

Table A4.2 Descriptive Statistics Comparing Propensity Score Matched Pell Recipient Scholars to Matched Pell Recipient Non-Scholars,[a] in Percentages

		Scholar (n=723)	Non-Scholar (n=723)
Gender	Female	58.64	57.54
	Male and Unkown ©	41.36	42.46
Ethnicity	African American	22.13	21.72
	White ©	54.36	54.91
	Missing or Prefer Not to Answer	17.84	17.57
	Other Minority	5.67	5.81
Living Situation in 9th Grade	Live with One Parent	35.41	34.99
	Do Not Live with Parent	4.15	3.73
	Live with Two Parents or Unknown Living Situation ©	60.44	61.27
Parent Education Level	Parent(s) Went to College	20.89	19.64
	Parent(s) Did Not Go to College or Unknown ©	79.11	80.36
Main Language Spoken in the Home	Spanish or Another Language	1.38	1.11
	English or Unknown ©	98.62	98.89
Percentage Minority Students in High School	High Percentage	43.15	44.40
	Less than High Percentage ©	56.85	55.60
Percentage of Students in High School Who Receive Free/Reduced Lunch	High Percentage	46.47	46.89
	Less than High Percentage ©	53.53	53.11
9th Grade GPA	Missing/Did Not Answer	7.19	8.02
	Mostly As	6.92	7.05
	Mixed As and Bs and Mostly Bs ©	49.65	49.10
	Mixed Bs and Cs and Mostly Cs	31.12	30.57
	Mixed Cs and Ds or Lower	5.12	5.26
Degree Attainment	Four Year	23.24	25.59
	Two Year	7.05	9.27
	Persist, No Degree	13.69	13.28
	Non-Persister, No Degree	56.02	51.87

a. The match is based on propensity scores using a one-to-one procedure. The number of students in each group may diminish as a result of this method, because the aim is to find the closest match based on specified characteristics, and not all students in the program may match well to those who do not participate in the program.

Table A4.3 Multinomial Logistic Regression of Attainment Comparing Pell Recipient Scholars to Pell Recipient Non-Scholars Using Propensity Score Matching (n=1446)

	Four Year			Two Year			Persist, No Degree		
	Odds Ratio	Std. Err.	Sig	Odds Ratio	Std. Err.	Sig	Odds Ratio	Std. Err.	Sig
Pell Recipient Scholar	0.841	0.108		0.705	0.14		0.955	0.153	

Note: Compared to Non-Persister, No Degree
***p<0.001; **p<0.01; *p<0.05
Log likelihood: -1663.515
LR Chi-square: 4.20
Pseudo R-Square: .00

Table A4.4 Multinomial Logistic Regression of Attainment Comparing Pell Recipient Scholars to Pell Recipient Non-Scholars Using Propensity Score Matching, Including Observable Control Variables (n=1446)

	Four Year			Two Year			Persist, No Degree		
	Odds Ratio	Std. Err.	Sig	Odds Ratio	Std. Err.	Sig	Odds Ratio	Std. Err.	Sig
Female	1.161	0.163		1.407	0.305		1.174	0.201	
African American	1.121	0.241		0.81	0.291		1.03	0.26	
Missing or Prefer Not to Answer	1.244	0.264		0.927	0.313		1.137	0.295	
Other Minority	0.828	0.272		1.806	0.692		3764	0.304	
Live with One Parent	0.894	0.132		1.056	0.234		0.831	0.149	
Do Not Live with Parent	0.754	0.27		0.784	0.436		0.287	0.177	*
Parent(s) Went to College	1.222	0.201		0.771	0.219		1.292	0.254	
Spanish or Another Language	2.691	1.459		0.694	0.755		0.487	0.522	
High Percentage Minority	1.15	0.226		0.68	0.208		1.022	0.243	
High Percentage Free/Reduced Lunch	0.637	0.115	*	0.929	0.252		1.321	0.287	
9th Grade GPA Missing/Did Not Answer	0.861	0.258		1.828	0.79		0.791	0.304	
9th Grade GPA Mostly As	2.683	0.66	***	1.093	0.513		1.635	0.56	
9th Grade GPA Mixed Bs and Cs and Mostly Cs	0.457	0.075	***	0.773	0.183		0.98	0.181	
9th Grade GPA Mixed Cs and Ds or Lower	0.414	0.145	*	0.803	0.37		0.797	0.308	
Pell Recipient Scholar	0.83	1.1		0.705	0.141		0.954	0.154	

Note: Compared to Non-Persister, No Degree
  ***p<0.001; **p<0.01; *p<0.05
  Log likelihood: -1610.303
  LR Chi-square: 110.62***
  Pseudo R-Square: .033

NOTES

CHAPTER 1

1. The concept of academic capital developed and tested in this book differs fundamentally from the better known term *academic capitalism*, which refers to the organizational behaviors of colleges and universities that adapt to economic globalization and private corporate behavior (Slaughter & Leslie, 1997; Slaughter & Rhoades, 2004).

2. Two points about this finding: (a) This departs from and alters critical positions taken previously (St. John, 2003, 2006a) because the data support changes in a conclusion from the 1990s, that raising standards resulted in lower completion rates; but (b) these trends do not prove a causal relationship between graduation requirements and completion of high school diplomas. In fact, empirical models show that college-continuation rates are not associated with graduation requirements (St. John, 2006a). Further analyses are needed. It is important to continue to track these trends and to assess these relationships. If this finding holds, it is indeed good news because the opportunity to prepare for college should be considered a basic right in the United States (St. John, 2006a).

3. The American Recovery and Reinvestment Act did provide some new funding, giving us a new opportunity to examine links between funding and outcomes.

4. Experiments with random assignment of benefits would have been necessary to make causal claims. None of these programs were intended as experiments, but instead their designs were informed by prior research.

5. Berkner and Chavez (1997) originally defined these steps as expectations, academic preparation, test taking, and college application. This narrow framework had serious problems because far more students take entrance exams and apply for college than actually enroll (Becker, 2004; Fitzgerald, 2004; J. B. Lee, 2004).

6. We stated the assumed linkages in the proposal for the book. We received great feedback from one of the reviewers and tightened the logic of these statements before we began to write up the studies in part I. Thus, while we are not testing hypotheses per se, this section illustrates an ongoing process of theory deconstruction, testing, and reconstruction.

7. None of the statistical methods used in this book are classified as causal; therefore, we make no causal claims. However, we do use insights from the qualitative and quantitative analyses to discuss directional relationships, consistent with the limits of the methodologies used.

8. In the TFCS program, all students who were eligible for the federal free and reduced-cost lunch programs could sign up. In WSA, low- and lower-middle-income students could apply, but there was an additional selection process using noncognitive variables.

9. Research evidence relative to TFCS and GMS is discussed in the text: Neither program had significantly different completion rates for funded students who enroll compared to unfunded students who enrolled. GMS had a significant relationship with enrolling in graduate school, an indicator of increased attainment. For WSA, we did not have persistence data for appropriate comparison groups. Both TFCS and

WSA had significant associations with enrollment compared to nonenrollment, so having students complete college at the same rate as less represented, nonfunded students yielded improved attainment.

10. The emergent concept of give back refers to a strong commitment to support the next generation in community and family networks.

11. The concept of cross-generation uplift emerged as central in this study.

12. One of the reviewers noted this problem. We bracketed and reviewed different portions of focus group transcripts related to each topic, but students tended to come back to ideas in recurrent ways. Thus, it was not possible to avoid some recurrence of concepts. In addition, in the case of WSA we wanted to provide readers with the opportunity to trace the cases across outcomes, so noted a few case reminders. In this case, we decided the insights gained through this in-depth approach were worth the risk of repetition.

13. The concept of family literacy is usually constrained to early literacy (St. John, Loescher, & Bardzell, 2003), but this book explores how this concept applies to building critical college literacy within families.

14. We use the term *social processes* as behaviors that can be undertaken as part of conscious tacit action within educational and social systems. We also recognize that patterns may be either tacit or form as part of personal knowledge through social interaction in families.

15. Human capital and social capital theory are basically functional and positive concepts that deny the alternative, which is the possibility of regress. This book uses a "postprogressive" stance that recognizes the possibility of both progress and regress (St. John, 2009b).

16. Social behavior patterns are defined here as replicating habits that exist and can emerge within families and other social systems. These patterns may function at a tacit level of behavior. Through dialogue and intervention, it is possible to raise awareness of these processes within communities. The African American tradition, which includes an emphasis on faith and community, illustrates the patterns noted here.

CHAPTER 2

1. St. John (2007, 2009a, 2009b) describes this "critical-empirical approach" as derived from Habermas's analytic method in building a theory of communicative action (Habermas, 1984, 1987, 1990) and of critiquing the limits of his own theory (Habermas, 2005).

2. The award maximums changed over time. In 2009–2010, the maximums were $4,200 for public 2-year colleges, $6,500 for public 4-year colleges, and $9,500 for independent colleges. This information was provided by Lorraine Solaegui, Director of Research on Education at the College Success Foundation as part of her review.

3. This generic statement of quantitative methods applied to our approach to analyses of all three programs. Since WSA was the only program for which we had data cutting across all of the outcomes examined, it was appropriate to include this statement on methods at this point in the text.

4. Students in the high school classes of 2001 and beyond also agreed to complete a college preparatory curriculum (i.e., a Core 40 Diploma).

5. Other members of the research advisory committee were: William Trent, University of Illinois; William Sedlacek, University of Maryland; Walter Allen, University of California-Los Angeles (UCLA); and Sylvia Hurtado, formerly at the University of Michigan and now at UCLA.

6. As a partial departure from our intent of going back to the original, we worked with St. John's (2003) reconstruction of concern about college costs from human capital theory, a reconstruction that has gone through various forms of testing with both quantitative and qualitative studies, as noted in the text.

7. It is important to recognize that ACE is the major lobbying organization for higher education (Cook, 1998). When ACE publishes and disseminates a report, it is considered official information representing U.S. higher education.

8. Federally subsidized loans pay in-school interest costs, making it possible to have a manageable debt at the end of college. When students must borrow beyond the federal limits for subsidized loans (about $4,000 during the period studied), accrued interest compounds, increasing debt level.

9. While this type of care can be misguided, at least from the frames of most advocates of postsecondary encouragement, those of us who have grown up in families with a history of college should keep our minds open.

10. St. John (2009b) reviews the foundations of the three monotheistic traditions in relation to both their social and developmental dimensions. We carry this rethinking to the context of socially progressive values.

11. At the time this book was written, the Great Recession of 2008 had already lingered into a new decade. As a result, the conditions of financial fear were worse than in previous decades, at least for many downwardly mobile, middle-income families facing employment challenges.

12. Too little is known about the social processes that foster cross-generation uplift. Based on our work, it

would be premature to suggest direct links between policy and changes in social processes that supported ACF.

13. The rules of regression analysis essentially require this assumption, although there are alternatives. For example, it is possible to consider the interaction between encouragement and parent occupation status. But that step merely tests a statistical relationship and does not deal with the inherent moral problem of treating the independent variables as though the values did not differ in a fundamental way for the two groups.

14. As noted, chapter 7 included quantitative analyses of the three programs but qualitative analyses for only the WSA and GMS programs.

CHAPTER 3

1. The factor analyses use data from records of students who took the Scholars Pledge, a database that did not include students who did not apply.

2. The significance tests used in Table 3.3 test for differences across rows, but not down columns, so it is not possible to judge significance for different rates of enrollment across center using this table.

3. This argument is similar to the point we made earlier about community colleges, but it is framed from a different vantage. Both arguments value the freedom to make informed choices and social agency in families. There is a strong social expectation that all children should attend college. Yet, in some family cultures going to work after high school is valued over going to college; it is important to understand the value, especially when it is reinforced by information-seeking behavior. Similarly, our concern about students being steered to community colleges was that social expectations could limit choices The point is that socially imposed pathways can be forms of reproduction (e.g., steering prepared low-income students into community colleges) or of prejudice (e.g., the expectation the information should lead to college enrollment). The critical issue, in our view, is that social agency of families should be appropriately understood and valued.

4. Most colleges, including public colleges in Indiana, only collect information on income for students who apply for aid. So income is not reported from families that do not have a perception of financial need.

5. In addition, an effort was made to interview parents in TFCS, which was not the case for WSA. The implicit theories of access embedded in the designs of the two programs differed. TFCS relied on parent engagement as a core component of advocacy and access while WSA relied on the linkages between students and teachers.

6. Since causal impact studies have not been reported for WSA, causation cannot be asserted.

CHAPTER 4

1. As a member of the Research Advisory Committee for WSA, St. John had the opportunity to meet with staff from the College Success Foundation to review and discuss the original paper (St. John & Hu, 2007). This comment is based on feedback and discussion.

2. A comment by St. John: "I include the GI Bill because in reviewing these cases I am aware how very different my life circumstances would have been had my father not gone to Europe in World War II, fought in the Battle of the Bulge, and returned to take advantage of the GI Bill to complete college. Most of my many cousins in my father's family grew up in difficult circumstances and never really broke the poverty cycle. My father actively encouraged three of his siblings to go on to college, and they lived with us part of the time while they attended. One made it, finishing in her 50s, and her children attained some college. My conclusion is that uplift is difficult within generations—one sibling supporting another—and not easily transmitted across generations within extended families."

3. The term *cheer advisor* refers to the coach of the cheerleading squad. The term *TA* means teaching assistant, a student who helps out with a course.

4. These same examples can be interpreted as being related to the faith traditions: the strong role of ritual in the Catholic tradition could reinforce educational attainment (Heft, 2004); and the secularization and deep commitments to justice in the Jewish tradition could explain the emergence of a supportive caring social setting (Walzer, 1983).

5. Starting in 2011, Indiana will require the Core 40 (college preparatory) diploma and a curriculum that requires advanced math and language courses for high school graduation.

6. The analyses consider low-income students (Twenty-first Century Scholars and other Pell recipients) who attended public colleges.

7. Many of the WSA students spoke about preparation as a problem in college (see next chapter). The fact

that many of the WSA students in the early cohorts were selected late explains why selection did not have as substantial an influence on preparation as it did for later cohorts.

CHAPTER 5

1. The Lumina Foundation (2008) evaluation included a qualitative study focusing on the use of support services by Scholars. However, the report did not include detailed data on interviews that focused on the college choice process.
2. Student persistence theory and research (Braxton, 2000; Pascarella & Terenzini, 2005) has largely focused on retention within a single campus. As Leslie's case illustrates, persistence can mean continuing to pursue a dream, an educational goal, even if it means transferring to a different college.
3. The research on persistence, which focuses on the first 2 years of college, generally makes an assumption that persistence is related to the fit between the student and the college (Braxton, 2000; Pascarella & Terenzini, 2005). In this book, we explore the idea of individual fit from the vantage of students rather that institutions. Viewed this way, finding a fit is part of an extended college choice process that may include transfer.
4. The social integration models of persistence (Braxton, 2000; Tinto, 1975) focus on both academic and social integration which can be a process of finding an academic or social fit in college. These notions are explored further as part of the analyses in this book.
5. Previous analyses of state indicators and national longitudinal studies (Class of 1992) indicate tuition is positively associated with enrollment because, as a given state's tax rate increases, the state provides more access by raising tuition (St. John, 2006a). The analyses in this chapter, along with prior studies using state indicators for state finance, reveal that the combination of high tuition and high grants do improve access, especially for low-income students.

CHAPTER 6

1. The difference in the number of respondents compared to the actual number of awardees is attributable to response rate, about 60%, less than might be expected in the evaluation of a grant program. In addition, a small number of recipients don't go on to college right after high school, and this subgroup is less likely to respond.
2. The effect size analysis is: (mean recipients minus mean nonrecipients)/(pooled standard deviation).
3. *La Raza* is Spanish for "the race." (http://en.wikipedia.org/wiki/La_Raza). There is also a national organization by this name (http://www.nclr.org).

CHAPTER 7

1. The initial study used federal student aid applications as a source of information for applications to in-state private colleges or to out-of-state colleges (St. John, Musoba, Simmons, & Chung, 2002). Since data for federal aid applications were not available for this study, it was not possible to track students into other types of colleges
2. The 2005 report (St. John, Gross, & Chung, 2005) used the number of students who had been reported as having received financial aid from the TFCS program, 855 students. In response to requests made during this study, we examined different, and eventually more accurate, indicators of being a Twenty-first Century Scholar (see Table 7.2).
3. Some 4-year campuses offer 2-year degrees. In addition, many students transfer from 4- to 2-year campuses (Hossler, Gross, & Dadashova, 2009).
4. The effect size analyses is: (mean recipients minus mean non recipients)/(pooled standard deviation).
5. The rates were provided by Gregory Wolniak, National Opinion Research Center, transmitted by e-mail March 9, 2009, 9:05 a.m.

CHAPTER 8

1. For example, in 1966 St. John's father and mother, a school teacher and beautician, were not eligible for student aid, but could afford to send their oldest child to a private college. College costs remained relatively low until the 1980s when tuition began to rise faster than inflation (St. John, 1994).
2. Enablement is often used in relation to social processes that foster dysfunction. In the studies in part I,

enablement denoted support services which played a constructive role in enabling transformation toward uplift.

3. There is clearly a set of correlations between cognitive measures of academic success and degree attainment (Adelman, 2004; St. John, 2006a), but these measures alone do not indicate success as it is socially constructed; that is, people can achieve and gain personally in a privatized society without any consideration of extending opportunity to others across generations. The noncognitive aspect of preparation is especially important with respect to a broader notion of success that includes a commitment to cross-generation uplift through giving back in the form of taxes and personal action.

4. Readers are reminded that students who received GMS awards were selected when applying for college. Since application for college and aid are artifacts of having college knowledge, these students must have already had some knowledge. We choose not to speculate about early academic capital formation for these students in comparison with their peers.

5. This conclusion is beyond the content of the analyses in part I, but is informed by personal experience and observations in schools (St. John, Griffith, & Allen-Haynes, 1997; St. John, 2009a).

6. Originally, this study was included as an appendix to chapter 5. However, due to space constraints, this appendix could not be included in the present work. It can be accessed at http://www.umich.edu/~mpas/LuminaReport.pdf.

7. Specifically, federal need analysis has a "zero expected family contribution" as the highest level of financial need. This threshold not only assumes students will not receive money from the family, but also that the child will work or borrow to pay for college, not to give back to the family.

CHAPTER 9

1. On the Ford funded project Promoting Equity in Higher and Urban Education we completed a state-by-state analysis of minority representation. Most of the Big 10 States—i.e., Indiana, Michigan, Minnesota, Illinois, Ohio, and Wisconsin—lag behind the rest of the nation in access to 4-year colleges for African Americans; see, http://www.ncid.umich.edu/promotingequity/

2. E-mail correspondence with Shirley Ort, Associate Provost and Director of Financial Aid at the University of North Carolina. UNC has hosted a national meeting on this model and maintains a list of universities that have documented aid commitments similar to UNC.

APPENDIX 1

1. Although the Cronbach's alpha of .623 may be considered a low reliability for a factor, some leniency may be permitted. Social science research typically requires a cutoff of .70, but some researchers consider an alpha of .60 as legitimate (Garson, 2008), even though an alpha of below .70 is not as ideal as one above (because below .70, the standard error of measurement may increase to over half of a standard deviation). It is important to keep in mind that this leniency is most applicable to exploratory research (Garson, 2009). In our case, the factors revealed such fundamental constructs related to social capital that we felt it necessary to continue using them in our statistical analyses. Furthermore, the qualitative studies conducted by Enersen et al. (2008) cross-validated our statistical findings. Because this cross-validation existed, we determined it was appropriate to proceed with these analyses to inform our theory of academic capital formation. When another data set with explicit data associated with building social capital in relation to college preparation and college-going becomes available, further testing of the theory of academic capital formation should be undertaken.

APPENDIX 3

1. The coding for test scores compares high scores and low scores to midscores. Readers are reminded that the entire group is composed of high-achieving students, so scores in the low category for this sample would probably not be low compared to the general population.

2. An odds ratio the odds for one outcome compared to another. In this text, only variables that are statistically significant are mentioned. Full analyses are presented in Table A3.1.

APPENDIX 4

1. Krystal Williams collaborated on an earlier version of the analyses in this appendix.

REFERENCES

Adelman, C. (1995). *The new college course map and transcript files: Changes in course-taking and achievement, 1972–1993.* Washington, DC: National Center for Education Statistics.

Adelman, C. (1999). *Answers in the tool box: Academic intensity, attendance patterns, and bachelor's degree attainment.* Washington, DC: National Center for Education Statistics.

Adelman, C. (2004). *Principal indicators of student academic histories in postsecondary education, 1972–2000.* Washington, DC: U.S. Department of Education, Institute of Education Sciences.

Advisory Committee on Student Financial Assistance (ACSFA). (2001). *Access denied: Restoring the nation's commitment to equal educational opportunity.* Washington, DC: Author.

Advisory Committee on Student Financial Assistance (ACSFA). (2002). *Empty promises: The myth of college access in America.* Washington, DC: Author.

Advisory Committee on Student Financial Assistance (ACSFA). (2008). *Apply to succeed: Ensuring community college students benefit from need-based financial aid.* Washington, DC: Author.

Alejandro, R. (1998). *The limits of Rawlsian justice.* Baltimore, MD: Johns Hopkins University Press.

Alexander, K. L., & Eckland, B. K. (1974). Sex differences in the educational attainment process. *American Sociological Review, 39*(5), 668–682.

Allen, W. R. (1992, Spring). The color of success: African-American college student outcomes at predominantly white and historically black public colleges and universities. *Harvard Educational Review, 62*(1), 26–43.

Allen, W. R., Bonous-Hammarth, M., & Suh, S. A. (2004). Who goes to college? High school context, academic preparation, the college choice process, and college attendance. In E. P. St. John (Ed.), *Readings on equal education: Vol. 20. Improving access and college success for diverse students: Studies of the Gates Millennium Scholars Program* (pp. 71–114). New York, NY: AMS Press.

Allen, W. R., Harris, A., & Dinwiddie, G. (2008). Saving grace: Comparison of African American Gates Millennium Scholarship recipients and non-recipients. In W. T. Trent & E. P. St. John (Eds.), *Readings on equal education: Vol. 23. Resources, assets, strengths among diverse students: Understanding the contributions of the Gates Millennium Scholars Program* (pp. 17–48). New York, NY: AMS Press.

Allen-Haynes, L., St. John, E. P., & Cadray, J. (2003). Rediscovering the African American tradition: Restructuring in post-desegregation urban schools. In L. F. Mirón & E. P. St. John (Eds.), *Reinterpreting urban school reform: Have urban schools failed, or has the reform movement failed urban schools?* (pp. 249–275). Albany, NY: SUNY Press.

Baum, S., & McPherson, M. S. (2009). Obama's plans for higher education: A good beginning, but more is needed. *The Chronicle of Higher Education, 55*(30), A56.

Bean, J. (1990). Why students leave: Insights from research. In D. Hossler & J. P. Bean (Eds.), *The strategic management of college enrollments* (pp. 147–169). San Francisco, CA: Jossey-Bass.

Becker, G. S. (1964). *Human capital: A theoretical and empirical analysis with special reference to education.* New York, NY: Columbia University Press.

Becker, G. S. (1975). *Human capital: A theoretical and empirical analysis, with special consideration of education* (2nd ed.). New York, NY: National Bureau of Economic Research.

Becker, W. E. (2004). Omitted variables and sample selection in studies of college-going decisions. In E. P. St. John (Ed.), *Readings on equal education: Vol. 19. Public policy and college access: Investigating the federal and state roles in equalizing postsecondary opportunity* (pp. 65–86). New York, NY: AMS Press.

Berkner, L., & Chavez, L. (1997). *Access to postsecondary education for the 1992 high school graduates.* Washington, DC: U.S. Dept. of Education, Office of Educational Research and Improvement.

Bial, D. (2004). *Alternative measures for college admissions, a relational study of a new predictor for success: The promise of the Bial Dale College Adaptability Index and the success of the POSSE program* (Unpublished doctoral dissertation). School of Education, Harvard University, Cambridge, MA.

Blau, P. M., & Duncan, O. D. (1967). *The American occupational structure.* New York, NY: Wiley.

Bound, J., & Turner, S. (2002). Going to war and going to college: Did World War II and the GI Bill increase educaitonal attainment for returning veterans. *Journal of Labor Economics, 20.*

Bourdieu, P. (1977). *Outline of a theory of practice* (R. Nice, Trans.). Cambridge, UK: Cambridge University Press.

Bourdieu, P. (1990). *Reproduction in education, society, and culture.* London, UK: Sage.

Bowen, W. G., & McPherson, M. S. (2009). *Crossing the finish line: Completing college at America's public universities.* Princeton, NJ: Princeton University Press.

Brantlinger, E. A. (1994). *The politics of social class in secondary schools: Views of affluent and impoverished youth.* New York, NY: Teachers College Press.

Braxton, J. M. (2000). Reinvigorating theory and research on the departure puzzle. In J. M. Braxton (Ed.), *Reworking the student departure puzzle* (pp. 257–274). Nashville, TN: Vanderbilt University Press.

Braxton, J. M., & Lien, L. A. (2000). The viability of academic integration as a central construct in Tinto's interactionist theory of college student departure. In J. M. Braxton (Ed.), *Reworking the student departure puzzle* (pp. 11–28). Nashville, TN: Vanderbilt University Press.

Braxton, J. M., McKinney, J., & Reynolds, P. (2006). Cataloging institutional efforts to understand and reduce college student departure. In E. P. St. John & M. Wilkerson (Eds.), *New directions for institutional research: Vol. 130. Reframing persistence research to support academic success* (pp. 25–32). San Francisco, CA: Jossey-Bass..

Cabrera, A. F., Nora, A., & Castañeda, M. B. (1993). College persistence: Structural equations modeling test of an integrated model of student retention. *The Journal of Higher Education, 64*(2), 123–139.

Carter, D. F. (1999). The impact of institutional choice and environments on African American and White students' degree expectations. *Research in Higher Education, 40,* 17–41.

Chen, R. (2008.). Financial aid and student dropout in higher education: A heterogeneous research approach. In W. G. Tierney (Ed.), *Higher education: Handbook of theory and research* (Vol. 23, pp. 209–239). New York, NY: Springer.

Choy, S. P. (2002a). *Access and persistence: Findings from 10 years of longitudinal research on students.* Washington, DC: American Council on Education.

Choy, S. P. (2002b). *Findings from the condition of education, 2002: Nontraditional undergraduates.* Washington, DC: National Center for Education Statistics.

Cohen, J., Cohen, P., West, S., & Aiken, L. S. (2003). *Applied multiple regression/correlation analysis for the behavioral sciences.* Mahwah, NJ: Erlbaum.

Coleman, J. S. (1965). *Education and political development.* Princeton, NJ: Princeton University Press.

Coleman, J. S. (1988). Social capital in the creation of human capital. *American Journal of Sociology, 94,* S95–S120.

Commission on the Skills of the American Workforce, (2007). *Tough choices, tough times: The report of the new commission on skills of the American workforce.* Washington, DC: National Center on Education and the Economy.

Conklin, K. D., & Curran, B. K (2005). Action agenda for improving America's high schools. Sponsored by Achieve, Inc., and the National Governors Association. Retrieved from www.achieve.org/achieve.nsf/ActionAgenda_Overview?Open Form.

Cook, C. E. (1998) *Lobbying for higher education: How colleges and universities influence federal policy.* Nashville, TN: Vanderbilt University Press.

Daun-Barnett, N. (2008). *Preparation and access: A multi-level analysis of state policy influences on the academic antecedents to college enrollment* (Unpublished doctoral dissertation). University of Michigan, Ann Arbor, MI.

DesJardins, S. L., & McCall, B. P. (2008, January). *Investigating the causal impact of the Gates Millennium Scholars Program on the correlates of college completion, graduation from college, and future educational aspirations of low-income minority students.* Paper presented in fulfillment of contract with the Bill and Melinda Gates Foundation.

DesJardins, S. L., & McCall, B. P. (2009, November). *The impact of Washington State Achievers Scholarship on student outcomes.* Paper Presented at the Association for the Study of Higher Education Conference, Vancouver, BC.

Durkheim, E. (1951). *Suicide.* (J. A. Spaulding & G. Simpson, Trans.). Glencoe, IL: Free Press.

Emeka, A., & Hirschman, C. (2006). Who applies for and who is selected for Washington State Achievers Scholarships? In E. P. St. John (Ed.), *Readings on equal education: Vol. 21. Public policy and equal educational opportunity: School reforms, postsecondary encouragement, and state policies on postsecondary education* (pp. 167–194). New York, NY: AMS Press.

Enersen, D. L., Servaty-Seib, H. L., Pistilli, M. P., & Koch, A. K. (2008). *Twenty-first Century Scholars, their parents and guardians, and the sites that serve them.* Prepared for Lumina Foundation for Education. Lafayette, IN: Purdue University. Retrieved from http://www.purdue.edu/sats/documents/TfCSPre-CollegeRepor.pdf

Erikson, E. H. (1969). *Gandhi's truth: On the origins of militant nonviolence.* New York, NY: Norton.

Feldman, K. A., & Newcomb, T. M. (1994a). *The impact of college on students: Vol. 1. An analysis of four decades of research* (Foundations of Higher Education series). Piscataway, NJ: Transaction. (Original work published 1969)

Feldman, K. A., & Newcomb, T. M. (1994b). *The impact of college on students: Vol. 2. Summary tables* (Foundations of Higher Education series). Piscataway, NJ: Transaction. (Original work published 1969)

Finn, C. E., Jr. (1990). The biggest reform of all. *Phi Delta Kappan, 71*(8), 584–592.

Fisher, A. S. (2007). State valuation of higher education: An examination of possible explanations for privatization. In E. P. St. John (Ed.), *Readings on equal education: Vol. 22. Confronting educational inequality: Reframing, building understanding, and making change* (pp. 219–244). New York, NY: AMS Press.

Fitzgerald, B. K. (2004). Federal financial aid and college access. In E. P. St. John (Ed.), *Readings on equal education: Vol. 19. Public policy and college access: Investigating the federal and state roles in equalizing postsecondary opportunity* (pp. 1–28). New York, NY: AMS Press.

Fogel, R. W. (2000). *The fourth great awakening and the future of egalitarianism.* Chicago, IL: Chicago University Press.

Freeman, K. (2005). *African Americans and college choice: The influence of family and school.* Albany, NY: SUNY Press.

Friedman, B. M. (2005). *The moral consequence of economic growth.* New York, NY: Vintage.

Garson, G. D. (2008). Measures of internal consistency. In *Scales and standard measures.* North Carolina State University, College of Humanities and Social Sciences. Retrieved from http://faculty.chass.ncsu.edu/garson/PA765/standard.htm

Garson, G. D. (2009). Internal consistency reliability. In *Reliability analysis.* North Carolina State University College, of Humanities and Social Sciences. Retrieved from http://faculty.chass.ncsu.edu/garson/PA765/reliab.htm

Gilpin, R. (2001). *Global political economy: Understanding the international economic order.* Princeton, NJ: Princeton University Press.

Gladieux, L. E., & Wolanin, T. (1976). *Congress and the colleges: The national politics of higher education.* Lexington, MA: Lexington Books.

Gratz v. Bollinger, 539 U.S. 244 (2003).

Grutter v. Bollinger, 539 U.S. 306 (2003).

Habermas, J. (1984). *Theory of communicative action: Vol. 1. Reason and the rationalization of society* (T. McCarthy, Trans.). Boston, MA: Beacon Press.

Habermas, J. (1987). *The theory of communicative action: Vol. 2. Lifeworld and system: A critique of functionalist reasoning* (T. McCarthy, Trans.). Boston, MA: Beacon Press.

Habermas, J. (1990). *Moral consciousness and communicative action.* Cambridge, MA: MIT Press.

Habermas, J. (2005).*Truth and justification.* Edited and translated by B. Fulmer. Cambridge: MIT Press.

Hansen, W. L. (1983). The impact of student financial aid on access. In J. Froomkin (Ed.), *The crisis in higher education* (pp. 84–96). New York, NY: Academy of Political Science.

Hansen, W. L., & Weisbrod, B. A. (1967). *An income net worth approach to measuring economic welfare.* Madison, WI: Institute for Research on Poverty, University of Wisconsin.

Hansen, W. L., & Weisbrod, B. A. (1969). *Benefits, costs, and finance of public higher education.* Chicago, IL: Markham.

Harbowski, F. A., Maton, K. I., Greene, M. L., & Grief, G. L. (2002). *Overcoming the odds: Raising academically successful African American women.* Oxford, UK: Oxford University Press.

Harbowski, F. A., Maton, K. I., & Grief, G. L. (1998). *Overcoming the odds: Raising academically successful African American males.* Oxford, UK: Oxford University Press.

Harper, S. (2008). Institutional seriousness concerning Black male student engagement: Necessary conditions and collaborative partnerships. In S. Harper & S. J. Quaye (Eds.), *Student engagement in higher education: Theoretical perspectives and practical approaches for diverse populations* (pp. 137–156). New York, NY: Routledge.

Harper, S. R., & Quaye, S. J. (Eds.). (2008). *Student engagement in higher education: Theoretical perspectives and practical approaches for diverse populations.* New York, NY: Routledge.

Hartle, T. W., Simmons, C. A. M., & Timmons, B. H. (2005). *What every student should know about federal financial aid.* Washington, DC: American Council on Education.

Harvey, D. (2005). *A brief history of neoliberalism.* New York, NY: Oxford University Press.

Hearn, J. C. (1993). The paradox of growth in federal aid for college students, 1965–1990. In J. C. Smart (Ed.), *Higher education: Handbook of theory and research* (Vol. 9, pp. 94–153). New York, NY: Agathon.

Heft, J. L. (Ed.) (2004). *Beyond violence: Religious sources for social transformation.* New York, NY: Fordham University Press, Second Edition.

Heller, D. E. (1997). Student price response in higher education: An update to Leslie and Brinkman. *The Journal of Higher Education, 68*(6), 624–659.

Heller, D. E. (2002). The policy shift in state financial aid programs. In J. C. Smart (Ed.), *Higher education: Handbook of theory and research* (Vol. 17, pp. 221–261). New York, NY: Agathon.

Heller, D. E. (2004). NCES research on college participation: A critical analysis. In E. P. St. John (Ed.), *Readings on equal education: Vol. 19. Public policy and college access: Investigating the federal and state roles in equalizing postsecondary opportunity* (pp. 29–64). New York, NY: AMS Press.

Heller, D. E. (2006). State support of higher education: Past, present, and future. In D. M. Priest & E. P. St. John (Eds.), *Privatization and public universities* (pp. 11–37) Bloomington, IN: Indiana Education Policy Center.

Henry, M., Lingard, B., Rizvi, F., & Taylor, S. (2001). *The OECD, globalization and education policy.* Amsterdam, the Netherlands: Pergamon Press.

Hilberg, S., & Means, B. (2006, March 24, 2006). *Achievers scholars case study: Focus group and life history transcript data.* Prepared for the Bbill & Melinda Gates Foundation. Menlo Park, CA: SRI InternationalHilberg, S., Joshi, A., & Means, B. (2006). *Washington State Achievers Scholarship Program Case Study: Final Report.* Presented by invitation to The Bill and Melinda Gates Foundation, Research Advisory Council, Seattle, WA

Hoffman, N., Vargas, J., Venezia, A., & Miller, M. S. (Eds.). (2007). *Minding the gap: Why integrating high school with college makes sense and how to do it.* Cambridge, MA: Harvard Education Press.

Hossler, D., Braxton, J. M., & Coopersmith, G. (1989). Understanding student college choice. In J. C. Smart (Ed.), *Higher education: Handbook of theory and research* (Vol. 5, pp. 231–288). New York, NY: Agathon.

Hossler, D., & Gallager, K. (1987). Studying student college choice: A three-phase model and the implications for policymakers. *College and University, 62,* 207–221.

Hossler, D., Gross, J. P. K., & Dadashova, A. (2009). Tracking the new mobility in college enrollment patterns: Comparing lateral transfer, reverse transfer, and nonpersisting students. In D. Hossler, J. Gross, & M. Ziskin (Eds.), *Readings on equal education: Vol. 24. Enhancing institutional and state initiatives to increase student success: Studies of the Indiana Project on academic success.* New York, NY: AMS Press.

Hossler, D., Gross, J. P. K., & Ziskin, M. (2009). Lessons learned: A final look. In D. Hossler, J. Gross, & M. Ziskin, (Eds.), *Readings on equal education: Vol. 24. Enhancing institutional and state initiatives to increase student success: Studies of the Indiana Project on Academic Success..* New York, NY: AMS Press.

Hossler, D., Schmit, J., & Vesper, N. (1999). *Going to college: How social, economic, and educational factors influence the decisions students make.* Baltimore, MD: Johns Hopkins University Press.

Hossler, D., Ziskin, M., Gross, P. J., Kim, S., & Cedric, O. (2009). A meta analysis of the impact of student financial aid on student persistence. *Higher Education: Handbook of Theory and Research.*

Hu, S. (2008). Do financial aid awards in college affect graduates' democratic values and civic engagement? *Journal of College and Character, 10*(1), 1–16.

Hu, S. (2009). *Mentoring and student persistence, engagement, and degree completion: A study of the mentoring components of the Washington State Achievers (WSA) Program.* Paper prepared for the Institute of Higher Education Policy (IHEP).

Hu, S., & Wolniak, G. C. (in press). Initial evidence on the influence of college student engagement on early career earnings. *Research in Higher Education.*

Huber, E., & Stephens, J. D. (2001). *Development and crisis of the welfare state: Parties and policies in global markets.* Chicago, IL: University of Chicago Press.

Hune, S., & Gomez, G. G. (2008). Examining the college opportunities and experiences of talented, low-income Asian American and Pacific Islander Gates Millennium Scholars and non-recipients. In W. T. Trent & E. P. St. John (Eds.), *Readings on equal education: Vol. 23. Resources, assets, and strengths among success diverse students: Understanding the contributions of the Gates Millennium Scholars Program* (pp. 73–106). New York, NY: AMS Press.

Institute for Higher Education Policy. (2010). *Expanding access and opportunity: The impact of the Gates Millennium Scholars Program.* Washington, DC: Author. Retrieved from http://www.ihep.org/assets/files/publications/a-f/(Report)_Expanding_Access_and_Opportunity-Gates_Scholars.pdf

Jackson, G. A. (1978). Financial aid and student enrollment. *The Journal of Higher Education, 49*(6), 548–574.

Jencks, C. (1972). *Inequality: A reassessment of the effect of family and schooling in America.* New York, NY: Basic Books.

Jencks, C., & Peterson, P. E. (Eds.). (1991). *The urban underclass.* Washington, DC: Brookings Institution.

Kane, T. J. (1995). *Rising public college tuition and college entry: How well do public subsidies promote access to college?* (Working paper series, No. 5146). Cambridge, MA: National Bureau of Economic Research.

King, J. E. (1999a). Conclusion. In J. E. King (Ed.), *Financing a college education: How it works, how it's changing* (pp. 198–202). Westport, CT: American Council on Education/Oryx Press.

King, J. E. (1999b). Crisis or convenience: Why are students borrowing more? In J. E. King (Ed.), *Financing a college education: How it works, how it's changing* (pp. 165–176). Westport, CT: American Council on Education/Oryx Press.

King, J. E. (Ed.). (1999c). *Financing a college education: How it works, how it is changing.* Westport, CT: American Council on Education/Oryx Press.

King, J. E. (2002). *Crucial choices: How students' financial decisions affect their academic success.* Washington, DC: American Council on Education.

King, J. E. (2003). Nontraditional attendance and persistence: The cost of students' choices [Special issue]. *New Directions for Higher Education, 2003*(121), 69–83.

King, J. E. (2004). *Missed opportunities: Students who do not apply for financial aid* (ACE Issue Brief). Washington, DC: American Council on Education.

Kuh, G. D. (1995). The other curriculum: Out-of-class experiences associated with student learning and personal development. *Journal of Higher Education, 66,* 123–155.

Kuh, G. D. (1996). Guiding principles for creating seamless learning environments for undergraduates. *Journal of College Student Development, 37,* 135–148.

Kuh, G. D., & Hu, S. (2001). Learning productivity at research universities. *Journal of Higher Education, 72,* 1–28

Kuh, G. D., Kinzie, J., Schuh, J. H., Whitt, E. J, & Associates (2005). *Student success in college: Creating conditions that matter.* San Francisco, CA: Jossey-Bass.

Lee, J. B. (2004). Access revisited: A preliminary reanalysis of NELS. In E. P. St. John (Ed.), *Readings on equal education: Vol. 19. Public policy and college access: Investigating the federal and state roles in equalizing postsecondary opportunity* (pp. 87–96). New York, NY: AMS Press.

Lee, M. (2008). Achieving the impossible dream: Reflections from Gates Scholars. In W. T. Trent & E. P. St. John (Eds.), *Readings on equal education: Vol. 23. Resources, assets, and strengths among successful diverse students: Understanding the contributions of the Gates Millennium Scholars Program* (pp. 253–282). New York, NY: AMS Press.

Leslie, L. L., & Brinkman, P. T. (1988). *The economic value of higher education.* New York, NY: Macmillan.

Levidow, L. (2005). Neoliberal agendas for higher education. In A. Saad-Filho & D. Johnston (Eds.), *Neoliberalism: A critical reader* (pp. 156–163). Ann Arbor, MI: Pluto Press.

Levin, H. M. (1996). Accelerated schools: The background. In C. R. Finnan, E. P. St. John, J. McCarthy, & S. P. Slovacek (Eds.), *Accelerated schools in action: Lessons from the field.* Thousand Oaks, CA: Corwin Press.

Levin, H. M., & McEwan (2000). *Cost effectiveness analysis: Methods and applications* (2nd ed.). Thousand Oaks, CA: Sage.

Levine, A., & Nidiffer, J. (1996). *Beating the odds: How the poor get into college.* San Francisco, CA: Jossey-Bass.

Lin, N. (2001). *Social capital: A theory of social capital and social structure.* New York, NY: Routledge.

Locks, A. M. (2008). *Institutional commitment to policies and practices that support racial and ethnic diversity in the post-affirmative action era: Examining sense of belonging and diversity engagement* (Unpublished dissertation). University of Michigan, Ann Arbor, MI.

Loury, L. D. (2004). Sibling and gender differences in African-American college attendance. *Economics of Education Review, 23*(3), 213–219.

Lumina Foundation. (2008). *Indiana's Twenty-first Century Scholars Program: A statewide story with national implications.* Indianapolis, IN: Author.

Lynn, M., Yosso, T. J., Solorzano, D. G., & Parker, L. (2002). Critical race theory and education: Qualitative research in the new millennium. *Qualitative Inquiry, 8*(1), 3–6.

Macey, D. (2000). *The Penguin dictionary of critical theory.* New York, NY: Penguin.

Manoil, K. (1999). First steps. In E. P. St. John, J. S. Bardzell (Eds.), *Improving early reading and literacy: A guide for developing research-based programs* (pp. 38–41). Bloomington, IN: Indiana Education Policy Center.

Manoil, K. M. (2008). *The relationship of school and classroom instructional variales on teachers' implmention of early literacy parent involvement strategies.* Ph. D. Dissertation, Indiana University, Bloomington, IN..

Manski, C. F., & Wise, D. A. (1983). *College choice in America.* Cambridge, MA: Harvard University Press.

Marcuse, H. (1991). *One dimensional man: Studies in the ideology of advanced industrial society.* Boston, MA: Beacon Press. (Original work published 1964)

McDonough, P. M. (1997). *Choosing colleges: How social class and schools structure opportunity.* Albany, NY: SUNY Press.

McDonough, P. M., Antonio, A. L., & Trent, J. W. (1997). Black students, Black colleges: An African American college choice model. *Journal for a Just and Caring Education 3*(1), 9–36.

McGregor R. D. (1960). *The human side of enterprise.* New York, NY: McGraw-Hill.

McPherson, M. S. (1978). The demand for higher education. In D. W. Breneman & C. E. Finn, Jr. (Eds.), *Public policy and private higher education* (pp. 143–146). Washington, DC: Brookings Institution.

McPherson, M. S., & Schapiro, M. O. (1991a). Does student aid affect college enrollment? New evidence on a persistent controversy. *American Economic Review, 81,* 309–318.

McPherson, M. S., & Schapiro, M. O. (1991b). *Keeping college affordable: Government and educational opportunity.* Washington, DC: The Brookings Institution.

McPherson, M. S., & Schapiro, M. O. (1993). Measuring the effects of student aid: An assessment of some methodological and empirical problems. In M. S. McPherson, M. O. Schapiro, & G. C. Winston (Eds.), *Paying the piper: Productivity, incentives, and financing in U.S. higher education* (pp. 187–228). Ann Arbor: University of Michigan Press.

McPherson, M. S., & Schapiro, M. O. (1998). *The student aid game: Meeting need and rewarding talent in American higher education.* Princeton, NJ: Princeton University Press.

Mirón, L. F., & St. John, E. P. (Eds.). (2003). *Reinterpreting urban school reform: Have urban schools failed, or has the reform movement failed urban schools?* Albany, NY: SUNY Press.

Moses, R. P., & Cobb, C. E. (2001). *Racial equations: Civil rights from Mississippi to the algebra project.* Boston: Beacon.

Musoba, G. D. (2004). Postsecondary encouragement for diverse students: A reexamination of the Twenty-first Century Scholars Program. In E. P. St. John (Ed.), *Readings on equal education: Vol. 19. Public policy and college access: Investigating the federal and state roles in equalizing postsecondary opportunity* (pp. 153–180). New York, NY: AMS Press.

Musoba, G. D. (2006). Accountability vs. adequate funding: Which policies influence adequate preparation for college? In E. P. St. John (Ed.), *Readings on equal education: Vol. 21. Public policy and equal educational opportunity: School reforms, postsecondary encouragement, and state policies on postsecondary education* (pp. 75–125). New York, NY: AMS Press.

National Commission on the Financing of Postsecondary Education. (1973). *Financing postsecondary education in the United States.* Washington, DC: Government Printing Office.

Nussbaum, M. C. (1999). *Sex and social justice.* Oxford, UK: Oxford University Press.

Nussbaum, M. C. (2000). *Women and human development: The capabilities approach.* New York, NY: Cambridge University Press.

Nussbaum, M. C. (2004). *Hiding from humanity: Disgust, shame, and the law.* Princeton, NJ: Princeton University Press.

Oakes, J. (1985). *Keeping track: How schools structure inequality.* New Haven, CT: Yale University Press.

Oakes, J. (2003). *Critical conditions for equity and diversity in college access: Informing policy and monitoring results.* Berkeley: University of California All Campus Consortium on Research for Diversity. Retrieved from http://www.escholarship.org/uc/item/427737xt

Oakes, J. (2005). *Keeping track: How schools structure inequality.* New Haven, CT: Yale University Press.

Oakes, J. (2008). Keeping track: Structuring equality and inequality in an era of accountability. *Teachers College Record, 110*(3), 700–712.

Oakes, J., & Saunders, M. (2004). Education's most basic tools: Access to textbooks and instructional materials in California's public schools. *Teachers College Record, 106*(10), 1967–1988.

Oakes, J., & Saunders, M. (Eds.). (2008). *Beyond tracking: Multiple pathways to college, career, and civic participation.* Cambridge, MA: Harvard Education Press.

Parsons, M. D. (2004). Lobbying in higher education: Theory and practice. In E. P. St. John & M. D. Parsons (Eds.), *Public funding of higher education: Changing contexts and new rationales* (pp. 215–230). Baltimore, MD: Johns Hopkins University Press.

Pascarella, E. T., & Terenzini, P. T. (1991). *How college affects students: Vol. 1. Findings and insights from twenty years of research.* San Francisco, CA: Jossey-Bass.

Pascarella, E. T., & Terenzini, P. T. (2005). *How college affects students: Vol. 2. A third decade of research.* San Francisco, CA: Jossey-Bass.

Pasque, P, A. (2007). Seeing more of the educational inequalities around us: Visions toward strengthening relationships between higher education and society. In E. P. St. John (Ed.), *Readings on equal education: Vol. 22. Confronting educational inequality: Reframing, building understanding, and making change* (pp. 37–84). New York, NY: AMS Press.

Patton, L. D., Morelon, C., Whitehead, D. M., & Hossler, D. (2006). Campus-based retention initiatives: Does the emperor have clothes? In E. P. St. John & M. Wilkerson (Eds.), *New directions for institutional research: Vol. 130. Reframing persistence research to support academic success* (pp. 9–24). San Francisco, CA: Jossey-Bass.

Paulsen, M. B. (1990). *College choice: Understanding student enrollment behavior* (ASHE-ERIC Higher Education Report No. 6). Washington, DC: The George Washington University, School of Education and Human Development.

Paulsen, M. B. (2001a). The economics of human capital and investment in higher education. In M. B. Paulsen & J. C. Smart (Eds.), *The finance of higher education: Theory, research, policy and practice* (pp. 55–94). New York, NY: Agathon Press.

Paulsen, M. B. (2001b). The economics of the public sector: The nature and role of public policy in higher education finance. In M. B. Paulsen & J. C. Smart (Eds.), *The finance of higher education: Theory, research, policy & practice* (pp. 95–132). New York, NY: Agathon.

Paulsen, M. B., & St. John, E. P. (1997). The financial nexus between college choice and persistence. In R. A. Vorhees (Ed.), *Researching student aid: Creating an action agenda* (pp. 65–82) (New Directions for Institutional Research, No. 95). San Francisco, CA: Jossey-Bass.

Paulsen, M. B., & St. John, E. P. (2002). Social class and college costs: Examining the financial nexus between college choice and persistence. *The Journal of Higher Education, 73*(3), 189–236.

Pelavin, S. H., & Kane, M. B. (1988). *Minority participation in higher education.* Prepared for the U.S. Department of Education, Office of Planning, Budget and Evaluation. Washington, DC: Pelavin Associates.

Pelavin, S. H., & Kane, M. B. (1990). *Changing the odds: Factors increasing access to college.* New York, NY: College Board.

Perna, L. W. (2004). Understanding the decision to enroll in graduate school: Sex and racial/ethnic group differences. *Journal of Higher Education, 75*(5), 487–527.

Perna, L. W. (2005a). A gap in the literature: The influence of the design, operations, and marketing of student aid programs on the formation of family college-going plans and resulting college-going behaviors of potential students. *Journal of Student Financial Aid, 35*(3), 7–15.

Perna, L. W. (2005b). The key to access: Rigorous academic preparation. In W. G. Tierney, Z. B. Corwin, & J. E. Colyar, *Preparing for college: Nine elements of effective outreach* (pp. 113–134). Albany, NY: SUNY Press.

Rawls, J. (1971). *A theory of justice.* Cambridge, MA: Belknap Press of Harvard University Press.

Rawls, J. (2001). *Justice as fairness: A restatement.* Cambridge, MA: Belknap Press of Harvard University Press.

Reynolds, J. R., & Burge, S. W. (2008). Education expectations and the rise in women's post-secondary attainments. *Social Science Research, 37*(2), 485–499.

Rizvi, F. (2004). Globalization and the dilemmas of Australian higher education. *Access: Critical Perspectives on Communication, Cultural, and Policy Studies, 24*(1), 33–42.

St. John, E. P. (1994). *Prices, productivity and investment: Assessing financial strategies in higher education* (ASHE/ERIC Higher Education Report, No. 3). Washington, DC: George Washington University, School of Education and Human Development.

St. John, E. P. (2002). *The access challenge: Rethinking the causes of the new inequality* (Policy Issue Report No. 2002-01). Bloomington, IN: Indiana Education Policy Center.

St. John, E. P. (2003). *Refinancing the college dream: Access, equal opportunity, and justice for taxpayers.* Baltimore, MD: Johns Hopkins University Press.

St. John, E. P. (Ed.). (2005). *Readings on equal education: Vol. 20. Improving access and college success for diverse students: Studies of the Gates Millennium Scholars Program.* New York, NY: AMS Press.

St. John, E. P. (2006a). *Education and the public interest: School reform, public finance, and access to college.* Netherlands: Springer Press.

St. John, E. P. (2006b). Financial inequality and academic success: Rethinking the foundations of research on college students. *American Behavioral Scientist, 49*(12), 1604–1619.

St. John, E. P. (2007). Finding social justice in educational policy: Rethinking theory and approaches in policy research. In F. K. Stage (Ed.), *New directions in institutional research*: Vol. 133. *Using qualitative data to answer critical questions* (pp. 67–80). San Francisco, CA: Jossey-Bass.

St. John, E. P. (2008). Financial inequality and academic success: rethinking the foundations of research on college students. In W. T. Trent & E. P. St. John (Eds.), *Readings on equal education: Vol. 23. Resources, assets, and strengths among successful diverse students: Understanding the contributions of the Gates Millennium Scholars Program* (pp. 201–228). New York, NY: AMS Press.

St. John, E. P. (2009a). *Action, reflection and social justice: Integrating moral reasoning into professional development.* Cresskill, NJ: Hampton Press.

St. John, E. P. (2009b) *College organization and professional development: Integrating moral reasoning and reflective practice.* New York, NY: Routledge.

St. John, E. P. (2010). Lessons learned from Indiana's Twenty-first Century Scholars program: Toward a comprehensive approach to improving college preparation and access for low-income students. In A. Kezar (Ed.), *Recognizing and serving low-income students in higher education: An examination of institutional policies, practices, and culture* (pp. 29–48). New York, NY: Routledge.

St. John, E. P., Asker, E. H., & Hu, S. (2001). College choice and student persistence behavior: The role of financial policies. In M. B. Paulsen & J. C. Smart (Eds.), *The finance of higher education: Theory, research, policy and practice* (pp. 419–436). New York, NY: Agathon.

St. John, E. P., Cabrera, A. F., Nora, A., & Asker, E. H. (2003). Economic influences on persistence reconsidered: How can finance research inform the reconceptualization of persistence models? In F. K. Stage, D. F. Carter, D. Hossler, & E. P. St. John (Eds.), *Theoretical perspectives on college students* (pp. 29–47) (ASHE Reader Series). Boston, MA: Pearson. (Original work published 2000)

St. John, E. P., Carter, D. F., Chung, C. G., & Musoba, G. D. (2006). Diversity and persistence in Indiana higher education: The impact of preparation, major choices, and student aid. In E. P. St. John (Ed.), *Readings on equal education: Vol. 21. Public policy and educational opportunity: School reforms, postsecondary encouragement, and state policies on higher education* (pp. 341–386). New York, NY: AMS Press.

St. John, E. P., & Chung, C. G. (2004a). Student aid and major choice: A study of high-achieving students of color. In E. P. St. John (Ed.), *Readings on equal education: Vol. 20. Improving access and college success for diverse students: Studies of the Gates Millennium Scholars Program* (pp. 217–248). New York, NY: AMS Press.

St. John, E. P., & Chung, C. G. (2004b). The impact of GMS on financial access: Analyses of the 2000 cohort. In E. P. St. John (Ed.), *Readings on equal education: Vol. 20. Improving access and college success for diverse students: Studies of the Gates Millennium Scholars Program* (pp. 115–153). New York, NY: AMS Press.

St. John, E. P., & Elliott, R. J. (1994). Reframing policy research: A critical examination of research on federal student aid Programs. In J. C. Smart (Ed.), *Higher education: Handbook of theory and research* (Vol. 10, pp. 126–180). New York, NY: Agathon.

St. John, E. P, Fisher, A. S., Lee, M., Daun-Barnett, N., & Williams, K. (2008). *Educational opportunity in Indiana: Studies of the Twenty-first Century Scholars Program using state student unit record data systems.* Report prepared for the Lumina Foundation. http://www.umich.edu/~mpas/LuminaReport.pdf

St. John, E. P., Griffith, A. I., & Allen-Haynes, L. (1997). *Families in schools: A chorus of voices in restructuring.* Portsmouth, NH: Heinemann.

St. John, E. P., Gross, J. P. K., Chung, A. S. (2005). *Improving academic success: Degree attainment by Indiana's Twenty-first Century Scholars.* Indianapolis, IN: Lumina Foundation for Education.

St. John, E. P., Gross, J. P. K., Musoba, G. D., & Chung, A. S. (2006). Postsecondary encouragement and academic success: Degree attainment by Indiana's Twenty-first Century Scholars. In E. P. St. John (Ed.), *Readings on equal education: Vol. 21. Public policy and equal educational opportunity: School reforms, postsecondary encouragement, and state policies on postsecondary education* (pp. 257–291). New York, NY: AMS Press.

St. John, E. P., & Hu, S. (2004, April). *The Washington State Achievers Program: How does it influence student postsecondary educational opportunities?* Paper presented at the annual meeting of the American Educational Research Association, San Diego, CA.

St. John, E. P., & Hu, S. (2006). The impact of guarantees of financial aid on college enrollment: An evaluation of the Washington State Achievers Program. In E. P. St. John (Ed.), *Readings on equal education: Vol. 21. Public policy and equal educational opportunity: School reforms, postsecondary encouragement, and state policies on postsecondary education* (pp. 211–256). New York, NY: AMS Press.

St. John, E. P., & Hu, S. (2007). School reform, scholarship guarantees, and college enrollment: A study of the Washington State Achievers program. In E. P. St. John (Ed.), *Readings on equal education: Vol. 22. Confronting educational inequality: Reframing, building understanding, and making change.* New York, NY: AMS Press.

St. John, E. P., Hu, S., Simmons, A. B., & Musoba, G. D. (2001). Aptitude versus merit: What matters in persistence? *Review of Higher Education, 24*(2), 131–152.

St. John, E. P., Hu, S., & Weber, J. (2000). *State policy and the affordability of public higher education: The influence of state grants on persistence in Indiana* (Policy Research Report, No. 00-02). Bloomington, IN: Indiana Education Policy Center.

St. John, E. P., Hu, S., & Weber, J. (2001). State policy and the affordability of public higher education: The influence of state grants on persistence in Indiana. *Research in Higher Education, 42,* 401–428.

St. John, E. P., Kim, J., & Yang, L. (in press). *Globalization and social justice: Vol. 1. Privatization and inequality: Comparative studies of college access, education policy, and public finance.* New York, NY: AMS Press.

St. John, E. P., Loescher, S. A., & Bardzell, J. S. (2003). *Improving reading and literacy in grades 1–5: A resource guide to research-based Programs.* Thousand Oaks, CA: Corwin.

St. John, E. P., McKinney, J., & Tuttle, T. (2006). Using action inquiry to address critical challenges. In E. P. St. John & M. Wilkerson (Eds.), *New directions for institutional research: Vol. 130. Reframing persistence research to support academic success* (pp. 63–76) San Francisco, CA: Jossey-Bass.

St. John, E.P., & Moronski, K. (in press). The late great state of California: The legacy of the master plan, the decline in access, and a new crisis. In E. P. St. John, J. Kim, & L. Yang (Eds.), *Globalization and social justice: Vol. 1. Privatization and inequality: Comparative studies of college access, education policy, and public finance.* New York, NY: AMS Press.

St. John, E. P., & Musoba, G. D. (2010). *Pathways to academic success: Expanding opportunity for underrepresented students.* New York, NY: Routledge.

St. John, E. P., Musoba, G. D., & Simmons, A. B. (2003). Keeping the promise: The impact of Indiana's Twenty-first Century Scholars Program. *The Review of Higher Education 27*(1), 103-123.

St. John, E. P., Musoba, G. D., Simmons, A. B., & Chung, C. G. (2002). *Meeting the access challenge: Indiana's Twenty-first Century Scholars Program.* (New Agenda Series, Vol. 4, No. 4). Indianapolis, IN: Lumina Foundation for Education.

St. John, E. P., Musoba, G. D., Simmons, A. B., Chung, C. G., Schmit, J., & Peng, C-Y. J. (2002). *Meeting the access challenge: An examination of Indiana's Twenty-first Century Scholars Program.* Bloomington, IN: Indiana Education Policy Center.

St. John, E. P., & Parsons, M. D. (Eds.). (2004). *Public funding of higher education: Changing contexts and new rationales.* Baltimore: Johns Hopkins University Press. (Paperback edition, 2005)

St. John, E. P., Paulsen, M. B., & Carter, D. F. (2005, September). Diversity, college costs, and postsecondary opportunity: An examination of the college choice-persistence nexus for African Americans and Whites. *The Journal of Higher Education, 76*(5), 545–569.

St. John, E. P., Paulsen, M. B., &. Starkey, J. B. (1996). The nexus between college choice and persistence. *Research in Higher Education, 37*(2), 175–220.

St. John, E. P., Pineda, D., & Moronski, K (2009). *Promoting equity in higher education: Legal, financial, and educational remedies to racial and income inequality in college access.* Report to the Lumina Foundation. Ann Arbor, MI: School of Education. Retrieved from http://www.ncid.umich.edu/promotingequity/reports/promoting_equity_paper.pdf

St. John, E. P., Rowley, L., & Hu, S. (2009). Diversity and leadership: A study of high-achieving students of color. *Journal of Negro Education, 78*(1), 17–28.

St. John, E. P., Simmons, A. B., & Musoba, G. D. (2002). Merit-aware admissions in public universities: Increasing diversity. *Thought & Action, 17*(2), 35–46.

St. John, E. P., Starkey, J. B., Paulsen, M. B., & Mbaduagha, L. A. (1995). The influence of prices and price subsidies on within-year persistence by students in proprietary schools. *Educational Evaluation and Policy Analysis, 17*(2), 149–165.

St. John, E. P., & Wilkerson, M. (Eds.), (2006). *Reframing persistence research to support academic success* (New Directions for Institutional Research No. 130). San Francisco, CA: Jossey-Bass.

Schoeni, R. F., & Ross, K. E. (2005). Material assistance from families during the transition to adulthood. In R. A. Settersten, Jr., F. F. Furstenberg, Jr., & R. G. Rumbaut (Eds.) *On the frontier of adulthood: Theory, research, and public policy, pp. 396-416.* Chicago, IL: University of Chicago Press.

Schultz, C. (1969). *The politics of public spending.* Washington, DC: The Brookings Institution.

Sedlacek, W. E. (2004). *Beyond the big test: Noncognitive assessment in higher education.* San Francisco, CA: Jossey-Bass.

Sedlacek, W. E., & Sheu, H. B. (2004). Correlates of leadership activities of Gates Millennium Scholars. In E. P. St. John (Ed.), *Readings on equal education: Vol. 20. Improving access and college success for diverse students: Studies of the Gates Millennium Scholars Program* (pp. 249–264). New York, NY: AMS Press.

Sedlacek, W. E., & Sheu, H. B. (2006). Early academic behaviors of Washington State Achievers. In E. P. St. John (Ed.), *Readings on equal education: Vol. 21. Public policy and equal educational opportunity: School reforms, postsecondary encouragement, and state policies on postsecondary education* (pp. 195–210). New York, NY: AMS Press.

Siddle Walker, V. (1996). *Their highest potential: An African American school community in the segregated south.* Chapel Hill: The University of North Carolina Press.

Siddle Walker, V., & Snarey, J. (Eds.). (2004). *Race-ing moral formation: African American perspectives on care and justice.* New York, NY: Teachers College Press.

Sirotnik, K. A., Oakes, J. (Eds.). (1986). *Critical perspectives on the organization and improvement of schooling.* Boston, MA: Kluwer-Nijhoff.

Slaughter, S. E., & Leslie, L. L. (1997). *Academic capitalism: Politics, policies, and the entrepreneurial university.* Baltimore, MD: Johns Hopkins University Press.

Slaughter, S. E., & Rhoades, G. (2004). *Academic capitalism and the new economy: Markets, state, and higher education.* Baltimore, MD: Johns Hopkins University Press.

Solaegui, L. (2009, December 7). *Selection design using noncognitive factors.* A talk at the University of Michigan sponsored by the Projects Promoting Equity in Urban and Higher Education, National Center for Institutional Diversity, University of Michigan.

Stanton-Salazar, R. D. (1997). A social capital framework for understanding the socialization of racial minority children and youths. *Harvard Educational Review, 67*(1), 1–40.

Theobald, N. (2003). The need for issues-driven school funding reform in urban schools. In L. F. Mirón & E. P. St. John (Eds.), *Reinterpreting urban school reform: Have urban schools failed, or has the reform movement failed urban schools?* (pp. 33–52). Albany, NY: SUNY Press.

Tierney, W. G. (1992). An anthropological analysis of student participation in college. *Journal of Higher Education, 63*(6), 603–618.

Tierney, W. G. (2006). *Trust and the public good.* New York, NY: Peter Lang.

Tierney, W. G., & Venegas, K. (2007). The cultural ecology of financial aid decision making. In E. P. St. John (Ed.), *Readings on equal education: Vol. 22. Confronting educational inequality: Reframing, building understanding, and making change* (pp. 1–36). New York, NY: AMS Press.

Tinto, V. (1975). Dropout from higher education: A theoretical synthesis of recent research. *Review of Educational Research, 45*(1), 89–125.

Tinto, V. (1987). *Leaving college: Rethinking the causes and cures of student attrition.* Chicago, IL: University of Chicago Press.

Tinto, V. (1993). *Leaving college: Rethinking the causes and cures of student attrition* (2nd ed.). Chicago, IL: University of Chicago Press.

Tinto, V. (2000). Linking learning and leaving: Exploring the role of the college classroom in student departure. In J. M. Braxton (Ed.), *Reworking the student departure puzzle* (pp. 81–94). Nashville, TN: Vanderbilt University Press.

Trent, W. T., Gong, Y., & Owens-Nicholson, D. (2004). The relative contribution of high school origins to college access. In E. P. St. John (Ed.), *Readings on equal education: Vol. 20. Improving access and college success for diverse students: Studies of the Gates Millennium Scholars Program* (pp. 45–70). New York, NY: AMS Press.

Trent, W. T., & St. John, E. P. (Eds.). (2008). *Readings on equal education: Vol 23. Resources, assets, and strengths among successful diverse students: Understanding the contributions of the Gates Millennium Scholars Program.* New York, NY: AMS Press.

U.S. Department of Education (1983). *A nation at risk.* Washington, DC: Author.

U.S. Department of Education (2006) *A Test of Leadership: Charting the Future of U. S. Higher Education*, Washington, DC: Author.

Voorhees, R. (2001). Community colleges. In M. B. Paulsen & J. C. Smart (Eds.), *The finance of higher education: Theory, research, policy, and practice* (pp. 480–500). New York, NY: Agathon.

Walker, G. W., Golde, C. M., Jones, L., Bueshel, A. C., Hutchings, P. (2008). *The formation of scholars: Rethinking doctoral education for the Twenty-first century.* The Carnegie Foundation for Advancement of Teaching. San Francisco, CA: Jossey-Bass.

Walpole, M. (2007). *Economically and educationally challenged students in higher education: Access to outcomes* (ASHE Higher Education Report: Vol. 33, No 3). San Francisco, CA: Jossey-Bass.

Walzer, M. (1983). *Spheres of justice: A defense of pluralism and equality.* New York, NY: Basic Books.

Williams, K. L., Penida, D., & St. John, E. P. (2009, November 4–6). *New evidence of (un)equitable representation over time: Examining trends in Latino/a and African American college enrollment at U.S. public institutions, 1992-2004.* Presented at the Association for the Student of Higher Education Annual Conference, Vancouver, BC. Retrieved from http://www.ncid.umich.edu/promotingequity.

Wolin, R. (2006). *The Frankfurt School revisited and other essays on politics and society.* New York, NY: Routledge.

Wood, D., Kaplan, R., & McLoyd, V. C. (2007). Gender differences in the educational expectations of urban, low-income African American youth: Role of parents and the school. *Journal of Youth and Adolescence, 36*(4), 417–427.

Wooden, O. (2007). High school guidance counselors as reproductive forces in the lives of African American students: A study of a Georgia high school. In E. P. St. John (Ed.), *Readings on equal education: Vol. 22. Confronting educational inequality: Reframing, building understanding, and making change* (pp. 245-280). New York, NY: AMS Press.

INDEX